Your First 20 Hours with Business Central

A guided tour through basic use and setup of Microsoft Dynamics 365 Business Central

Written By
Jeremy Vyska

Your First 20 Hours with Business Central

Copyright ©2021 Spare Brained Ideas AB

All rights reserved. No part of this book may be reproduced, stored in a retrieval system, or transmitted in any form, without prior written permission of the author, except in the case of brief quotations embedded in critical articles or reviews.

Every effort has been made to ensure the accuracy of the information, guidance, and steps presented in this book. However, this book is sold without warranty of results, express or implied. The author cannot be held liable for any damages caused or alleged to have been caused directly or indirectly.

First Published: 2021 April

sparebrained.com

ISBN: 979-8-7764-9772-8

Imprint: Amazon.com

Preface

This book is meant to be an introductory level tour through the basics of setting up a Microsoft Dynamics 365 Business Central system *from scratch*.

This should *always* be done with consideration of local laws, regulations, and accounting practices. Professional assistance is *strongly* recommended to ensure correct configuration.

Microsoft Dynamics 365 Business Central is a powerful ERP system with more possibilities and options than most companies will ever utilize, and that is before including *any* of the brilliant solutions and extensions available in the AppSource ecosystem or Microsoft Dynamics 365 Business Central solution ecosystems at large. As a result, you should consider this a map of the initial parts of the system, but you should continue to explore additional learning options, such as through Microsoft Learn, the Dynamics User Group Skill-Up platforms, work with many excellent trainers in our industry.

WHO SHOULD READ THIS BOOK?

The target for this book is someone who has very low familiarity with Microsoft Dynamics 365 Business Central but has some basic knowledge of how business processes work and light accounting knowledge.

This book will hopefully be helpful to both new users of Microsoft Dynamics 365 Business Central and to technical people cross-training to work with it for the first time.

How to Read this Book

It is strongly recommended that you have a test company or a **Sandbox** copy of a company to be able to follow along with as you read. For some of the first chapters, we will also refer to looking at a CRONUS company – this is a demonstration and training company that Microsoft includes with the system. Typically, this is made to have data and language relevant to your local regulations and language.

About the Author

Jeremy has been working with the Business Central (NAV/Navision) product for over 20 years. With a storied career encompassing development, consulting, implementation, support, and training, he has been both a small business owner of solution centers/partners and professional "fixer" for partners and ISV/vertical solution providers. He takes great joy in teaching and finding new and clever ways to benefit everyone.

Feedback & Questions

Visit https://sparebrained.com/contact or email us at support@sparebrained.com to get in touch.

To help us in resolving issues:

This file is print version **1.0**, publish date of **2021-11-25**.

Piracy

Hey, please don't, it is not very expensive.

Acknowledgements From the Author

First off, thank you to my lovely wife, who has been the best parts for over half my life so far and my whole career. Your patience is greatly appreciated.

Secondly, if I thanked all the amazing help I've had over my career, we'd have a nice book, so I will thank everyone who participated in making this book happen.

Philip von Bahr, my partner at Spare Brained Ideas, your relentless drive to make "good to great" is worth more than you can ever know, even if we fight a bit about commas and semicolons.

Farah Khaddour – thank you! Good sass is always appreciated, even *if* it hadn't come with an amazing amount of help with language and clarity.

The DynamicsCon Team – thank you! The networking, even if virtual, was a key driver to the decision to make this book to help more great people join the community

Thank you also to Belinda Allen for validating that we were on the right track with some early reviews!

To Søren Alexandersen – Thank you for encouraging me to get me engaged with the community at just the right time.

And lastly, thank you to all the wonderful people from the community I've gotten to know in the past year. I hope this effort helps you as much as (and more than) you have helped me!

Table of Contents

Preface 3
    Who Should Read this Book? 3
    How to Read this Book 4
    About the Author 4
    Feedback & Questions 4
    Piracy 4
    Acknowledgements From the Author 5
Table of Contents 7
PART 1: Getting to Know BC 14
    Chapter 1: Getting to Know the UI 16
        Role Centers 16
        The Many Types of Pages 23
        Lists 24
        Cards 28
        Documents 30
        Worksheets 32

Reports	34
Tablet & Phone	36
Skills You will Want to Master	38
Summary	53
Chapter 2: Understanding How Everything Connects	**55**
What's In the Box?	55
Data Organized Neatly	58
The Data Must Flow	61
Summary	64
PART 2: Building Your Foundation	**65**
Chapter 3: Product and Business Posting Groups	**67**
Quick Explanation of Posting Groups	67
Entering VAT Posting Groups	71
Entering General Posting Groups	73
Summary	74
Chapter 4: Customer / Vendor / Inventory Posting Groups	**75**
Customer Posting Groups	75
Vendor Posting Groups	76
Inventory Posting Groups	76
Location(s)	77
Summary	79
Chapter 5: Company Information, Periods and No. Series	**81**
Company Information	81
Accounting Periods	82
No. Series	84
Chapter 6: Module Setup Tables – G/L, A/P, A/R, Inventory	**90**
General Ledger (G/L) Setup	90
Purchases & Payables (A/P) Setup	93

Sales & Receivables (A/R) Setup 95

Inventory Setup 99

Payment Terms and Methods 100

Summary 102

Chapter 7: Customer / Vendor / Item Templates 104

Configuration Templates 105

Configuration Templates - Customer 107

Configuration Templates - Vendor 111

Item Templates, Part 1 114

Items and Units of Measure 114

Item Category Codes 116

Item Templates, Part 2 118

Chapter 8: Data Migration – Importing Master Data 120

Generating the Template 120

Chart of Accounts – General Ledger Accounts 122

Customer Import File 126

Vendor Import File 127

Item Import File 127

Performing the Import 129

Reviewing Data Migration Results 136

Summary 138

Chapter 9: Updating Posting Groups 140

Chart of Accounts - Subcategory 141

Chart of Accounts - Indentation 145

General Posting Setup - Creation 147

General Posting Setup - Configuration 149

VAT Posting Setup 150

Customer Posting Setup 151

- Vendor Posting Setup 152
- Bank Account Posting Groups 153
- Inventory Posting Setup 154
- Summary 155

Chapter 10: Languages, Currencies, Exchange Rates 156
- Languages 156
- Currencies 160
- Summary 170

Chapter 11: Bank Accounts 172
- Setting Up a Bank Account 172
- Additional Considerations 174
- Summary 174

PART 3: Starting Up 176

Chapter 12: Adjusting Inventory into Stock 178
- Item Journals Tour 179
- Journal Batches 180
- Preparing an Item Journal Excel File 181
- Posting The Item Journal 185
- Posting Results Review 186
- Reversing the G/L Inventory Value 192

Chapter 13: Opening Balances 194
- Opening Balances – General Strategy 194
- Bank Accounts 195
- Customers 197
- Vendors 200
- Tax & VAT Opening Balances 202
- General Ledgers 203
- Summary 205

PART 4: Basic Operations 206

Chapter 14: Purchasing 207
- Creating Purchase Orders 207
- Getting to Know the PO 212
- Attaching Documents 215
- Posting – Receive & Invoice 218
- Purchasing – Partial Posting 222
- Purchase Invoices 226
- Sending Purchase Documents 228

Chapter 15: Selling 235
- Creating Sales Orders 236
- Getting to Know the Sales Order 242
- Sending Sales Orders 247
- Posting & Review 250
- Reviewing the Posting Results 253
- Selling in Another Currency 256
- Sales – Partial Shipping 259
- Sales – Combined Invoicing 261
- Adding Tracking to a Posted Shipment 267
- Sending a Statement 270

Chapter 16: Making Payments 273
- Preparing Your Payment Journal(s) 274
- Manually Creating a Payment Line 276
- Suggest Vendor Payments 280

Chapter 17: Receiving Payments 287
- Preparing Your Cash Receipt Journals 287
- Creating a Receipt Line 288
- Creating Partial Receipts 294

Chapter 18: Correcting Errors 297
- Sales Return Orders 297
- Sales Corrective Credit Memos 305
- Purchase Return Orders 309
- Purchase Corrective Credit Memos 312
- Changing Applications 313
- Undo Shipments 319
- Undo Receipts 322

Chapter 19: Recurring Tasks 323
- Closing Fiscal Years / Income Statement 323
- Closing Months 333
- Updating Exchange Rates 333
- Posting Inventory Costs 341

PART 5: Wrapping Up 347

Chapter 20: Continued Learning & Resources 349
- Books 351
- Microsoft Learn 353
- Online Courses 354
- Community Resource Overview 354

PART 6: Appendices 357
- Appendix A: Example Imports 358
- Appendix B: Companies 367

PART 7: Index 371

PART 1: GETTING TO KNOW BC

Chapter 1 will cover many different parts within the layout that you may encounter throughout Business Central. It is a good foundation to understand how the system looks and how the interface works.

Chapter 2 will cover how the system functions, explaining what modules can be found in the product, and reviewing essential concepts used by every module.

Chapter 1: Getting to Know the UI

In this chapter, we will go over what you will see when you work with Microsoft Dynamics 365 Business Central (often shortened to Business Central or even "BC") and how to find your way around the User Interface (UI). Understanding how the system looks and works will be useful for every part of the system and you will be off to a great start.

ROLE CENTERS

When you first access your new Business Central system, you start right out on the "home" page: the **Role Center**.

The Role Center is designed to give a work role specific view into the system, and a jumping off point to the most needed parts of the system, this means that there are many different Role Centers that are tailored to the different needs of different users.

The built-in Role Centers are:

- Accountant
- Administration of users, user groups and permissions
- Business Manager
- Company Hub
- Inventory Manager
- Manufacturing Manager
- Project Manager
- Sales and Relationship Manager
- Sales Order Processor
- Service Manager
- Shipping and Receiving – WMS
- Team Member

- Warehouse Worker - WMS

For our walkthrough of Business Central, we will use on the **Business Manager** role.

Looking at the very top bar, you find components like these:

Element	What is it?
1	If you are using Business Central on Microsoft's platform, this button will be visible allowing you to easily navigate to other parts of Microsoft's cloud, such as Office 365. If you are using on-premises, this button will not be visible.
2	This is the **Tell Me** feature. This allows you to Search for functionality in the system. This searches through the Action Bar of the current page, as well as other Pages and Reports throughout the system. Alt-Q is the default shortcut on Windows Keyboards, and a great speed booster. We will reference this component often as: 🔍 **Tell Me** We will also mark searchable content like: 🔍 **Customers**
3	This Notifications area is not currently used in Business Central, but it may become so someday.
4	The **My Settings** area of the system. Here you can Personalize, change My Settings, a shortcut to the Company Information setup area, and a few more useful options. We will reference this component often as: ⚙ **Settings**
5	The **Help Me** feature. This provides quick links to help & support pages, but is also a valuable resource in troubleshooting.
6	The User menu, which gives you access to sign out.

> **Note:** The screenshots and demonstration data used throughout this book are from the CRONUS International company, which is the base "W1" or "Worldwide" version of the product. There are many localized versions to fit better in other regions.

Here we can see the general structure of a Role Center in Microsoft Dynamics 365 Business Central:

Figure 1-1 - Role Center Structure

PART 1: GETTING TO KNOW BC
CHAPTER 1: GETTING TO KNOW THE UI

THE NAVIGATION ELEMENTS

The Navigation Menus, Navigation Bar, and the Action Bar are the main Navigation elements of the Role Center.

1. The Navigation Menu – This is the main functional area of the system this Role Center promotes.
2. The Navigation Bar – These are the most used Lists for this Role Center. When you search for Lists in the 🔍 **Tell Me** functionality and use the Bookmark feature, they will be added to this Navigation Bar.
3. The Headline component – This is a rotating highlight of Key Items about your business. Often, this area is customized to match your top needs by a Partner.
4. The Action Bar – These are the most used Actions for this Role Center. This often includes launching directly into creating new Documents.

ACTIVITIES AREA

This section of the Role Center is to show **Cues** - visual KPI's of your more important measures throughout the system, displayed and grouped in different ways. Typically, one can click through on them to dig more into the numbers. Often, they can also be configured to Color coding to rapidly indicate healthy/unhealthy states for your organization.

5. Wide Cues – Usually these are financial indicators, as they are a good display for larger numbers.
6. Cues – Typically these are count-based indicators, such as counts of Open Documents or Overdue Documents.

INSIGHTS AREA

This section of the Role Center is to show Charts and Lists, providing deeper insights than a single indicator can provide.

7. Charts – These can be built-in charts, but also Power BI charts.
8. Lists – These are lists of information important enough to show on the main Role Center.

CHANGING ROLE CENTER

You can switch between Role Centers yourself to try them out via the ⚙ **Settings** (**1**) menu option, then **My Settings** (**2**), then the ⋯ (**3**) button:

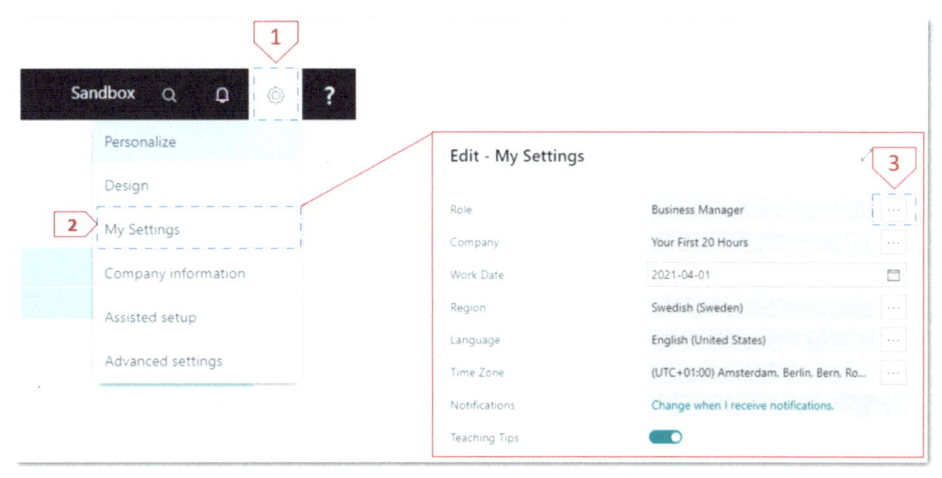

Figure 1-2 - Changing Role Centers

TRY IT!

The different Role Centers have different utility to different audiences. If you are setting up BC for your team, it is a good idea to switch through some of them to look. Try switching through the following roles:
- Business Manager
- Sales Order Processor
- Inventory Manager

Take note of the differences in:
- Navigation Menus
- Action Menus
- Cues in the Activities

THE MANY TYPES OF PAGES

Almost everything you see when you are using Business Central is a **Page**. Pages are the mechanism used to display data and to allow users to interact with data. There are many types of pages in the system, including these essential types:

- Role Centers – They are a display-only Page that we discussed above.
- Lists – Displays data in a table form.
- Cards – Displays a single entity or record, such as the **Item Card**.
- Documents – Usually displays two main parts – a single Header and a set of connected Lines.
- Worksheets – Used for creating worksheets or journals, which often involve many lines of information being entered into the system.

LISTS

List type pages are used to give user viewing or editing to a collection of multiple things ('entities') at the same time. Some notable examples are views like the Customer list, the Item list, but also editing lists, such as many setup tables, like Payment Terms or Currencies.

Let us look at the Item list:

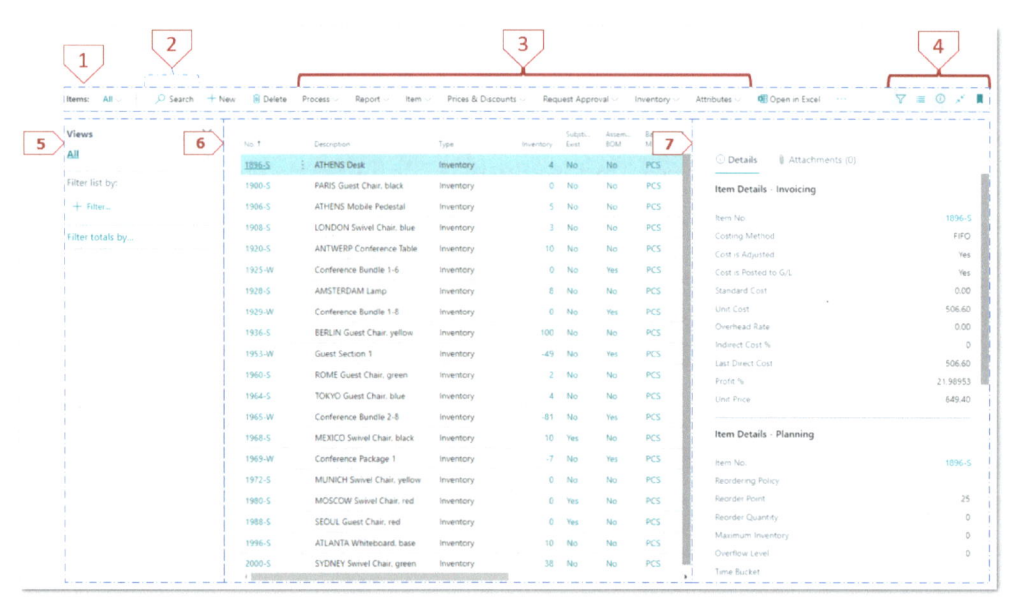

Figure 1-3 - Anatomy of a List Page

Element	What is it?
1	The **Action Bar** is your menu for the List Page you are on.
2	The **Search** function to search the contents of the List.
3	The **Promoted Actions** are the actions that you need most often.
4	The **View Controls** help you adjust some of the view settings.
5	The **Filter Pane** allows you to apply or see filters on this Page.
6	The **Content Area**, which typically shows the List.
7	The **FactBox Area** shows deeper information about the current row.

At the top, the **Action Bar** (**1**) is the Menu bar showing Actions and Reports for the List.

This can include reports related to the list, functions that affect the selected record, or navigating to related information and functions without having to open the Card. An example of this is in the Customer list Action Bar that contains reports such as the **Top 10 Customer List** and the **Aged Accounts Receivable**. You can also rapidly create Sales Documents for the selected Customer right from the list. The most needed actions are **Promoted** (**3**), which makes them sorted into groups and readily available.

On the far right of the **Action Bar**, there are the **View Controls** (**4**) that allow you to reshape the content area, showing or hiding parts:

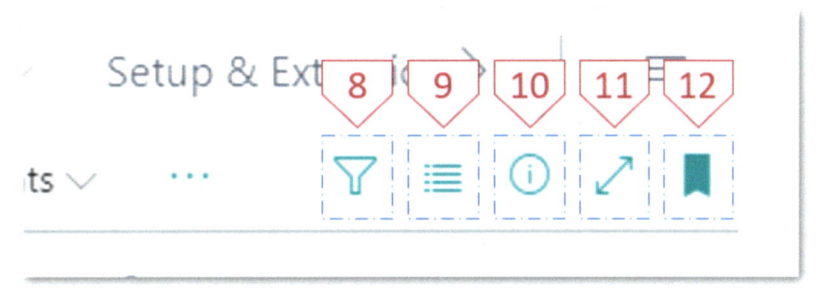

Figure 1-4 - Page View Settings Controls

Element	What is it?
8	The **Filter** button (▽) allows you to show/hide the Filter Pane (**5**). (See the Filtering section under Skills You Want to Master later in this chapter)
9	The **List Display Mode** button (≡) shows the current view mode of the list. (More below)
10	The **Info** button (ⓘ) shows and hides the FactBox area. (More below)
11	The **Page Toggle** button (↗) toggles pages between slim and wide mode.
12	The **Bookmark** button (▢/▮) indicates if the Page has been bookmarked, putting it on your Role Center.

The **List Display Mode** allows you to swap the **Content Area** (**6**) between **List**, the **Tall Tiles** view, and the **Tiles** views:

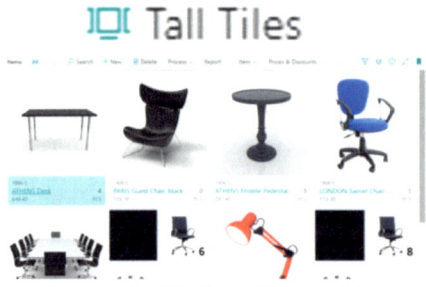

Figure 1-5 - List Page Display Modes

Tile views may be useful when you have images for records, such as Customers and Vendors by their logos, or Items with pictures of the items.

The FactBox area (**7**) is where you find the smaller 'sections' of information related to the record you are looking at. One such example can be found on the Customer list, where there are multiple FactBoxes added:

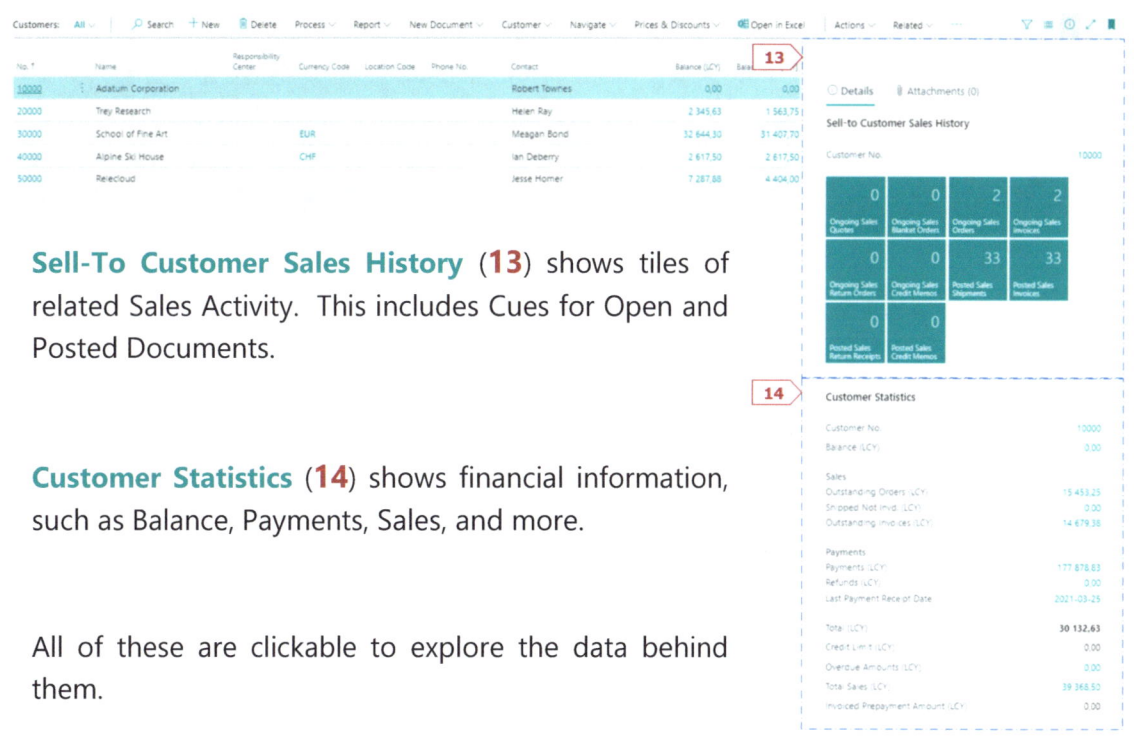

Sell-To Customer Sales History (**13**) shows tiles of related Sales Activity. This includes Cues for Open and Posted Documents.

Customer Statistics (**14**) shows financial information, such as Balance, Payments, Sales, and more.

All of these are clickable to explore the data behind them.

Figure 1-6 - FactBox Examples

Within the FactBox area, there are also often spaces for "Links" (useful to link to customer websites for customers, or to specifications/MDS for Items that maybe live on your site or on SharePoint) and "Notes", a freeform space that allows BC Users to place various 'good to know' information about the entity you are on.

> Note: The "Search" functionality in the Action Bar works like magic, in that it searches across all columns, but it *can* perform much more slowly than a filter within the exact column you need! See more about Filtering later in this chapter.

CARDS

Card type pages are used when you are editing a single Object ('entity'). Notable examples of this are the Customer Card and the Item Card. The Card type page is also used for Setup Data, such as Sales & Receivables Setup. (see **Chapter 6**)

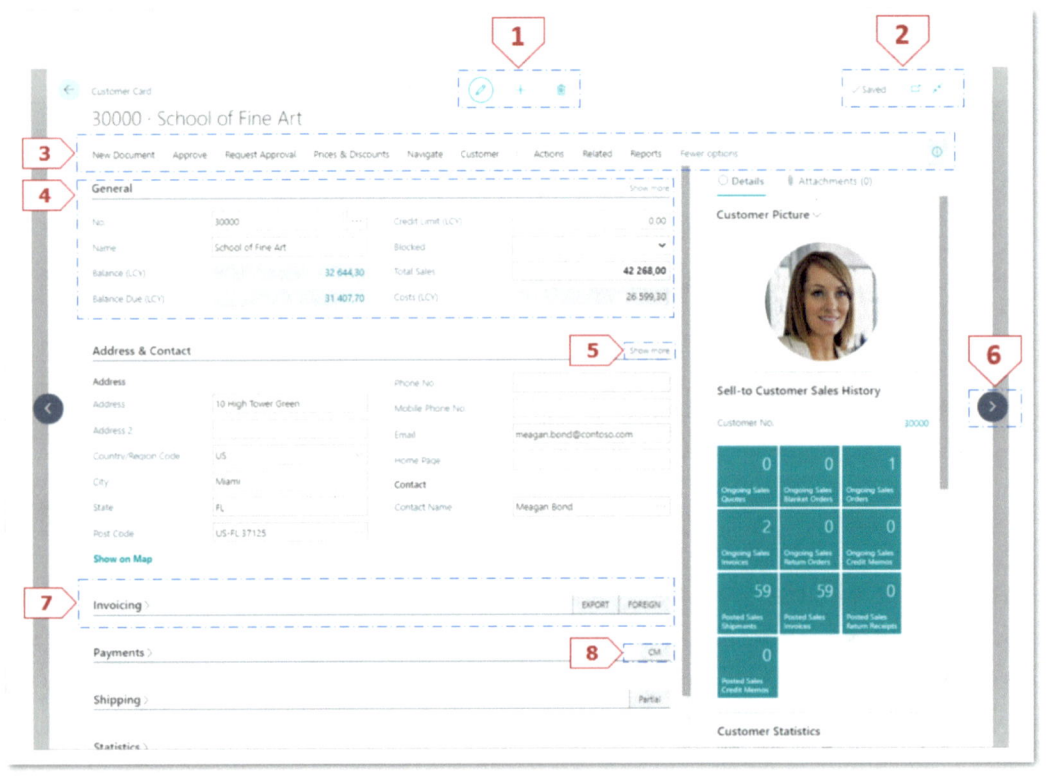

Figure 1-7 - Card Page Anatomy

Element	What is it?
1	**System Actions** - switching between view/edit mode, creating a new entity of the same type, or deleting the record.
2	**Saving Indicator**, the **New Window** button, and the **Slim/Wide Toggle**.
3	The **Action Bar** is your menu for the Card Page you are on.
4	A section of a Card grouping fields together is a **FastTab**, which can be expanded and collapsed by clicking on the name.
5	Some fields are used infrequently and can be hidden away. They are shown with the **Show more** control (the same control switches to **Show less** to hide again).

PART 1: GETTING TO KNOW BC
CHAPTER 1: GETTING TO KNOW THE UI

6	On the left and right edges of some Cards, you may be able to use the **Back** and **Forwards** arrows to move through the data, one Card at a time.
7	An example of a collapsed **FastTab**.
8	When a FastTab is collapsed, some fields are important to still see the value of. These **Promoted Fields** will show their value in the same space.

Documents

Document type pages are very similar to **Card** pages but also have **Lists** embedded as part of them; a "Subpage".

You will see this often for Sales Documents, Purchase Documents, and more. For example, the **Sales Order** looks like:

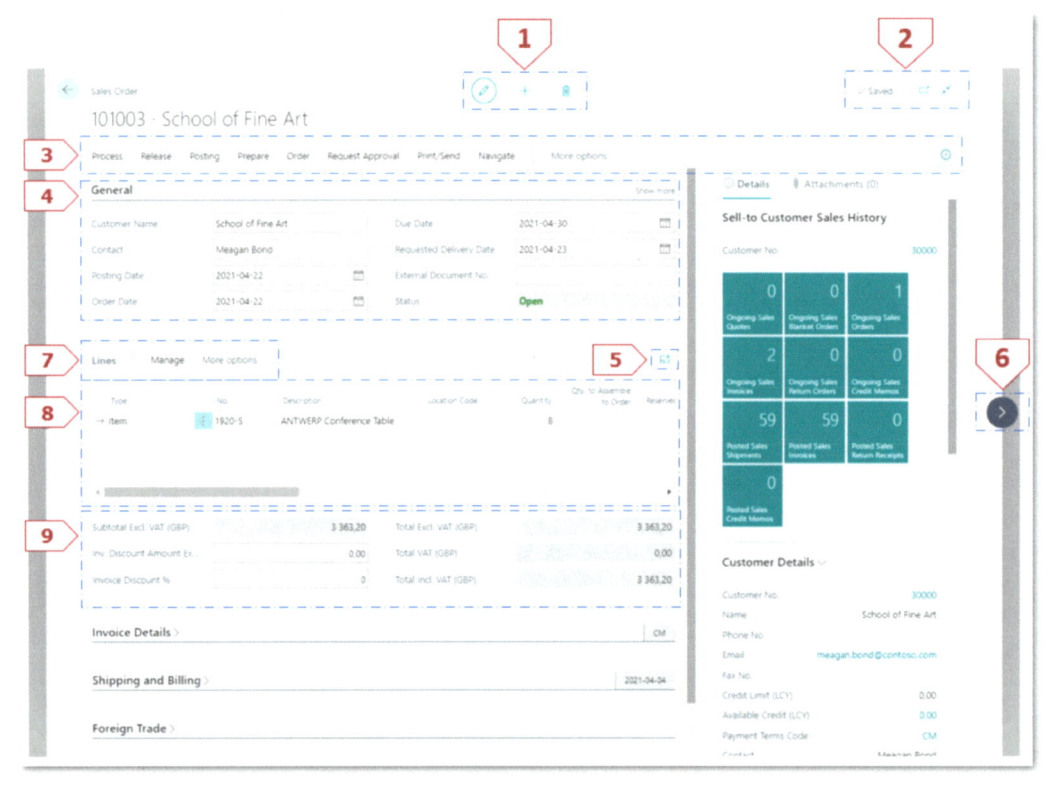

Figure 1-8 - Document Page Anatomy

Element	What is it?
1	**System Actions** - switching between view/edit mode, creating a new entity of the same type, or deleting the record.
2	**Saving Indicator**, the **New Window** button, and the **Slim/Wide Toggle**.
3	The **Action Bar** is your menu for the Document Page you are on.
4	A section of a Document is a **FastTab**, which can be expanded and collapsed by clicking on the name.

5	The ⬈ **Expand Lines** button maximizes the Subpage area to fill the screen.
6	On the left and right edges of some Documents, you may be able to use the **Back** and **Forwards** arrows to move through the data, one at a time.
7	Each Subpage area also has an **Action Bar** for the actions of the Line selected.
8	The Subpage is an editable **List** page with a variety of the same features of Lists, such as multi-selection of lines.
9	Some Subpages will also provide a **Totals** section.

WORKSHEETS

Worksheet type pages are very similar to **List** type pages but are used when entering many lines of information into the system at one time. An example of these pages is the **General Journal**:

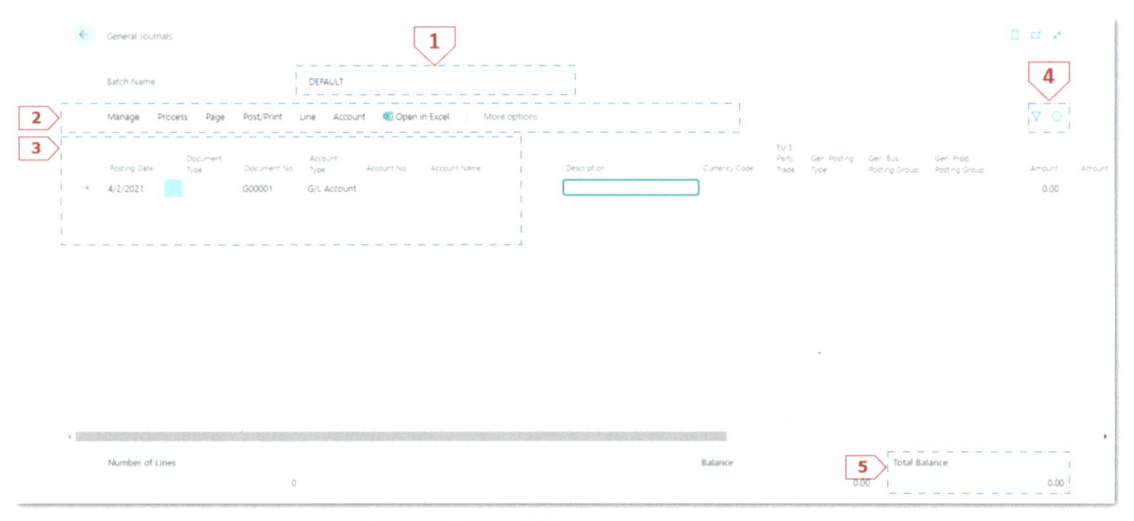

Figure 1-9 - Worksheet Page Appearance

Element	What is it?
1	The **Batch Name** allows users to work with different batches of lines.
2	The **Action Bar** is your menu for the Worksheet Page.
3	The **Lines** area is the data of the worksheet.
4	Worksheet pages can also be filtered on, as well as show/hide the FactBox area.
5	Financial Worksheet pages have a **Total Balance** for the lines.

REPORTS

Reports in Business Central come in two main kinds:

- Printable Reports – these create some sort of document for you to print or send.
- Processing Reports – these perform specific tasks in the system.

When you run Printable Reports, which are often in the Action Bar on most Pages:

1. Typically, it presents you with an **Options & Filtering** window. (as shown below)
2. The data is prepared for display.
3. The data is sent to a Layout to be displayed, which usually go to one of these:
    a. PDF
    b. Word
    c. Printer
    d. Email

Processing Reports are typically handled in a similar sequence:

1. It presents you with an **Options & Filtering** window. (see example below)
2. The task is performed and then you will be notified when it is completed.

A great example of a report showing the Options & Filtering window is the **Sales – Confirmation** report:

You select the **Printer** (**1**).

The **Options** (**2**) section are specific settings that this report might need you to choose 'at runtime', which may have default or required settings.

The **Filter** (**3**) section allows you to see or set what 'subset' of data should be used. We can see that we are filtering on **Document Type** of **Order**, with order **No.** of **101002**, and strangely, **Bill-To Customer** of **10000**.

We could technically remove the filter from the **No.** field and print all the Order Confirmations for all Orders that have **Bill-To Customer** of **10000** in one go. Filtering will be covered later in this chapter, as it is a powerful tool you should have!

You can **Print** (**6**) or **Preview** (**7**).

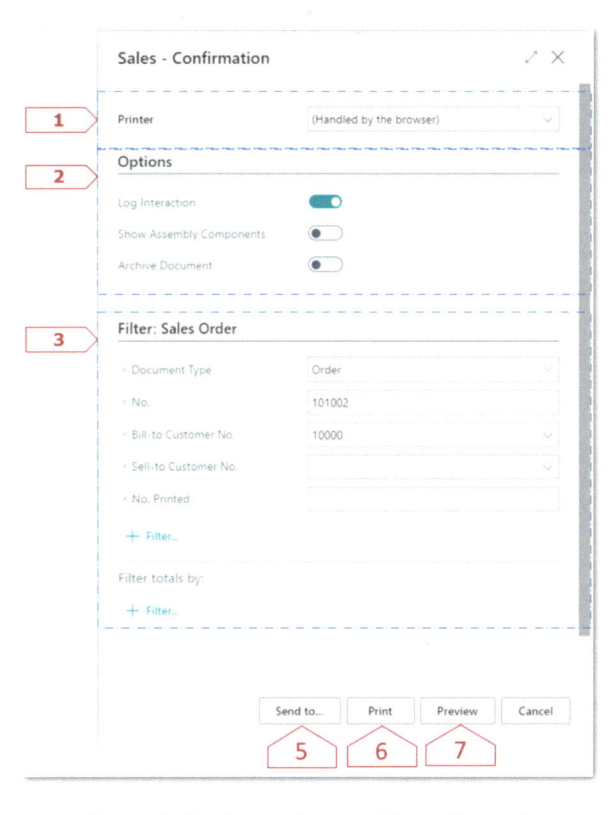

Figure 1-10 - Report Request Dialog Example

There can be some additional options in the bottom section:

In this case, we have a **Send To...** (**5**) button which allows us to create a PDF or Word document from the same report. For other reports (for list reports instead of Documents), you might also have the option to send to Excel.

You may also have the option to **Schedule** reports, which allows you to queue up reports to run later. One possible use of this could be that during the morning you could, for example, schedule 5 or 6 long-running reports to run automatically in the evening after everyone is done for the day. The reports will end up in your **Report Inbox** on the Role Center once the scheduled creation is done.

PART 1: GETTING TO KNOW BC
CHAPTER 1: GETTING TO KNOW THE UI

TABLET & PHONE

It is worth mentioning - Microsoft Dynamics 365 Business Central natively supports an app (the *Universal App*), which is currently available in:

- **Google Play** for Android devices.
- **App Store** for Apple devices.
- **Microsoft Store** for Windows.

If you are using Microsoft Dynamics 365 Business Central Cloud, it works straight away, *as easily as setting up an email*. If you are using BC on-premises (or private cloud), this may require additional setup.

When working on a Tablet or Phone, you will have live access (*online only!*) to all the data and functions, but in a UI that is specifically designed for mobile.

PREVIEW THE MOBILE UI IN YOUR WEB BROWSER

You can take a quick preview of what those look like by simply adding "tablet" or "phone" to *your BC URL*, for example:

In the URL for my local test system (http://bc18-w1/BC/) I use http://bc18-w1/BC/**tablet** and I get the Tablet UI on my PC.

In most web browsers, you can enable an "Inspect" view of BC (by right-clicking in your Business Central window and selecting **Inspect** (**1**) and even emulate different **devices** (**2**) like the **iPhone X** (**3**) to get a better view of what everything will look like *in that format*:

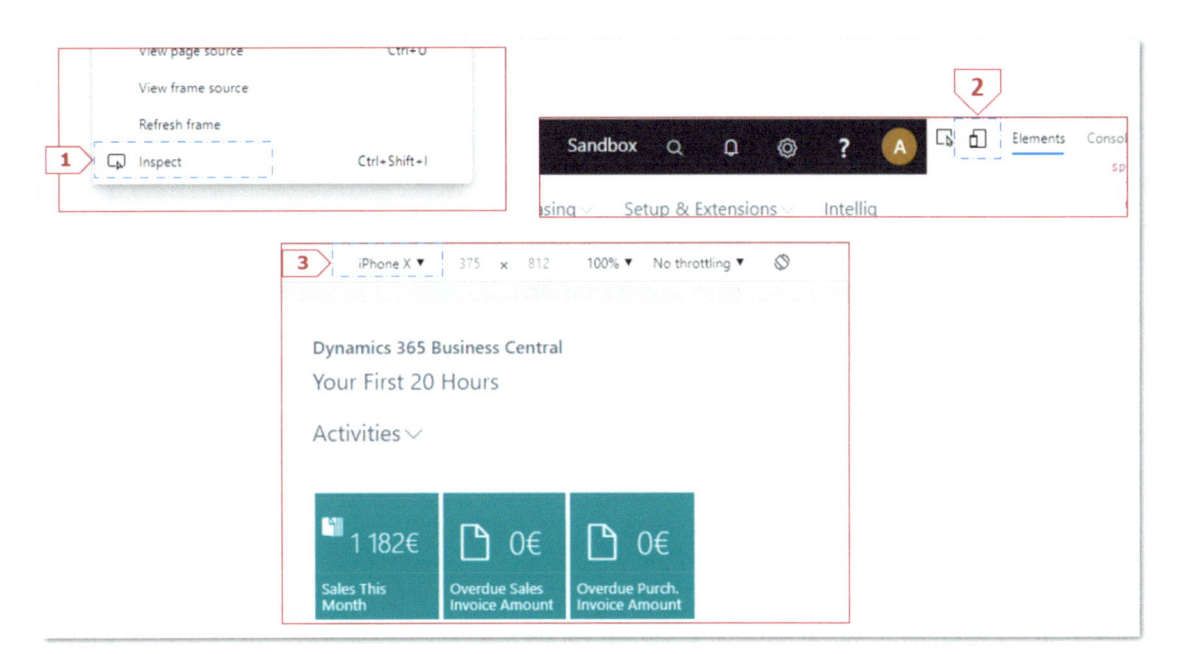

Figure 1-11 - Browser tools to emulate devices

Skills You will Want to Master

The following section will highlight some skills that you will be able to use throughout the system and once learned, you will want to share these with the rest of your staff or coworkers.

Filtering

Within the **Filter list by** section of the ▽ Filter Pane, you can manually add filters. Each filter consists of two parts:

- *Which field do you want to filter with?*
- *What filter do you wish to apply?*

When you add a new filter, it will ask for both parts. When selecting which field to filter, it will group things together for you to choose from:

1. Visible fields on the page, in the order they appear.
2. Available fields that live in the table underlying the data.

You can manually begin to search for a field by writing its name to quickly filter on it. Even though **Payment Terms Code** is not a field on the 🔍 **Customers** list (as an example), you could filter on that field since it is *living* on the **Customer Card**:

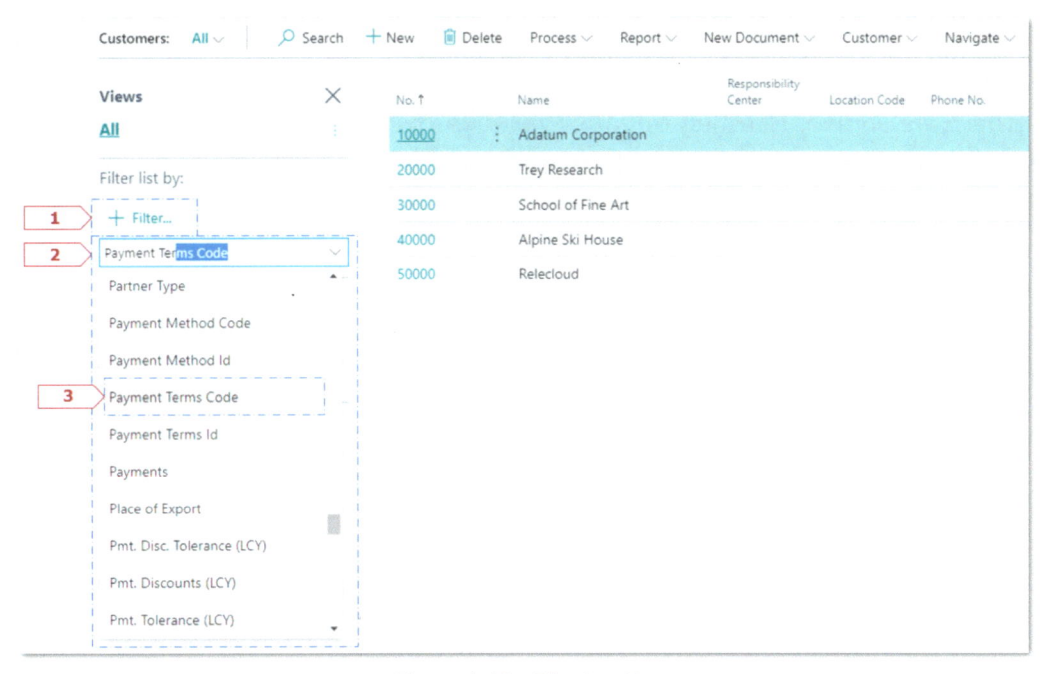

Figure 1-12 - Filtering Lists

By clicking on **+ Filter...** (**1**), you can type name of a field (**2**) or select from the list (**3**). After selecting the field, it will provide you with a space to enter *what filter* you would like to apply to the selected field(s):

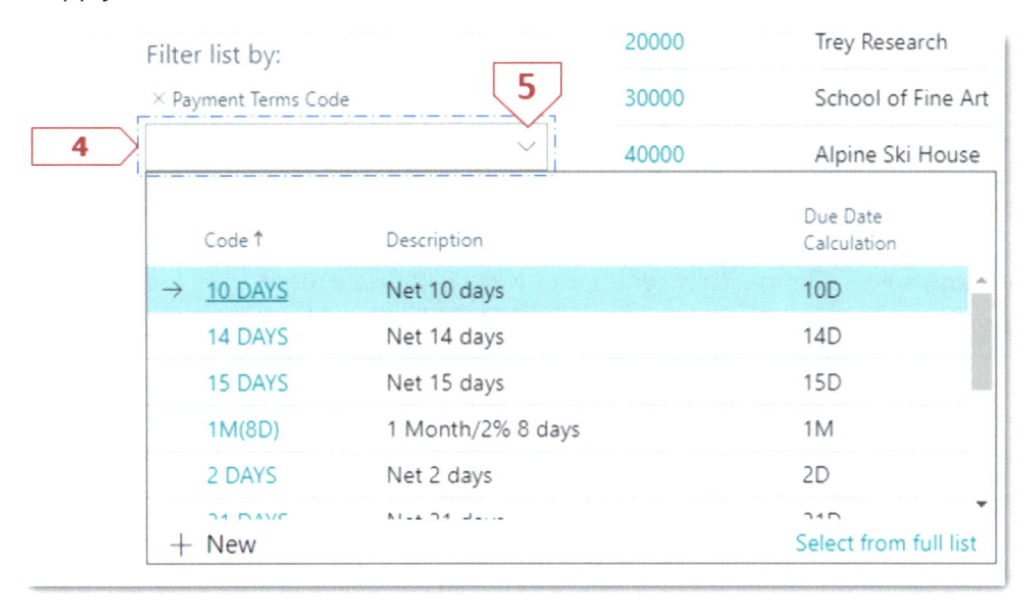

Figure 1-13 - Filtering by a field

PART 1: GETTING TO KNOW BC
CHAPTER 1: GETTING TO KNOW THE UI

In the **Payment Terms Code** example, we enter a code (**4**) or could select a single value via the drop-down (**5**) from the list of 🔍 **Payment Terms**.

There are some interesting options available to you as a user for filtering. We will address several of them here - some basic ones, and some notable ones.

We recommend reading more on the Docs page for [Entering Filtering Criteria](#).

Symbol	Explanation	Example
@	Makes the filter case insensitive.	@london
*	An indefinite number of symbols.	Lon*
?	Match a specific number of characters, example would match on "London" and "Lindon".	L?ndon
>	Greater than.	>200
<	Less than.	<1200
<= or >=	Greater than or equal to; Less than or equal to.	<=1200
&	Combine multiple filters.	>=200&<=1200
|	Either/Or filter.	1200|1300
..	This one is a 'range' interval, and context driven. It works with text, numbers, dates and more. At the beginning, "Up to and including". Between values, "Between and including". At the end, "Including and after".	..2000 1000..2000 9000.. ..SO-010010 CUS100..CUS199 VEND500..
%me	Any time you are filtering on a user field, you can just use **%me** for your own account.	
%mycustomers	On the Role Center, there is a **My Customers** panel. Any customer in that list is available using this shortcut 'token' when filtering on a **Customer No.** field.	
%myvendors	Same as above, but for vendors.	
%myitems	Same as above, but for items.	

When entering dates, there is also a huge *superpower* of how it helps you quickly enter values. There are more than we will cover in this book available on the Microsoft

Docs site – [Entering Dates](#) page, but here are some things to know (all of these may vary based on your chosen Language in Settings):

In a date field you can enter two, four, six, or eight digits:

- If you enter *only* two digits, this is interpreted as the day, and it will add the month and the year of the work date.
- If you enter four digits, this is interpreted as the day and the month, and it will add the year of the work date. The order of the day and month is determined by your region settings. Even if your region settings have the year before the day and month, four digits are interpreted as the day and month.
- If the date you want to enter is in the range 01/01/1930 through 12/31/2029, you can enter the year with two digits; otherwise, enter the year with four digits.

You can also use shortcuts like:

- 't' or 'today' for today's date.
- 'w' or 'workdate' for the **Work Date** you are set to (under **Settings**).
- 'mo', 'tu' etc. – the weekday name of the **Work Date** week.
- For filtering on dates, you can also use 'p#', where the # is the Accounting Period (often months). Entering 'p2' in a date filter will filter automatically for the entire month of February for the **Work Date** year.

PART 1: GETTING TO KNOW BC
CHAPTER 1: GETTING TO KNOW THE UI

PERSONALIZE

Sometimes when you are working with Pages in BC, you might know the data exists for *something*, but is not showing on the page you are looking at.

One such example: on the **Customers** list, you know the **Customer Card** has a field for which currency the customer uses – however, that field only shows on the Customer Card, not the **Customers** list. Under **Settings**, you can choose **Personalize**; this opens the personalization view:

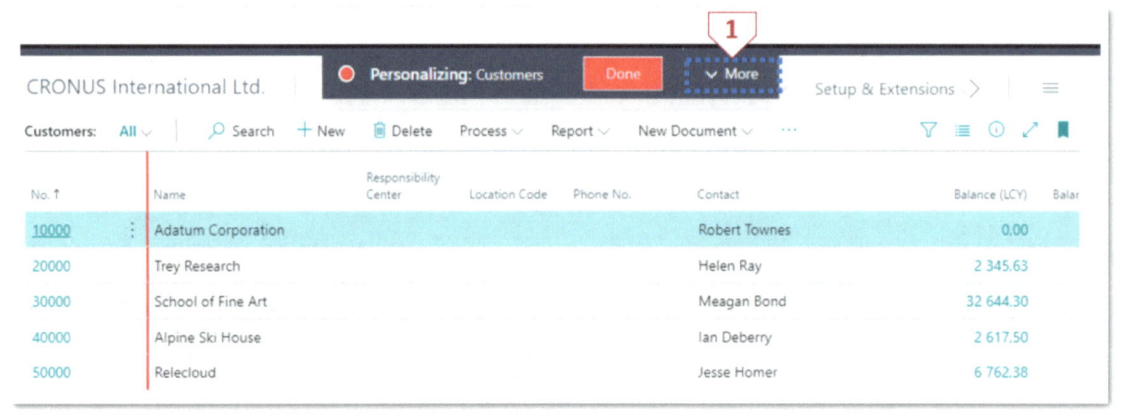

Figure 1-14 - Initial Personalizing View

You will now be able to adjust the page in a small array of ways, such as reordering fields, hiding fields, and more.

In our example, we want to add a field, which is not visible by default. If we select the **More** (**1**) option in the Personalizing panel, we see we can add a **Field** (**2**):

Figure 1-15 - Personalizing Steps

This will present us with a list of fields we might want to drag onto the list, including our **Currency Code** (**4**):

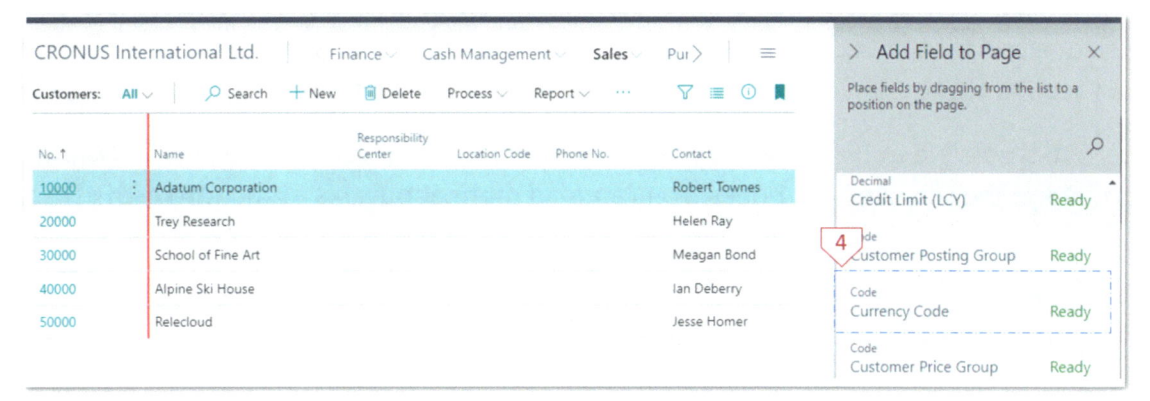

Figure 1-16 - Personalizing - Adding Fields

We will drag that field into the list headers, before the **Location Code** column (in the headers (**5**)):

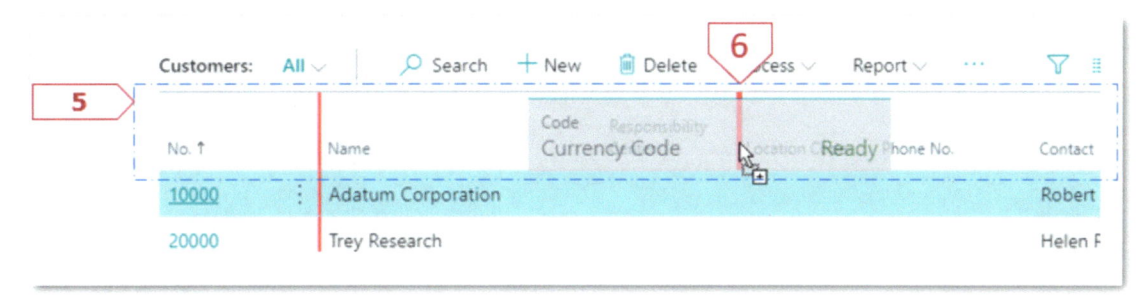

Figure 1-17 - Personalizing - Adding Fields

You will know that it is landing in the right place when the pink line (**6**) appears.

Lastly, click **Done** (**3**) (Figure 1-15). You will then see the newly added column, **Currency Code** (**7**):

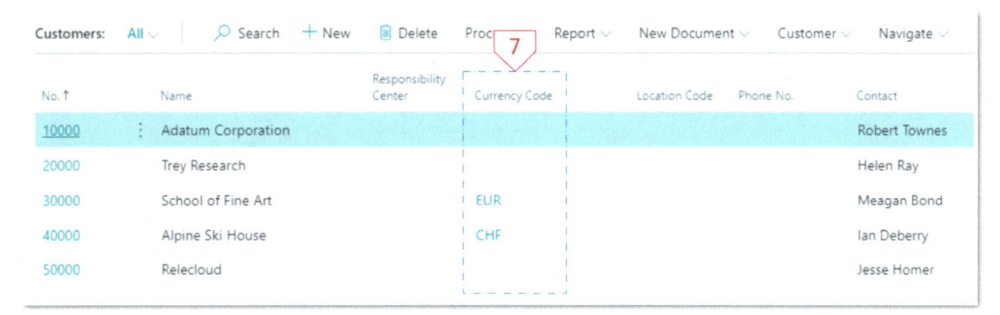

Figure 1-18 - Personalizing - Field Added

PART 1: GETTING TO KNOW BC
CHAPTER 1: GETTING TO KNOW THE UI

This is how you can make the system fit your workflow a little better. Note that Personalizations are tied to your user (they are *personal*!), so only *you* see them, but you will see the changes on every machine you access the system from.

It is possible to make these sorts of minor adjustments for a whole Profile, but that is beyond the scope of this book. You can read more about this at the **Microsoft Docs** site:

https://docs.microsoft.com/en-us/dynamics365/business-central/dev-itpro/developer/devenv-design-profiles-using-client

DIG INTO DETAILS

From time to time, you may become interested in knowing more about data that *might not be visible*, but you do not need it showing all the time, or the data is not even visible on the list of **Personalization** fields you can add. When that happens, we can open the **Page Inspector**.

Under the **Help** menu, click on **Help & Support**, here you will get some additional information and links. There is a link at the *bottom* of this list to **Inspect pages and data**. If you open this while you are on the **Customers** list, you can see it shows a new panel about the Customer list page:

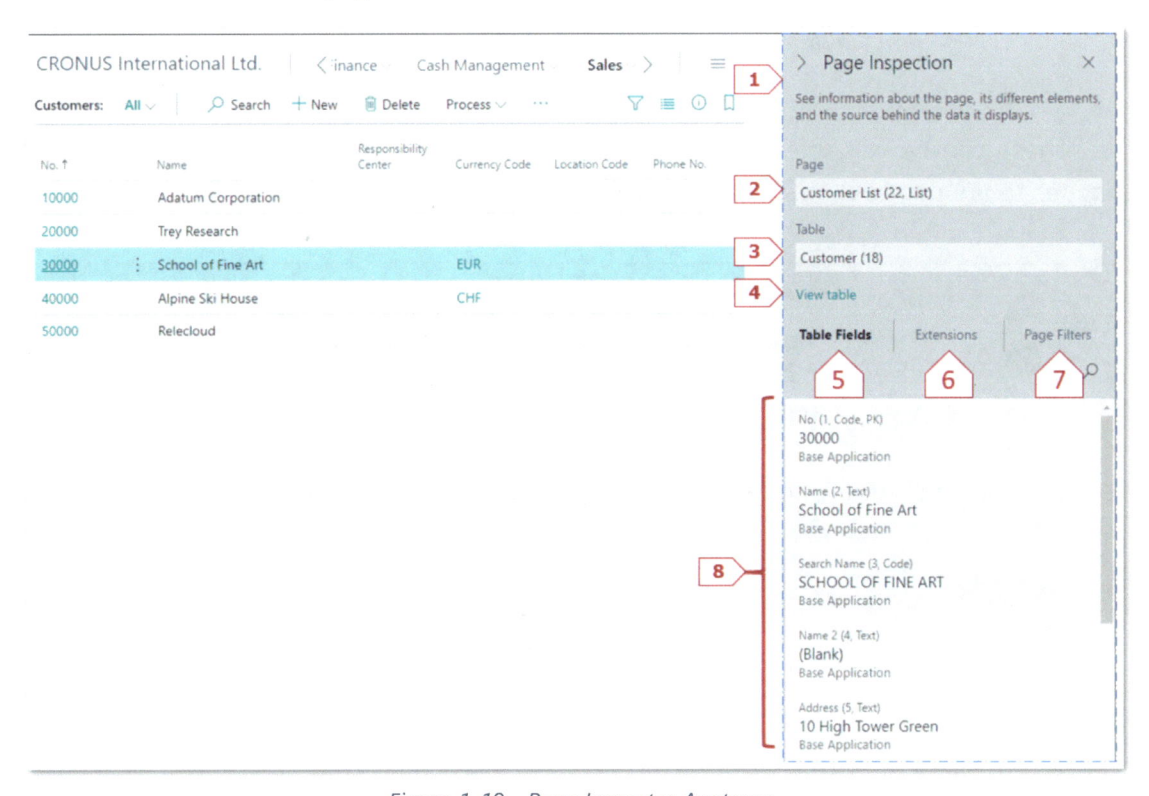

Figure 1-19 - Page Inspector Anatomy

The **Page Inspection** pane (**1**) shows:

- What **Page** (**2**) is displaying is great information if you are working with a Partner to customize your system, or trying to help someone, and you need to *ensure* that you both are on literally the same page.

- In **Table** (**3**), this shows which Table ID the data comes from, which is very helpful when troubleshooting with a Partner.
- You can click **View Table** (**4**) to see all the data that exists in the underlying Table.
- The Section numbered (**8**) is a list of things that can be changed by the toggles (**5**, **6**, and **7**):
    - When you click **Table Fields** (**5**), you can scroll through the fields to see the data. Additionally, using the 🔍 **Magnifying Glass**, you can search by Field Name to see specific data,
    - When you select the **Extensions** (**6**) toggle, you will see which Extensions (see Note below) are installed in your system and are currently affecting the view you are looking at.
    - When viewing the **Page Filters** (**7**), it shows you if there are any filters being applied.

These can be valuable tools and information when working with partners making changes to your system or to support staff you are working with.

> ℹ️ Note: What are Extensions? Extensions are how Business Central is modified. Extensions can be fully developed products released via the AppSource marketspace (run by Microsoft) or changes developed by a partner for one specific system.
>
> An Extension contains all the data, logic, and UI changes that affect your system. Extensions can add more fields or actions to a Page, or hide elements, or add entire modules, changing the system in very large ways.

CONTROLLING NOTIFICATIONS / MESSAGES

As you are working through the system, you will often be asked a set of confirmation questions like this:

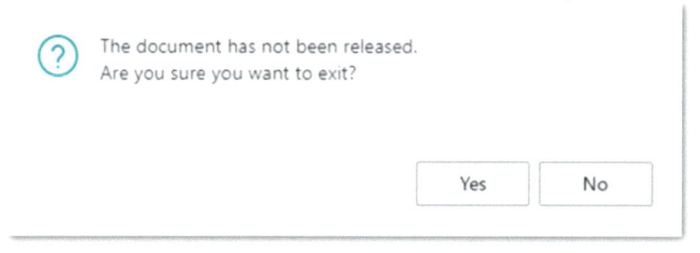

Figure 1-20 - Example Notification Dialog Box

In the ⚙ **Settings** -> **My Settings** window, there is a link to **Change when I receive notifications** (**1**):

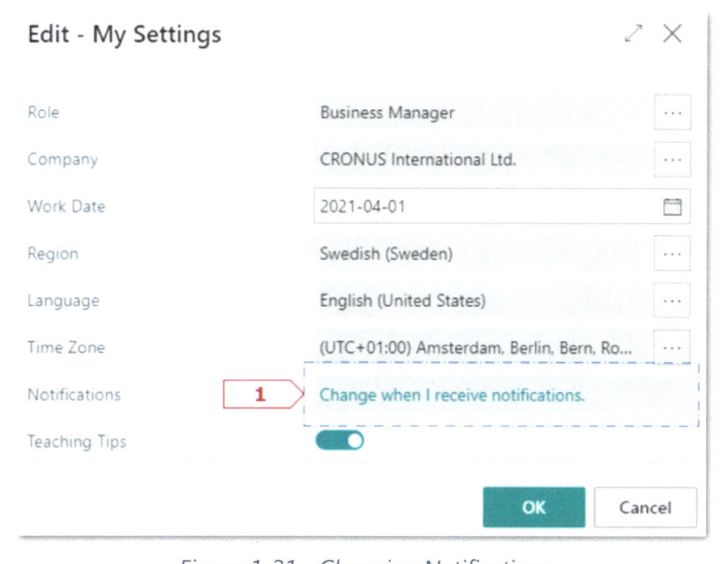

Figure 1-21 - Changing Notifications

This opens the **My Notifications** list that allows you to enable or disable many notifications, including our **Warn about unreleased orders** (**2**) example:

PART 1: GETTING TO KNOW BC
CHAPTER 1: GETTING TO KNOW THE UI

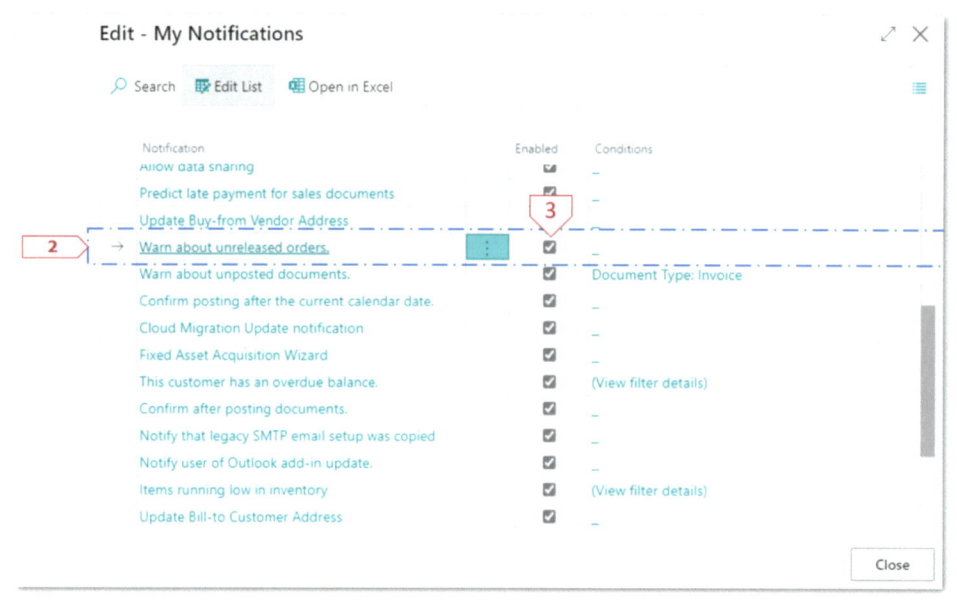

Figure 1-22 - Configuration of My Notifications

Some of these are of great benefit, but others you may want to disable by clearing the check mark in **Enabled** (**3**).

You should *definitely* teach your team about this – they will thank you!

WORK DATE

It can sometimes be of great value to have the system 'assume' you are working on another date, such as performing a month or year closing process, where you will enter a prior date over and over.

You can change the **Work Date** to a different date via the **Settings** -> **My Settings** window menu. When you create Documents, journal entries, and more, the system will act as if you are working on that date. This way, Posting Dates and Document Dates will default to your Work Date. This only affects your login, so other people can continue working as normal.

Super helpful!

DRILL-DOWN / FLOWFIELDS

Many places in the system will appear to be hyperlinks - the blue text you can click on.

When you click on them, they bring you to related records about the information you clicked. This is very common on the Role center and in FactBoxes. On the **Customer Card**, we can see the **Balance (LCY)** (**1**) field is an example of such:

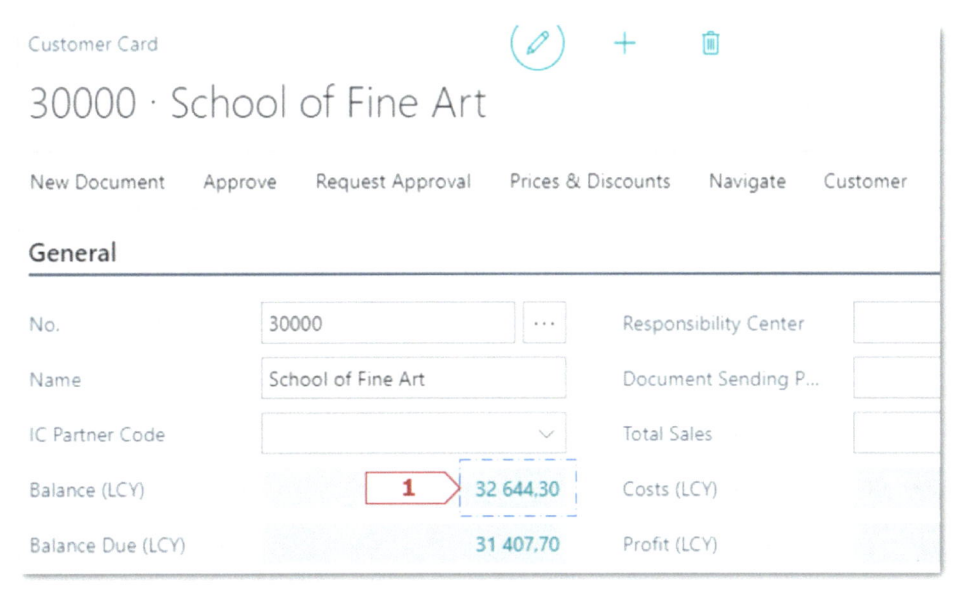

Figure 1-23 - Example Drill-Down / FlowField

When we click on the balance, it is taking us to the open **Customer Ledger Entries** that comprises the balance, which in this case is based on the **Remaining Amount (LCY)** (**2**):

Figure 1-24 - Customer Ledger Entries

Under the hood, Microsoft Dynamics 365 Business Central is not *storing* that **Balance (LCY)** anywhere – it is calculated every time it is displayed, making it show you up-to-date information as much as possible.

PART 1: GETTING TO KNOW BC
CHAPTER 1: GETTING TO KNOW THE UI

PAGE 49

This calculation system is one of the shining beacons of the product from its early days, referred to as **Sum Index Flow Technology**. This technology was designed to be able to quickly *sum* values from related tables and *flow* that sum into a field based on *filters*. While that technology has grown to support more things over time, the framework remains, as we still refer to these fields as **FlowFields**.

This Customer **Balance (LCY)** field is just such a **FlowField**, showing a calculation on information living in another table – the Customer Ledger Entries.

This is technology is heavily used on the **Chart of Accounts**, where it uses the filtering part, the **FlowFilter**, which shows as **Filter totals by** (**3**).

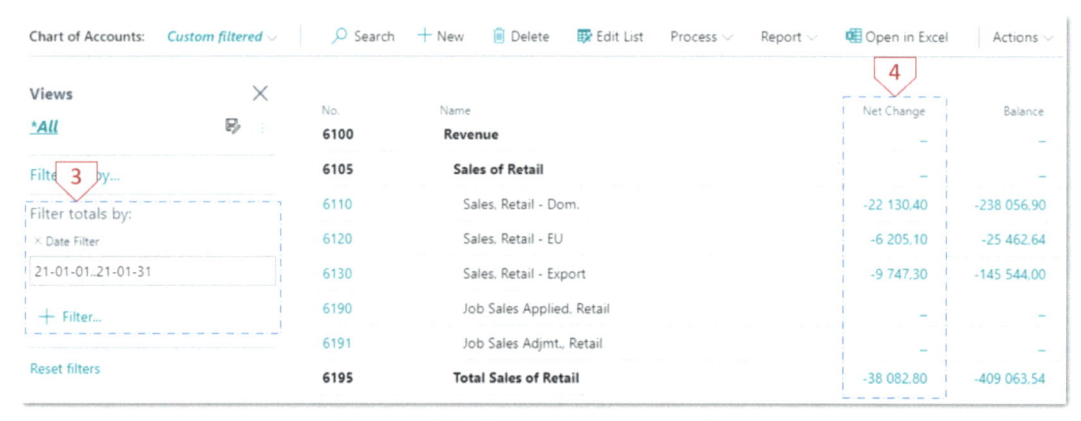

Figure 1-25 - Filter totals by / FlowFilters

On the Chart of Accounts, this is the technology that helps you see the **Net Change** (**4**) by a specific month, quarter, day – any date range.

ROLE EXPLORER

In the upper right corner of the Role Center Navigation Area, you will find the link to the Role Explorer:

Figure 1-26 - Opening Role Explorer

When you click on that, it will show you a summary of many of the parts of the Role Center in a large list so you can more easily browse through all your Role Center actions and links:

Figure 1-27 - Role Explorer

From here, you can also **Explore All** to see functionality that is not normally part of your Role Center. This can be of particularly large help when you are filling in or assisting a teammate who has different responsibilities!

PART 1: GETTING TO KNOW BC
CHAPTER 1: GETTING TO KNOW THE UI

PAGE 51

Keyboard Shortcuts

On the Microsoft Docs site, there is a great "Cheat Sheet" of the keyboard shortcuts of working with the system that is worth going and checking out:

[Working with the General Functionality in Business Central - Business Central | Microsoft Docs](#)

Here are some of the highlights from that list:

General functions
Keyboard shortcuts

Ctrl+F1 Business Central Help	Shift+F12 (≡) Role Explorer	Ctrl+Alt+F1 Inspect page and data
Alt+T My Settings	Alt+N (+) Create a new record	Alt+O Add a new note for the selected record
Alt+Q (🔍) Open Tell Me	Alt+Shift+N Close a newly created record and create a new one	Alt+F2 (ⓘ) Toggle FactBox area
F5 Refresh data	Alt+Shift+W (◲) Pop-out a page to a separate window	Ctrl+F12 (↗) Switch between slim/wide page

Data in lists
Keyboard shortcuts

Alt+F7 Sort column in asc/desc order	Ctrl+Shift+F3 Toggle filter pane; focus on totals filters	Ctrl+Enter Change focus from filter pane back to list
Shift+F3 (▽) Toggle filter pane; focus on data filters	F3 (🔍) Toggle the search box	Ctrl+Alt+Shift+F3 Reset filters
Alt+F3 Filter on selected cell value	Shift+Alt+F3 Add filter on selected field	

Entering Data
Keyboard shortcuts

F8 Copy from the cell above	Ctrl+Insert Insert a new line in documents	F6 Move to the next FastTab or part
Enter/Shift+Enter Go to next/previous Quick Entry field	Ctrl+Delete Delete the line in documents, journals, and worksheets	Shift+F6 Move to the previous FastTab or part (sub-page)
Ctrl+Shift+Enter Go to next Quick Entry field outside a list	Ctrl+Shift+F12 (⛶) Toggle Focus Mode	Alt+F6 Toggle collapse/expand for the current field group (FactBox)

Figure 1-28 - Example Shortcut Keys

Summary

With this understanding of Role Centers, Cards, Lists, and Documents, you will have more insight into how content is displayed as you work throughout the system. You will now be able to get to the information you need faster and work more efficiently as you master the system.

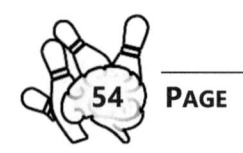

Chapter 2: Understanding How Everything Connects

In this chapter, we are going to go over the general idea of how Microsoft Dynamics 365 Business Central works. What are the main functional areas? How is information roughly classified? How does information flow through the system?

While it might not feel like a very hands-on topic to get started with, if you understand the *idea* of how the patterns of a **module** (group of functionalities) works, when you want to start using a new module, you will find you can quickly grasp how it should work – or where to look if you are having trouble.

What's In the Box?

Microsoft Dynamics 365 Business Central is referred to as an Enterprise Resource Planning (ERP) system. This means that it helps a business to manage and plan their resources. This can mean money, inventory, and resources (people, equipment, etc.). In this case, the system also has some additional and related management components. Let us review the "functional" areas of the system:

Figure 2-1 - Modules in Business Central

1. Financial Management – This is the core of managing the flow of money/value through your entire system.
2. Purchasing & Payables – This is the module that contains everything about Vendors and your relationship/activity with them.
3. Sales & Receivables – This is the module that contains almost everything about selling to Customers and your activity with them.

4. Inventory – The Inventory system is about managing items, along with their costs. There is a LOT of features in this beyond simple Item tracking, such as multiple Location support or even assembly management for kit items.
5. Jobs – When it comes to projects, you need to manage the cost, billing, and budgets. The Jobs module is typically not called Projects (in English – localizations vary) because it is not a 100% complete project management toolset, but it can be used to provide many of those aspects.
6. Resources – Resources allow you to track equipment and people. This integrates tightly with Jobs and Service but can be used stand-alone to add sales of resources, such as delivery fees for trucks.
7. CRM – While not a fully developed Customer Relationship Management module, there are many of the supporting components, such as Contact management, segmenting, and marketing pieces.
8. Manufacturing – The manufacturing module is all about supporting production of goods from raw materials, subassemblies, and even outsourced production. It has significant tools to plan your JIT processes.
9. Service – Some items, when sold, need to be maintained and supported over time. The Service Module handles support contracts, warranties (and cost management of those warranties) or billable service calls. This integrates heavily with the Resources system to also support complex zone and skill management.
10. Warehousing – Very complex inventory systems require their own management to handle Picking and Put-Aways, or even cross-docking. This integrates very tightly with the Inventory module. Because this is a separate module, you can easily support different Locations with different configurations.
11. Intercompany and Consolidations – While heavily focused on Financials, this module also supports systems for easily handling Intercompany sales and purchasing.
12. Additional cross-module systems – there are many supporting subsystems that work throughout the Business Central system to additionally enhance how parts work, such as Number Series, Dimensions, Workflows and more.

Data Organized Neatly

All the data in the system is stored in something called Tables, a collection of fields (like Excel columns) stored on one or many records (like Excel rows). These are *generally* of differing conceptual types, which can help you quickly understand what role they play, where to find them, and how they are used.

Master Data

These are Core Entities that are used in many places. **Customers** or **Items** are both two common examples of Master Data. They consist of lots of information about a given data entity. Often, they have single-value settings that will come from Supplemental or Setup tables, such as on the Customer, where there is a field for "Payment Terms" which comes from the Reference Table "Payment Terms".

Core Entities usually have Subsidiary Table settings that can have a list of values. A common example of this is that Items have a list of **Item Units of Measure** which tells the system which **Units of Measure** (Reference data) are valid for a given Item (Master).

You will *generally* see these as a List, with a Card to work with each entity. The single-value settings will be a field on the card with a drop-down. Subsidiary settings are available via the Action Bar and will open as a separate list page.

Supplemental Data

Supplemental Data tables are lists of possible settings that are valid for the user to select from. Two examples later in this book are **Languages** and **Currencies**, which are lists that are usually provided to the user to select a value. This allows you to easily add and update settings as needs grow over time. You will typically see these as Lists. Sometimes they will have a Card to edit their settings if they are complex enough.

Setup Data

Setup Data is a single record of information that will be used in many places - an easy example of this is the **Company Information** setup. In each BC Company, you would only have one legal entity, so, you have a single Company Information record providing information to any part of the system that needs (for example) your company's address. There is typically one core Setup table for each module – for example, the Sales & Receivables Setup for the Sales & Receivables Module.

DOCUMENTS

Document Data consists of at least two main tables; a Header and a Line. Looking at one example: on a 🔍 **Sales Quote**, you have 1 header record and as many lines as you need, related to the Header. There can be related supporting data for each Header and Line Record.

For the Header, you might have attached Documents. You will access these via the Action Bar on a Document page.

For each Line, you might have Reservations (to lock availability) or Item Tracking Lines (for Lot or Serial tracking). You will access these via the Action Bar of the List Part that is showing the lines.

The role of Documents is to operate as a "worksheet" for operational staff to enter, update, and maintain the information about that document until it is posted.

When Documents are "Posted", they will often be removed from the list of open Documents to then be copied to the relevant Document History table.

The Document History table is typically unchangeable and is usually the route to your ability to reprint/resend documents, such as a 🔍 **Posted Sales Credit Memo**.

> ℹ️ Note: This is a key concept that challenges many new users. When you Post a Sales Order *completely*, it is gone! You will have one or more related Document History entries, including multiple Posted Sales Shipments and Posted Sales Invoices.
>
> Due to the flexibility in Invoicing, you may also have a Posted Sales Invoice that contains lines from several different Sales Orders. This can get even more complex with Prepayment Invoices and Sales Order Archiving!

Journals

At its heart, Microsoft Dynamics 365 Business Central is an accounting system. To add information to the **Ledgers**, this is always done through a **Journal**, even if automatically for you (more on that soon). Journals are a Worksheet where you enter information about a given Transaction. Until it is "posted", it is an in-progress piece of information typically not considered 'real' data.

Journals typically are organized by Journal Template and Journal Batch. What information is on each Template and Batch varies by module, but Templates are to provide many default settings for all Journals of a given type. Batches are a way to have multiple journals being created/edited at the same time.

When a Journal is "posted", it is moved to the Ledger.

Ledgers

Ledgers are the permanent record of transactions. Typically, the only way to affect Ledgers is to post new entries that offset them. As an example, if Payment Journal is posted where someone accidentally entered an extra zero, you cannot delete that error or change the amount. You will need to post a new Journal entry that creates a matching reversing entry. This is typically a requirement of accounting systems to pass auditing scrutiny. Microsoft Dynamics 365 Business Central delightfully provides many tools to help make those sorts of corrections simpler, some of which will be reviewed in **Chapter 18**.

Some modules also have supporting ledgers to record activity specific to that area of the system, for example, if a **Customer** has 3 open invoices, and makes a Payment to pay all 3, there will be a single **Payment** entry in the **Customer Ledger Entry**. However, there is a Subledger called the **Detailed Customer Ledger Entry** that acts as a *mini ledger* for each transaction. When the Payment is "applied" to the Invoice, it will create a new Ledger Entry in the Detailed Customer Ledger Entry to show the reduction in 'open' balance. More on this in both **Chapter 17** and **Chapter 18**!

THE DATA MUST FLOW

As mentioned in the last section, the Ledgers are the permanent core memory of the system, and to get data into them, you create Journals, which are "posted" – recorded in the ledger. So how do Documents make data happen? How does a single Sales Order of a single Item make all the following Ledger Entries?

Module	Ledger	Account / Code	Amount	Description
Inventory	Item Ledger Entry	1920-S	-1	This affects the "Inventory" for the Item 1920-S by negative 1
Inventory	Value Entry	1920-S	(complex)	This is how the Cost of Goods Sold is deducted from the Sale
S&R	Cust. Ledger Entry	10000	525,50	The customer 10000 now will show a balance of 525,50 owed for this Invoice
S&R	Detailed Cust. Ledger Entry	10000	525,50	An entry called "initial Entry" goes into the Subledger for this invoice, making the Open Amount 525,50
Financials	VAT Entry	(complex)	105,10	In my case, the VAT is registered to record the Tax Debt
Financials	General Ledger Entry	Sales, Retail	-420,40	The sale is registered on my Income Statement G/L Account
Financials	General Ledger Entry	Sales VAT 25%	-105,10	The tax obligation is recorded on my Balance Sheet G/L Account
Financials	General Ledger Entry	Accounts Receivables	525,50	The Customer Debt to me is recorded on my Balance Sheet G/L Account

Additionally, the following History Documents have been created:

- Posted Sales Shipment
- Posted Sales Invoice

As you can see from the **Post: Ship** action leading to **Item Ledger Entry** (Figure 2-2), there is a connection over to the Inventory module, and there is information that flows to the **General Ledger Entries** (Financials Module), but for the most part, we are within the Sales & Receivables Module.

The flow roughly looks like so:

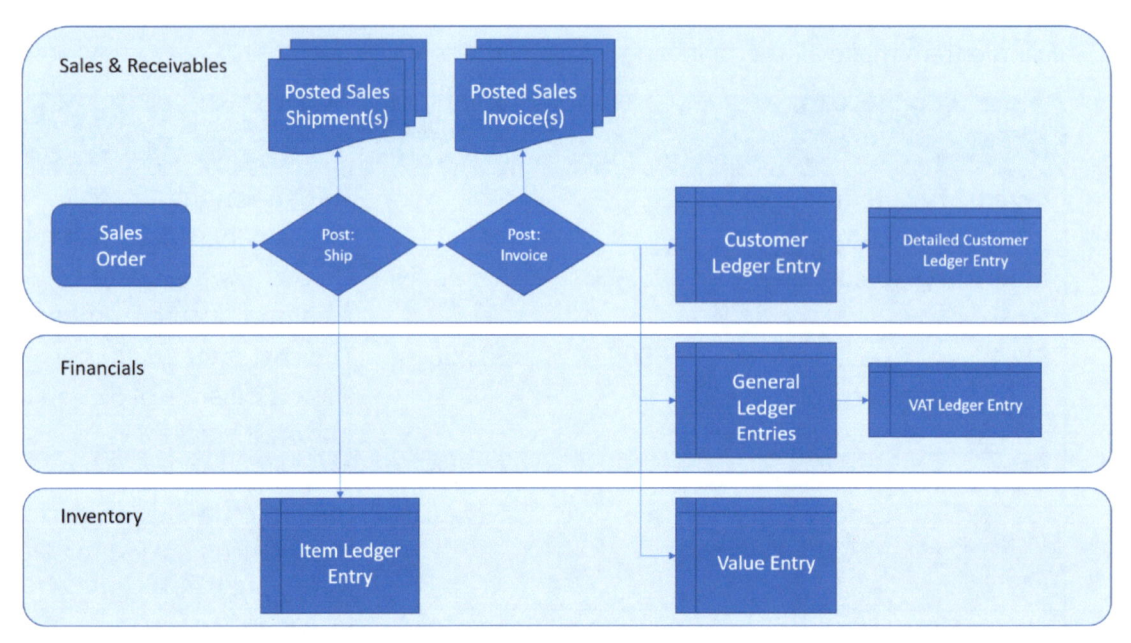

Figure 2-2 - Document to Ledgers Workflow

As you can see, the Sales Order Document travels a lot of places.

First, when you **Post** the **Sales Order** in the **Shipment** mode, it creates a Posted Sales Shipment -- this will be a History Document. It will also (depending on settings) create related changes in the inventory module (to reflect the change in Item stock levels).

When you **Post** the **Sales Order** in the **Invoice** mode, the financial implications are 'realized'. This results in a **Posted Sales Invoice**, which is the Document History.

This will also create ledger entries in the **Customer Ledger Entry** and **Detailed Customer Ledger Entry** for the Sales & Receivables module to be able to show you:

- customer balance information
- per-invoice level payment information (so you can send a Customer a statement showing which invoices are unpaid by how much)

This will also create ledger entries in the **General Ledger** to be able to account for:

- sales results
- tax obligations
- customer debt

This is all happening under the hood via journals. The posting process does all the following:

- creates history documents
- creates relevant journals
- posts relevant journals

This means that you *can* just post an invoice for a customer without ever entering a document if you do not need to be able to produce the document from Microsoft Dynamics 365 Business Central. As detailed further in **Chapter 13**, if you are bringing over open balances from a prior system, you will probably want to just enter the open invoices via journals and post them. This will create all the correct ledger entries without having to recreate all the Document data.

This pattern of "Document to Journal to Ledger" is used throughout almost every module. Odds are quite high that if you see the word **Post**, it is going to follow this flow.

One question you *probably* had earlier, while looking at the Ledger Entries going to our General Ledger, was *"How did it know which accounts to use?"*. That is for the next chapter!

> ## Try It!
>
> With a CRONUS company, you should be able to use "Tell Me" to get to the Sales Order list. Create a new Sales Order via the **New** Action. In the **Customer Name**, click the **...** (AssistEdit) to select a customer from the list – most likely, any will do.
>
> In the **Lines** section, change **Type** to **Item**. Enter **1920-S** in the **No.** field, then enter **1** in **Quantity**. (Your first sales order, done!)
>
> In the Action Bar, select **Posting** and choose **Post...**, then with **Ship and Invoice** selection, click **OK**. It will offer to open the Posted Invoice. Choose **Yes**.
>
> On the **Posted Sales Invoice**, in the Action Bar, select **Invoice** and choose **Find entries...** to see all the results. You will see our example list and can click on the **No. of Entries** columns to drill-down into the details behind each number.

Summary

You now have a pretty good grasp of the general areas of the system. You now know what underlying patterns are used and should have a better chance of understanding new modules. You should also now have a sense of how Documents, Journals, and Ledgers connect.

The good news for you – the rest of the book from herein is very hands-on!

PART 2: BUILDING YOUR FOUNDATION

Chapters 3 through 5 will cover essential frameworks in Microsoft Dynamics 365 Business Central – posting groups, Locations, and Company-wide Setup.

Chapter 6 will walk you through the Setup for each Module we will use in this guide.

Chapter 7 will walk you through preparing the Customer, Vendors, and Items for import.

Chapter 8 will be the Master Data Import process itself.

Chapter 9 will be connecting the Posting Groups to your newly imported Chart of Accounts.

IMPORTANT NOTE:

As of April 1, 2021, Microsoft Dynamics 365 Business Central has the option to use your localized CRONUS data as the default setup for your new Companies at creation. This guide assumes you create an Empty company, but we will mostly align closely with CRONUS International to ensure you will still find value in this guide for how and why you might want to adjust the defaults. Check **Appendix B** about **Companies** for more information.

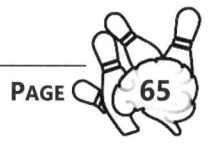

Chapter 3: Product and Business Posting Groups

We are going to be setting up the core Financials shortly, but first we will review how Posting Groups work in BC, so we can prepare some of them before we import the General Ledger Accounts.

QUICK EXPLANATION OF POSTING GROUPS

When you post a sales order with a customer to sell them an item (the example in **Chapter 2**), you will get a variety of entries against G/L Accounts. It would neither be practical to have to memorize which accounts are for which customers and items, nor to teach that to everyone else who will have to use the system.

Business Central handles that via something called **Posting Groups**. They are a map of which entities interact with which G/L Accounts.

In our sales order example, which accounts receivable account should we use? You might have different accounts setup for different fiscal/tax regions, or maybe even for probability of being collected.

This is handled via the **Customer Card**, where there are a few 'Posting Group' settings:

Posting Group	Role
General Business Posting Group	The General Business Group controls where the Sales revenue and Purchases expenses will land, based on the Customer and Vendor Card settings.
VAT Business Posting Group	The VAT Business Posting Group is a secondary layer to indicate where the Tax portion of transactions go.
Customer Posting Group	The Customer Posting Group controls where the Accounts Receivable lands.

In our sales order example (from **Chapter 2**), we also have an item involved. The **Item Card** has a few Posting Group settings as well:

Posting Group	Role
General Product Posting Group	The General Product Posting Group controls where the Cost of Goods Sold will land.
VAT Product Posting Group	The VAT Product Posting Group helps you be able to configure the rates based on the type of item (or resource!) you are buying/selling.
Inventory Posting Group	The Inventory Posting Group controls which Inventory Accounts will be affected (in combination with Locations).

When everything is all brought together in a Document, you now have the pieces of the puzzle, which maps to the Setup tables:

1. Gen. Business Posting Group + Gen. Product Posting Group -> General Posting Setup
2. VAT Business Posting Group + VAT Product Posting Group -> VAT Posting Setup
3. Location + Inventory Posting Group -> Inventory Posting Setup

> **Note:** Like most parts of Business Central, you set the information on the Master table, then when a Document is created, the information is brought to the Document as a default.
>
> You would have Posting Groups defined on a Customer Card, but for a special-order scenario, maybe you need to override the Gen. Business Posting Group – this is possible and allowed but should be done with care.

Aleksander Totovic has a fantastic series of posts on his blog outlining these configurations in detail:

https://totovic.com/favorits/postinggroups/

One great example diagram from his series about how posting groups connect is:

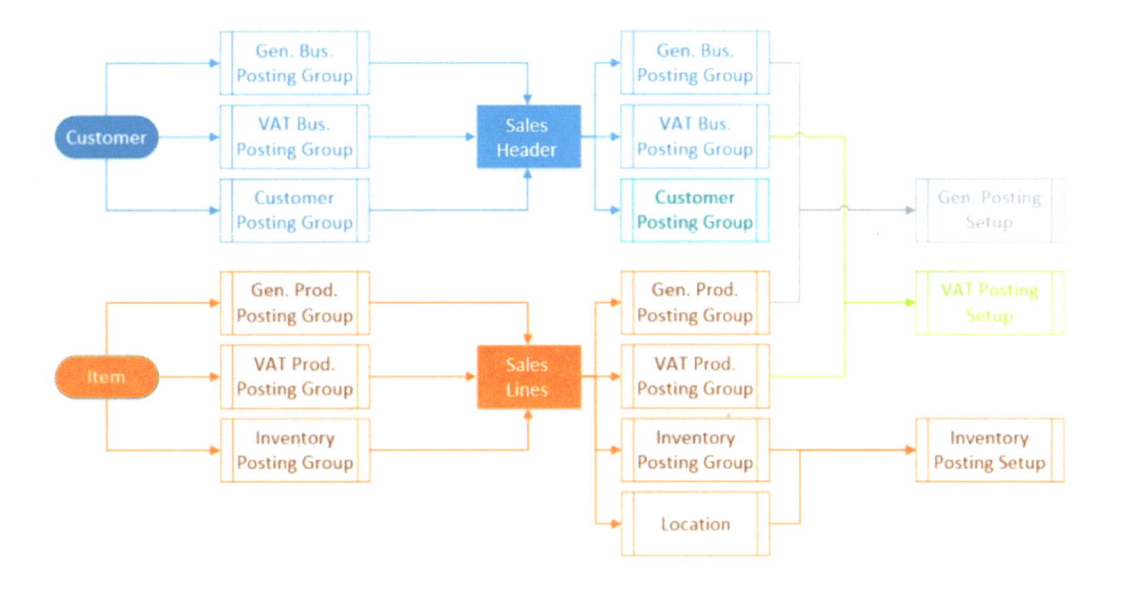

Figure 3-1 - How Gen. Posting Groups Combine

PART 2: BUILDING YOUR FOUNDATION
CHAPTER 3: PRODUCT AND BUSINESS POSTING GROUPS

For the CRONUS databases in Europe, the Business Posting Groups are often broken down into the following categories:

- DOMESTIC – Domestic Customers and Vendors
- EU – Customers and Vendors in the EU
- EXPORT - Non-EU / Export Customers and Vendors
- INTERCOMP – Intercompany transactions

This usually aligns with the local tax regulations. Since you set Sales and Purchasing Accounts separately in the configurations, you can use the same Business Posting Groups for both Customers and Vendors.

ACTION: Your Business and Product Posting Plan

You will need to have a variety of these Posting Groups setup so you can use them on some of the Templates you are going to make. Consider requesting advice from your accounting and tax team to make sure you have a good map of what you need to set up.

With that plan, write down the list of groups you will want to make. The **Code** should be 20 characters or less – shorter is easier. You can put a longer Description when you enter the values.

Gen. Business	Gen. Product

VAT Business	VAT Product

ENTERING VAT POSTING GROUPS

I recommend entering the VAT Posting groups first, as we will use those on the General Posting groups.

The easiest way for us to access each of the relevant setup areas is to use the **Tell Me** functionality to locate the **VAT Business Posting Groups** and the **VAT Product Posting Groups**. Both tables are just a **Code** and **Description** setting.

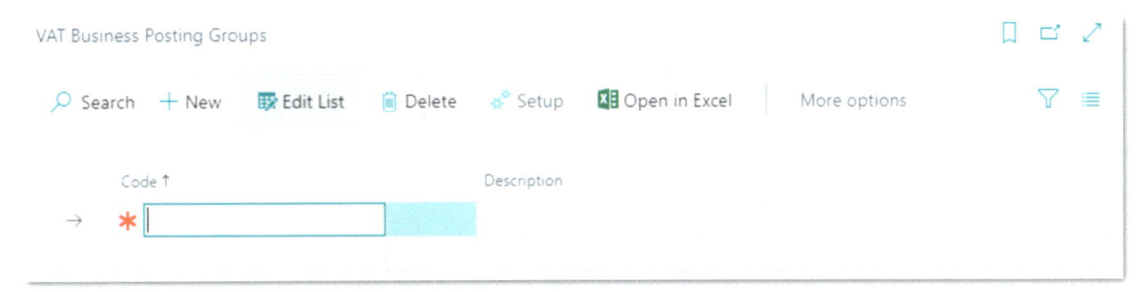

Figure 3-2 - VAT Business Posting Group List

For my VAT Business Posting Group, I will use these:

Code	Description
DOMESTIC	Domestic Customer and Vendors
EU	EU Customers and Vendors
EXPORT	Non-EU Customers and Vendors

For my VAT Product Posting Group, I will use:

Code	Description
EXCLUDE	Non-VAT
VAT12	VAT 12%
VAT25	VAT 25%
VAT6	VAT 6%
VATONLY	VAT Only

PART 2: BUILDING YOUR FOUNDATION
CHAPTER 3: PRODUCT AND BUSINESS POSTING GROUPS

ACTION: Enter VAT Business and Product Groups

In your Business Central system, create your 🔍 **VAT Business Posting Groups** and 🔍 **VAT Product Posting Groups** according to your previously written plan earlier.

> ℹ️ Note: Business Central is developed in Europe, where VAT is the tax system.
>
> In other regions, like North America, the product has been localized to work with local regulations. For guidance, please consult with local partners.

ENTERING GENERAL POSTING GROUPS

Now with the previous steps completed, we will enter the 🔍 **Gen. Business Posting Groups**:

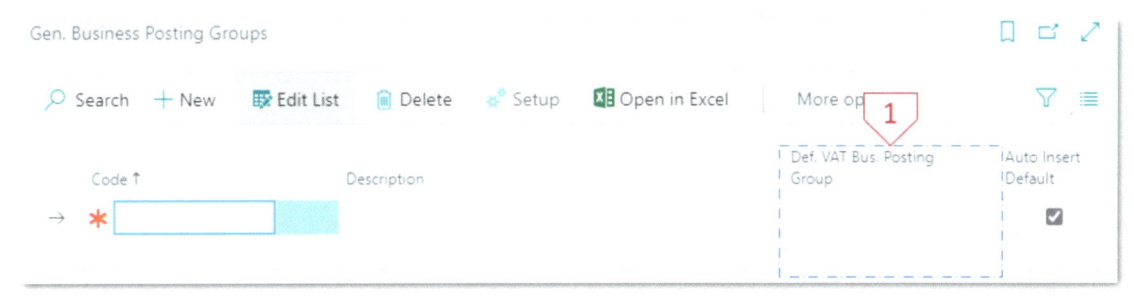

Figure 3-3 - Gen. Business Posting Groups List

You can see this is mostly the same simple information. Additionally, we have the option of specifying the **Def. VAT Bus. Posting Group** (**1**) that should be defaulted when this **Gen. Business Posting Group** is used. (In our scenario, our **Gen. Business Posting Groups** align nicely with our local tax regulations.) This makes it very efficient when assigning posting groups on master data cards.

We will use:

Code	Description	Def. VAT Bus. Posting Group	Auto Insert Default
DOMESTIC	Domestic Customers and Vendors	DOMESTIC	Yes
EU	EU Customers and Vendors	EU	Yes
EXPORT	Non-EU Customers and Vendors	EXPORT	Yes
INTERCO	Intercompany		Yes

For 🔍 **General Product Posting Groups**, this one is a little more specific to the company buying and selling items and services. A moving company might want to book their Employee Time (as Resources) to one set of accounts, but all other sold material (as Items) as another set of accounts. A different company that sells home repair supplies might have general categories they break their sales down by on the G/L (plumbing, heating, etc.).

In our scenario, we will keep it simple, assuming this company just buys and sells Items:

Code	Description	Def. VAT Prod. Posting Group	Auto Insert Default
MISC	Misc. With VAT	VAT25	Yes
NO VAT	Misc. Without VAT	EXCLUDE	Yes
GOODS	General Goods	VAT25	Yes

> Note: We are intentionally creating a problem for ourselves later by using the generic **GOODS** for the Gen. Product Posting Group here.
>
> When we build our Sales section of the Chart of Accounts, we will want the Sales broken out into the Seasonal and Non-Seasonal items.
>
> In Chapter 8, **GOODS** will be re-worked to be two new groups: **NORMAL** and **SEASONAL**.

ACTION: Enter Gen. Business and Product Groups

In your Business Central system, create your **General Business Posting Groups** and **General Product Posting Groups** according to your previously written plan.

Summary

This chapter was building part of the foundation and laying the groundwork. Now you can use some of these Posting Groups in our Templates later in **Chapter 5**. You will notice we have not done anything involving the G/L Accounts fields just yet. We will be revisiting these Posting Groups in **Chapter 7** to set those up.

Chapter 4: Cust./Vendor/Inv. Posting Groups

The good news for you is that you are now a savvy navigator of the Posting Group concept, now we will finish some of the "foundation" work for our future Master Data.

Curiously, many of the following essential Posting Groups are going to be *missing* from the Manual Setup checklist. You will get where you need to be fastest by using the **Tell Me** (Alt-Q) functionality.

CUSTOMER POSTING GROUPS

You will generally want as many **Customer Posting Groups** as you want to have different Accounts Receivables on your General Ledger. Sometimes it can be better to segment your customers into different Customer Posting Groups, even if they use the same Aged Accounts Receivable to start with, because you *can* update which accounts receivable the Posting Groups use.

For our **Customer Posting Group** setup in our demonstration, we are going to keep it aligned with our Tax strategy from a naming/setup perspective, even though we will use just a single A/R account for now.

Code	Description
DOMESTIC	Domestic Customer and Vendors
EU	EU Customers and Vendors
EXPORT	Non-EU Customers and Vendors

As you enter your own Customer Posting Groups, you will notice for the first time that you see some Account settings. We cannot configure those yet, as we have not imported/created any G/L Accounts for now, but we will revisit these settings in **Chapter 9**.

ACTION: Enter Customer Posting Groups

In your Business Central system, create your 🔍 **Customer Posting Groups**.

VENDOR POSTING GROUPS

In Business Central, the Sales and Payables modules are often reflections of each other and work very similarly. The 🔍 **Vendor Posting Groups** are used to control which Accounts Payable each Vendor gets posted to.

Since the concept behind it is identical to Customer Posting Groups, we will stick with what works:

Code	Description
DOMESTIC	Domestic Customer and Vendors
EU	EU Customers and Vendors
EXPORT	Non-EU Customers and Vendors

ACTION: Enter Vendor Posting Groups

In your Business Central system, create your 🔍 **Vendor Posting Groups**.

INVENTORY POSTING GROUPS

If you are the sort to pop open the setup page before reading the text, you were possibly surprised to find that there are almost no fields to set on the 🔍 **Inventory Posting Groups** page:

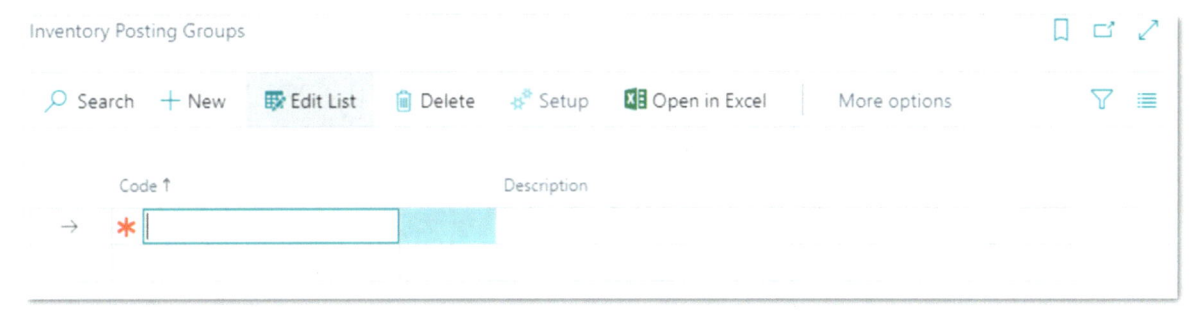

Figure 4-1 - Inventory Posting Group List

Much like the Gen. Product Posting Group, the Setup for Inventory is only considered in *combination* with a Location (even a Blank Location). You will see that in more detail in **Chapter 9**.

This is a breakdown set of categories of inventory values that could be held on our books. On a per-Location basis, what "Inventory Value" would you want to see on the G/L?

For our setup scenario, our company has "normal" items that are carried year-round and some "seasonal" items that are only sold for parts of the year, such as spring or winter items. This gives us the ability to see how much the value of our Inventory is carried month to month and whether it is seasonal or not.

Code	Description
NORMAL	Standard Inventory offering
SEASONAL	Seasonal inventory items

ACTION: Enter Inventory Posting Groups

In your Business Central system, create your **Inventory Posting Groups**.

LOCATION(S)

As previously mentioned, **Inventory Posting Groups** work in combination with **Locations**. This will be our very first Master Data item in the company. Locations can be setup to be automatically numbered, which we will address in the next chapter, but many organizations prefer having Location Codes be named descriptively.

PART 2: BUILDING YOUR FOUNDATION
CHAPTER 4: CUST./VENDOR/INV. POSTING GROUPS

Locations are logical barriers between your stock stored in different places. Each Location can have its own inventory policies. The settings on the location determine if the location will be "Basic" inventory versus "Warehouse Managed Stock" (WMS). Locations can be across the street or on the other side of the world.

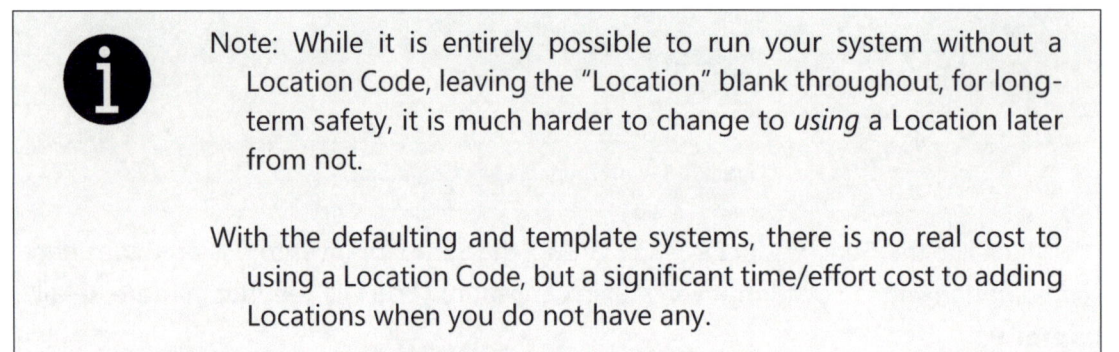

> **Note:** While it is entirely possible to run your system without a Location Code, leaving the "Location" blank throughout, for long-term safety, it is much harder to change to *using* a Location later from not.
>
> With the defaulting and template systems, there is no real cost to using a Location Code, but a significant time/effort cost to adding Locations when you do not have any.

For our scenario, we will have one Location configured as a "Basic" location. Since a popular industrial area in my city is "Askim" (Ah-whwim), we will set up **ASKIM** as our Location:

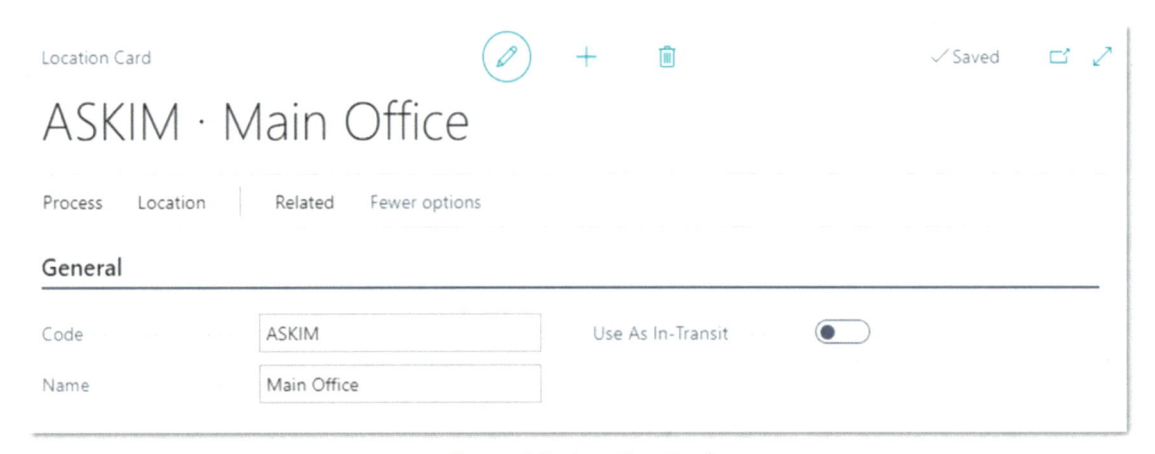

Our recommendation: start with Locations!

Figure 4-2 - Location Card

For a simple **Location**, you only need to have a **Code**, and nothing else. Everything else is a nice-to-have information, for now.

ACTION: Create your Location(s)

In your Business Central system, create your 🔍 **Locations**. In our scenario, we are using a simple non-Warehousing location. If you need a more complex setup, please work with a Partner!

SUMMARY

We have now completed creating some additional Posting Groups that we will use heavily during our Master Data import & creation process. Much as last chapter, we are not yet tying any setup information to G/L Accounts, so we will be coming back to finish these setup areas.

Chapter 5: Company Info., Periods and No. Series

Before we move into the next steps, we need to tidy up some infrastructure in our system. In this chapter, we are taking care of a couple of small key setup stages, then doing a deep dive into a system that will be vital for years to come.

COMPANY INFORMATION

This Master Setup is used heavily in all the documents we will produce in the system, from simple things like "what is your address" to being able to set the company's logo that will show on customer facing reports.

As mentioned back in **Chapter 1**, we can jump straight to the **Company Information** under **Settings**.

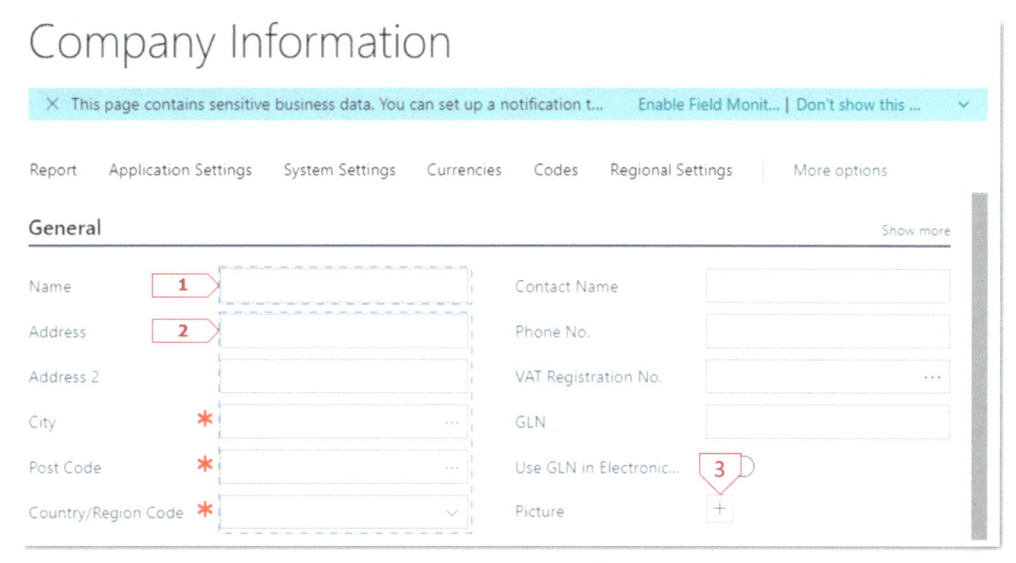

Figure 5-1 - Company Information

PART 2: BUILDING YOUR FOUNDATION
CHAPTER 5: COMPANY INFO., PERIODS AND NO. SERIES

The appearance will vary based on localizations and extensions, but for our scenario, we will mainly be filling in some fictional **Name** (**1**) and **Address** (**2**) information, plus adding a **Picture** (**3**) which will appear on reports.

ACTION: Create your Company Information

Fill in your company information. Our primary focus is the General FastTab for now.

ACCOUNTING PERIODS

Many companies use the Calendar Year and Months as their Accounting Year and Periods. However, Microsoft Dynamics 365 Business Central needs to be able to support all manner of settings. This is handled via the **Accounting Periods** list:

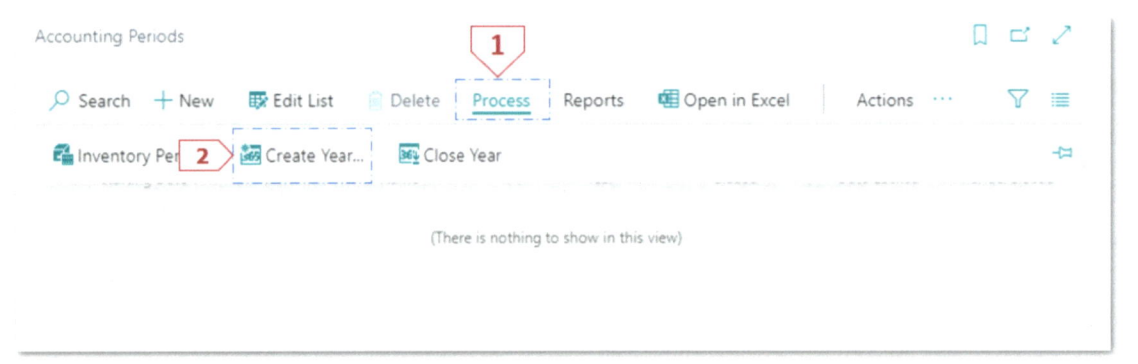

Figure 5-2 - Accounting Periods

Under the **Process** (**1**) action bar item, you will find there is a **Create Year...** (**2**) option. This will require some settings:

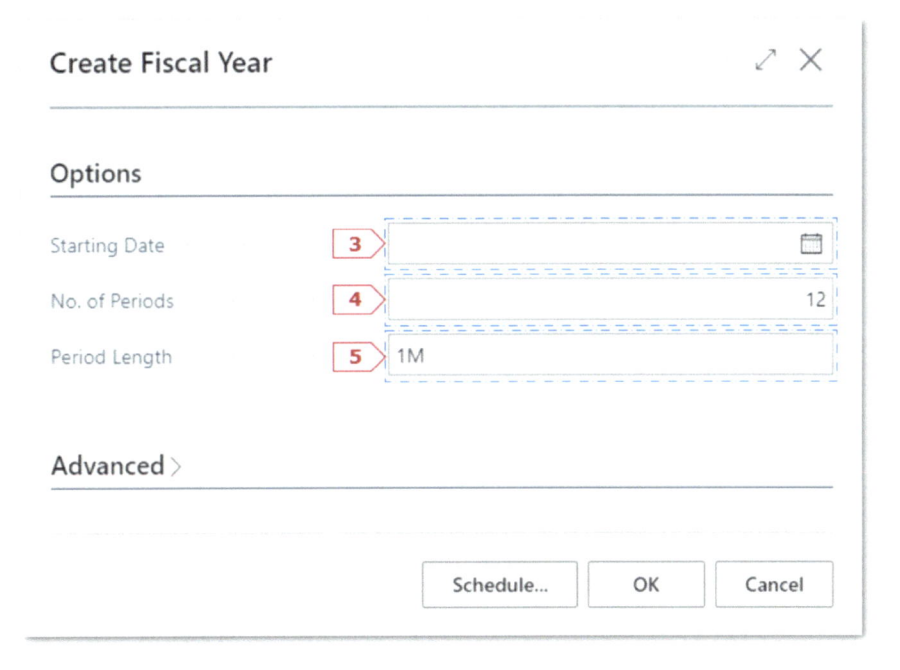

Figure 5-3 - Create Fiscal Year Settings Dialog

If you use Calendar based accounting, or use months with a different closing date, this is a nice and easy request to fill in; for example, if your Year End is December 31, enter **January 1** as your **Starting Date** (**3**), with **12** as your **No. of Periods** (**2**). If your Year End is June 30, enter **July 1** as your **Starting Date**. You can also choose the **Period Length** (**5**) of your accounting periods.

In our scenario, we will use **January 1** as the **Starting Date** and run the routine. This creates the following entries:

PART 2: BUILDING YOUR FOUNDATION

CHAPTER 5: COMPANY INFO., PERIODS AND NO. SERIES

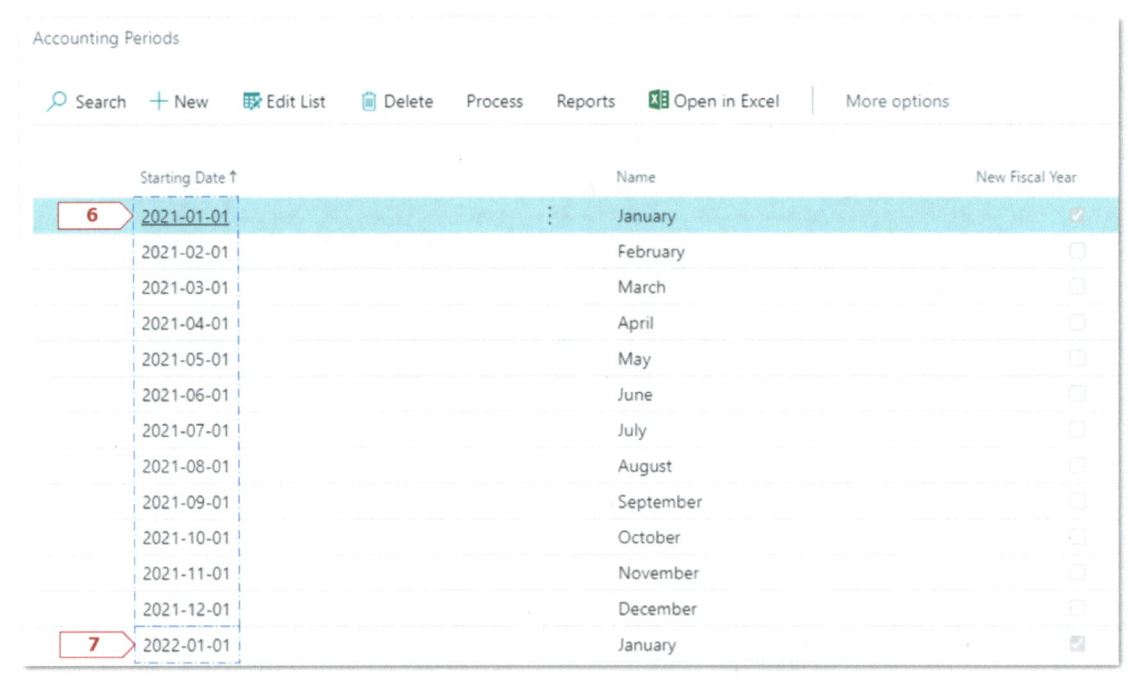

Accounting Periods			
Starting Date ↑		Name	New Fiscal Year
6 → 2021-01-01		January	✓
2021-02-01		February	☐
2021-03-01		March	☐
2021-04-01		April	☐
2021-05-01		May	☐
2021-06-01		June	☐
2021-07-01		July	☐
2021-08-01		August	☐
2021-09-01		September	☐
2021-10-01		October	☐
2021-11-01		November	☐
2021-12-01		December	☐
7 → 2022-01-01		January	✓

Figure 5-4 - Accounting Periods List with Months

We nicely get the whole year (**6**), plus the first period in the next year (**7**).

ACTION: Create your Accounting Periods

Create your year in 🔍 **Accounting Periods**. You can use the **Create Year…** functionality, or if you require to do something special, you can manually **Edit List** to enter the information you need.

NO. SERIES

This area of Microsoft Dynamics 365 Business Central will take you a while to set up.

Anywhere the system could automatically create a Number for you (Customer Number, Item Number, Sales Order Number, Posted Sales Shipment Number, etc.), you ~~have to~~ *get to* configure how it will generate that next number/code. To give you a sense of how many different areas this is used in, the CRONUS demonstration company has about 150 different number series set up.

For each 🔍 **No. Series**, you need to decide:

FORMAT & INCREMENTATION

What should the number look like?

This is a 20-length alpha-numeric, so you can have '1000' to '9999' as valid values, or 'C100' to 'C999'.

You can also decide how many digits to bump up each time a number is pulled. You could have 'C100' to 'C990' skipping 10s, to get C110, C120. 1 is the typical value unless you have a special need.

Just be aware that the last set of digits in your pattern is what gets increased. So, if you setup a series like SO-00001-2021, it will think you want SO-00001-2022 to be the next value.

MANUAL NUMBERING

Should it be possible for a user to change it? (Noted as **Manual Nos.** later.) If the Customers are all made like 'C100','C101', etc. – when the user wants to change a Customer to have the Customer No. set to 'BOB', is that allowed?

ALLOW GAPS?

Some documents and transaction types are not allowed to have gaps in them due to accounting rules. That might make sense for a Posted Invoice series but might make no sense at all for Items.

ANNUAL PATTERNS

You can even setup a number series to have a **Start Date** and **End Date** so that you can automatically use different numbers for different years, for example, you might want POYYYY-1000 where YY is the 4 digits of the year.

DIFFERENT SERIES FOR THE SAME DATA

Some companies might need to have different number strategies for the same data, for example, items that are raw material might get a 7-digit integer number, but items that are finished goods sold to a customer get a 'I-xxxx' number, can be managed here as well.

Bear in mind that *typically* different number series are used in different places, so you *could* have a Customer 1000 and a Vendor 1000, as well as a Posted Sales Invoice 1000, and a Posted Purchase Invoice 1000 – but do you want to do that to yourself?

ACTION: Plan Your Number Series

Using the following partial list and the above explanations, plan for your numbering; you will have to make some estimates if the numbers are enough. When you gain a thousand customers per year, a 4-digit series will run out fast, as an example.

Code	Description	Example Starting No.	Your Starting No.	Increment	Manual	Allow Gaps	Date Driven
CONT	Contact	CT000001					
CUST	Customer	C0001					
GJNL-GEN	General Journal	G00001					
GJNL-PMT	Payment Journal	G90001					
GJNL-PURCH	Purchase Journal	G80001					
GJNL-RCPT	Cash Receipts Journal	G70001					
GJNL-REC	Recurring General Journal	G60001					
GJNL-SALES	Sales Journal	G50001					
IC_GJNL	Intercompany Gen. Jnl	IC00001					
IJNL-GEN	Item Journal	INV00001					
IJNL-PHYS	Physical Inventory Journal	PINV00001					
IJNL-RCL	Item Reclass. Journal	RINV00001					
IJNL-REVAL	Revaluation Journal	VINV00001					
ITEM	Items	10000					
P-CR	Purchase Credit Memo	PCM-00001					
P-CR+	Posted Purchase Credit Memo	PPCM-00001					
P-INV	Purchase Invoice	PI-00001					
P-INV+	Posted Purchase Invoice	PPI-00001					

Code	Description	Example Starting No.	Your Starting No.	Increment	Manual	Allow Gaps	Date Driven
P-ORD	Purchase Order	PO-00001					
P-QUO	Purchase Quote	PQ-00001					
P-RCPT	Purchase Receipt	PRCT-00001					
P-RETORD	Purchase Return Order	PRET-00001					
P-SHPT	Posted Purchase Shipment	PSHP-00001					
S-CR	Sales Credit Memo	SCM-00001					
S-CR+	Posted Sales Credit Memo	PSCM-00001					
S-INV	Sales Invoice	SI-00001					
S-INV+	Posted Sales Invoice	PSI-00001					
S-ORD	Sales Order	SO-00001					
S-QUO	Sales Quote	SQ-00001					
S-RCPT	Posted Sales Receipt	SRCT-00001					
S-RETORD	Sales Return Order	SRO-00001					
S-SHPT	Sales Shipment	SSHP-00001					
VEND	Vendor	V0001					

Note that there are many more beyond the above list you may need, but, with the above list, you will have all that will be used in this guide.

For the actual **No. Series**, you will need to enter some of the information in one place and some in another. It is a little bit like a Document – the **No. Series** as the Header and **No. Series Line** as the Line. Here are the information fields that needs to be set in the **No. Series**:

- Code
- Description
- Default Nos. (You will *almost always* want this checked)
- Manual Nos. (Per your Plan)
- Date Order (Some regions have legal requirements that enforce Document Numbering is done in Chronological order, which this supports)

You will notice that you cannot enter the **Starting No.** and **Ending No.** fields directly, as they are FlowFields down into the **No. Series Line**, where the information will live. After you have created an Entry in the **No. Series** table, you will need to **Navigate** via the Action Bar to the **Lines**. On the Lines, you can enter the information about:

PART 2: BUILDING YOUR FOUNDATION
CHAPTER 5: COMPANY INFO., PERIODS AND NO. SERIES

- Starting No.
- Ending No.
- Warning No. (The user will get a warning notice when the No series is at or above this value)
- Increment-By No.
- Allow Gaps in Nos.

If you are only going to have one sequential series, such as for customers, you can skip the **Start Date** field.

Opening the **No. Series**, you will see all the configured series. With a Series selected, such as **CUST** in CRONUS, you can **Navigate** (**1**) -> to the **Lines** (**2**):

Figure 5-5 - No. Series List

This will bring up the **No. Series Lines** list:

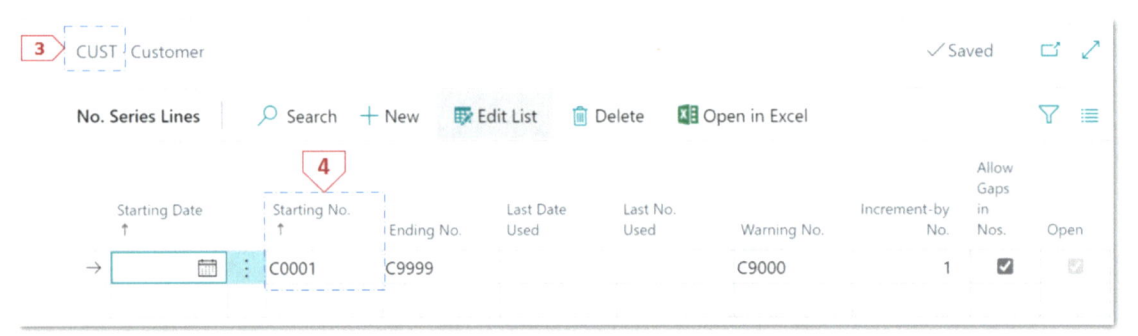

Figure 5-6 - No. Series Lines - Customer Example

88 PAGE PART 2: BUILDING YOUR FOUNDATION
CHAPTER 5: COMPANY INFO., PERIODS AND NO. SERIES

Here on the **CUST** series (**3**), when we use it on the Customer and create the first Customer, it will be numbered **C0001** (from the **Starting No.** (**4**)). At this point, the **No. Series Line** will be updated, and the **Last Date Used** will be set to our Today, along with the **Last No. Used** will be updated to say **C0001**.

> Note: If you are moving to BC from another system and you want to maintain the numbering you used before, such as for customers, you *can* just enter the Last No. Used manually and start with that.
>
> In my case, if I already had 200 customers, I could set the Last No. Used to C0299 and now I will have all my BC created Customers from C0300 and up.
>
> You could also accomplish this via the Starting No.

ACTION: Enter All the Number Series

With your plan from above, it is time to enter each No. Series and Line into the **No. Series** system.

Chapter 6: Module Setups – G/L, A/P, A/R, Inventory

For this part, we will be putting to use some of the setup work you have done so far, as well as wrapping up some of the last parts of the settings that we will need to import the master data in a smart way.

GENERAL LEDGER (G/L) SETUP

The **General Ledger Setup** is the main Setup table for the Financials core of the system. It has several fields, some of which are significantly beyond the scope of this workbook.

GENERAL FASTTAB

Reviewing the key fields we will need in our scenario:

General

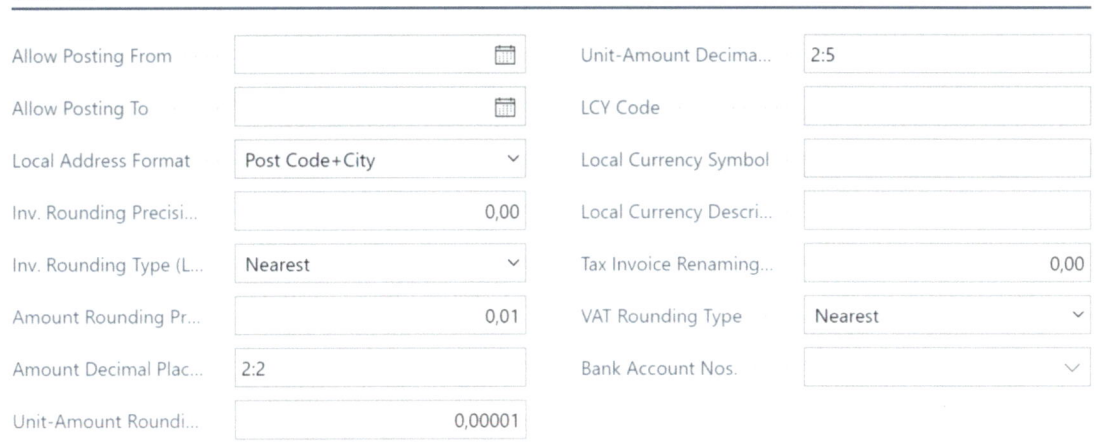

Allow Posting From		Unit-Amount Decima...	2:5
Allow Posting To		LCY Code	
Local Address Format	Post Code+City	Local Currency Symbol	
Inv. Rounding Precisi...	0,00	Local Currency Descri...	
Inv. Rounding Type (L...	Nearest	Tax Invoice Renaming...	0,00
Amount Rounding Pr...	0,01	VAT Rounding Type	Nearest
Amount Decimal Plac...	2:2	Bank Account Nos.	
Unit-Amount Roundi...	0,00001		

Figure 6-1 - General Ledger Setup - General FastTab

- **Allow Posting From** and **Allow Posting To** allow you to restrict what period people are *allowed to* Post in. This is often configured by most companies to restrict posting to at least the current year, if not just the Current period (month). You can override this on a per-user basis (in the User Setup area), so, it is recommended that these are both set. (More about this in **Chapter 19**.)
- **Local Address Format** will control how the addresses are formatted on Documents / Reports.
- **Inv** / **Amount** / **Unit-Amount Rounding** fields are controls that allow you to handle what sort of precision should be given to different parts of the system and which direction.
  - A precision value of **1** would force the rounding to whole digits; **0,01** (**0.01** for some regions, as decimal formats vary) would have you rounding **0.9123** to **0.91**, this affects the *calculations* of what is stored. For our scenario, we will turn on our Invoice Rounding to **1** so we can see it in action later, but that *will* mean we will need a Rounding Account later.
  - **Decimal Places** controls just the *display* versions of how things should show.
    The first digit is the minimum decimal places to show, and the second is how many are the maximum. **2:2** will always show 2 decimals, whereas **2:5** will show at least 2 decimals and up to 5. In the example of a **0,9123** amount, having the **2:2** setting will display as **0,91**; having the **2:5** setting will display as **0,9123** (this method only shows what exists, as an example for this scenario 0,9123**5** would show the entire 0,9123**5**).

PART 2: BUILDING YOUR FOUNDATION
CHAPTER 6: MODULE SETUPS – G/L, A/P, A/R, INVENTORY

- **LCY Code** is a 3-character abbreviation of "**L**ocal **C**urrenc**Y**" is. For an international use of this workbook, we will use the Euro as our test currency, so we will set EUR as our LCY code. You will note if you are following along, the system knows what to do with EUR and will default the next settings.
- **Local Currency Symbol** will be shown in some reports and on some pages. For our scenario, we will use the (€) symbol.
- We could have our Bank Accounts get their **Bank Account No.** numbers automatically via the **Bank Account Nos.** connection to **No. Series**, but many users prefer to have specific codes for their accounts. A company with Credit Suisse bank accounts in EUR and in GBP may want to have bank accounts coded as "CS-EUR" and "CS-GBP", therefore, making it easier to understand.

DIMENSIONS FASTTAB

This is a complex topic, unfortunately beyond the scope of this book, but it would be wise to chat with a partner and your accountant to get the settings on this right.

ACTION: General Ledger Setup

Create your 🔍 **General Ledger Setup** using the above information as a guide, setting it up in a way that makes sense for your needs.

Purchases & Payables (A/P) Setup

The 🔍 **Purchases & Payables Setup** Table is the main setup table for the Purchases & Payables module (as the name implies).

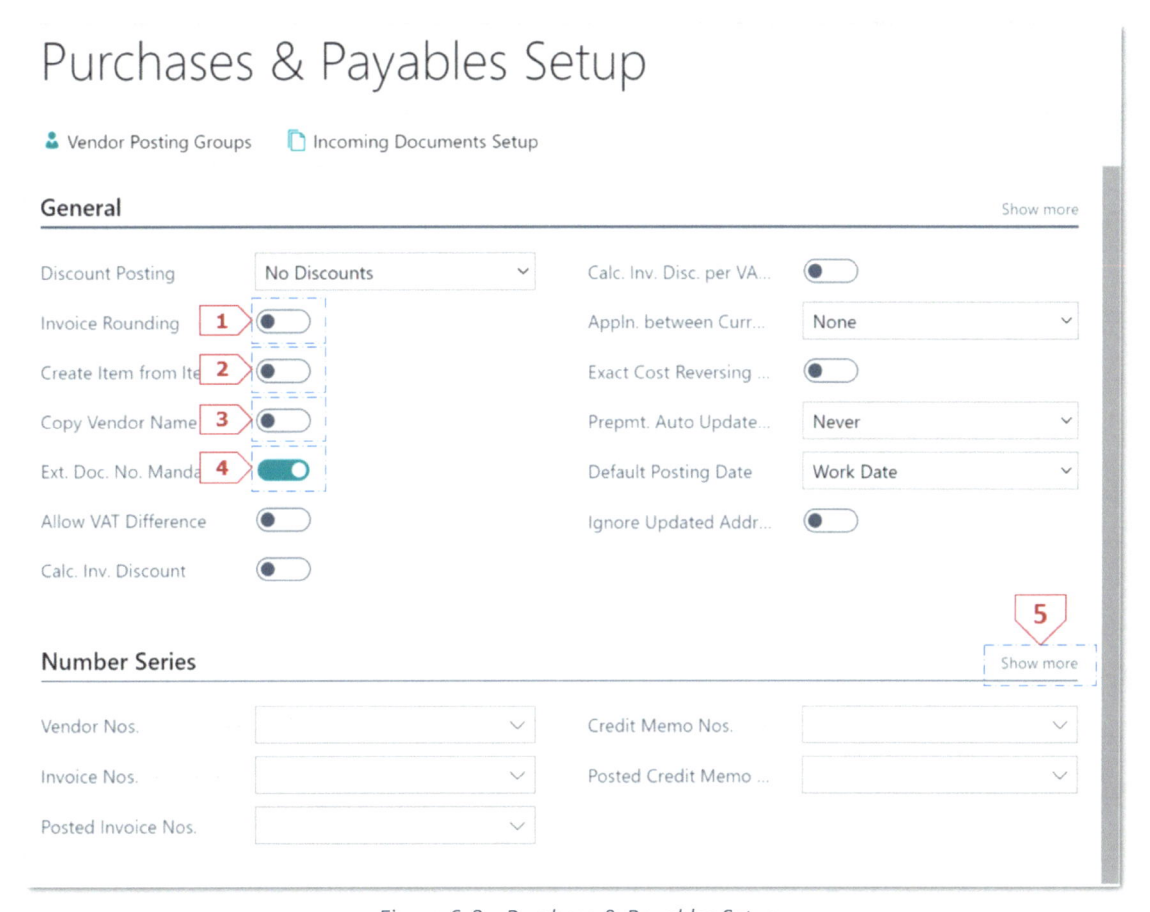

Figure 6-2 - Purchase & Payables Setup

General FastTab

- **Invoice Rounding** (**1**) - On our payables side, we do not want Business Central to round our purchase invoices, so this will remain disabled.
- **Create Item from Item No.** (**2**) - While it is nice of Business Central to give us the functionality to 'automagically' create items when a user enters an Item Number that is not recognized, that seems optimistic about entry error rates. We will leave that disabled.

- **Copy Vendor Name to Entries** (**3**) - This setting ensures that the Vendor Name will be listed in the Vendor Ledger Entries, without which, we would only have the Vendor No. field. In our scenario, we will enable this.
- **Ext. Doc. No. Mandatory** (**4**) - If you want to require a **Vendor Invoice Number** on your Purchase documents, that is what this "Ext(ernal) Doc(ument) No. Mandatory" field controls.

NUMBERING FASTTAB

In the **Number Series** section, we will select the relevant **No. Series** values from our earlier list:

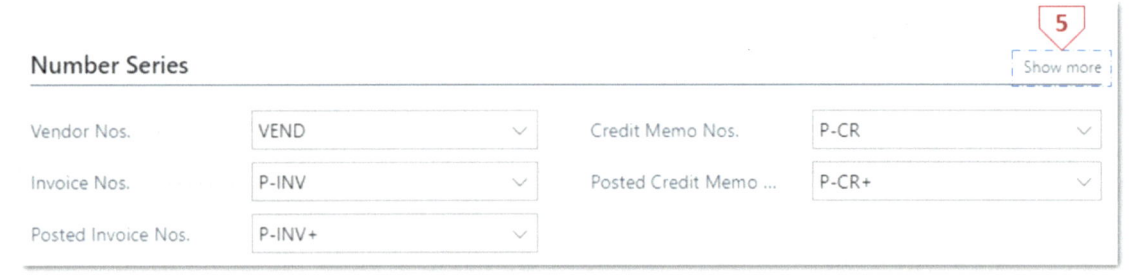

Number Series				Show more (5)
Vendor Nos.	VEND	Credit Memo Nos.	P-CR	
Invoice Nos.	P-INV	Posted Credit Memo ...	P-CR+	
Posted Invoice Nos.	P-INV+			

Figure 6-3 - P&P Setup - Numbering FastTab Collapsed

Also, in this section, we need to click the **Show More** (**5**) to be able to set the **Order Nos.** series, which we will need in Chapter 14, and a few return related settings for Chapter 18:

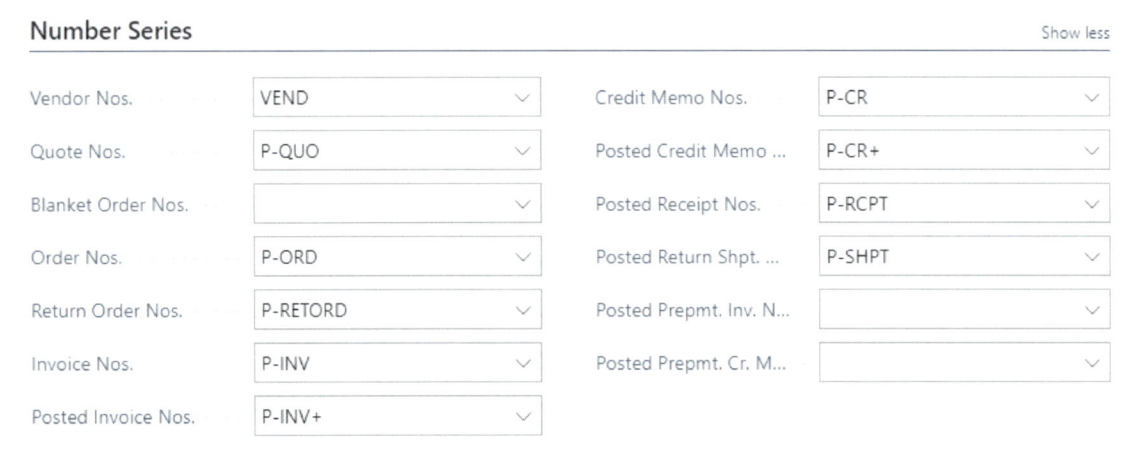

Number Series				Show less
Vendor Nos.	VEND	Credit Memo Nos.	P-CR	
Quote Nos.	P-QUO	Posted Credit Memo ...	P-CR+	
Blanket Order Nos.		Posted Receipt Nos.	P-RCPT	
Order Nos.	P-ORD	Posted Return Shpt. ...	P-SHPT	
Return Order Nos.	P-RETORD	Posted Prepmt. Inv. N...		
Invoice Nos.	P-INV	Posted Prepmt. Cr. M...		
Posted Invoice Nos.	P-INV+			

Figure 6-4 - P&P Setup - Numbering FastTab Expanded

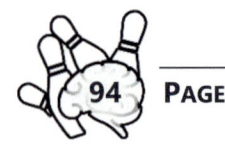

ACTION: Purchases & Payables Setup

Create your 🔍 **Purchases & Payables Setup** using the above information as a guide, setting it up in a way that makes sense for your needs.

SALES & RECEIVABLES (A/R) SETUP

The 🔍 **Sales & Receivables Setup** is the main setup for the Sales & Receivables module.

GENERAL FASTTAB

The General Section is very similar to the Purchases & Payables Setup, though it has a few more options:

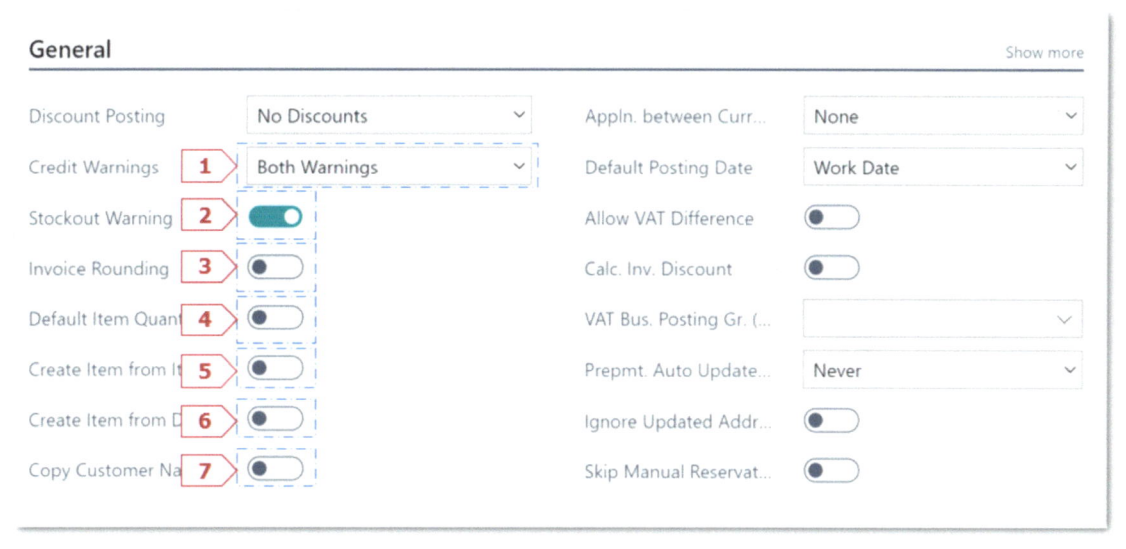

Figure 6-5 - Sales & Receivables Setup - General FastTab

- **Credit Warnings** (**1**) are useful if you setup Credit for Customers and want the system to give you and your team warnings when customers are approaching or are over their credit limit.

- **Stockout Warning** (**2**) is one piece of the "Stock Warning" system (it can vary on an Item Level as well). This will present the user with a warning if they are trying to enter a Sales Order for an item with insufficient stock for it.
- We will turn on **Invoice Rounding** (**3**) for the Sales module in our scenario. This respects the Invoice Rounding information from the General Ledger Setup we addressed earlier.
- If you typically sell just "1" of an item, you can pre-default the Quantity of the Sales Line with the **Default Item Quantity** (**4**) setting, which is helpful. In our scenario, we will leave this disabled.
- As with the Purchasing side, we will leave both the **Create Item from Item No.** (**5**) and **Create Item from Description** (**6**) settings disabled, as that relies too heavily on *error-free* information entry.
- Much as on the Payables side, having the **Copy Customer Name to Entries** (**7**) to populate the customer's Name on the Customer Ledger Entries is helpful, so we will enable this.

NUMBERING

The **Number Series** section is a lot longer than the **Purchases & Payables Setup**. We will fill out ours from the plan above:

Number Series

Customer Nos.	CUST	Posted Return Receip...	S-RCPT
Quote Nos.	S-QUO	Reminder Nos.	
Blanket Order Nos.		Issued Reminder Nos.	
Order Nos.	S-ORD	Canceled Issued Remi...	
Return Order Nos.	S-RETORD	Fin. Chrg. Memo Nos.	
Invoice Nos.	S-INV	Issued Fin. Chrg. M. ...	
Posted Invoice Nos.	S-INV+	Canceled Issued Fin. ...	
Credit Memo Nos.	S-CR	Posted Prepmt. Inv. N...	
Posted Credit Memo ...	S-CR+	Posted Prepmt. Cr. M...	
Posted Shipment Nos.	S-SHPT	Direct Debit Mandate...	

Figure 6-6 - Sales & Receivables Setup - Numbering FastTab

We will leave most of the settings blank around Reminders, Finance Charges, and Prepayment, as those systems are beyond the scope of this workbook.

ARCHIVING

Something worth mentioning is the **Archiving** section:

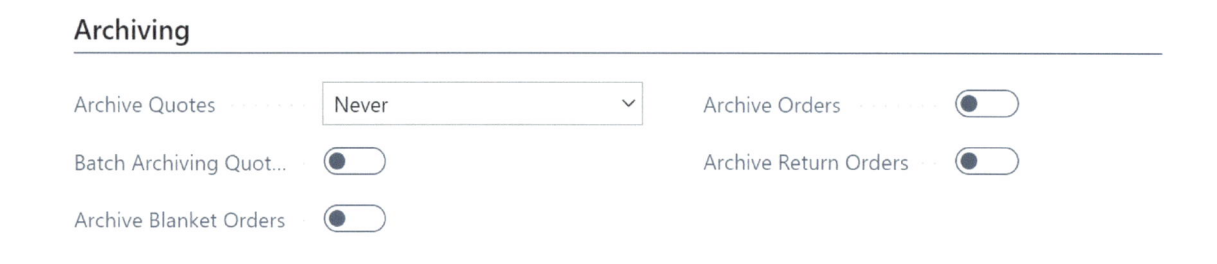

Figure 6-7 - Sales & Receivables Setup - Archiving FastTab

The Archiving system is one of the only ways you can have a 'snapshot' of the Order at the time it becomes a completely posted (and often deleted) document, by enabling the **Archive Orders** functionality. The **Archived Sales Orders** will be created as a result. Review carefully with a partner if that gives you enough information beyond the usual Posted Documents.

ACTION: Sales & Receivables Setup

Create your **Sales & Receivables Setup** using the above information as a guide, setting it up in a way that makes sense for your needs.

INVENTORY SETUP

The 🔍 **Inventory Setup** is the main Setup table of the Inventory module. This is where we have a few key settings:

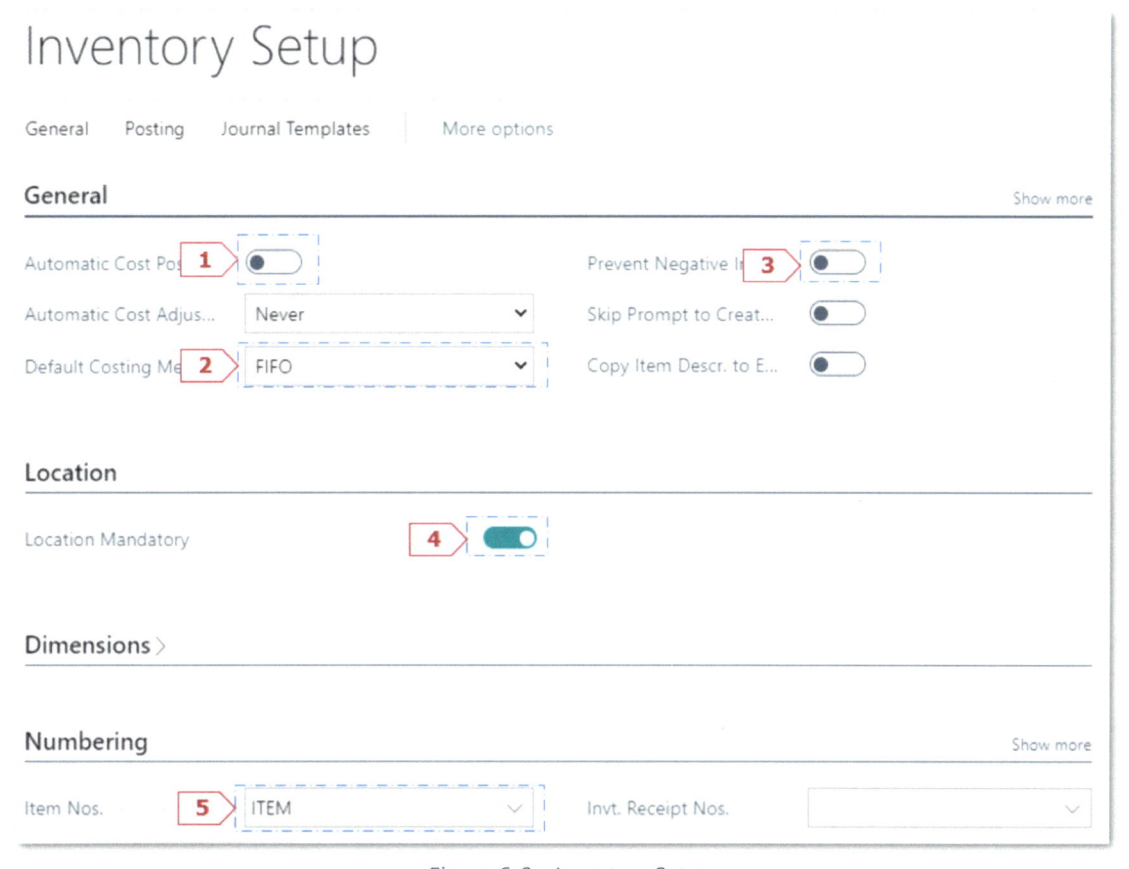

Figure 6-8 - Inventory Setup

Automatic Cost Posting (**1**) is something you should discuss with your partner about whether this is optimal for your organization or not. When this is enabled, the system will automatically create a lot of COGS related entries and adjustments for items based on item values – but it will do so while you are posting documents, which *can* create a performance impact. If this is not enabled however, you will need to run some **Adjust Cost** routines manually to handle the costing getting to the G/L accounts. For our scenario, we will leave this disabled so we can review the routines in **Chapters 12** and **Chapter 19**.

Here you can also specify the **Default Costing Method** (**2**) for new Items. You can also enable some safety catches, such as **Prevent Negative Inventory** (**3**) and **Location Mandatory** (**4**). As mentioned earlier, you *can* run the system with no Locations. If that is what you are doing, you will need **Location Mandatory** turned off. With our scenario having a single Location to start, we will enable this to ensure it is always set before posting is allowed.

Lastly, we will set the **Item Nos.** (**5**) to the relevant No. Series from earlier.

ACTION: Inventory Setup

Create your **Inventory Setup** using the above information as a guide, setting it up in a way that makes sense for your needs.

PAYMENT TERMS AND METHODS

For getting our Customer and Vendor Templates setup in the next Chapter, we will also need to set up some of the Payment settings:

PAYMENT TERMS

The **Payment Terms** setup is a relatively simple List:

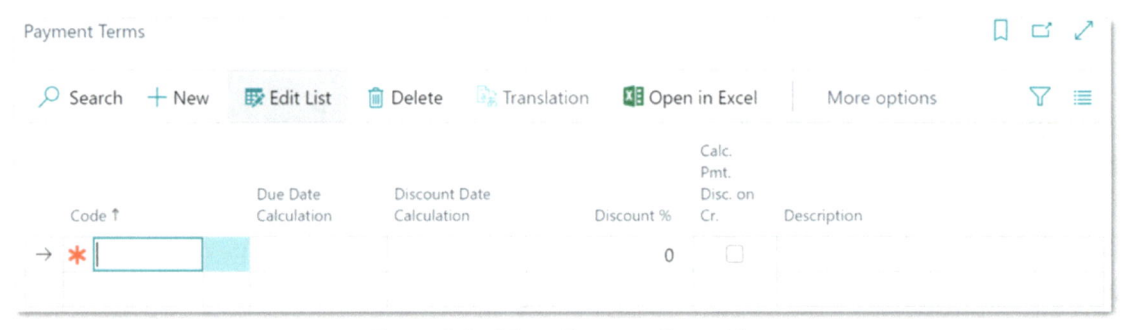

Figure 6-9 - Nice - Payment Terms List

For our scenario, we will configure two Payment terms:

PART 2: BUILDING YOUR FOUNDATION
CHAPTER 6: MODULE SETUPS – G/L, A/P, A/R, INVENTORY

- **NET30** – a simple "NET 30 days" payment term – the whole balance is due within 30 days of a document.
- **NET30(5)** – a "NET 30 days" payment term, but in this case, if payment is made within 5 days, then there is a 10% discount.

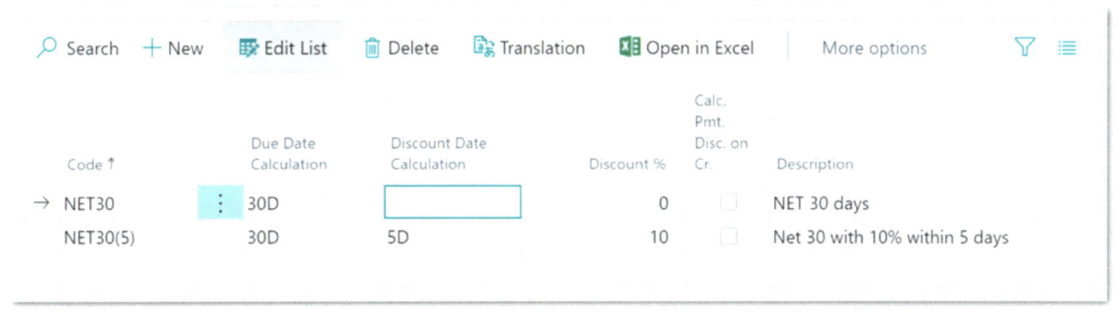

Code ↑	Due Date Calculation	Discount Date Calculation	Discount %	Calc. Pmt. Disc. on Cr.	Description
→ NET30	30D		0	☐	NET 30 days
NET30(5)	30D	5D	10	☐	Net 30 with 10% within 5 days

Figure 6-10 - Example Payment Terms

You will want to see the Microsoft Docs for the Payment Terms or communicate with your partner if you need to do something more complex, such as "End of Month", etc.

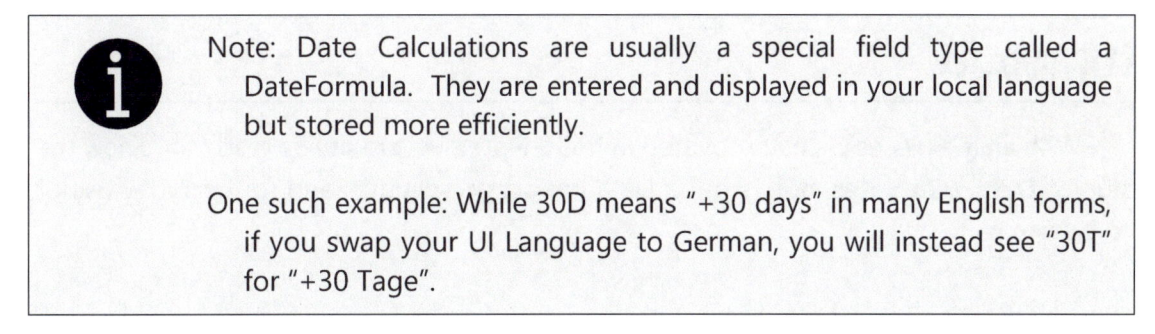

> **Note:** Date Calculations are usually a special field type called a DateFormula. They are entered and displayed in your local language but stored more efficiently.
>
> One such example: While 30D means "+30 days" in many English forms, if you swap your UI Language to German, you will instead see "30T" for "+30 Tage".

ACTION: Create your Payment Term(s)

You will want to have at least one **Payment Terms**, if not more. You can create a payment term with a **Due Date Calculation** of **0D** to make everything due immediately.

PAYMENT METHOD

For the **Payment Methods**, this is mainly information for our use. You can configure Payment Methods that are handled in an automatic fashion, such as a **CASH** payment method that immediately treats an Order as 'Paid' against a given G/L or Bank Account as soon as it is posted.

For our scenario, we will go with just a **WIRE** payment option, where everything is paid by bank transfers manually (**PAYPAL** was automatically inserted by an Extension):

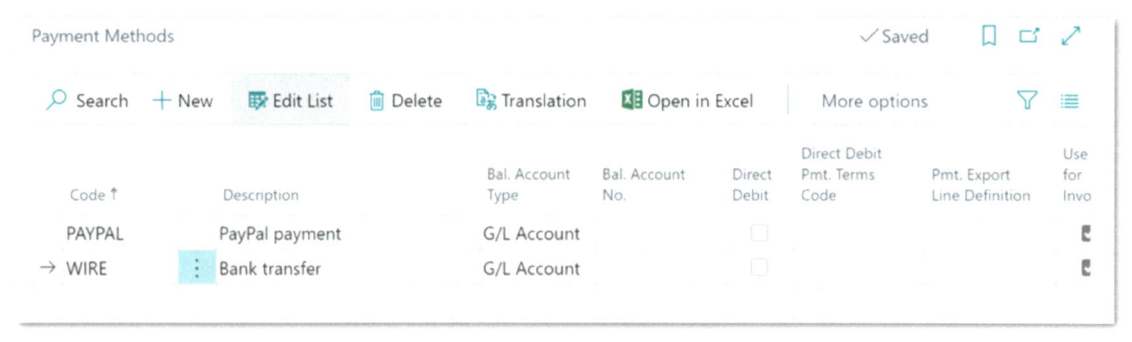

Code ↑	Description	Bal. Account Type	Bal. Account No.	Direct Debit	Direct Debit Pmt. Terms Code	Pmt. Export Line Definition	Use for Invo
PAYPAL	PayPal payment	G/L Account		☐			
→ WIRE	Bank transfer	G/L Account		☐			

Figure 6-11 - Payment Methods

SUMMARY

With all the pieces we have covered in this chapter, we are finally ready to review the value of **Data Templates**, both from a Data Import perspective, and for everyday use of the system.

Chapter 7: Customer / Vendor / Item Templates

To make the most efficient use of Customers, Vendors, and Items, Microsoft Dynamics 365 Business Central supports a template system that allows us to configure most of the common fields that we would need to set on each. We will make use of this during the Import in the next Chapter, but you will also save a lot of time in maintaining the system.

CONFIGURATION TEMPLATES

There is a powerful templating system for some of the master data tables:

- Customer (table 18)
- Vendor (table 23)
- Item (table 27)
- Contacts (table 5050)

🔍 **Configuration Templates** allow you to define which table the templates apply to and which fields you would like to set to which values. Taking one of our commonly needed Customer scenarios, we would have the following settings:

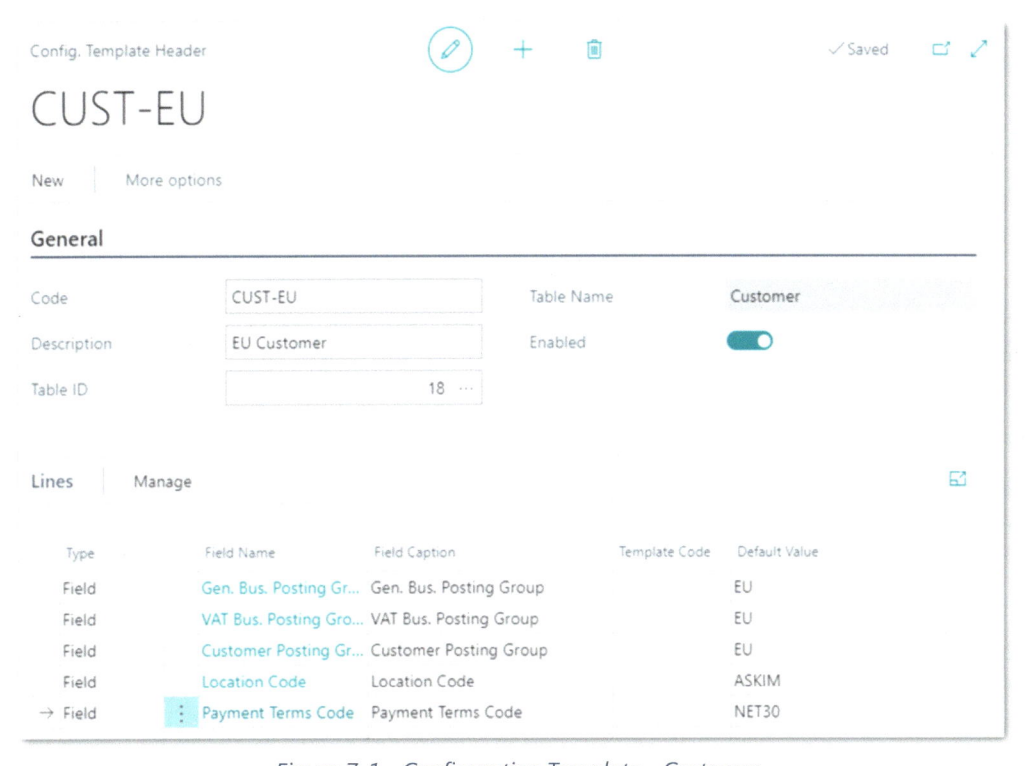

Figure 7-1 - Configuration Template - Customer

Created according to the example above (Figure 7-1); whenever we create a Customer, we would get a power boost:

- If there is only 1 template, it will automatically apply it.

PART 2: BUILDING YOUR FOUNDATION
CHAPTER 7: CUSTOMER / VENDOR / ITEM TEMPLATES

- If there are more than 1 template, it will ask which you would like to use.

> **Note:** There are a few different Template systems used in different parts of the Product. If you search for 🔍 **Customer Templates**, you will not get to this list.
>
> We are using the template system in this situation because it is used when creating new records manually *and* will be used during the Master Data Import process.

Templates have the Header (the **General** FastTab), which specifies which Table ID is involved, and then a list of fields that should receive settings.

CONFIGURATION TEMPLATES - CUSTOMER

To better understand the **Configuration Template** we will make for 🔍 **Customers**, here is a commonly used **Customer** in the CRONUS demonstration company:

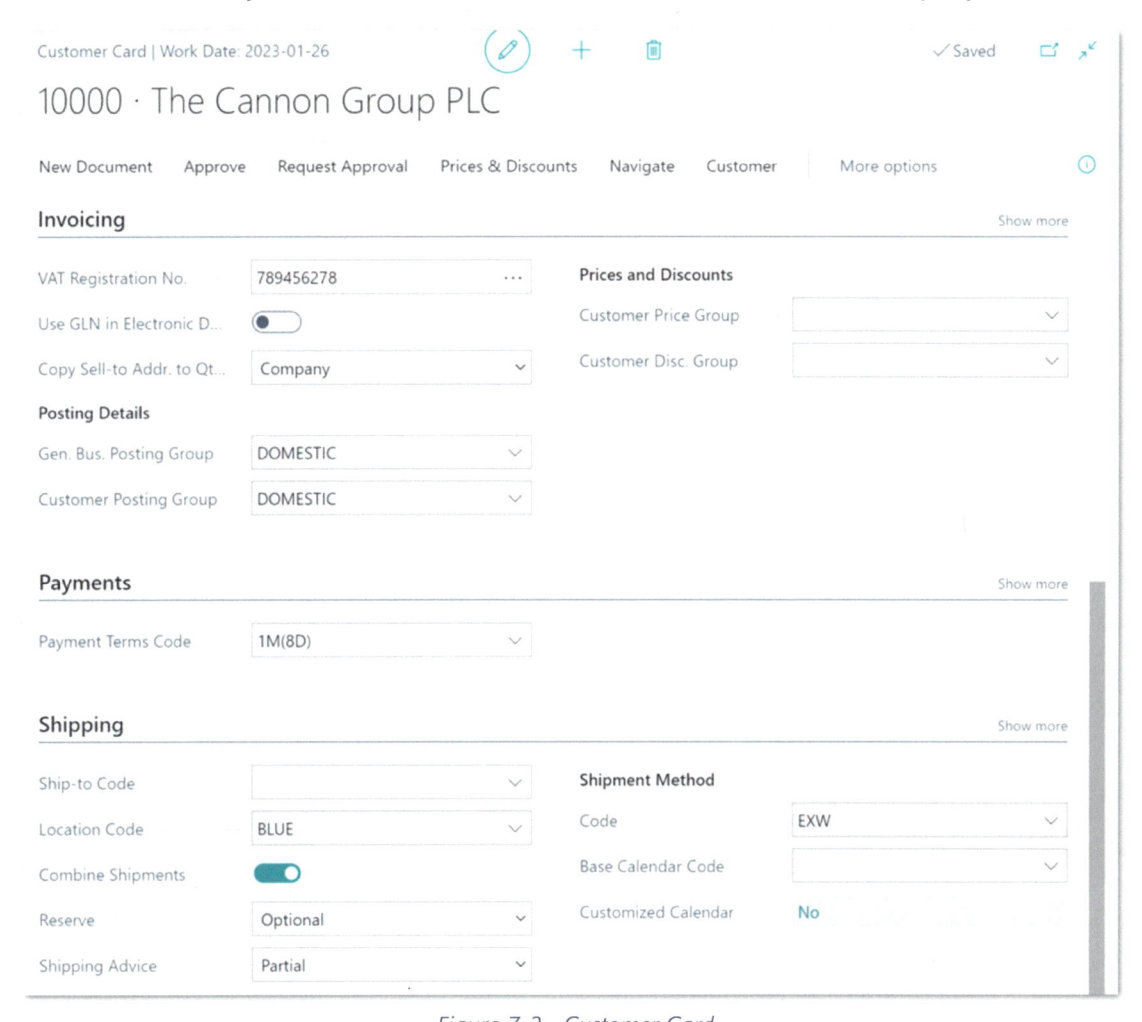

Figure 7-2 - Customer Card

In this screenshot, we can see the **Invoicing**, **Payments**, and **Shipping** sections, as those are the main configuration fields. We will find many customers sharing similar settings:

- In the **Invoicing** FastTab, we can see the **Gen. Bus. Posting Group** appearing with the **Customer Posting Group**.
- In the **Payments** FastTab, we see the **Payment Terms Code**.

- In the **Shipping** FastTab, we can see the **Location Code**.

These are the main fields that should be defaulted in our scenario to speed up creating customers.

Since our Customer Scenarios align with the Domestic, EU, and Non-EU we used earlier for the Posting groups, we have a nice and simple setup for three 🔍 **Customer Templates**:

EU Customers:

Type	Field Name	Field Caption	Template Code	Default Value
Field	Gen. Bus. Posting Gr...	Gen. Bus. Posting Group		EU
Field	VAT Bus. Posting Gr...	VAT Bus. Posting Group		EU
Field	Customer Posting G...	Customer Posting Group		EU
Field	Location Code	Location Code		ASKIM
Field	Payment Terms Code	Payment Terms Code		NET30

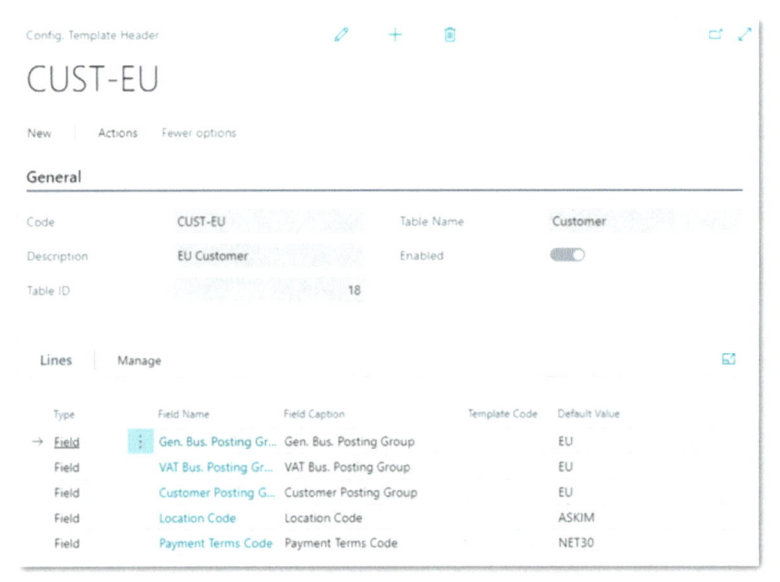

Config. Template Header — **CUST-EU**
- Code: CUST-EU
- Description: EU Customer
- Table ID: 18
- Table Name: Customer
- Enabled: ✓

Figure 7-3 - Configuration Template - Customer EU

Domestic Customers:

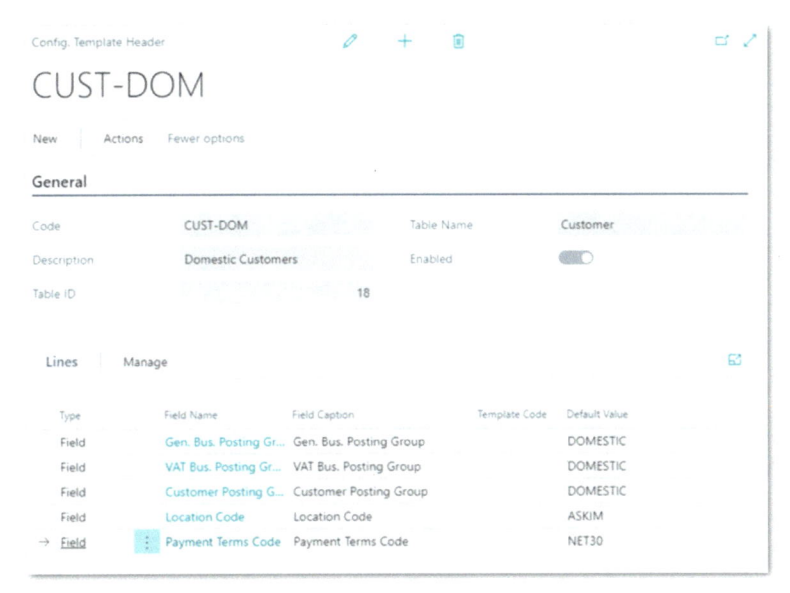

Figure 7-4 - Configuration Template - Customer Domestic

Export Customers:

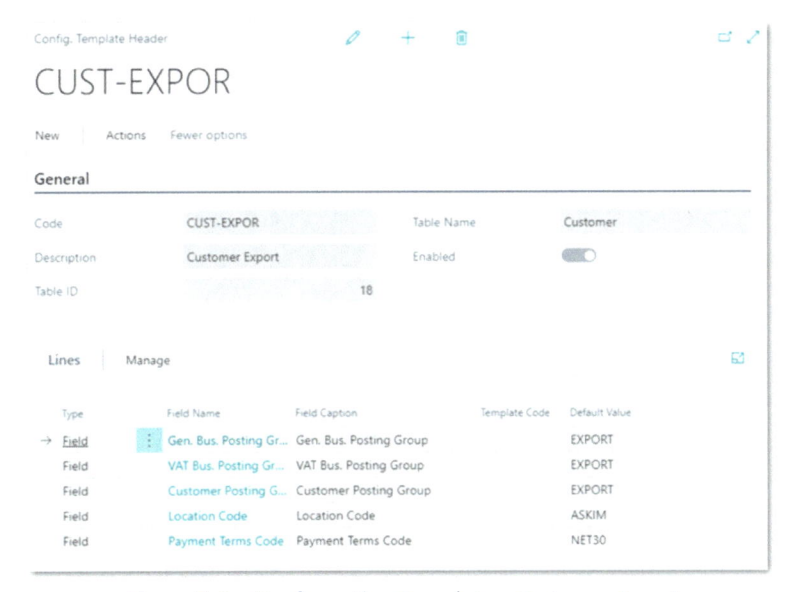

Figure 7-5 - Configuration Template - Customer Export

ACTION: Create Templates - Customer

You will want at least one Customer Template in your 🔍 **Configuration Templates** to apply the Posting Groups (based on your Posting Groups, you may need several). Now, think about all the different combinations you might like, to make an easy "one-click" creation.

Some examples:

- Maybe all customers belong to 2 or 3 salespeople.
- Maybe most of your customers come from a few different cities.
- maybe you often setup lots of new Sell-To Customers of a large Chain and need the Bill-To across all the Locations.

After you create the first one, note that you can use the **Copy Config. Template** in the Action Bar on new templates to copy the field settings from a source template, then just alter the values you need.

Configuration Templates - Vendor

As often happens with sales and purchasing, you will find that the Vendor Template is nearly a mirror of the Customer Template. Still within the 🔍 **Configuration Templates**:

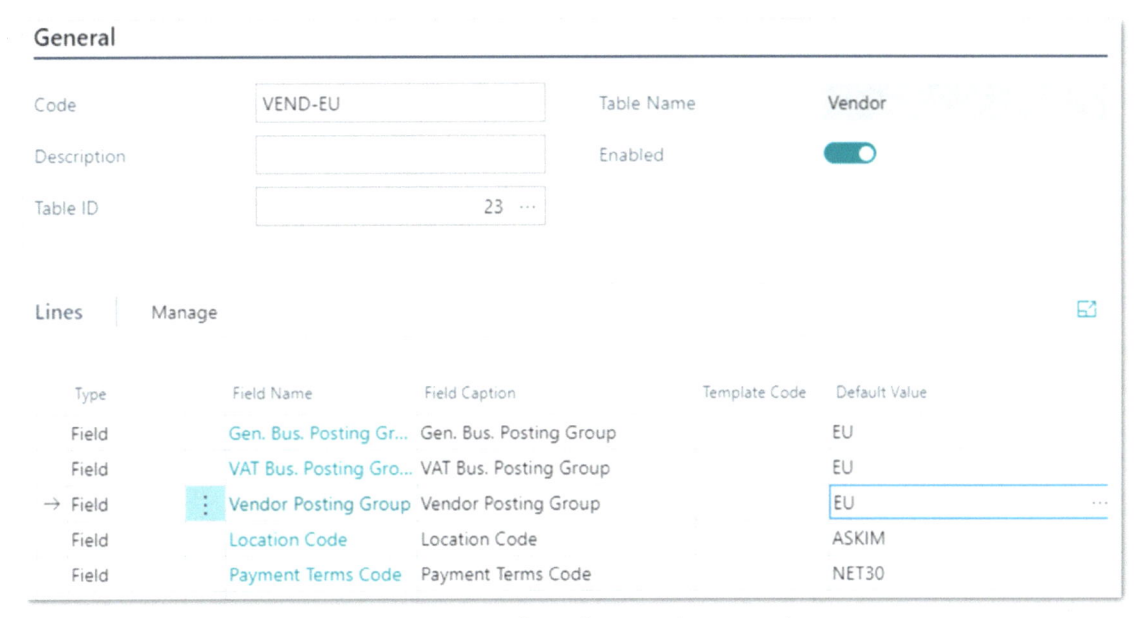

Type	Field Name	Field Caption	Template Code	Default Value
Field	Gen. Bus. Posting Gr...	Gen. Bus. Posting Group		EU
Field	VAT Bus. Posting Gro...	VAT Bus. Posting Group		EU
→ Field	Vendor Posting Group	Vendor Posting Group		EU
Field	Location Code	Location Code		ASKIM
Field	Payment Terms Code	Payment Terms Code		NET30

General — Code: VEND-EU, Table Name: Vendor, Table ID: 23, Enabled.

Figure 7-6 - Configuration Template - Vendor

Much as before, we can align our templates with the Posting Groups we made earlier, creating templates for the **EU**, **Domestic**, and **Export**.

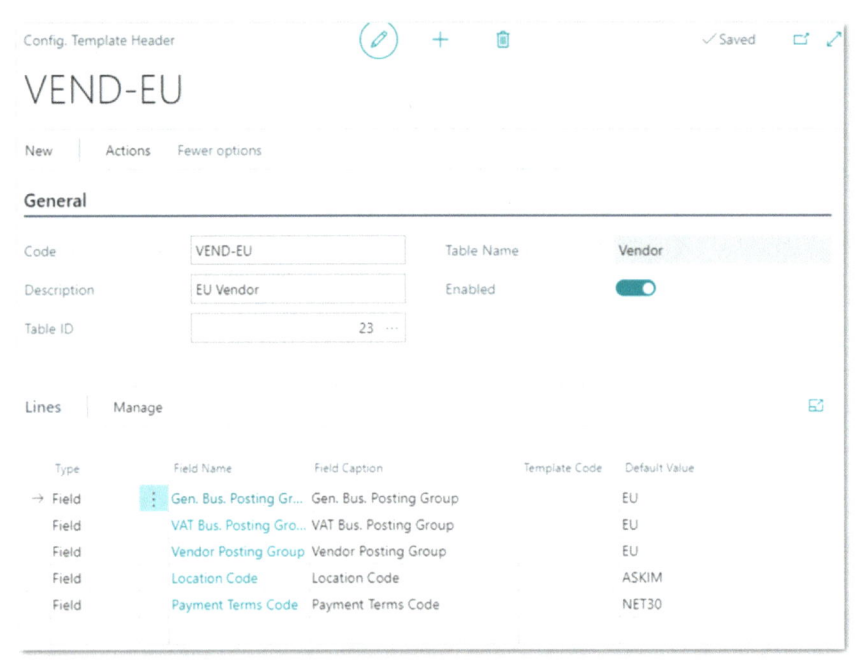

Figure 7-7 - Configuration Template - Vendor EU

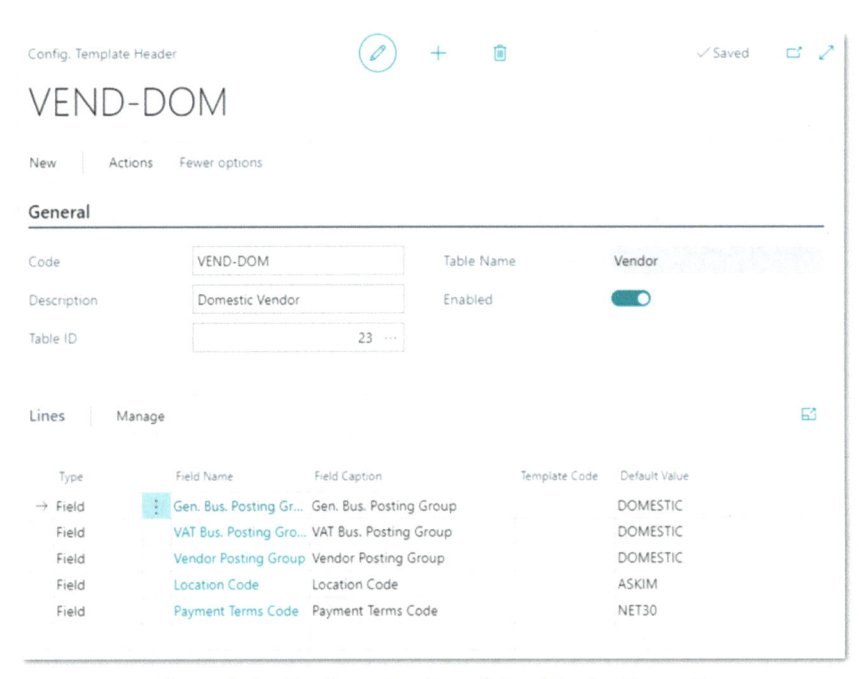

Figure 7-8 - Configuration Template - Vendor Domestic

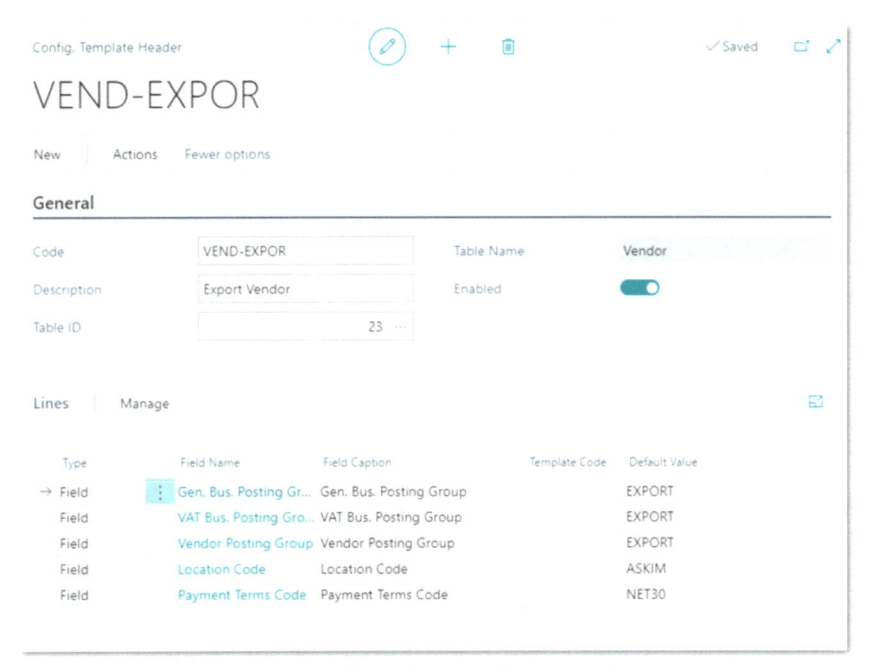

Figure 7-9 - Configuration Template - Vendor Export

ACTION: Create Vendor Templates

You will want at least one Vendor Template in your 🔍 **Configuration Templates** to apply the Posting Groups. Based on your Posting Groups, you may need several.

ITEM TEMPLATES, PART 1

The **Configuration Templates** for **Items** work very similarly. However, for the Item Template, we may require more settings which results in us needing more Templates. Some critical Item settings such as the **Base Unit of Measure** and **Item Category Code** typically vary. Before configuring the Item Templates, we need to explore how those systems work.

ITEMS AND UNITS OF MEASURE

Business Central has support for simple and very complex **Unit of Measures** handling.

To take one example, maybe you just buy "1" each of something and sell it as "1" each, but in other scenarios, you might buy a 5000m spool of wiring and sell it in 100m packages.

Each **Item** needs to be able to handle these complex requirements on a *per-item* basis. This is solved via **Units of Measures** (**UOM**), and the following examples are from the CRONUS demonstration company:

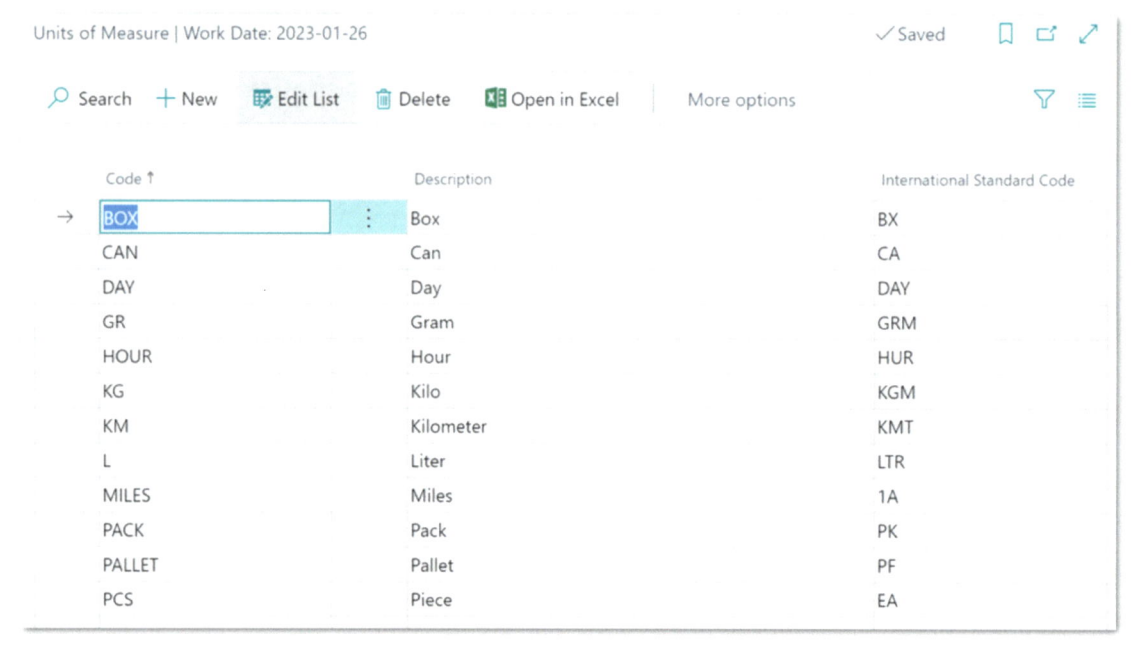

Code ↑	Description	International Standard Code
BOX	Box	BX
CAN	Can	CA
DAY	Day	DAY
GR	Gram	GRM
HOUR	Hour	HUR
KG	Kilo	KGM
KM	Kilometer	KMT
L	Liter	LTR
MILES	Miles	1A
PACK	Pack	PK
PALLET	Pallet	PF
PCS	Piece	EA

Figure 7-10 - CRONUS Unit of Measures List

So, in the above example, you buy and sell in **PCS**. However, in the complex example, you buy in **KM**, sell in **PACK**, but keep your inventory in **M** (meters, *not shown*).

The **Unit of Measures** list is a basic list of **Code** and **Description**, while relationship between different Units of Measure is configured on a *per-item* basis. A **Box** or **Pallet** of one Item can be a wildly different count from another Item. For our complex cabling example, **Item Units of Measure** would be:

Code ↑	Qty. per Unit of Measure	Height
M	1	0
PACK	100	0
KM	1 000	0

Figure 7-11 - Example Item Units of Measure List

This means that when you buy 2 KM from a supplier, upon the receipt, in your Item Ledger Entry, it will automatically store that as 2000 M, as the **M** is your **Base Unit of Measure**. You could then sell 3 Packs, with the **Unit of Measure** for PACK set to "100", and you would see that 300 M has been shipped, leaving 1700 in stock.

This is a very powerful feature, but it does mean that you will need to consider the **Unit of Measure** options for the Items you will buy & sell to create appropriate Item Templates.

For the Items we will be creating in our scenario, we will keep it simple and assume buy and sell in **PCS** only.

ACTION: Units of Measure

Based on your item requirements, you should set up the **Unit of Measures** list.

PART 2: BUILDING YOUR FOUNDATION
CHAPTER 7: CUSTOMER / VENDOR / ITEM TEMPLATES

ITEM CATEGORY CODES

Item Categories help you quickly filter on a given Category of Items. They also support complex nesting of different levels of Categories – so you could easily support "Outdoors -> Garden & Tools -> Lawn Mowers -> Accessories" as an example.

The Category system can also heavily control how something called **Item Attributes** work, allowing you to have configurable details about Items that you decide, but unfortunately, Item Attributes are a bit beyond the scope of this book.

As mentioned in our scenario, we will have **NORMAL** and **SEASONAL** items. Not only will we have those under different Inventory Posting Groups (for the financial and inventory tracking), but we will also set up some **Item Categories** for some of our example items:

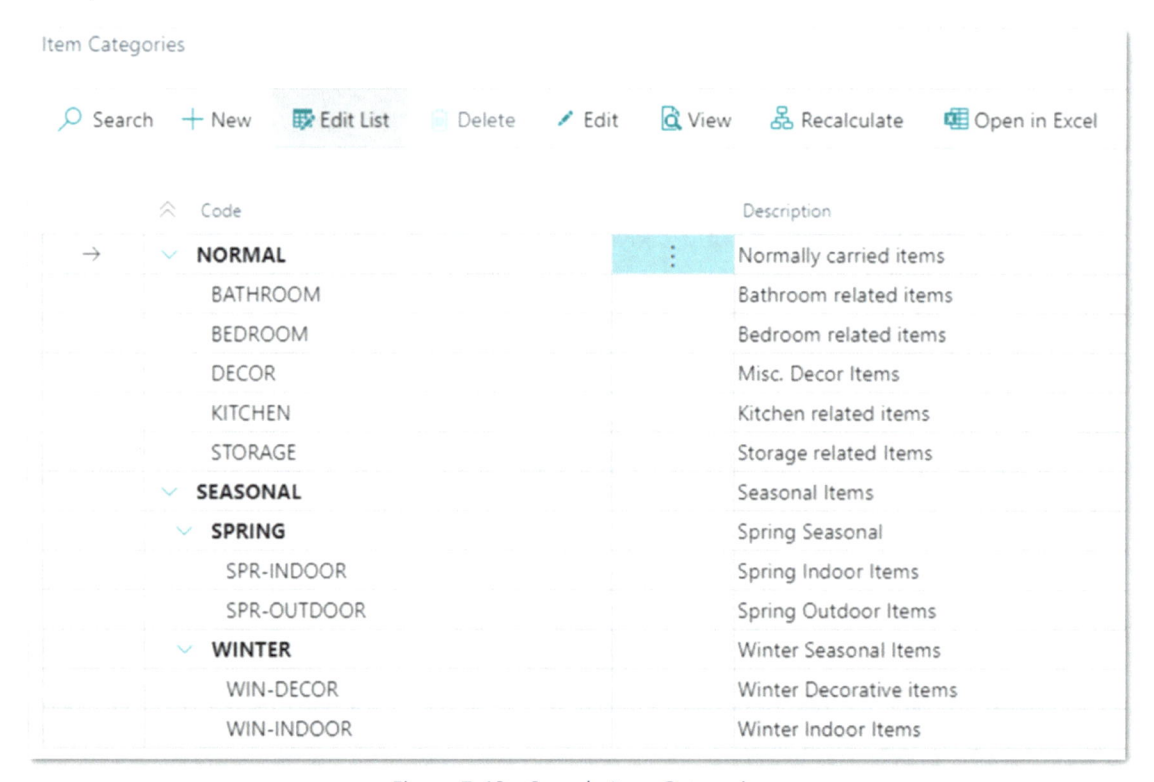

Code	Description
NORMAL	Normally carried items
BATHROOM	Bathroom related items
BEDROOM	Bedroom related items
DECOR	Misc. Decor Items
KITCHEN	Kitchen related items
STORAGE	Storage related Items
SEASONAL	Seasonal Items
SPRING	Spring Seasonal
SPR-INDOOR	Spring Indoor Items
SPR-OUTDOOR	Spring Outdoor Items
WINTER	Winter Seasonal Items
WIN-DECOR	Winter Decorative items
WIN-INDOOR	Winter Indoor Items

Figure 7-12 - Sample Item Categories

However, applying all these individual categories as templates, per Unit of Measure, would create a lot of work for setting up the Templates. In our scenario, we have a tiny list of example items, so, this will not save us any time. We will keep our templates limited to just the **NORMAL** and **SEASONAL** variants, so, just two Item Templates will be needed.

ACTION: Item Categories

If you want to utilize **Item Categories**, contact a partner to learn about **Item Attributes** to maximize the benefit of this system.

Item Templates, Part 2

Now that we know a bit more about what kind of information goes into an 🔍 **Configuration Templates** for **Items**, it is time to decide what sort of templates would benefit us.

In our scenario, we will simply have two (as previously mentioned):

- **NORMAL**
- **SEASONAL**

We will set the default **Base Unit of Measure** to the **PCS** value, as well as the Posting Groups, but otherwise, we will be setting the Item Category Codes to the top-level categories of each so we can filter.

Still within the 🔍 **Configuration Templates**; this time for the Item Table - **27**:

Normal

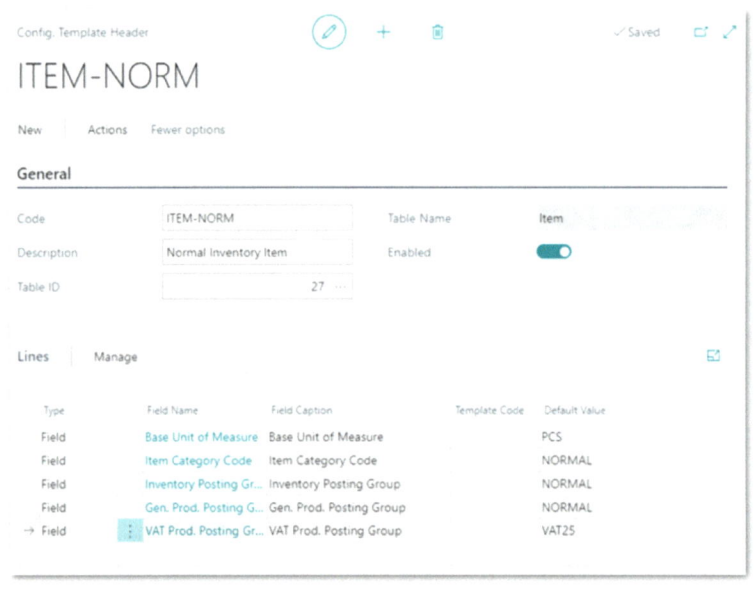

Figure 7-13 - Configuration Template - Item Normal

Seasonal

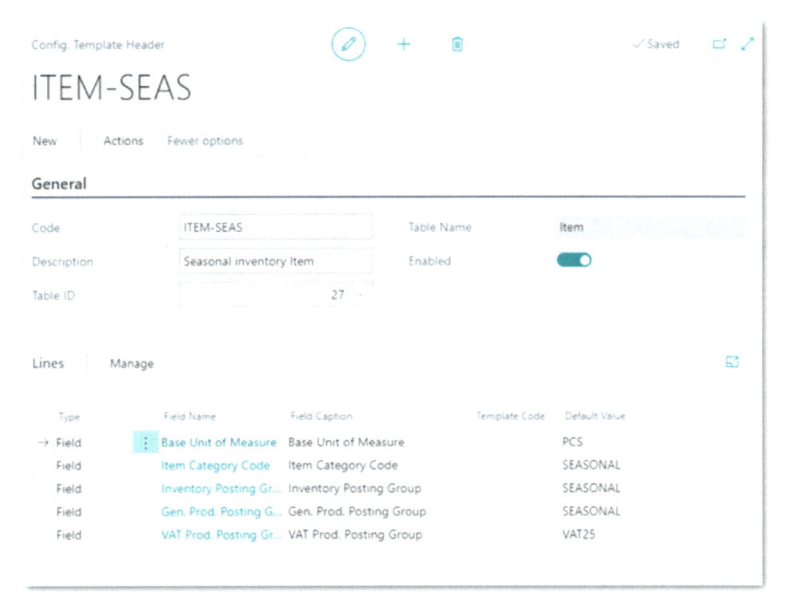

Figure 7-14 - Configuration Template - Item Seasonal

ACTION: Create Item Template(s)

You will want at least one Item Template in your **Configuration Templates** to apply a **Base Unit of Measure** and the **Posting Groups**. Based on your needs, you may need anywhere from one to a couple dozen.

Chapter 8: Data Migration – Importing Master Data

It is time to make the big jump – we are about to work on Importing Master Data. Microsoft Dynamics 365 Business Central has an import process that creates an Excel file for you, in which you can configure many of the Master Data parts, then Import them.

GENERATING THE TEMPLATE

Via the **Tell Me** function, we should search for the **Data Migration** window:

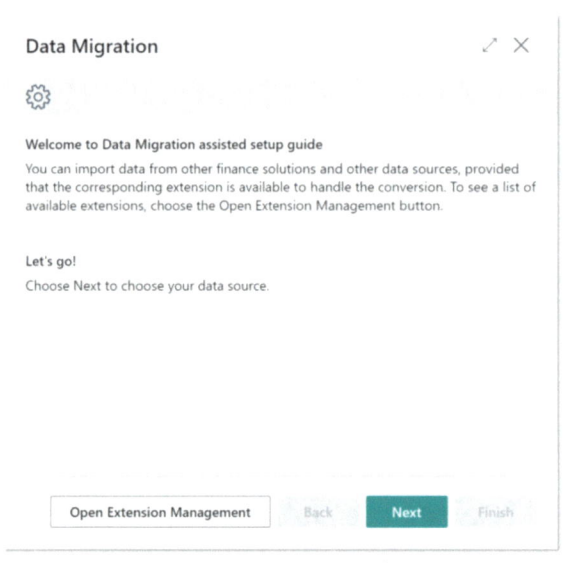

Figure 8-1 - Data Migration Welcome Page

In this new window, click on **Next** to move to the next step where you will be able to select the data source. The standard functionality only contains **Import from Excel**, which is the default. Clicking **Next** again brings you to the template page:

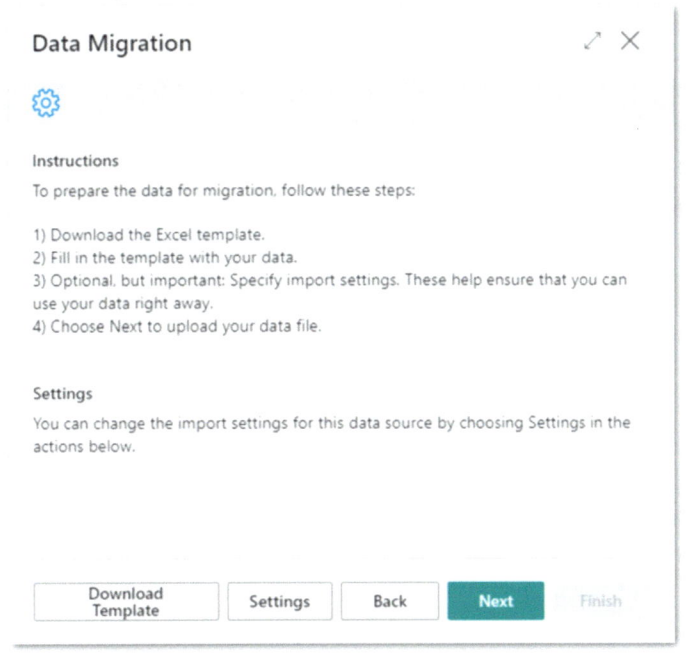

Figure 8-2 - Data Migration Instructions Page

Click on **Download Template**. This will generate and download an Excel file:

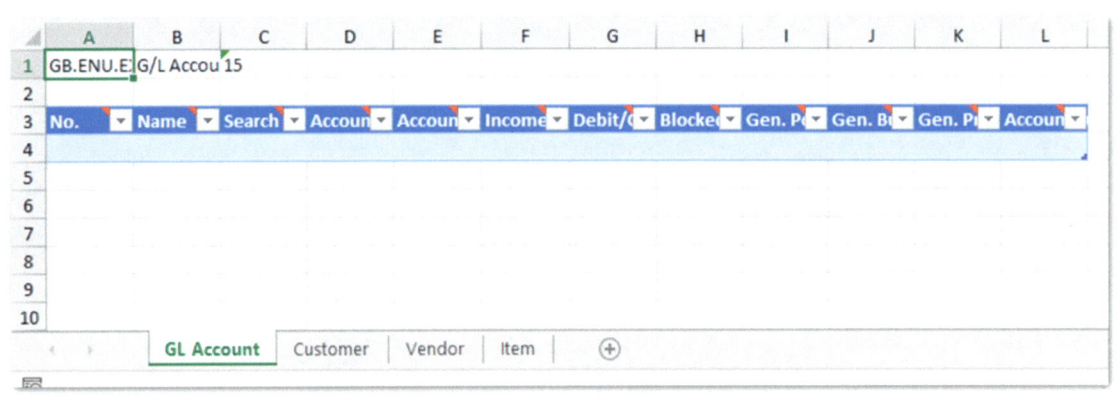

Figure 8-3 - Data Migration - Template GL Sheet

ACTION: Download Data Migration Template

Using the steps above to go through the **Data Migration**, please make sure to **Download Template** and look through the Excel file it generates.

PART 2: BUILDING YOUR FOUNDATION
CHAPTER 8: DATA MIGRATION – IMPORTING MASTER DATA

CHART OF ACCOUNTS – GENERAL LEDGER ACCOUNTS

GENERAL LEDGER ACCOUNTS - FUNCTIONALITY REVIEW

The **GL Account** sheet (the slash in *G/L Account* is not permitted in Excel) in the Excel file (Figure 8-3) will be how we generate the 🔍 **Chart of Accounts**. The Chart of Accounts is the setup list of General Ledger Accounts, structured in a way to align with accounting practices, as well as showing **Net Change** and **Balance** information for each configured General Ledger Account.

Each **General Ledger Account** has a **No.** (a unique ID field) and **Name**. They also have something called **Account Type**, which controls how the information gets structured, reported on, and how users are allowed to work with the Account. In this example section from the CRONUS company:

No.	Name	Net Change	Balance
6000	**INCOME STATEMENT**	–	–
6100	**Revenue**	–	–
6105	**Sales of Retail**	–	–
6110	Sales, Retail - Dom.	-10 503,70	-761 618,03
6120	Sales, Retail - EU	-43 209,73	-97 472,74
6130	Sales, Retail - Export	-16 710,22	-128 946,20
6190	Job Sales Applied, Retail	–	–
6191	Job Sales Adjmt., Retail	–	–
6195	**Total Sales of Retail**	-70 423,65	-988 036,97

Figure 8-4 - G/L Account Subset

"**6000** - INCOME STATEMENT" is a **Heading** Account Type. You cannot apply transactions to it, and it will never have any value.

"**6105** – Sales of Retail" is an Account Type of **Begin-Total**, a grouping account, indicating to the system where a group of accounts will begin. No transactions can be directly applied against it, and it will never have any sort of values.

"**6195** – Total Sales of Retail" is an Account Type of **End-Total**, a grouping account, indicating to the system where a group of accounts will end. No transactions can be directly applied against it. An End-Total account will have (either automatically or manually) a value in a field called **Totaling**:

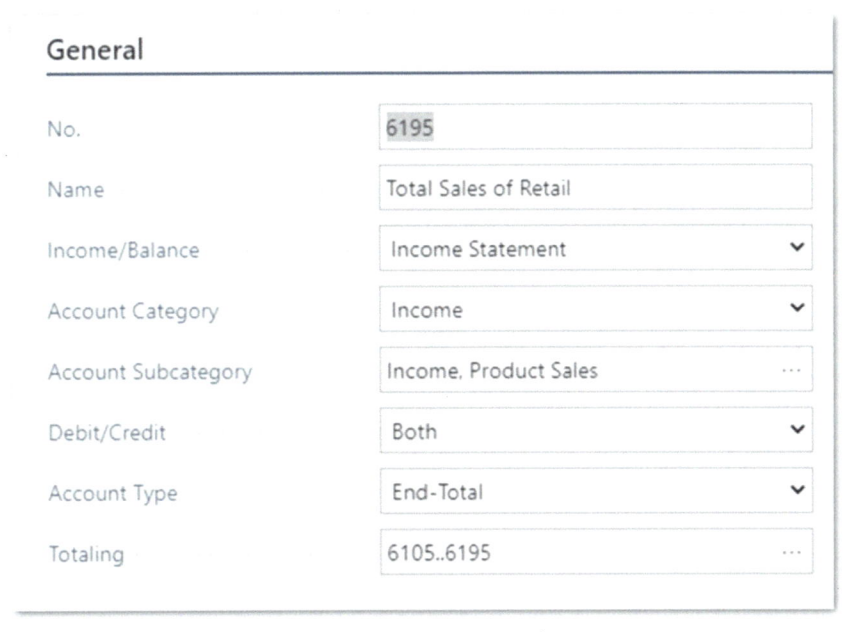

Figure 8-5 - G/L Account Card Excerpt

The **Totaling** setting **6105..6195** (Figure 8-5) sets account **No. 6195** to automatically summarize the values of all accounts from **6105** to **6195** (inclusive). In Figure 8-4, we can see that **6195** shows the sum of the values from **6110**, **6120**, and **6130** in the **Balance** and **Net Change**.

"**6110** – Sales, Retail – Dom." is an Account Type of **Posting**, which is a normal transactional account against which values will be posted.

Additionally, a General Ledger Account can have some useful properties on it:

- **Account Category** – These align with accounting basics, such as Assets, Liabilities.
- **Income/Balance** – Indicates if this is a Balance Sheet or an Income Statement.
- **Debit/Credit** – Controls which types of entries can be posted, the default being **Both**.

- **Gen. Posting Type**, **Gen. Bus. Posting Group**, and **Gen. Prod. Posting Group** give the values necessary to be able to use the G/L Account in the right combinations with transactions. Typically, these are needed on Sales & Purchase related Income Statement accounts so they can be used directly on Documents.

GL Account – Import File

You will see that our columns in the Import File mostly align with what we have previously indicated:

Figure 8-6 - Data Migration Template - GL Account

Each field will have a Note in Excel showing some of the values that are valid. On the **Account Type**, it is expecting you to enter one of the following options:

0: Posting

1: Heading

2: Total

3: Begin-Total

4: End-Total

Working through this step can take a little while, preparing your Excel file. Even if you are making a new Company and have no previous Chart of Accounts created, it is still considered faster to prepare your Chart using this import method.

Because a chart often has a significant number of accounts, the example for our scenario is not shown here within this section but can be found in **Appendix A**.

ACTION: Generate / Configure your Chart of Accounts

With your existing chart of accounts, create entries in the **GL Account** sheet in the Import Template File in Excel.

If you do not already have a 🔍 Chart of Accounts for your business, this should *absolutely* be done with help from an accountant familiar with the accounting practices required in the country or countries that you will be doing business with and reporting to. There are often substantial regulations for reporting and taxes around this and should not be taken lightly.

If you already have a Chart of Accounts for your business, it is possible you do not have the Begin/End Total accounts, so you may want to review what groups of accounts you want to make using the new grouping feature.

CUSTOMER IMPORT FILE

Much like the **GL Account** sheet, the **Customer** sheet has column headings that include notes explaining many of the values.

Figure 8-7 - Data Migration Template - Customer Headers

Many are self-explanatory, except for a few notes:

- Unlike our G/L Accounts, we can choose whether to specify the **No.** If you leave it blank here, customers will automatically receive their new Customer No. from the **Customer No. Series** that you set up on **Sales & Receivables Setup**.
- You will notice that we can optionally force specific **Customer Posting Groups**, **Payment Terms**, and **Gen. Business Posting Groups** here. These settings will override the Customer Template that we will select during the Import.

If you import your existing Customers with a blank **No.** so they receive a new auto-generated **Customer No.**, be aware that you could have issues connecting your **Opening Balances** (and open documents) to their old customer number from a prior system.

ACTION: Generate / Configure Your Customer List

With your existing customer list, create entries in the **Customer** sheet in the Import Template File in Excel.

If you need to apply different templates to different groups of customers, consider using multiple copies of the Import Template File. The Data Migration can be run multiple times.

VENDOR IMPORT FILE

The Import Columns on the **Vendor** sheet align closely with the Customer Import, with only the **Credit Limit** removed:

Figure 8-8 - Data Migration Template - Vendor Headers

The same clarifications and explanations from the **Customers** apply to this section as well, especially including any warnings about auditing compliance.

ACTION: Generate / Configure Your Vendor List

With your existing vendor list, create entries in the **Vendor** sheet in the Import Template File in Excel.

If you need to apply different templates to different groups of vendors, consider using multiple copies of the Import Template File. You can run the Data Migration multiple times.

ITEM IMPORT FILE

The Item sheet has quite a few columns, many of which will be ignored for our simple implementation:

Figure 8-9 - Data Migration Template - Item Headers

- **No.** can be left blank to so that all the Items import will be automatically be assigned an **Item No.** from the **Item No. Series** set on the 🔍 **Inventory Setup**.
- **Base Unit of Measure** can be left blank if using an Item Template.
- **Unit Price** is good to be set here, as it is easy to get them all in during this process.

- **Unit Cost**, **Standard Cost** – these fields are heavily affected by what costing methods you use. For FIFO (First-In, First-Out), this is not relevant, as Unit Cost will be calculated based on costing calculations that will run after we have purchased stock or adjusted in the value of stock.

You will note that we appear to be able to set the **Inventory** quantity in the Excel file for the items. We will not use this column, as **Chapter 12** will focus on bringing in the Item Inventory manually for more fine-tuned control.

The rest of the columns in the Import Template have to do with the replenishment methods available in the system. With these values set, it is entirely possible to generate Purchase Documents based on current or forecasted need. This is far more complex than what this book will cover – unfortunately, as it is a fascinating topic!

ACTION: Generate / Configure Your Item List

With your existing item and inventory list, create entries in the **Item** sheet in the Import Template File in Excel.

If you need to apply different templates to different groups of items, consider using multiple copies of the Import Template file. You can run the Data Migration multiple times.

PERFORMING THE IMPORT

In our scenario, we will set up three main Import file batches:

BATCH 1 – GL, EU PARTNERS, NORMAL ITEMS

The first Excel file contains:

1. All the General Ledger Accounts.
2. All EU Based Customers.
3. All EU Based Vendors.
4. All Items that are NORMAL category items.

BATCH 2 – DOMESTIC PARTNERS, SEASONAL ITEMS

The second Excel file contains:

1. All Sweden-based (DOMESTIC) Customers.
2. All Sweden-based (DOMESTIC) Vendors.
3. All Items that are SEASONAL category items.

BATCH 3 – EXPORT PARTNERS

The third Excel file only contains the EXPORT (Non-EU) Customers and Vendors.

*Since these Excel files are too large to include as screenshots, they are available in **Appendix A** in both table form and with download links.*

DATA MIGRATION - IMPORT

For each file, on the 🔍 **Data Migration** page, you will need to change the **Settings** (**1**):

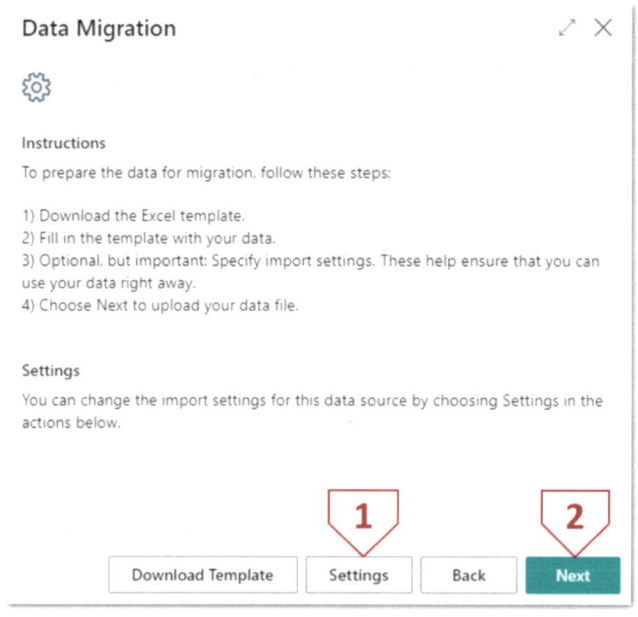

Figure 8-10 - Data Migration - Instructions Page

On the **Data Migration Settings** screen, here is where we can specify the **Configuration Templates** that we set up earlier. Our **Batch 1** setup looks as following:

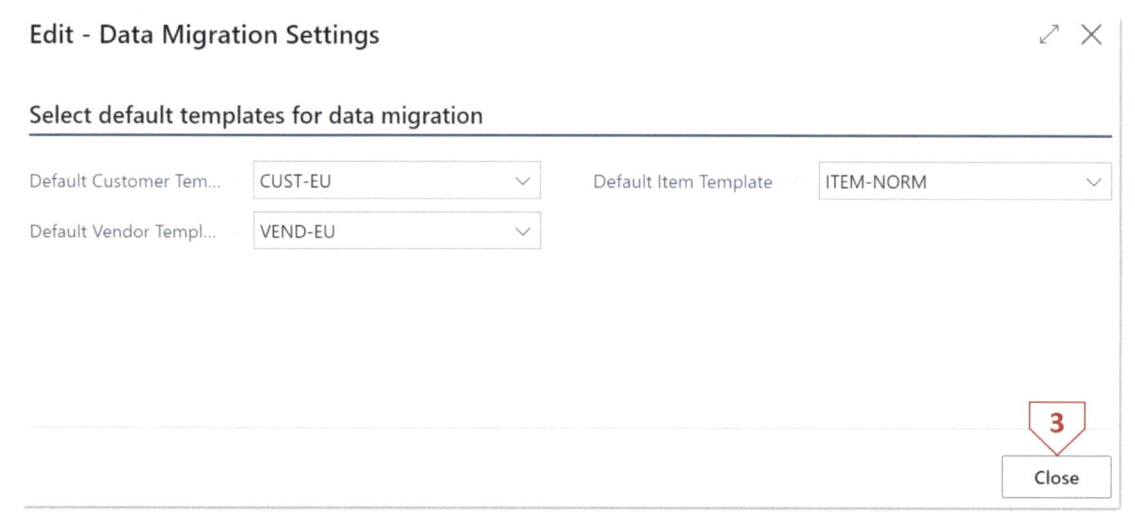

Figure 8-11 - Data Migration - Settings

Click **Close** (**3**) to return to the Data Migration. When you click **Next** (**2**), it will open a dialog to select which Excel file to import from:

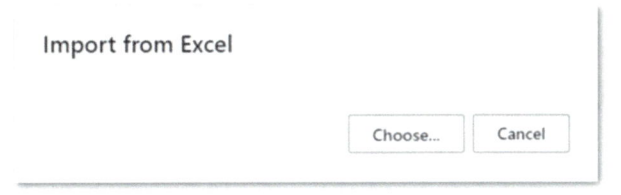

Figure 8-12 - Data Migration - Import Chooser

After selecting the file, we will see an information summary that shows what will be imported:

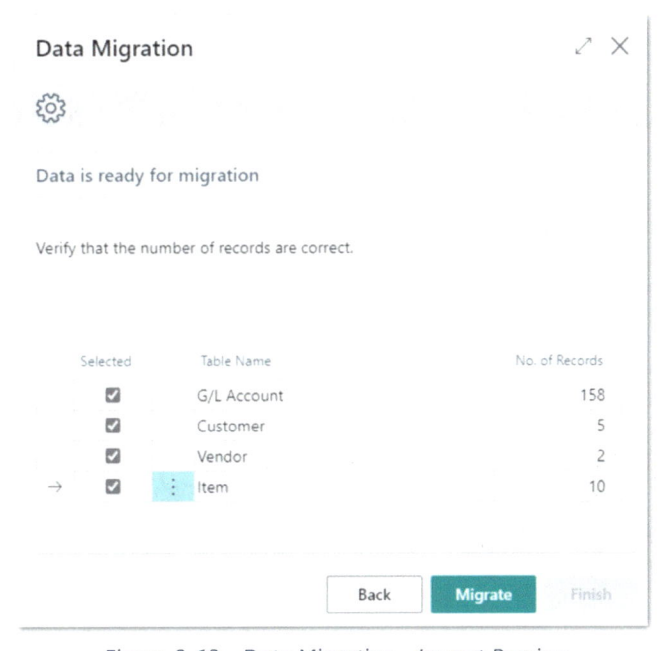

Figure 8-13 - Data Migration - Import Preview

By clicking **Migrate**, the import process will begin. Unless your data is flawless, you might get a warning about errors like this:

PART 2: BUILDING YOUR FOUNDATION
CHAPTER 8: DATA MIGRATION – IMPORTING MASTER DATA

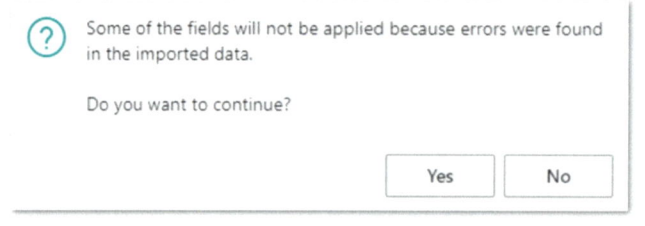

Figure 8-14 - Data Migration - Example Error Message

This is letting you know that there are going to be issues applying some portion of the data you are trying to import. However, it will proceed as much as possible. Unfortunately, there is no way (at this stage) to see which fields are in error.

Back in **Chapter 3**, we intentionally created a problem to have something to solve in this step. With your files and templates, you may not have any errors – if this is the case, you are welcome to skip ahead past the fixing process.

Once you proceed past the error warning (or if you did not receive any), you will get some progress indications as the import routines run. After it completes, you will get a summary of the results:

Figure 8-15 - Data Migration - Example Results Message

Resolving Import Errors

Now, on the final page of the **Data Migration**, you can click **Show Errors** to see what might have been incorrect (or simply click **Finish** if your data was correct):

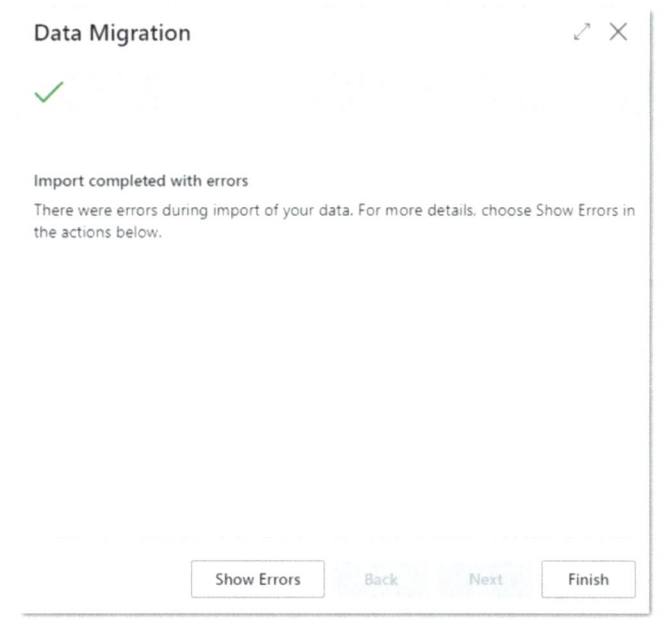

Figure 8-16 - Data Migration - Import Complete, with Errors

In our scenario, it shows the 6 errors as part of the **G/L Account** Import step:

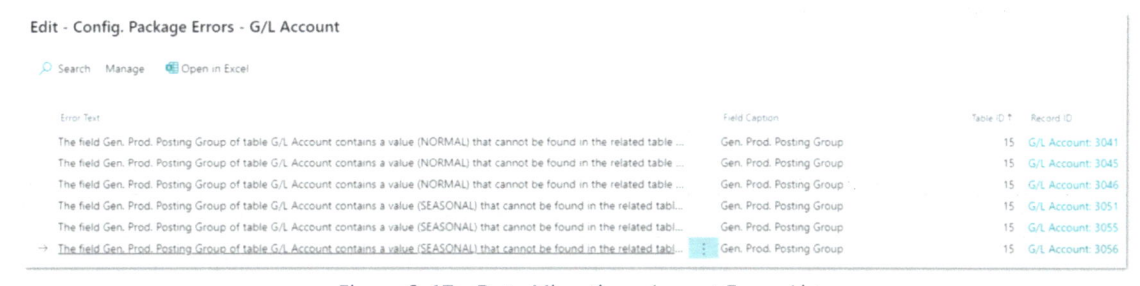

Figure 8-17 - Data Migration - Import Errors List

Here, we have specified the **Gen. Prod. Posting Group** of a few of our accounts to either **NORMAL** or **SEASONAL**, but as you recall, we had created a simple **GOODS** Gen. Prod. Posting Group earlier.

This represents a disconnect between how to track sales vs. inventory. The Items are set up to use the **Inventory Posting Group** of **NORMAL**, but just the basic **Gen. Prod. Posting Group** of **GOODS**. This means that we will be able to see the inventory value easily by **NORMAL** vs. **SEASONAL** items, but we cannot analyze the sales separately in the same way.
This is a very common problem when setting up the system; so, *how do we fix it?*

1. Add the **NORMAL** and **SEASONAL** Gen. Prod. Posting Groups.
2. Update each of our **Configuration Templates** to use the correct *new* posting groups.
3. Update the Items imported with the wrong **Gen. Prod. Posting Group**.
4. Remove the **GOODS** Gen. Prod. Posting Group

Unfortunately, if you re-run the Data Migration and re-import the files we specified before (while the G/L Accounts would be fine and be updated, because we specified the **No.** field), all the Customers, Vendors, and Items would be duplicated (because we have the **No.** field blank). There is no "matching" logic that would detect them as duplicates and then re-apply the data. If we re-created the first Excel file with the newly assigned No. values in the sheets, then we could perform the re-import safely (with no duplicates).

DATA MIGRATION – MORE IMPORTING

With the 2nd Excel file, we will use the following Template settings:

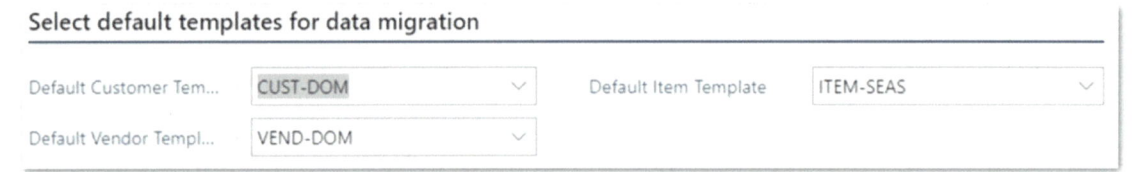

Select default templates for data migration			
Default Customer Tem...	CUST-DOM	Default Item Template	ITEM-SEAS
Default Vendor Templ...	VEND-DOM		

Figure 8-18 - Data Migration - Import Settings

Which previews to give the correct results:

Selected	Table Name	No. of Records
☐	G/L Account	0
☑	Customer	8
☑	Vendor	6
☑	Item	8

Figure 8-19 - Data Migration - Import Preview

And with the 3rd Excel file, use the following settings:

Select default templates for data migration

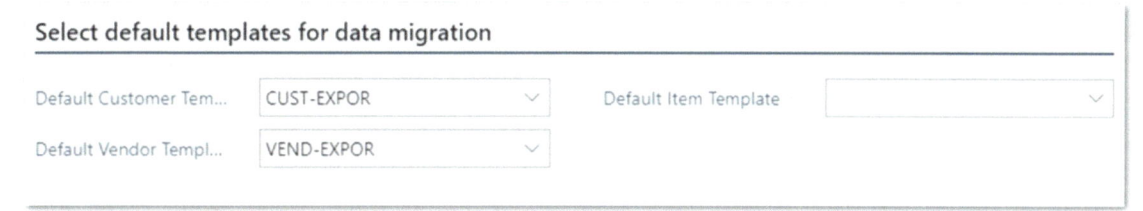

Default Customer Tem...	CUST-EXPOR	Default Item Template	
Default Vendor Templ...	VEND-EXPOR		

Figure 8-20 - Data Migration - Import Settings

Which previews to the right results as well:

Selected	Table Name	No. of Records
☐	G/L Account	0
☑	Customer	7
☑	Vendor	2
☐	Item	0

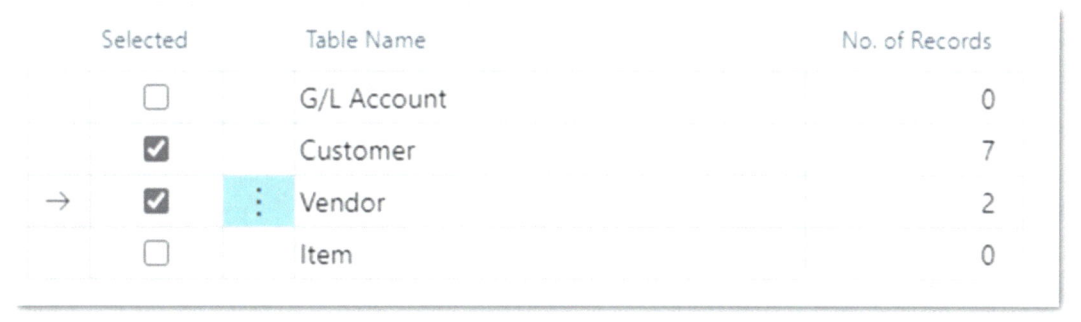

Figure 8-21 - Data Migration - Import Preview

REVIEWING DATA MIGRATION RESULTS

CHART OF ACCOUNTS

If we review the 🔍 **Chart of Accounts**, we will see that all our Accounts have been imported:

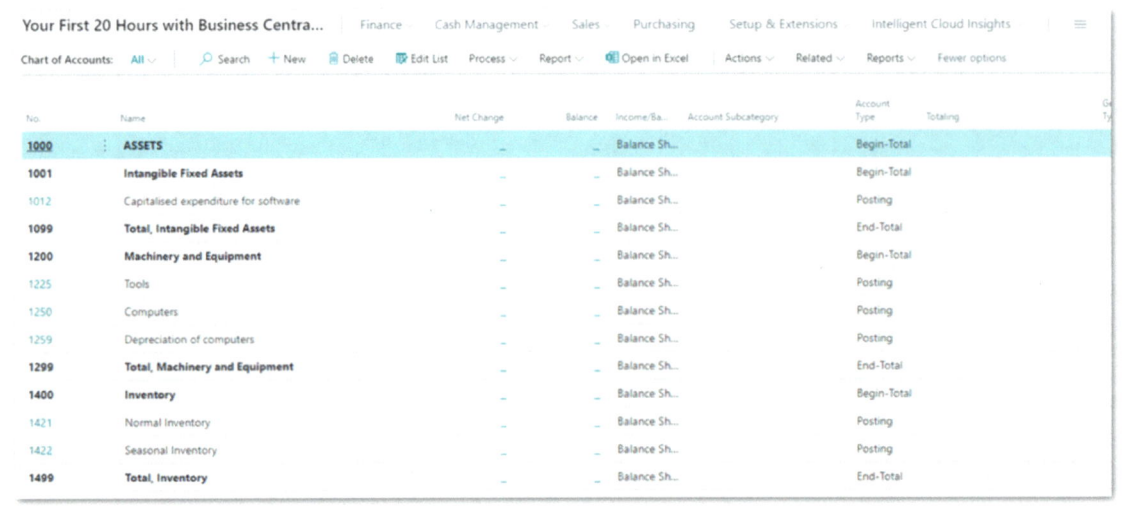

Figure 8-22 - Post-Migration Chart of Accounts

There are some additional post-migration processing steps that we are going to go into in the next chapter to make this ready for use.

CUSTOMERS

Looking next at the 🔍 **Customers** list, we can see things have been imported properly:

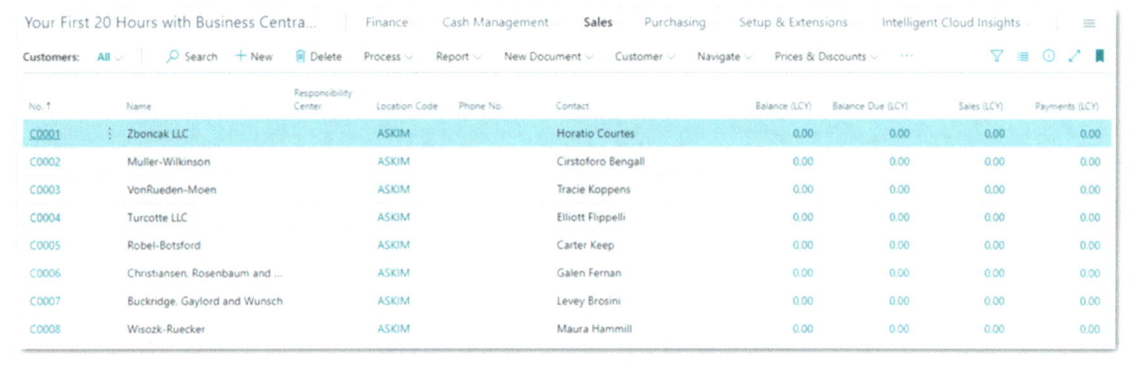

Figure 8-23 - Post Migration Customers

Based on all our hard work, they are ready to go!

VENDORS

Checking the 🔍 **Vendors** list, we can now see that the import is completed:

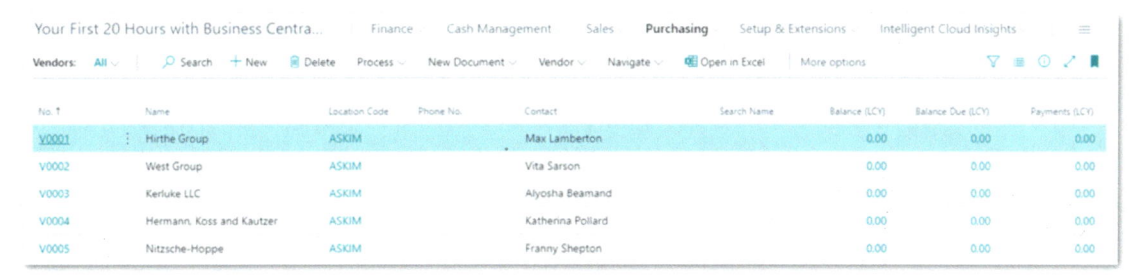

Figure 8-24 – Post Migration Vendors

ITEMS

And lastly, the 🔍 **Items** list also has data:

PART 2: BUILDING YOUR FOUNDATION
CHAPTER 8: DATA MIGRATION – IMPORTING MASTER DATA

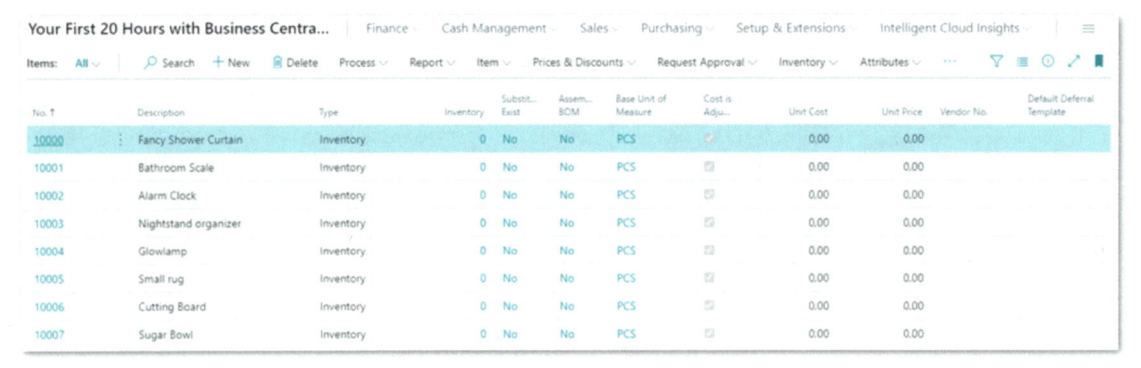

Figure 8-25 - Post Migration Items

SUMMARY

With this process, we have now generated all the key elements we need for our basic organization:

1. General Ledger Accounts (Chart of Accounts)
2. Customers
3. Vendors
4. Items

Chapter 9: Updating Posting Groups

Now that we have the 🔍 **Chart of Accounts** created, we can connect all the Posting Groups we created earlier to the appropriate accounts.

We will need to revisit:

- General Posting Setup
- VAT Posting Setup
- Customer Posting Groups
- Vendors Posting Groups
- Bank Posting Groups
- Inventory Posting Setup

But, before we proceed into that, we need to explore 🔍 **G/L Account Categories**.

Chart of Accounts - Subcategory

One field we did not try to handle during the Excel Import process is on the **General Ledger Account** card, the **Account Subcategory** (**1**) setting which is shown here:

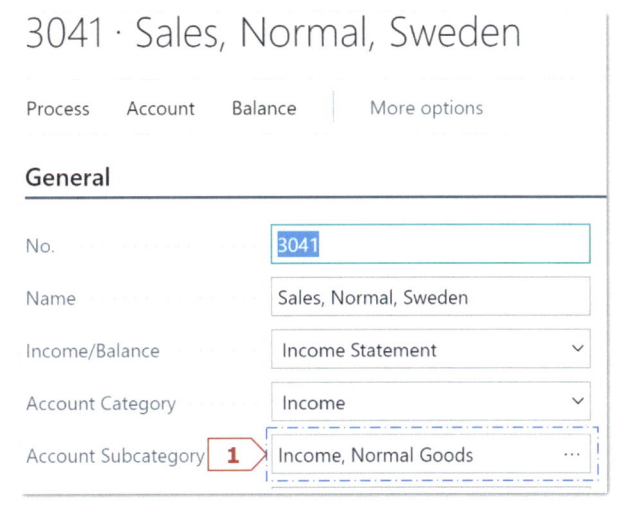

Figure 9-1 - G/L Account Card - Subcategory

This is mostly used as an informational field to help some reporting and filtering. The main setup area of where this Subcategory comes from is the **G/L Account Categories** setup list:

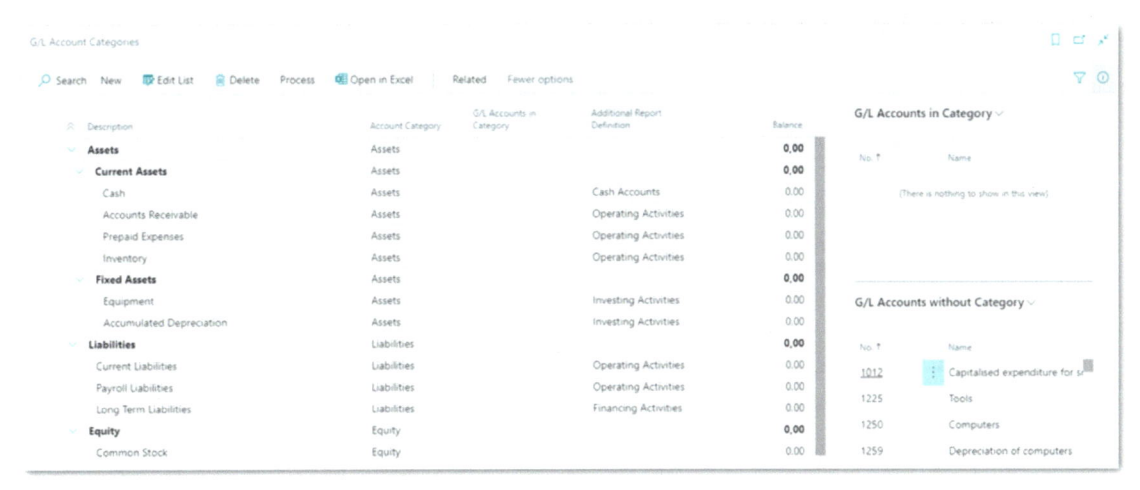

Figure 9-2 - G/L Account Categories List

Part 2: Building Your Foundation
Chapter 9: Updating Posting Groups

This list is also an interesting collective view of the **Balance** information by the categories.

Interestingly, the Balance is not a drill-down and you can neither delve into the numbers behind it, nor can you apply any additional filters, such as date. Even with using the **Create New – No Data** setting in the creation of a new company, you will find that these are still automatically generated.

You will also find that these probably do not quite align to your needs entirely, so, it is worth taking the time to adjust some of them.

In our scenario, the default mostly works, except for the income related categories (changing Services and Sales to **NORMAL** and **SEASONAL**) and some of the Jobs related categories.

Rather than changing every single G/L Account Card manually, from the **G/L Account Categories** list, you can click in the **G/L Accounts in Category** to browse the list *and* multi-select which G/L Accounts should be included. As shown below, when you click into the **Accounts Receivables**, you can hold down Shift (for a range) or Ctrl (for specific multi-select) and select all your Accounts Receivables from the list:

	No.	Name	Income/Ba...	Account Category	Account Type	Gen. Posting Type	Gen. Bus. Posting Group
○	1499	Total, Inventory	Balance Sh...		End-Total		
✓	1500	Accounts Receivable	Balance Sh...	Assets	Begin-Total		
✓	1510	Receivables, Domestic	Balance Sh...	Assets	Posting		
✓	1511	Receivables, EU	Balance Sh...	Assets	Posting		
✓	1512	Receivables, Non-EU	Balance Sh...	Assets	Posting		
✓	1525	Doubtful Receivables	Balance Sh...	Assets	Posting		
→ ✓	1599	Total, Accounts Receivables	Balance Sh...		End-Total		
○	1900	Liquid Assets	Balance Sh...	Assets	Begin-Total		

Figure 9-3 - G/L Account Selection

You will see that it brings the range back into the field, using the same Filtering syntax we covered about in **Chapter 1**:

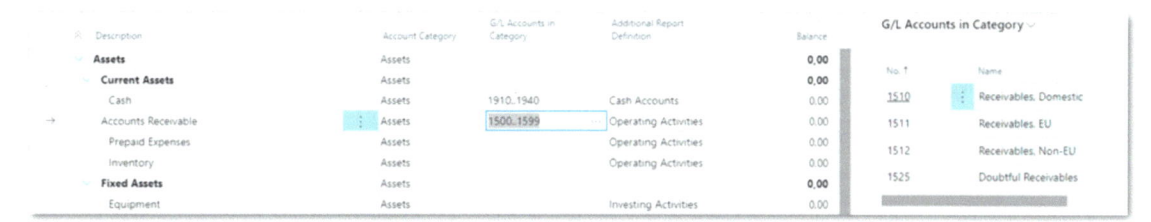

Figure 9-4 - G/L Account Range in Category

This means that you can *just* enter the values manually if you would like.

ACTION: Adjust your G/L Account Categories

Take the time to set the 🔍 **G/L Accounts in Category**. If you must, you can change categories, add more, or rename them.

UPDATE ACCOUNT SCHEDULES

After you have updated all your 🔍 **G/L Account Categories**, you should have a Notification up top as shown:

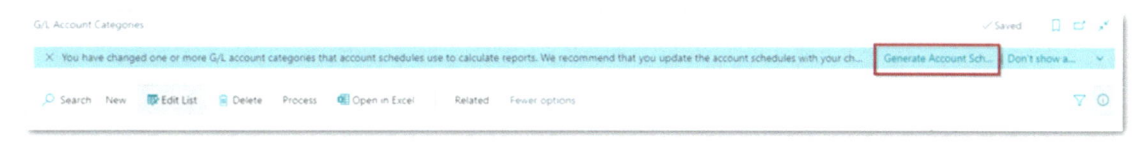

Figure 9-5 - G/L Account Category Notification Bar

Click on the **Generate Account Schedules** link and you will get a confirmation message:

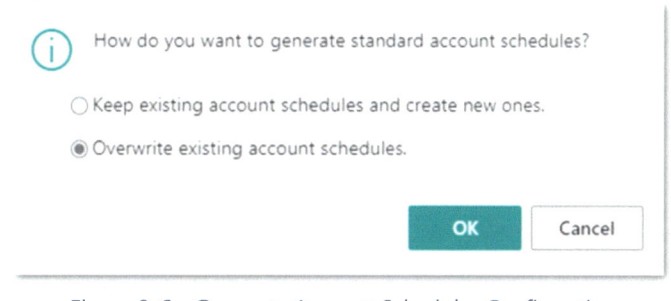

Figure 9-6 - Generate Account Schedules Confirmation

Because at this step, we have not setup **Account Schedules**, it is fine to select **Overwrite existing account schedules**. This will ensure your financial statements will contain all the correct G/L Accounts.

Chart of Accounts - Indentation

This step is the last preparation of your 🔍 **Chart of Accounts**. When we look at the Chart of Accounts, we can see all the **Name** values are left-aligned:

Figure 9-7 - Chart of Accounts - Non-indented

In the Action Bar, select **Process** (**1**) and then **Indent Chart of Accounts** (**2**):

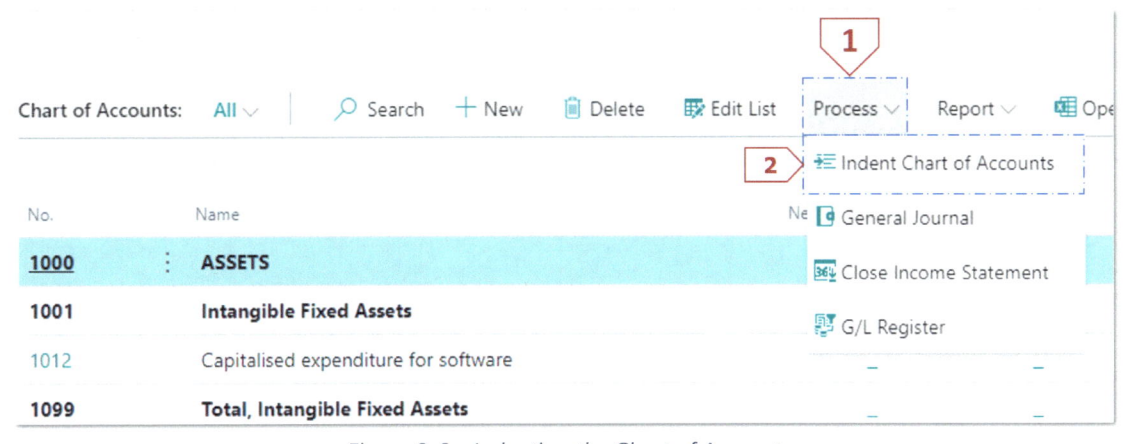

Figure 9-8 - Indenting the Chart of Accounts

PART 2: BUILDING YOUR FOUNDATION
CHAPTER 9: UPDATING POSTING GROUPS

This will change the indents of the **Name** field to align with their grouping, based on your **Begin-Total** and **End-Total** groups:

No.	Name	Net Change	Additional-Currency Net Change	Balance	Income/Ba...	Account Subcategory	Account Type
1000	**ASSETS**	-	-	-	Balance Sh...		Begin-Total
1001	**Intangible Fixed Assets**	-	-	-	Balance Sh...		Begin-Total
1012	Capitalised expenditure for software	-	-	-	Balance Sh...	Equipment	Posting
1099	**Total, Intangible Fixed Assets**	-	-	-	Balance Sh...		End-Total
1200	**Machinery and Equipment**	-	-	-	Balance Sh...		Begin-Total
1225	Tools	-	-	-	Balance Sh...	Equipment	Posting
1250	Computers	-	-	-	Balance Sh...	Equipment	Posting
1259	Depreciation of computers	-	-	-	Balance Sh...	Accumulated Depreciation	Posting
1299	**Total, Machinery and Equipment**	-	-	-	Balance Sh...		End-Total
1400	**Inventory**	-	-	-	Balance Sh...	Inventory	Begin-Total
1421	Normal Inventory	-	-	-	Balance Sh...	Inventory	Posting
1422	Seasonal Inventory	-	-	-	Balance Sh...	Inventory	Posting
1499	**Total, Inventory**	-	-	-	Balance Sh...	Inventory	End-Total
1500	**Accounts Receivable**	-	-	-	Balance Sh...	Accounts Receivable	Begin-Total
1510	Receivables, Domestic	-	-	-	Balance Sh...	Accounts Receivable	Posting
1511	Receivables, EU	-	-	-	Balance Sh...	Accounts Receivable	Posting
1512	Receivables, Non-EU	-	-	-	Balance Sh...	Accounts Receivable	Posting
1525	Doubtful Receivables	-	-	-	Balance Sh...	Accounts Receivable	Posting
1599	**Total, Accounts Receivables**	-	-	-	Balance Sh...	Accounts Receivable	End-Total

Figure 9-9 - Chart of Accounts – Indented

This will also automatically update the **Totals** field on the account, making **End-Total Type** accounts calculate the correct values in **Net Change** and **Balance**.

ACTION: Indent your Chart of Accounts

Following the steps above, on your **Chart of Accounts**, perform the **Indent Chart of Accounts** process. Verify all the **Total** settings.

GENERAL POSTING SETUP - CREATION

The 🔍 **General Posting Setup** is the way the Customer/Vendors from Document Headers connect to the Item/Resource/etc. from Document Lines to determine which G/L Accounts are involved. Sales of services to an EU customer might hit entirely different sales accounts from sales of items to a non-EU customer. This means we are creating a setup entry for all our combinations in this list:

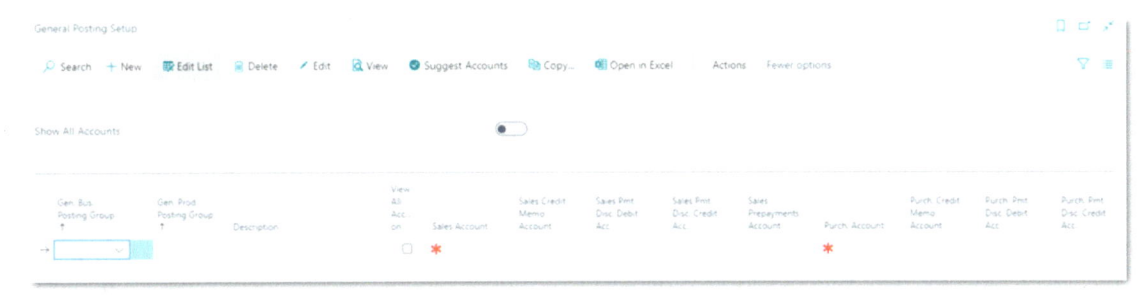

Figure 9-10 - General Posting Setup

Based on our earlier work, this means that we need to make a table like this with the following combinations:

		Gen. Bus. Posting Group			
		DOMESTIC	EU	EXPORT	INTERCO
Gen. Prod. Posting Group	NORMAL	Sales			
		Purch.			
	SEASONAL	Sales			
		Purch.			
	MISC	Sales			
		Purch.			
	NO VAT	Sales			
		Purch.			

As you saw, we have a *lot* more options than just which Sales Account and Purchasing Account to use. By default, you have account settings for the following showing:

- [Sales/Purchase] Credit Memo Account – We will use the same accounts, so that credits hit the same account as the original document.

- [Sales/Purchase] Pmt. Disc. Debit Account and Pmt. Disc. Credit Account (used by the Payment Discount system) – We will not be doing Prepayment handling in this company, so we can leave this blank.
- [Sales/Purchase] Prepayments Account – We will not be doing Prepayment handling in this company, so we can leave this blank.
- Direct Cost Applied Account – This account is used as a pass-through account for inventory costs.
- COGS Account – This account is for recording the Cost of Goods sold.
- Inventory Adjmt. Account – This is the account used to record the gain/loss when inventory is adjusted in or out.

Unfortunately, there is no function to "Generate Combinations" for us here, so we have a bit of entry work to do to get this:

Figure 9-11 - General Posting Setup Combinations

You will notice that we also have a combination where the **Gen. Bus. Posting Group** is set to **BLANK** – this will be used later in **Chapter 12** when we are importing the existing stock.

For our scenario, we will configure the **NORMAL** and **SEASONAL** **Gen. Prod. Posting Groups** to be used separately since we will more often need to adjust out seasonal items.

General Posting Setup - Configuration

When you click in the **Sales Account** or **Purch. Account**, you might find two possible types of lists:

Complete List

If you would change the G/L Account Categories from the system default, you will get the full list of all the posting accounts, like here:

Figure 9-12 - G/L Account List Chooser

You will know you are seeing *all* Posting Accounts because the **Account Type** column header will have the filter indicator, but the **Account Category** column heading will *not*.

Category List

If you have used the standard G/L Account Categories, you will see a much shorter list:

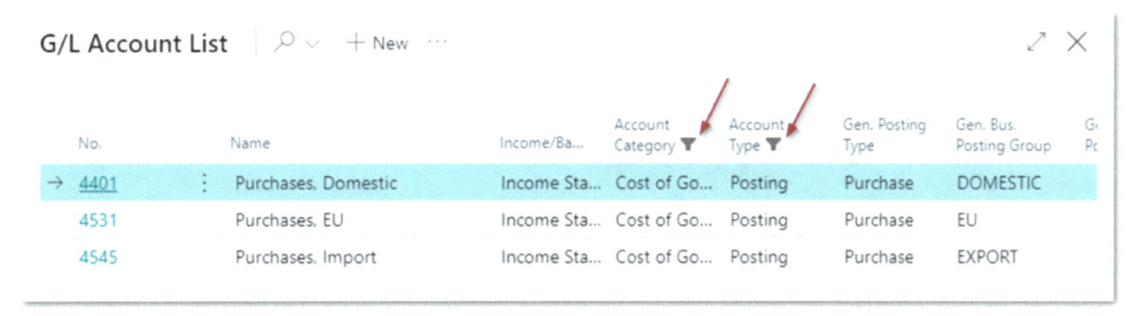

Figure 9-13 - G/L Account List Chooser, Filtered

PART 2: BUILDING YOUR FOUNDATION
CHAPTER 9: UPDATING POSTING GROUPS

You will be seeing a filtered list based on the relevant Account Category, which makes it easy to set up.

In our scenario, we end up with a list as such:

Gen. Bus. Posting Group	Gen. Prod. Posting Group	Description	View All Acc. on	Sales Account	Sales Credit Memo Account	Sales Pmt. Disc. Debit Acc.	Sales Pmt. Disc. Credit Acc.	Sales Prepay. Account	Purch. Account	Purch. Credit Memo Account	Purch. Pmt. Disc. Debit	Pur. Pmt. Disc. Credit	Purch. Prepay. Account	COGS Account	COGS Acco. (Inter...	Invent. Adjmt. Account	Invt. Accrual Acc. (Interim)	Direct Cost Applied Account
→	NORMAL		☐	*					*					4586	4580			4580
	SEASONAL		☐											4586	4581			4581
DOMESTIC	MISC		☐	3095	3095				4401	4401				4586				4580
DOMESTIC	NO VAT		☐	3095	3095				4401	4401				4586				4580
DOMESTIC	NORMAL		☐	3041	3041				4401	4401				4586				4580
DOMESTIC	SEASONAL		☐	3051	3051				4401	4401				4586				4581
EU	MISC		☐	3095	3095				4531	4531				4586				4580
EU	NO VAT		☐	3095	3095				4531	4531				4586				4580
EU	NORMAL		☐	3046	3046				4531	4531				4586				4580
EU	SEASONAL		☐	3056	3056				4531	4531				4586				4581
EXPORT	MISC		☐	3095	3095				4545	4545				4586				4580
EXPORT	NO VAT		☐	3095	3095				4545	4545				4586				4580
EXPORT	NORMAL		☐	3045	3045				4545	4545				4586				4580
EXPORT	SEASONAL		☐	3055	3055				4545	4545				4586				4581
INTERCO	MISC		☐	3095	3095				4401	4401				4586				4580
INTERCO	NO VAT		☐	3095	3095				4401	4401				4586				4580

Figure 9-14 - Example General Posting Setup

ACTION: Setup your General Posting Setup

Determine the combinations you need and determine which G/L accounts you need to set. With that information, populate the 🔍 **General Posting Setup**.

VAT Posting Setup

You might have wondered earlier when we setup the 🔍 **VAT Prod. Posting Groups** that we implied a rate in name but set no values for that percentage anywhere. Much like the General Posting Setup, the **VAT Posting Setup** is a "combination" setup between the **VAT Bus. Posting Group** and the **VAT Prod. Posting Group**:

VAT Bus. Posting Group ↑	VAT Prod. Posting Group ↑	Description	VAT Identifier	VAT %	VAT Calculation Type	Sales VAT Account	Purchase VAT Account	Reverse Chrg. VAT Acc.	VAT Clause Code	EU Service	Tax Category
→				0	Normal VAT	*	*			☐	

Figure 9-15 - VAT Posting Setup

In our scenario, we are bound to use a standard setup, since this reflects local regulations:

VAT Bus. Posting Group ↑	VAT Prod. Posting Group ↑	Description	VAT Identifier	VAT %	VAT Calculation Type	Sales VAT Account	Purchase VAT Account
→ DOMESTIC	VAT25		MOMS25	25	Normal VAT	2610	2640
DOMESTIC	VAT12		MOMS12	12	Normal VAT	2620	2642
DOMESTIC	VAT6		MOMS6	6	Normal VAT	2630	2645
DOMESTIC	EXCLUDE		INGEN MOMS	0	Normal VAT	2610	2640
DOMESTIC	VATONLY		ENDAST	0	Full VAT		2641
EU	VAT25		MOMS25	25	Reverse Charge VAT	2610	2640
EU	VAT12		MOMS12	12	Reverse Charge VAT	2620	2642
EU	VAT6		MOMS6	6	Reverse Charge VAT	2630	2645
EU	EXCLUDE		INGEN MOMS	0	Normal VAT	2610	2640
EXPORT	VAT12		MOMS12	0	Normal VAT	2620	2642
EXPORT	VAT25		MOMS25	0	Normal VAT	2610	2640
EXPORT	VAT6		MOMS6	0	Normal VAT	2630	2645
EXPORT	EXCLUDE		INGEN MOMS	0	Normal VAT	2610	2640

Figure 9-16 - Sample VAT Posting Setup

ACTION: Configure your VAT Posting Setup

For your configuration, your accounting team will likely need to help make certain you are complying with your local regulations for your **VAT Posting Setup**. You can typically refer to your CRONUS demonstration for your region, for reference.

Customer Posting Setup

In our **Customer Posting Setup**, we already have them configured and just need to point the Receivables Account to the relevant G/L Account, as shown:

	Code ↑	Description	View All Acc... on	Receivables Account
→	DOMESTIC		☐	1510
	EU		☐	1511
	EXPORT		☐	1512

Figure 9-17 - Sample Customer Posting Setups

ACTION: A/R Account on Customer Posting Groups

Based on your Chart of Accounts, assign a **Receivables Account** to each of your 🔍 **Customer Posting Groups**.

VENDOR POSTING SETUP

In our 🔍 **Vendor Posting Setup**, we already have them configured and just need to point the **Payables Account** to the relevant G/L Account:

	Code ↑	Description	View All Acc... on	Payables Account
	DOMESTIC		☐	2441
	EU		☐	2442
→	EXPORT		☐	2442

Figure 9-18 - Sample Vendor Posting Setups

ACTION: A/R Account on Vendor Posting Groups

Based on your Chart of Accounts, assign a **Payables Account** to each of your 🔍 **Vendor Posting Groups**.

BANK ACCOUNT POSTING GROUPS

While we have not setup Bank Accounts just yet (covered in **Chapter 11**), we can prepare the 🔍 **Bank Account Posting Groups** while we are fixing up all the Posting Groups. This is probably the simplest posting group in the system – it only has one option: which **G/L Account No.** to use.

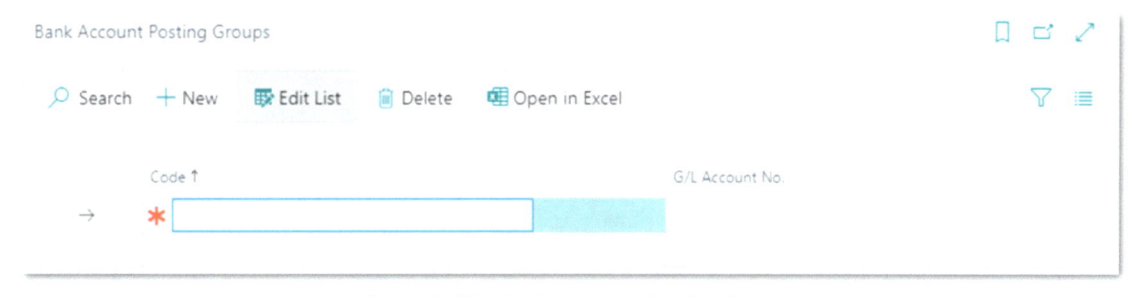

Figure 9-19 - Bank Account Posting Setups

We have only one Bank Account in our example scenario:

Code ↑	G/L Account No.
BANK-EUR	1940

Figure 9-20 - Sample Bank Account Posting Setup

ACTION: Setup Bank Account Posting Group(s)

Create your 🔍 **Bank Account Posting Groups**. Most typically, people have a G/L Account per Bank Account; if that is the case for you, simply set up as many Bank Account Posting Groups as the quantity of Bank Accounts you will have.

PART 2: BUILDING YOUR FOUNDATION
CHAPTER 9: UPDATING POSTING GROUPS

INVENTORY POSTING SETUP

Much like the General Posting Setup, each 🔍 **Inventory Posting Setup** is a combination between the **Location Code** and the **Inventory Posting Group Code**:

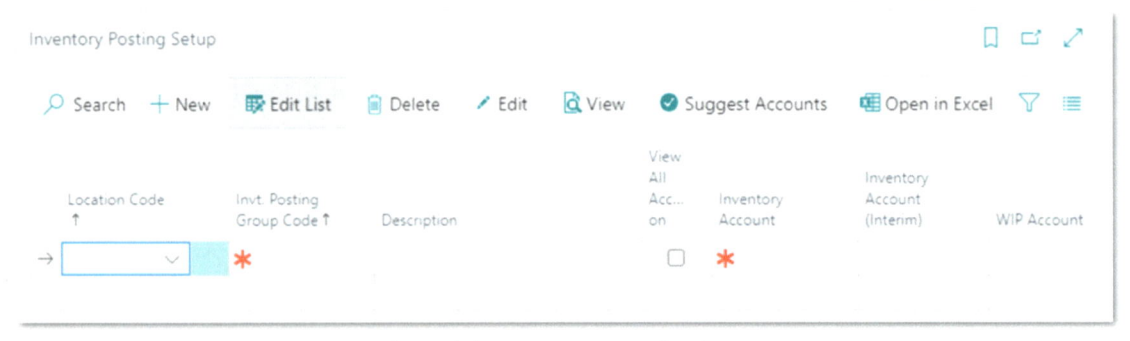

Figure 9-21 - Inventory Posting Setup

In our scenario, we have a single location, but we want to keep track of our Inventory Value based on **NORMAL** vs. **SEASONAL**, requiring two combinations to point to two different **Inventory Account**s:

Location Code ↑	Invt. Posting Group Code ↑	Description	View All Acc... on	Inventory Account
ASKIM	NORMAL		☐	1421
ASKIM	SEASONAL		☐	1422

Figure 9-22 - Sample Inventory Posting Groups

ACTION: Create Inventory Posting Setup(s)

Based on your **Locations** and your **Inventory Posting Groups**, create an 🔍 **Inventory Posting Setup** for each combination, pointing to your **Inventory Account**.

Also review with your accounting team if you need to set the **Inventory Account (Interim)**, as that is commonly needed if goods are physically received separately from the Invoice.

SUMMARY

With this, you *technically* are all set up – you *could* start doing some transactions right away. All your based Master Data is initialized and now each module is connected to the relevant Financial information. We have two more small chapters left in our **Building Your Foundation** part.

Chapter 10: Languages, Currencies, Exchange Rates

One of the strengths Microsoft Dynamics 365 Business Central has is that it has been a globally aware product for a very long time. This means that it has extensive support for languages and currencies. This chapter will review how you set up those areas, plus, highlight some of the related aspects of using them.

LANGUAGES

Business Central supports multiple languages in two major ways:

- User Interface – The way that users see the captions, action bar, and display elements from Business Central.
- Data application – multiple language support.

While the User Interface multi-language support is strong (available via the Settings menu), we are talking about the Data application side.

If you do a **Tell Me** search on **Languages**, you will see this *slim* result set:

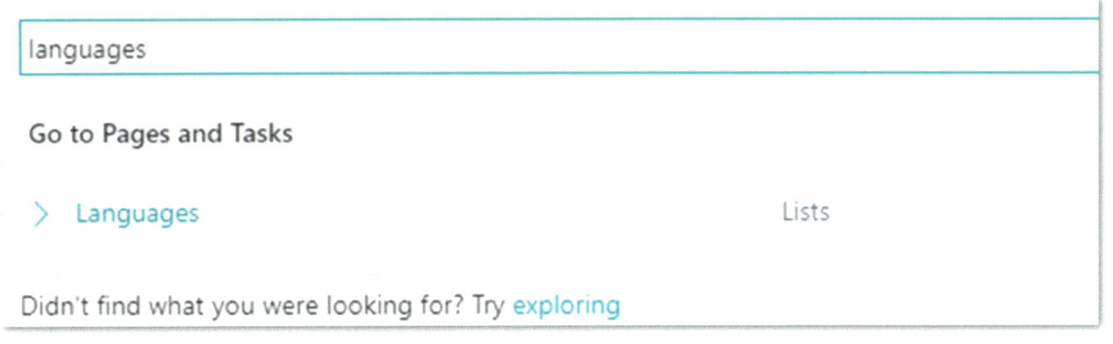

Figure 10-1 - Language Search

When you open **Languages**, the section will be empty by default:

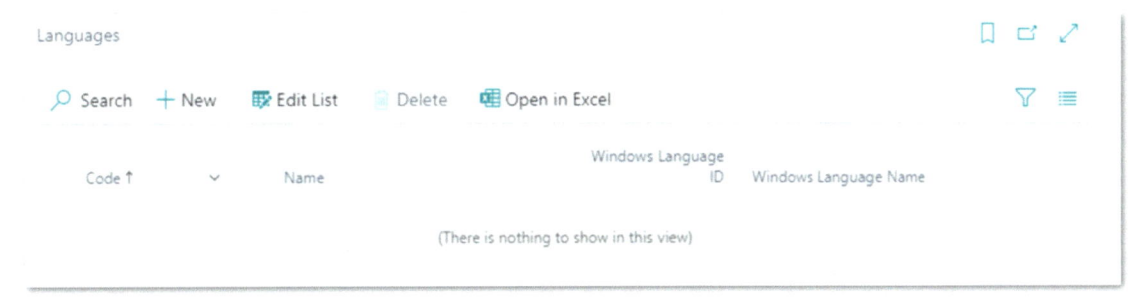

Figure 10-2 - Empty Languages List

It *looks* like there is nothing much to it; even searching on **Translation** makes you think there is nothing here (since it tries to give you results on **Transaction**):

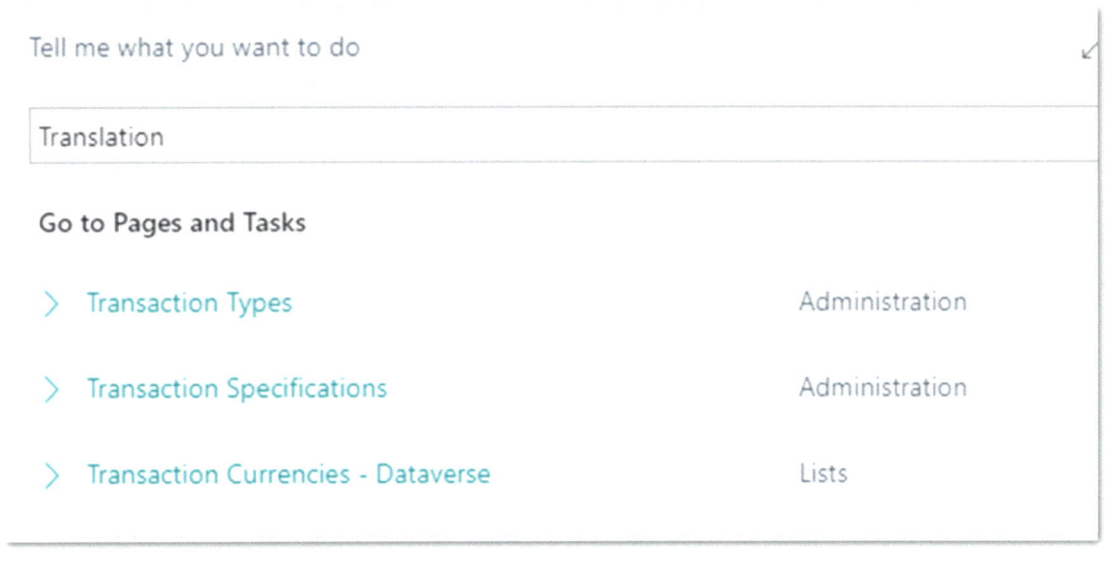

Figure 10-3 - Futile Search Results for Translations

PART 2: BUILDING YOUR FOUNDATION
CHAPTER 10: LANGUAGES, CURRENCIES, EXCHANGE RATES

However, on all the following places, you will find they support translations:

- Items
- Payment Terms
- Shipment Methods
- Payment Methods
- VAT Clauses / Tax Areas
- Units of Measure
- Extended Texts

Additionally, the **Language Code** can control which templates to use for some of the CRM/Marketing module components, but that is beyond the scope of this book.

To see an example of how the translations seamlessly flow, we can go to **Items** in CRONUS for a conference table:

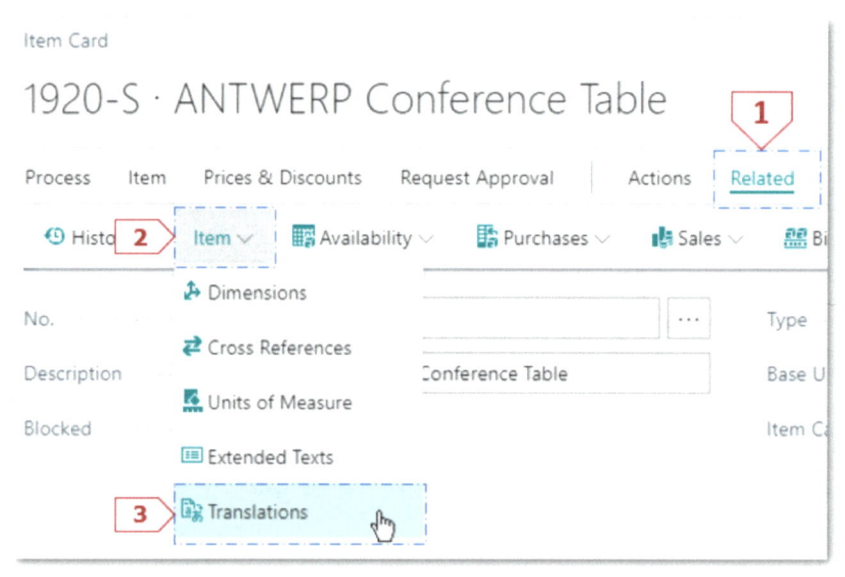

Figure 10-4 - Item Card – Translations Action

You can see that under the Action Bar; when you click **Related** (**1**) -> **Item** (**2**) there is the **Translations** (**3**) action. This opens the **Item Translations**:

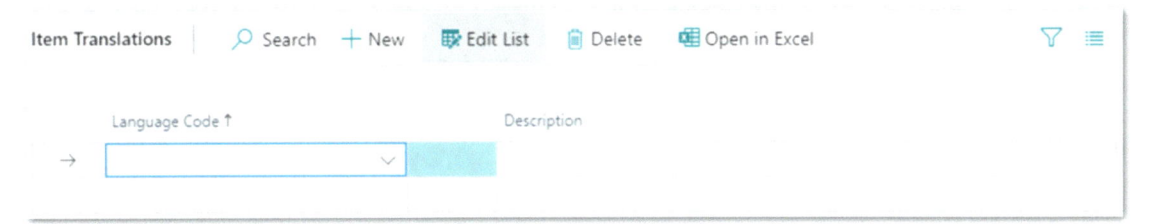

Figure 10-5 - Item Translations

Here, we could set the Swedish (SVE) translation for the table:

Figure 10-6 - Sample Item Translation

If you create a **Sales Order** for a Customer with their **Language Code** set to **SVE** (if the above setting is set), and add this conference table to the lines, you will see the **Description** in **Figure 10-7** is defaulted from the Translated version of the item:

Figure 10-7 - Sales Line with Item Description Translated

PART 2: BUILDING YOUR FOUNDATION
CHAPTER 10: LANGUAGES, CURRENCIES, EXCHANGE RATES

CURRENCIES

Business Central has a lot of powerful multi-currency features; the aspects we are going to cover are:

- Currency Setup.
- Additional Reporting Currency (**ACY**).
- Multi-Currency transactions.

As you recall from the section on the 🔍 General Ledger Setup, we had to specify which Currency is our local currency (**LCY**).

A variety of places throughout the system show information marked with the "**(LCY)**" tag to indicate that the information should be read in the local currency, as opposed to the currency of the transaction. To see one example in context, we will look at the **Customer Statistics** FactBox used on Sales Orders:

As you can see in **Figure 10-8**, the **Balance (LCY)** field is showing us the Customer's Balance information in our LCY, regardless of whether the Customer is set to use Euro or Yen.

Customer Statistics	
Customer No.	50000
Balance (LCY)	7 287.88

Figure 10-8 - Customer Statistics FactBox

SETTING UP CURRENCIES

If you are billing a Customer, or paying a Vendor in another currency, or handling bank accounts in multiple currencies - *how does the system handle that?* Via the 🔍 **Currencies** setup:

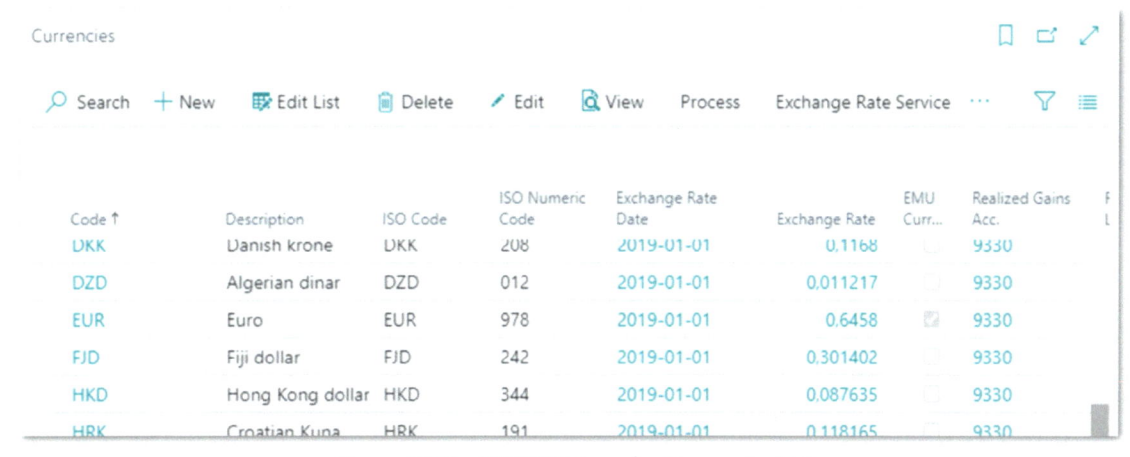

Figure 10-9 - CRONUS Samples Currencies List

Each Currency Code must be set up along with:

- An **Exchange Rate**.
- Realized and Unrealized **Gain/Loss Accounts**.

While we can see this is an editable Setup List page, much like the G/L Account, we can also go to a specific **Currency Card** to see more details:

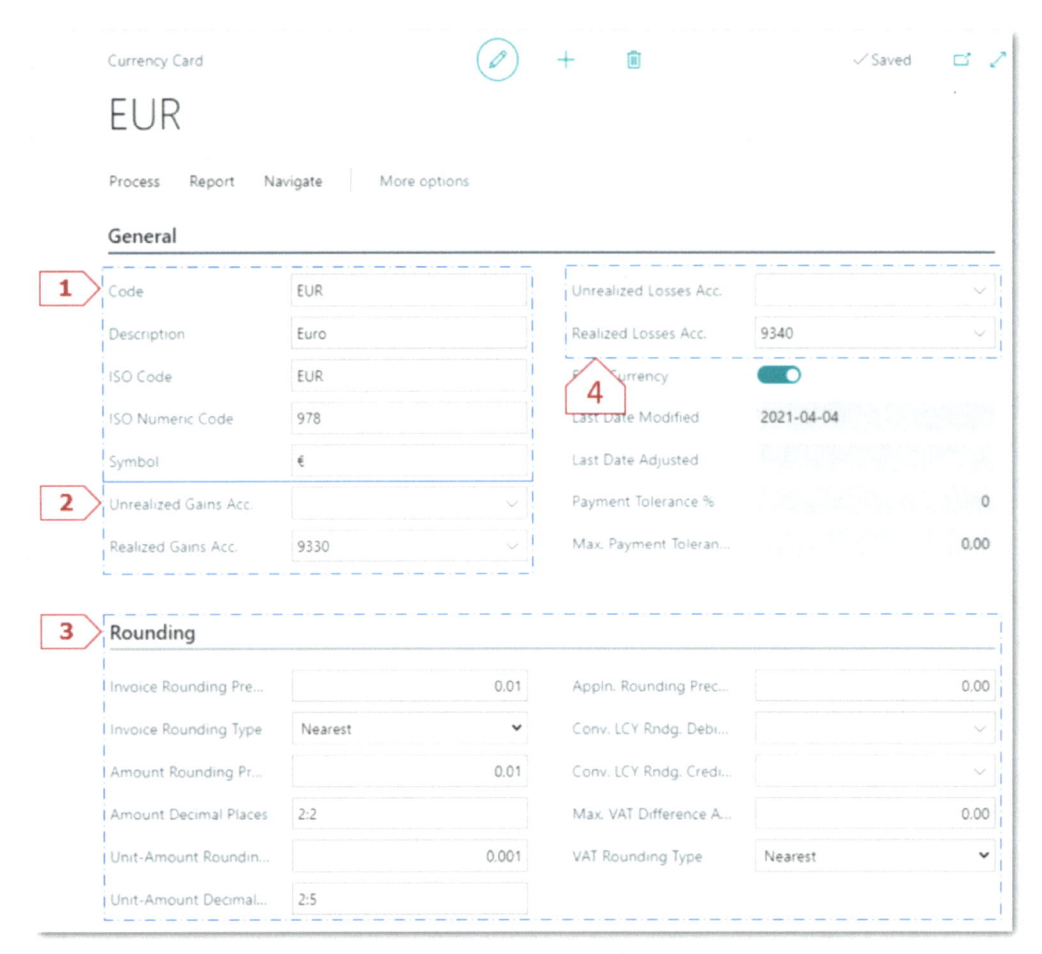

Figure 10-10 - Currency Card Anatomy

Element	What is it?
1	General currency settings.
2	Unrealized and Realized Gains Accounts.
3	Rounding settings, as different currencies have different rounding rules.
4	Unrealized and Realized Losses Accounts.

On the 🔍 **Currencies** list (Figure 10-9), you might have noticed that the **Exchange Rate** appears to be a **FlowField**. This is because each Currency's Exchange Rate has a related setup of **Currency Exchange Rates** under **Process** (**5**) -> **Exch. Rates** (**6**):

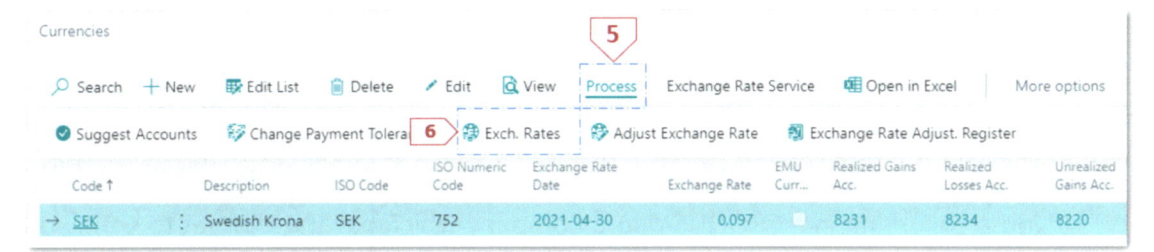

Figure 10-11 - Currency List - Opening Exchange Rates

This opens to a list of exchange rates by date:

Figure 10-12 - Currency Exchange Rates

The rates defined here determine how the currency conversion should be handled based on the transaction date and the rate's **Starting Date**. This means that you can post transactions on past or future dates, and the relevant exchange rate for that date will be used.

When you change the Exchange Rates on a Currency with open transactions, there will be some additional steps you will want to complete, but we will cover that in **Chapter 19**.

In our configuration, we will set up the Currency Code **SEK** for demonstration use. We have our system configured to use **EUR** as our LCY, so, we do not need to set that up here in the Currencies list.

ACTION: Create Your Currencies

Based on the transactions you will be doing, and financial positions you will have (such as Bank Accounts); set up your **Currencies**, making sure to assign the Gain / Loss accounts, as well as Exchange Rates.

ADDITIONAL REPORTING CURRENCY

Frequently, organizations either have reporting needs to an entity in another currency or do enough business in another currency that it would be valuable to know all your financials from that second currency value.

If you are working in a CRONUS demo company which has the **LCY** set to **GBP**, you might want to be able to see the Chart of Account information in another currency, such as **EUR**.

First, you will need to add Gain / Loss Accounts in the **Reporting** section of the **Currency Card** (from the **Currencies** list):

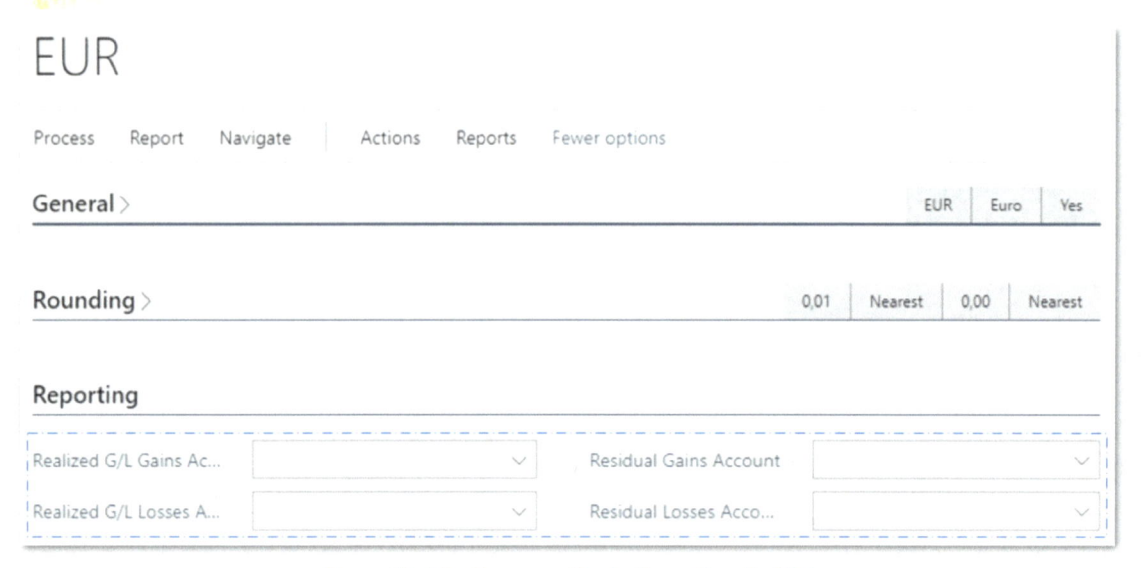

Figure 10-13 - Currency Card - Reporting FastTab

Second, you will set the **Additional Reporting Currency** (**1**) to the **General Ledger Setup**:

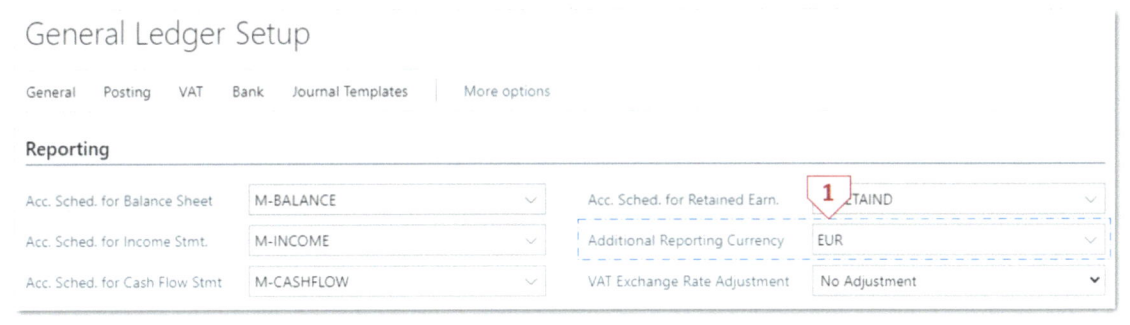

Figure 10-14 - General Ledger Setup - Reporting FastTab

With that done, a process will run to add the Additional Reporting Currency (**ACY**) values to all the G/L Ledger Entries:

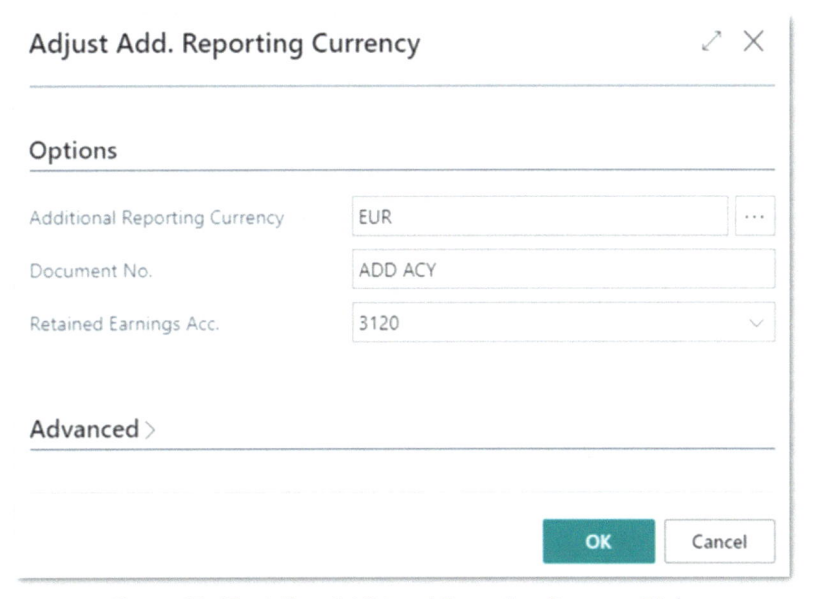

Figure 10-15 - Adjust Additional Reporting Currency Dialog

After verifying the settings and clicking **OK**, it will calculate if any changes are necessary, and then ask for you to confirm *if you really want to do this*:

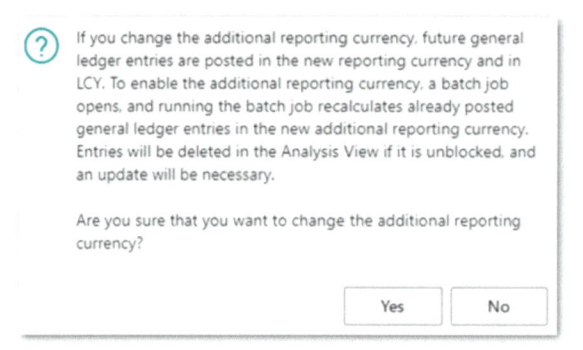

Figure 10-16 - Adjust Additional Currency Confirmation Message

If you are working with an empty company with no balances set anywhere yet, then this process will not have any affect yet.

While there is some support for a setting of **Show Amounts in Add. Reporting Currency** in the **Options** for some reports, like the **Closing – Trial Balance**, the main benefit will be in the UI (and for Microsoft Power BI, but that is a separate book entirely).

On the **Chart of Accounts**, you can add the **Additional-Currency Net Change** and **Addition-Currency Balance** fields to also see those balances in the Additional Reporting Currency, which can be very helpful.

As seen in **Chapter 1**, you will need to Personalize the Chart of Accounts and add the fields:

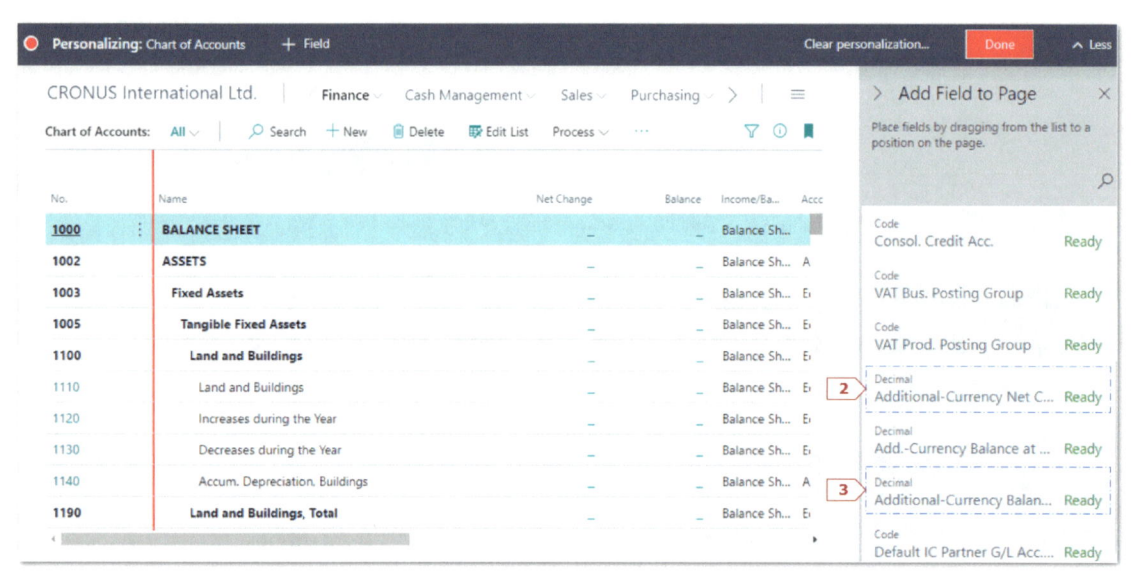

Figure 10-17 - Personalizing Chart of Accounts to Add Additional Currency Fields

You should add both:

- **Additional-Currency Net Change** (**2**)
- **Additional-Currency Balance** (**3**)

ACTION: Determine / Setup ACY

Investigate with your management and accounting teams if there are benefits to maintaining an additional reporting currency for your system. If so, complete the setup based on our steps above, setting the values in the **Currencies** area, configuring the Additional Currency on the **General Ledger Setup**, and personalizing the **Chart of Accounts**.

MULTI-CURRENCY TRANSACTIONS

The biggest benefit of setting up currencies comes from their use in transactions, such as Sales Orders and Purchase Orders. In addition, each **Customer** and **Vendor** can have a **Currency Code** set as their default, which will then be used as the default Currency Code on the Sales Orders and Purchase Orders for them.

For the following example, we will look at CRONUS International, again, with **GBP** (£) set as the LCY.

With the **Customer 30000** set to use the **Currency Code** of **EUR** and looking at a 🔍 **Sales Order** for that customer. You will see that everything is in **EUR**, from the **Unit Price Excl. VAT** (**1**) to the **Totals** (**2**):

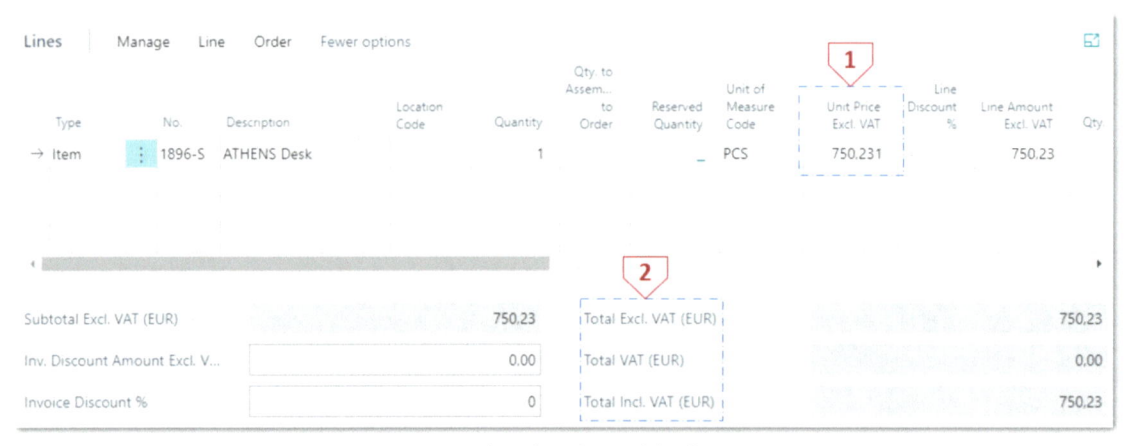

Figure 10-18 - Example Sales Lines with Alternate Currency

If you want to see the value of this Sales Order in your LCY, first locate **Orders** (**1**) in the Action Bar; here you will find the option **Statistics** (**4**):

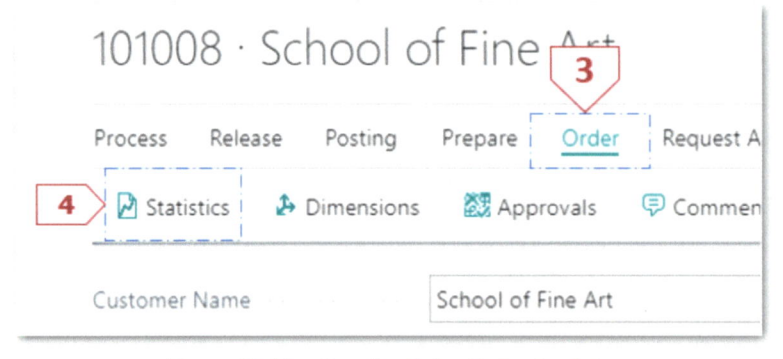

Figure 10-19 – Opening Sales Order Statistics

The **Sales Order Statistics** will show the **Sales (LCY)** (**5**) that is the **GBP** equivalent of the **750,23 EUR**, based on the Currency Exchange Rates we set earlier[1]:

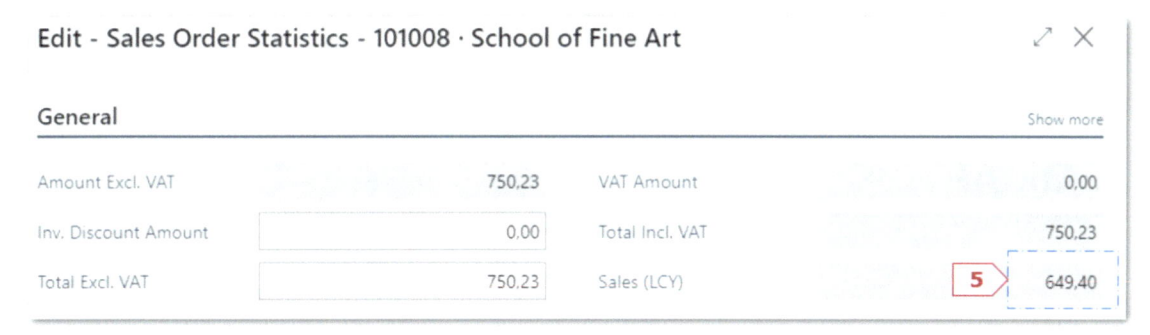

Figure 10-20 - Sales Order Statistics

When we invoice this order, if we look at the Customer Ledger Entries (via the Action bar from **Customers**), it should show us a great combination of information:

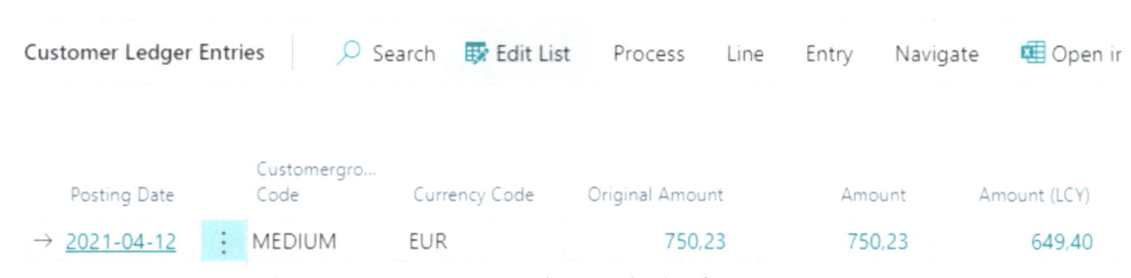

Figure 10-21 - Customer Ledger Entries in Alternate Currency

The **Original Amount** and **Amount** are both in the **Currency Code** of **EUR 750,23**.

The **Amount (LCY)** is in our **GBP** (**£**) **649,40**. All the related G/L, VAT and Value (item costing) Entries are also in the GBP amount of **649,40**.

This makes it very simple to reconcile transactions when discussing specific orders with customers and vendors.

For more information about how gain and loss entries are posted, see **Chapter 19**.

ACTION: Configure your Customers and Vendors

---

[1] You *can* specify a custom Currency Factor per document, but that is beyond the scope of this book.

If you have Customers or Vendors that you will invoice/pay in another currency, make sure the **Currency Code** is configured.

Assign the **Currency Code** to those 🔍 **Customers** and 🔍 **Vendors** that require it as their default.

Summary

By setting up currencies, this makes us ready to do business around the world, with ease. Consider discussing with your partner to also set up regular Exchange Rate update jobs to make this part of the system *shine!*

Chapter 11: Bank Accounts

For the last piece of Part 2 – Building Your Foundation: the Bank Account system.

Many parts of the world have localizations that change the way the banking module works to better align with local needs (checks for North America, EFT for EU, QR codes for Switzerland, and more).

If you need to be able to produce documents (such as checks) or transact electronically with your bank, odds are that you need this module.

If not, you *may* be able to skip this chapter and simply use a G/L Account as your Bank account, but we highly recommend that you review this choice with a local partner. Functionally, the Bank Account can be nearly interchangeable with a G/L Account in *most* journal transactions.

SETTING UP A BANK ACCOUNT

The banking module varies heavily on regional banking practices. To create a new Bank Account, in the 🔍 **Bank Accounts** list, click **New** (**1**):

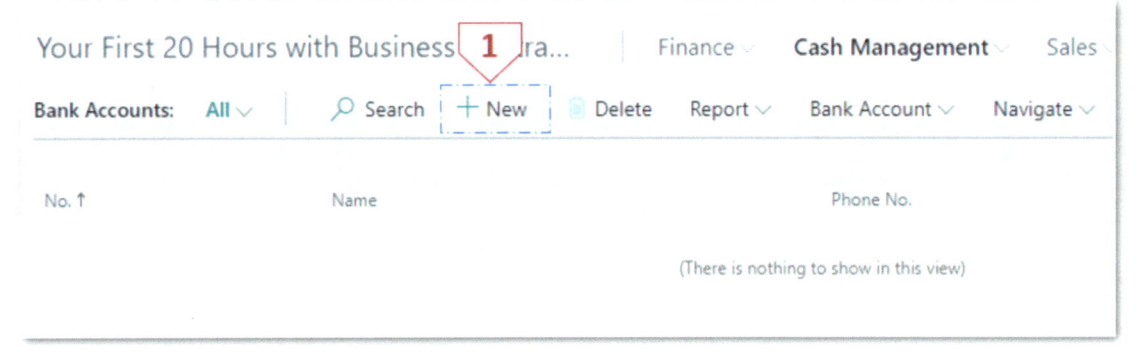

We will create the **NWW-EUR** bank account for our scenario:

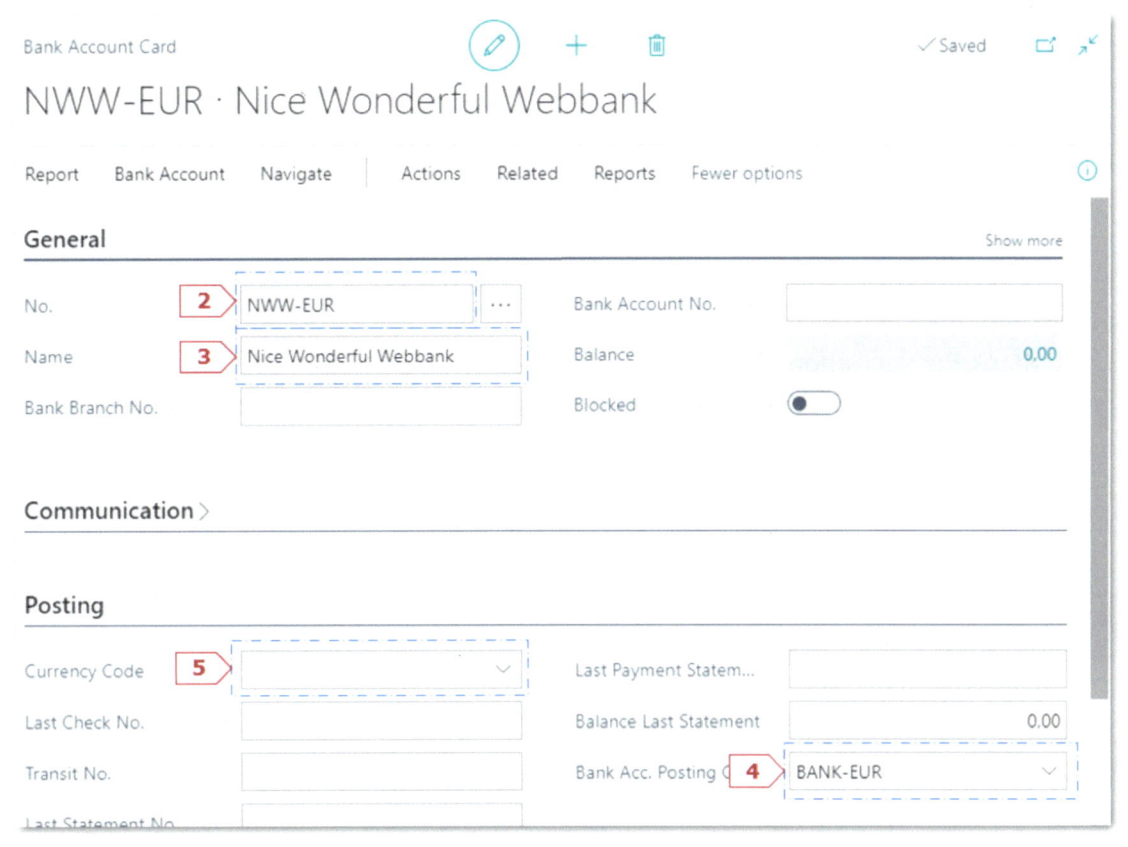

For our purposes, we only need three fields to be set on our **Bank Account**:

2. The **No.** field needs a value.
3. The **Name** field helps identify the account better in lists.
4. The **Bank Acc. Posting Group** is needed to connect the Bank Account to the G/L.

If you are banking in other currencies (see **Chapter 10**), you may also need to set the Currency Code (5).

ACTION: Consult Your Local Partner

This one is *so* localized that it is *strongly* encouraged you check with your local partner about any specific configuration you need to do, or extra training you will need around your banking module.

ADDITIONAL CONSIDERATIONS

Depending on your local banking environment, you may need to investigate any of the following (and more):

- Check layouts.
- Check printing.
- Check voiding.
- Bank Reconciliations & Statements.
- EFT / SEPA / PAIN / etc. – electronic billing and payments.

It is a good idea to have a **Bank Account** configured for each bank account that your company operates, even if you do not have complex needs for now.

SUMMARY

With the basic Bank Account configurations in place, we are ready to start loading in the initial Opening Balances and Item Stock!

PART 3: STARTING UP

Chapter 12 will focus on bringing in the **Opening Balances** for your **Chart of Accounts**, your **Customers**, your **Vendors**, and your **Bank Accounts**.

Chapter 13 will focus on adjusting in your starting inventory.

Chapter 12: Adjusting Inventory into Stock

If you have existing stock that will be brought into the Inventory Module, this is a great time to handle that - before the beginning balances of the General Ledger.

The process we will focus on here is:

- We will create 🔍 **Item Journals** to bring all the stock into the system; this includes doing the following:
    o Prepare an Excel file with all the entries.
    o Bring the entries into Business Central.
    o **Post** the journal entries.
    o Review the Item inventory levels.
    o Review the Financials created.
- We will create a financial adjustment to "zero out" all the affected accounts; this includes doing the following:
    o Prepare General Journal entries to reverse the Inventory values.
    o **Post** the General Journal.
    o Review the Financials.

This will ensure that the Chart of Accounts is all "clean" - that there are no balances at all that would interfere with their import in the next Chapter. In the next chapter, we will bring all the existing Inventory values into the system via the 🔍 **General Journal**.

ITEM JOURNALS TOUR

The 🔍 **Item Journals** are the main journals of the Inventory module, allowing you to manually adjust inventory levels up and down for items. When you Post the journal; the **Item Ledger Entries** will be created. These Item Ledger Entries are used as the source table for the FlowField named **Inventory** on the **Item Card**. Additionally, financial entries will be created if there are Costs/Amounts related to these journal lines.

The Item Journal is a Worksheet type page:

Figure 12-1 - Item Journal Anatomy

Element	What is it?
1	The **Batch Name** controls which batch we are working in. (more below)
2	The **Posting Date** that this adjustment should be registered on. You can both forward- and back-date entries.
3	The **Entry Type** has four options: **Purchase**, **Sales**, **Positive Adjmt.**, and **Negative Adjmt.** Typically, you will select either the positive or negative adjustments, as the purchase and sale of items is done through their respective modules.
4	The **Document No.** is used for the Find Entries functionality. (demonstrated in **Reviewing the Posting Results** in **Chapter 15**)
5	The **Item No.** selects which item the journal entry will affect.
6	The **Description** field allows the user to enter free text to describe the entry. Usually, this will default to the **Description** from the selected **Item**. (from the **Item No.** (**5**))
7	The **Location Code** selects which **Location** should be affected. Depending on your choices during Chapter 4, you may or may not be required to enter this field.
8	The **Quantity** field controls how many of the Item will be adjusted. This number should always be a positive value, as you can select the **Negative Adjmt.** type to decrease the inventory.

PART 3: STARTING UP
CHAPTER 12: ADJUSTING INVENTORY INTO STOCK

9	The **Unit of Measure Code** will default from the **Item No.** (**5**), but you can choose another Unit of Measure Code if needed. (More information in Chapter 7)
10	The **Unit Amount** field sets the value of the items you are adjusting up or down. (See **12**)
11	The **Amount** field will calculate automatically from the Quantity (**8**) and Unit Amount (**10**) field.
12	The **Unit Cost** field also sets the value of the items that you are adjusting up or down. The Unit Cost (**12**) and Unit Amount (**10**) fields are usually the same for adjustment entries. If using **Sales** as the Entry Type (**3**), Unit Cost (**12**) will be different from the Unit amount (**10**) to reflect the profit.

During the setup process, it is common for teams of users to need to create journal lines for many items, but find that it is more practical to work in Excel. You *could* work directly in the **Item Journal**, but we will use the Excel Import process instead.

JOURNAL BATCHES

Since we have not covered how Business Central uses **Journal Batches** before, this is a good opportunity.

Journal Batches allow multiple users to work with separate journal lines (like separate Sheets in Excel), as well as posting them separately. It is common to have batches setup for different users, so they do not accidentally change values that another user is working with.

For the opening balances of items, it can be helpful to break up item lists into separate batches if creating the journal lines will be performed by multiple users.

Additionally, Business Central can post smaller batches faster than larger batches, so posting 50 batches of 1000 items will post much faster than a single batch of 50,000 items.

PREPARING AN ITEM JOURNAL EXCEL FILE

The easiest way to work with the **Item Journal** in Excel is to rely on the seamless *copy and paste* functionality.

Opening the 🔍 **Item Journals**:

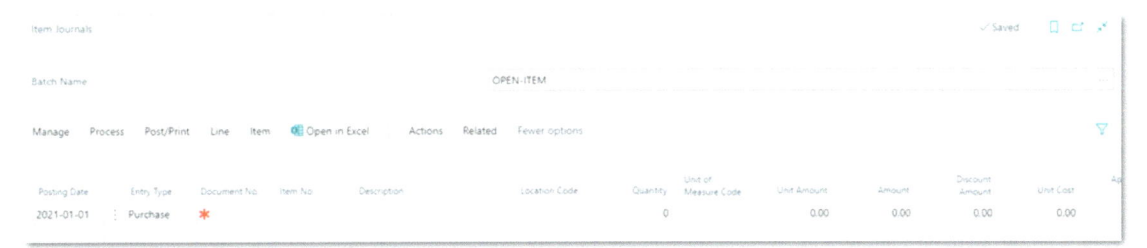

Figure 12-2 - Item Journal

If you press Ctrl-C, it will tell you "1 Row Copied".

When you then paste in Excel, you will see:

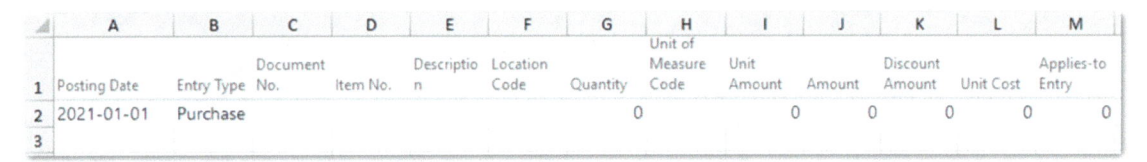

Figure 12-3 - Item Journal Copied to Excel

That's it! You now have your template layout, and you can resize the columns as you need. Take the time to go through and create the lines for the items you have imported; match the new **Item No.** with the **Quantity** of the inventory from your existing system, even if it is just a sticky note from a count of boxes on the shelves.

ADDITIONAL CONSIDERATIONS

If you have your items setup with **FIFO** and you bring all item quantities in on one line with a **Unit Amount**, all the opening balance item entries will be treated as that *one* cost/value.

If you have multiple Locations, each Item and Location combination will require a line of its own.

If you make use of Bins or Item Tracking (Lots and Serials), that is unfortunately beyond the scope of this book and you will want some partner assistance.

EXAMPLE FILE

Continuing our scenario from **Chapter 8**: Data Migration, we have a list of Items to work with. With the list copied and the Item Journal pasted to Excel, our scenario can be prepared as shown:

Posting Date	Entry Type	Document No.	Item No.	Description	Location Code	Quantity	Unit of Measure Code	Unit Amount	Amount	Discount Amount	Unit Cost	Applies-to Entry
2021-01-01	Positive Adjmt.	OPEN-ITEMS	10000	Fancy Shower Curtain	ASKIM	55 PCS		2	110	0	2	0
2021-01-01	Positive Adjmt.	OPEN-ITEMS	10001	Bathroom Scale	ASKIM	23 PCS		20	460	0	20	0
2021-01-01	Positive Adjmt.	OPEN-ITEMS	10002	Alarm Clock	ASKIM	54 PCS		55	2970	0	55	0
2021-01-01	Positive Adjmt.	OPEN-ITEMS	10003	Nightstand organizer	ASKIM	89 PCS		60	5340	0	60	0
2021-01-01	Positive Adjmt.	OPEN-ITEMS	10004	Glowlamp	ASKIM	115 PCS		20	2300	0	20	0
2021-01-01	Positive Adjmt.	OPEN-ITEMS	10005	Small rug	ASKIM	12 PCS		60	720	0	60	0
2021-01-01	Positive Adjmt.	OPEN-ITEMS	10006	Cutting Board	ASKIM	280 PCS		5	1400	0	5	0
2021-01-01	Positive Adjmt.	OPEN-ITEMS	10007	Sugar Bowl	ASKIM	30 PCS		3	90	0	3	0
2021-01-01	Positive Adjmt.	OPEN-ITEMS	10008	Small Storage Bin	ASKIM	13 PCS		1.5	19.5	0	1.5	0
2021-01-01	Positive Adjmt.	OPEN-ITEMS	10009	Drawer Organizer	ASKIM	5 PCS		50	250	0	50	0
2021-01-01	Positive Adjmt.	OPEN-ITEMS	10010	Spring-themed vase	ASKIM	41 PCS		15	615	0	15	0
2021-01-01	Positive Adjmt.	OPEN-ITEMS	10011	Spring floral mural	ASKIM	21 PCS		25	525	0	25	0
2021-01-01	Positive Adjmt.	OPEN-ITEMS	10012	Patio table	ASKIM	6 PCS		80	480	0	80	0
2021-01-01	Positive Adjmt.	OPEN-ITEMS	10013	Patio chair	ASKIM	48 PCS		60	2880	0	60	0
2021-01-01	Positive Adjmt.	OPEN-ITEMS	10014	Winter-themed vase	ASKIM	23 PCS		15	345	0	15	0
2021-01-01	Positive Adjmt.	OPEN-ITEMS	10015	Winter snowscape mural	ASKIM	19 PCS		25	475	0	25	0
2021-01-01	Positive Adjmt.	OPEN-ITEMS	10016	Boot tray	ASKIM	73 PCS		5	365	0	5	0
2021-01-01	Positive Adjmt.	OPEN-ITEMS	10017	Boot and glove dryer	ASKIM	33 PCS		30	990	0	30	0

Figure 12-4 - Item Journal Data in Excel

You will note that the formatting is not important, so you could copy and paste fields down, such as **Posting Date**, **Entry Type**, **Document No.**, and others. You can also use an Excel formula in the **Amount** column.

The rows in the Excel file can be copied and pasted back into the Item Journal:

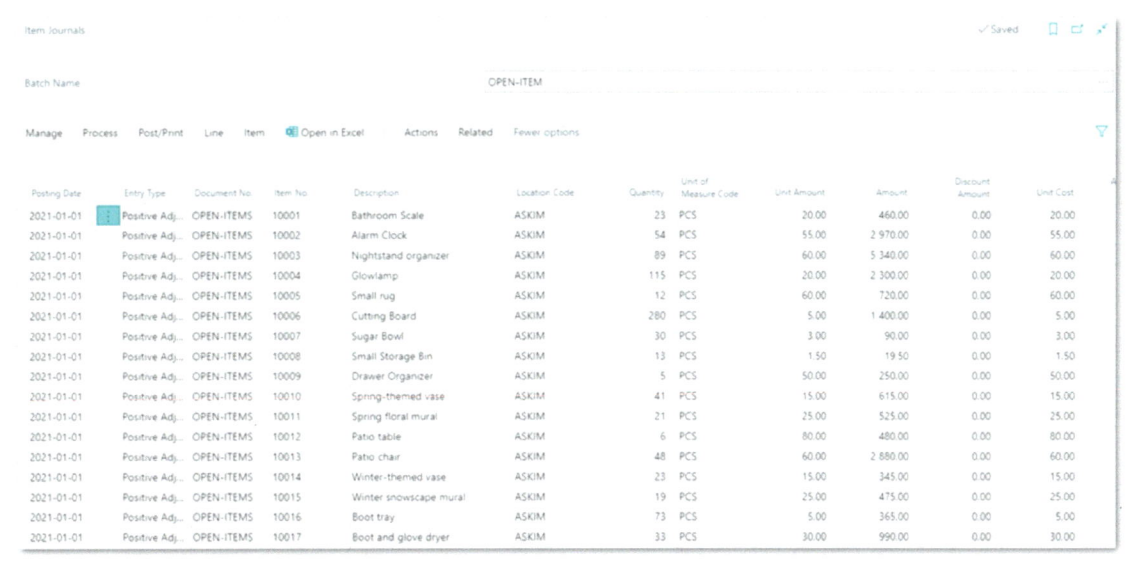

Figure 12-5 - Item Journal Lines Pasted in From Excel

(OPTIONAL) PASTING ERROR

It is possible to get this error message when you paste the Excel rows back into your journal lines:

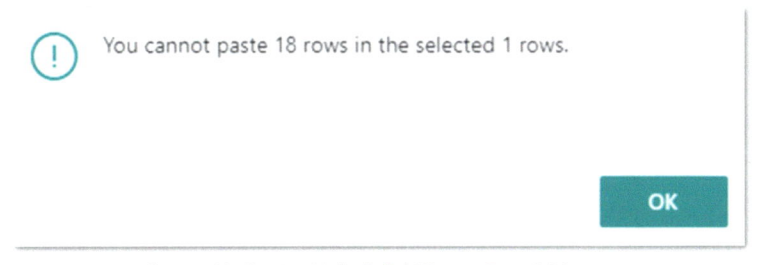

Figure 12-6 - An Unhelpful "Paste Error" Message

It can be difficult to tell what the issue is or how to fix it. In this case, it is simply a matter of deleting the row in your journal, which is accomplished via (**1**) -> Delete Line (**2**):

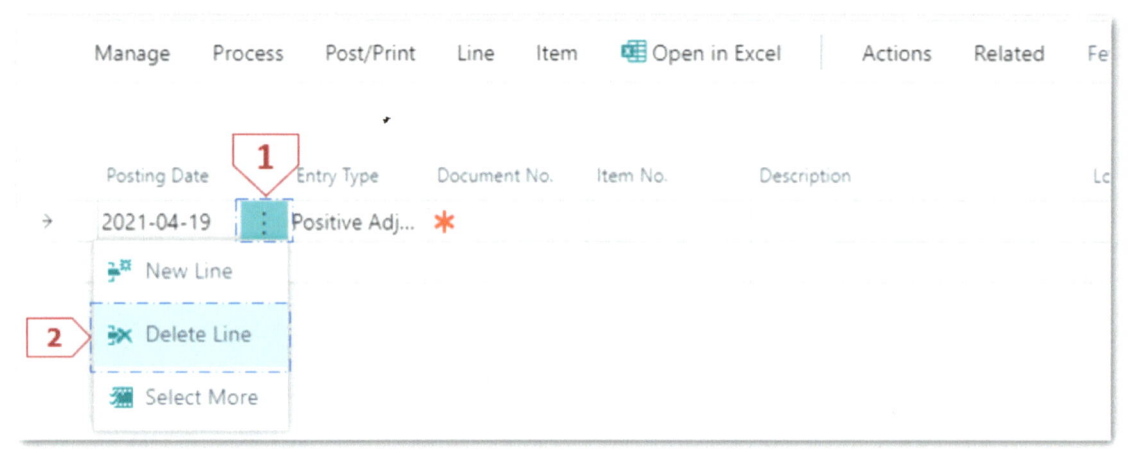

Figure 12-7 - Deleting an Item Journal Line

Then you should be able to paste the rows from Excel without issue.

ACTION: Create/Paste Your Item Journal

Following the steps outlined above, you will want to create an Excel file from the **Item Journals** page. Populate the columns for all your items, while paying close attention to:

- Posting Date
- Location Code
- Quantity
- Item Cost / Amount

Paste all your generated data back into the **Item Journals**.

POSTING THE ITEM JOURNAL

For the next steps, **Post** the Item Journal, which will create ledger entries in the item module:

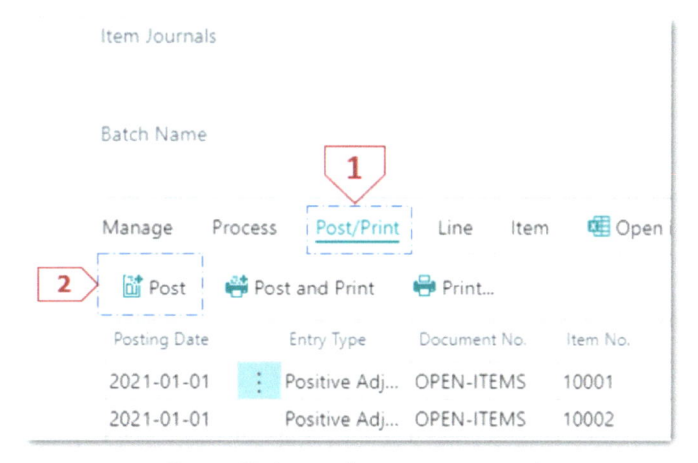

Figure 12-8 - Posting an Item Journal

It will ask you to confirm to proceed:

Figure 12-9 - An "Are you sure" Message about Posting an Item Journal

And once the process is completed, which could take some time if you have a lot of Items; you will see a *completed* confirmation window:

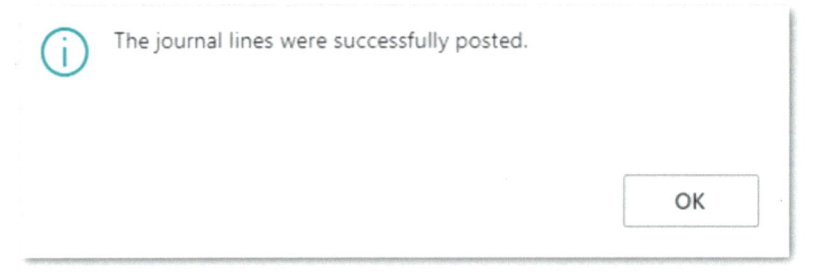

Figure 12-10 - Confirmation of Posting Complete

ACTION: Post Your Item Journal

In the 🔍 **Item Journals**, **Post** the values for your inventory. If you have created multiple batches, you should post all the batches before performing the following next steps.

POSTING RESULTS REVIEW

The first step in reviewing the results of the posting is in the 🔍 **Items** list:

Figure 12-11 - Items List now with Inventory

We can see several important things in this list:

- **Inventory** (**1**) now has a value, showing that our stock came into the inventory module.
- **Cost is Adjusted** (**2**) is **false** (unchecked) for all the items, showing that we have *not* impacted the financial module yet.
- **Unit Price** (**3**) is zero for all items.

COSTING AND FINANCIALS

The **Cost is Adjusted** field is **false**, *at the moment*, because back in **Chapter 6**, during the **Inventory Setup** section, we chose *not* to have **Automatic Cost Posting** enabled. (Automatic Cost Posting is the system that connects the Inventory module to the Financials module, which we will cover in **Chapter 19**) This means that if we look at the **Show more** (**4**) details on the **Costs & Posting** section of one of our Items:

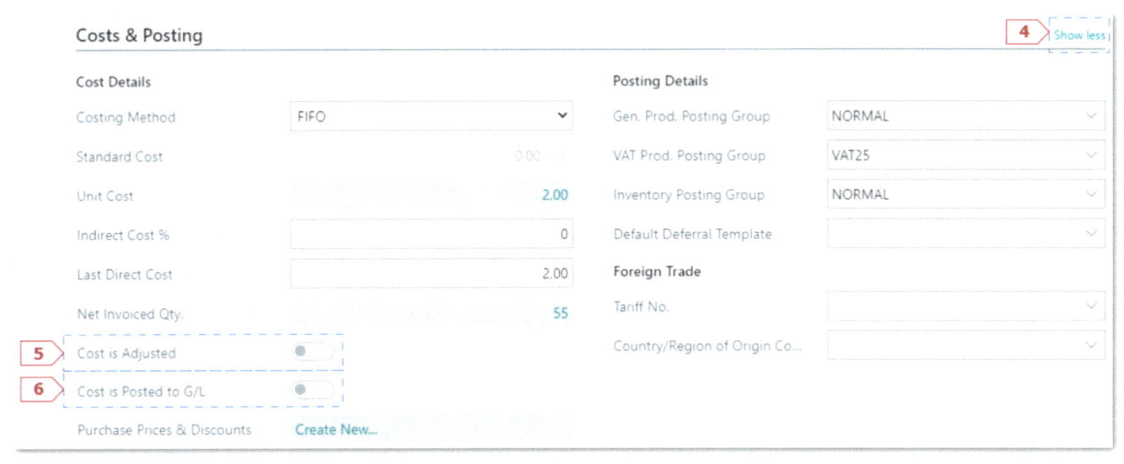

Figure 12-12 - Item Card - Costing Status Indicators

You will see that *two* important status indicators are set to **false/off**: both the **Cost is Adjusted** (**5**) and **Cost is Posted to G/L** (**6**). We will cover this process in more detail later in **Chapter 19**, but we need to run the **Adjust Cost – Item Entries** action and the **Post Inventory Cost to G/L** action.

Both of these actions are under the ⋯ (**7**) -> **Actions** (**8**) -> **Periodic Activities** (**9**) as **Adjust Cost – Item Entries** (**10**) and **Post Inventory Cost to G/L** (**11**):

PART 3: STARTING UP
CHAPTER 12: ADJUSTING INVENTORY INTO STOCK

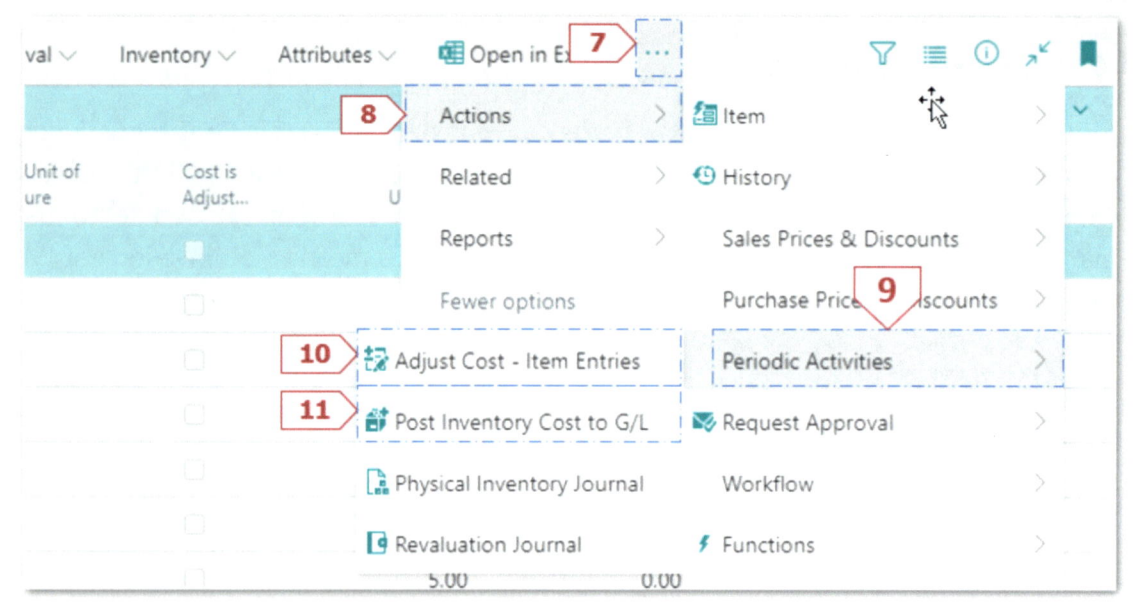

Figure 12-13 - Item Cost - Adjusting Actions

As a reminder, on the 🔍 **Items** list, we can also use the 🔍 **Tell Me** feature to search "on the current page" for actions and find the **Adjust Cost – Item Entries** action:

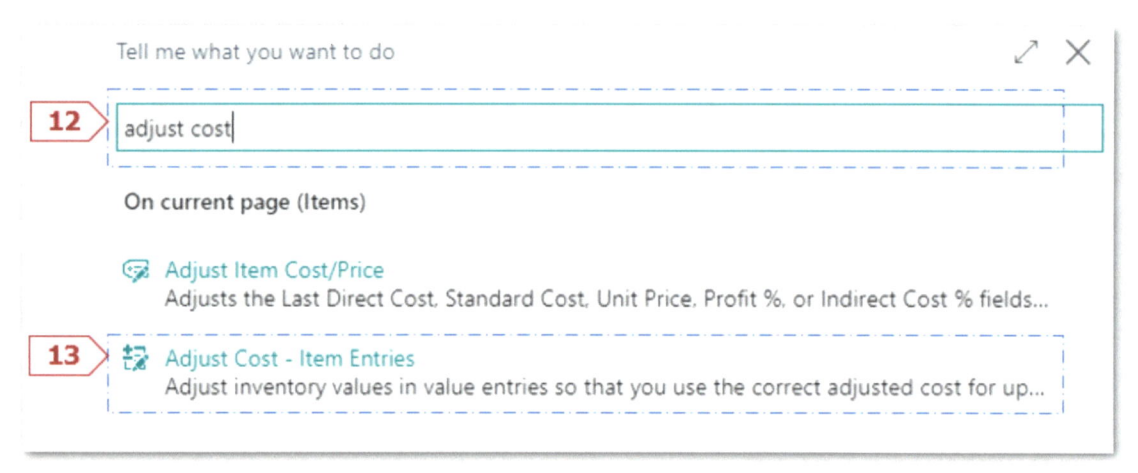

Figure 12-14 - Using "Tell Me" to Search for Page Actions

The **Adjust Cost – Item Entries** will give us the option to filter which Items we want to affect, but we want to run this process for all items.

Once your options are set; click **OK** to run the process:

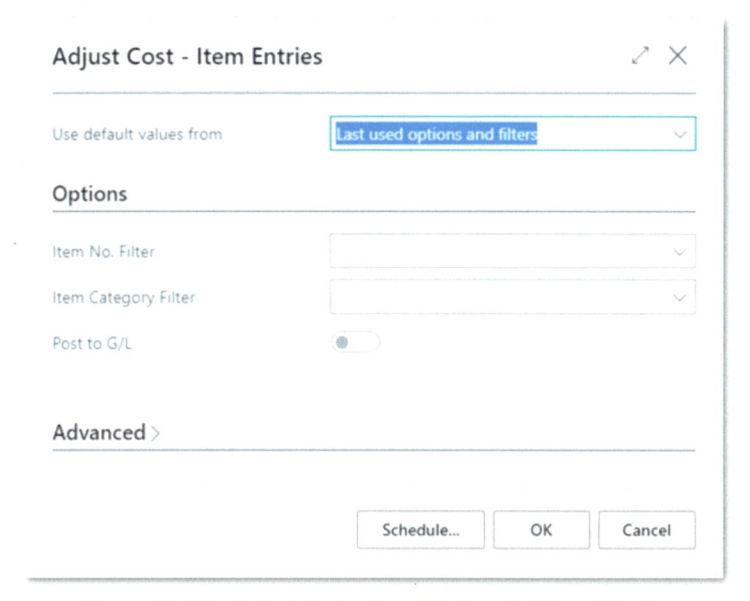

Figure 12-15 - Adjust Cost - Item Entries - Settings Window

The **Adjust Cost – Item Entries** routine will not do much for us now, as we have not performed any transactions on these items, but it is *necessary* to do the next step.

The **Post Inventory Cost to G/L** process will take all the value of the inventory adjustments and post them to the relevant G/L Accounts for Inventory and Inventory Adjustments, based on the **Inventory Posting Setup** work we did in **Chapter 9**. We are required to provide a **Document No.** (**14**), instruct it to **Post** (**15**), then click on **Preview** (**16**):

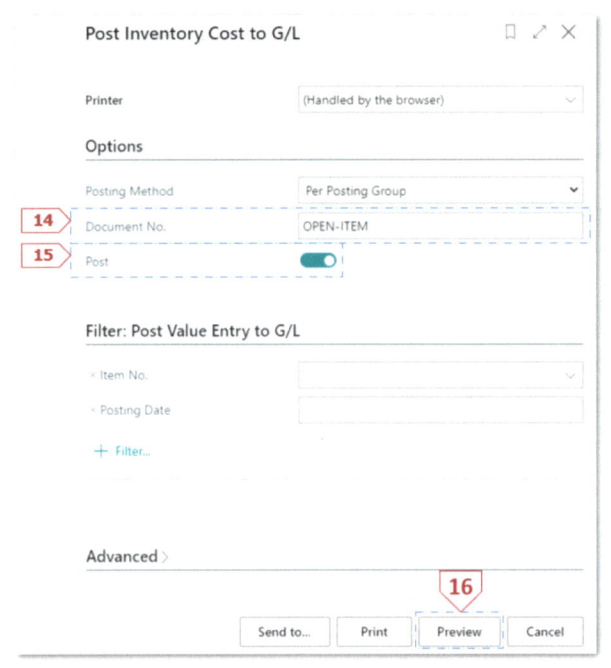

Figure 12-16 - Post Inventory Cost to G/L Settings Window

If you want a copy of the results of this report, you can choose to **Print**, but we will use **Preview**. Note that in this case, even though we are selecting **Preview**, it is a preview of the report, but the transactions will still post! If you would like to look at the transactions that *would be* posted, but *not actually* perform the Posting; deselect the **Post** option, then **Print**/**Preview** the report.

In our scenario, we will enable **Post**, then **Preview**. The resulting report will show you a detailed breakdown of which entries will be created:

Posted per Posting Group
Your First 20 Hours with Business Central

ADMIN

Entry No.	Item Ledger Entry Type	Document No.	Source No.	Inventory Posting Group	Posting Date	COGS	Inventory Adjustment	Direct Cost Applied	Overhead Applied	Purchase Variance	Mfg. Direct Cost Variance	Manufacturing Ovhd Variance	WIP Inventory	Inventory	Expected Cost
	10012	Patio table													
12	Positive Adjmt.	OPEN-ITEMS		SEASONAL	21-01-01		-480,00							480,00	No
	10013	Patio chair													
13	Positive Adjmt.	OPEN-ITEMS		SEASONAL	21-01-01		-2 880,00							2 880,00	No
	10014	Winter-themed vase													
14	Positive Adjmt.	OPEN-ITEMS		SEASONAL	21-01-01		-345,00							345,00	No
	10015	Winter snowscape mural													
15	Positive Adjmt.	OPEN-ITEMS		SEASONAL	21-01-01		-475,00							475,00	No
	10016	Boot tray													
16	Positive Adjmt.	OPEN-ITEMS		SEASONAL	21-01-01		-365,00							365,00	No
	10017	Boot and glove dryer													
17	Positive Adjmt.	OPEN-ITEMS		SEASONAL	21-01-01		-990,00							990,00	No
			Inventory Cost Posted to G/L				-20 334,50							20 334,50	

Total		Entry Type	Line Dimensions	General Posting Setup	Amount
	21-01-01	Inventory		ASKIM,NORMAL	13 659,50
	21-01-01	Inventory		ASKIM,SEASONAL	6 675,00
	21-01-01	Inventory Adjmt.		,NORMAL	-13 659,50
	21-01-01	Inventory Adjmt.		,SEASONAL	-6 675,00

Figure 12-17 - Print Preview of Posted Costs

We are mainly interested in the summary information in the bottom right, enlarged here to show more detail:

General Posting Setup	Amount
ASKIM,NORMAL	13 659,50
ASKIM,SEASONAL	6 675,00
,NORMAL	-13 659,50
,SEASONAL	-6 675,00

Figure 12-18 - Item Costs Summarized by G/L Account

This is showing us that the Inventory Value of the **ASKIM** location increased with two entries, broken down by the **Gen. Prod. Posting Groups** **NORMAL** and **SEASONAL**. These entries were balanced against the inventory adjustment accounts from those **Gen. Prod. Posting Groups**. Looking at the **Chart of Accounts**, we can see the inventory values (filtered (**17**) on the **Balance <>0**) in the **Net Change** (**18**):

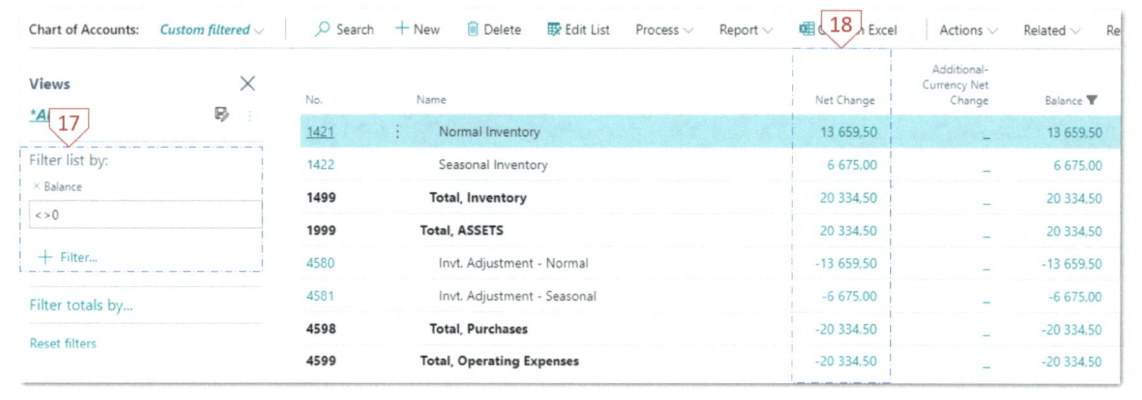

No.	Name	Net Change	Additional-Currency Net Change	Balance
1421	Normal Inventory	13 659,50	–	13 659,50
1422	Seasonal Inventory	6 675,00	–	6 675,00
1499	Total, Inventory	20 334,50	–	20 334,50
1999	Total, ASSETS	20 334,50	–	20 334,50
4580	Invt. Adjustment - Normal	-13 659,50	–	-13 659,50
4581	Invt. Adjustment - Seasonal	-6 675,00	–	-6 675,00
4598	Total, Purchases	-20 334,50	–	-20 334,50
4599	Total, Operating Expenses	-20 334,50	–	-20 334,50

Figure 12-19 - Inventory Accounts Affected by Cost Posting

ACTION: Adjust and Post Inventory Costs

Following the steps above, from the **Items** list, execute the following actions: **Adjust Cost – Item Entries** and **Post Inventory Cost to G/L**.

Review the **Chart of Accounts** after, as you will need the new **Balance** information of the affected accounts.

REVERSING THE G/L INVENTORY VALUE

Because we will be bringing in our existing Opening Balances for the whole **Chart of Accounts** in the next Chapter, which includes the Inventory Accounts, we need to zero out the G/L Accounts we have affected with our transactions.

For this process, you will want to make a new set of **General Journal** entries that reverse the entries from the **Post Inventory Cost to G/L** report. In our example, the reversal lines look like the following:

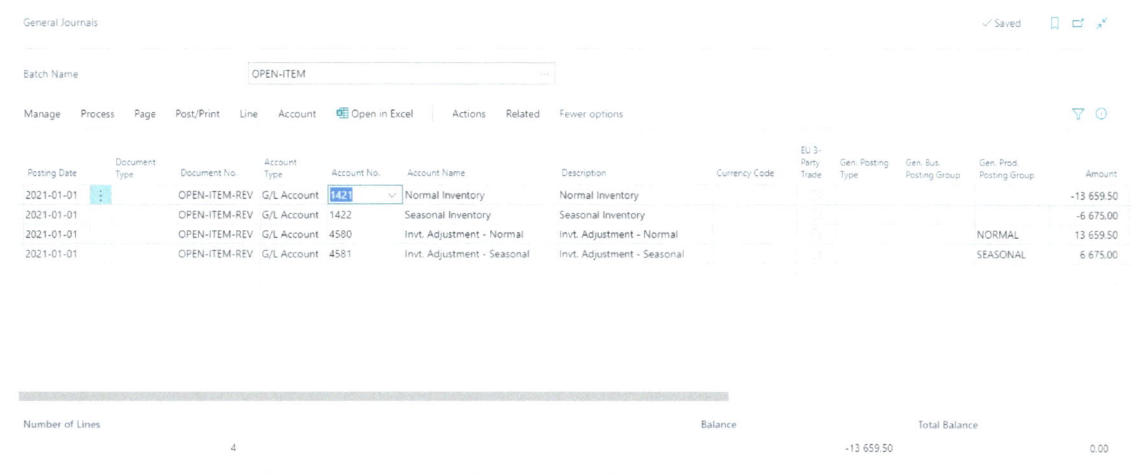

Figure 12-20 - General Journal Entries to Reverse Inventory Costs

As seen on the same **Posting Date**, we will want to have each affected G/L Account present, with the reverse amount. Since this is a Worksheet page, you should see that the **Total Balance** in the bottom right balances out to 0 when you are done.

These entries should be **Post**ed. When that is complete, you will know you have the correct results by again filtering the 🔍 **Chart of Accounts** on **Balance <> 0** and get *no result*:

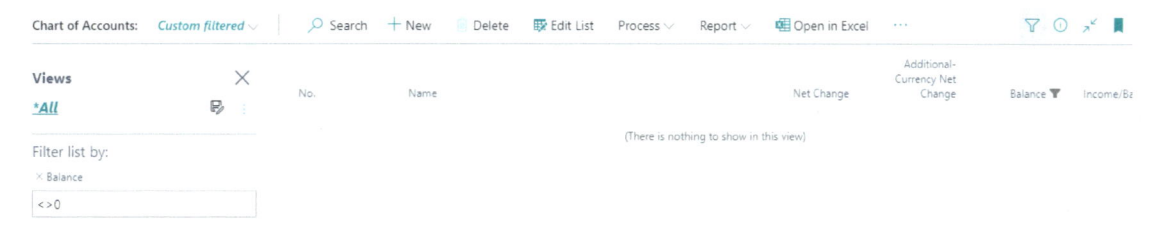

Figure 12-21 - Chart of Accounts - No Accounts with Balance

ACTION: Reverse Inventory Financial Entries

Following the steps above, create 🔍 **General Journal** entries that reverse the entries from the **Post Inventory Cost to G/L** report, **Post** the Entries, then review the 🔍 **Chart of Accounts** with **Balance** filtered to "**<>0**" to ensure that no accounts have any balances.

PART 3: STARTING UP
CHAPTER 12: ADJUSTING INVENTORY INTO STOCK

Chapter 13: Opening Balances

At the start of any business, it will have some assets and information that needs to be brought in.

In this chapter, we will focus on creating the Opening Balances of:

- Chart of Accounts
- Bank Accounts
- Customers
- Vendors

OPENING BALANCES – GENERAL STRATEGY

For the General Ledger and Bank Accounts, this is as easy as crafting the correct General Journals.

For the bank accounts, customers, and vendors, the overall strategy is simple – each of those has a Posting Group that controls which G/L Account will be affected on the Chart of Accounts. We post the opening balances balanced against the same G/L Account, which causes the financial entries on that G/L Account to be cancelled out to a zero total.

This allows us to then bring in the opening balance for that G/L Account and *not* have double entries.

In our scenario, if our bank, **NWW-EUR**, is set to use G/L Account **1940** (via the Bank Posting Group), when we increase the balance of NWW-EUR by **85000€**, that will create an entry on G/L Account **1940** of 85000€. So, when we import G/L Account **1940**'s opening balance, if that already includes the 85000€, we now have doubled the value of that G/L Account.

For Customers and Vendors, you will be creating Journal Entries for the entire open balance. You will not be recreating the existing documents, but this means that you *will* need to keep archives of your existing documents for auditing and regulatory purposes.

It is also strongly recommended that you prepare all the opening balances in General Journal Batches so that you can post them in groups, making sure each step is correct.

We are taking about the *simplest* method of bringing in the opening balances – a snapshot *as-of the date* we are going live. It is also possible that you can break up your opening balances, from your existing system, into fiscal periods (using the Posting Date), creating summary entries for each G/L Account, for each month.

Please consult with your accountant and local partner to ensure that the process meets your local regulations and business needs.

> Note: This is a good time to remind you that during the Opening Balance chapter, it is a good idea to make use of the **Work Date** functionality under **Settings** to make sure you are creating all these entries on the right **Posting Date**!

All the values used in this section for our scenario are available in **Appendix A**.

BANK ACCOUNTS

For our scenario, we only have the one Bank Account, **NWW-EUR**, and we have an existing balance of **50544,69 EUR**. This means our **General Journal** should contain the following single entry:

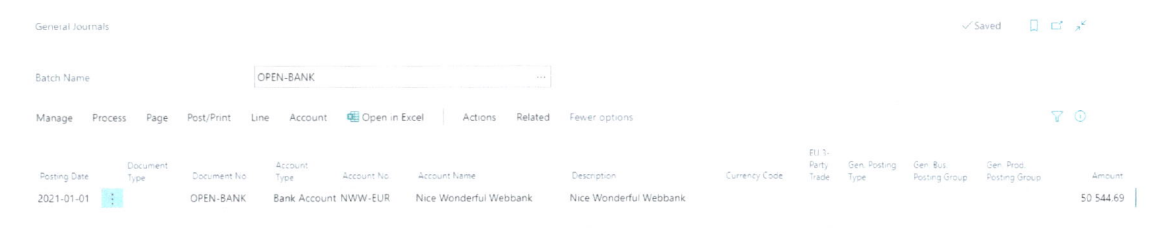

Figure 13-1 - General Journal with Bank Opening Balance

PART 3: STARTING UP
CHAPTER 13: OPENING BALANCES
PAGE 195

We could create the balancing offset entry for this posting manually as a new line (sometimes called **double entry**), but the Business Central has a more efficient method of allowing you to simply enter the Balance Account on the same line ('single entry'):

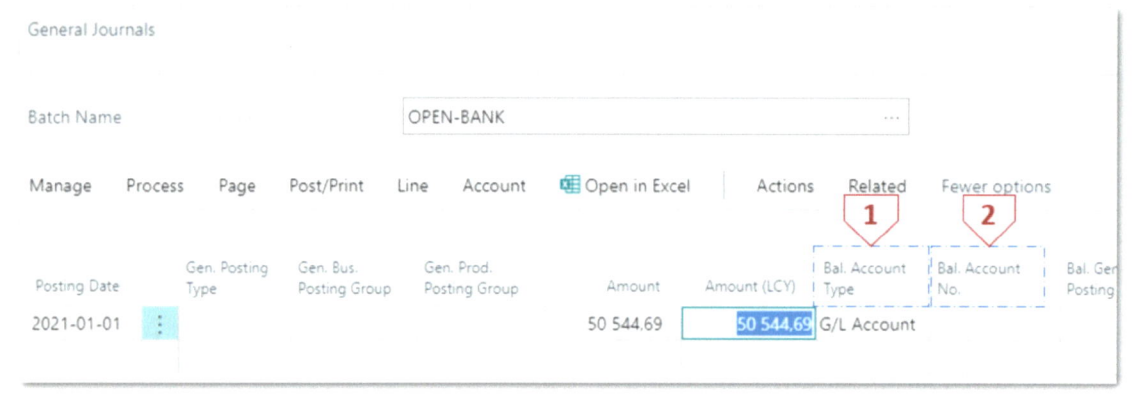

Figure 13-2 - General Journal with Bank Opening Balance, Showing Balance Information

We can set the **Bal. Account Type** (**1**) to **G/L Account** and the **Bal. Account No.** (**2**) to the G/L Account we have setup for our Bank Posting Group, which in our case is **1940**.

When we **Post** this entry, it should effectively be *self-reversing*, which we can check by looking at our 🔍 **Chart of Accounts**; it should still have no accounts with a **Balance**:

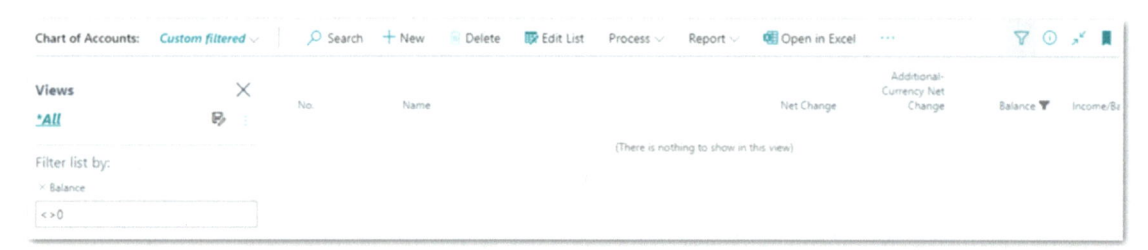

Figure 13-3 - Chart of Accounts - Showing no Accounts with Balance

We can additionally confirm that *everything worked* by checking the **Balance** (**3**) on the 🔍 **Bank Accounts** for our **NWW-EUR** account:

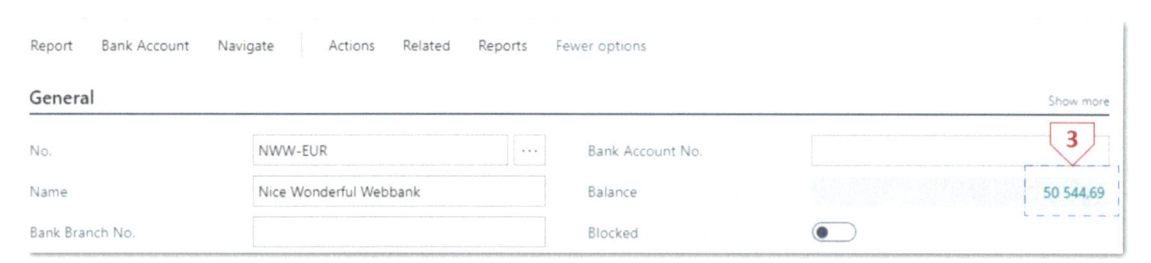

Figure 13-4 - Bank Account Card with Balance

PAGE

PART 3: STARTING UP
CHAPTER 13: OPENING BALANCES

ACTION: Import Your Bank Account Balances

Following the steps above, create 🔍 **General Journal** entries that create the opening balance information for each **Bank Account**, **Post** the Entries, review the 🔍 **Chart of Accounts** with **Balance** filtered to "**<>0**" to ensure no accounts have balances, and then check the **Balance** on the 🔍 **Bank Accounts**.

CUSTOMERS

As previously mentioned, (in Opening Balances – General Strategy), we will bring in the opening balance for each customer as a total open balance. This means that whether a customer has 3 open invoices waiting to be paid, or 200, the total of those will be treated as a single entry to apply payments to.

Generating detailed invoice/payment matching information will not be possible using this method. If you *do* need the document level detail, work with a partner to help you generate journal lines at a per-document level more efficiently.

Business Central has a shortcut to help us with Customer Opening Balances built right into the 🔍 **General Journal**:

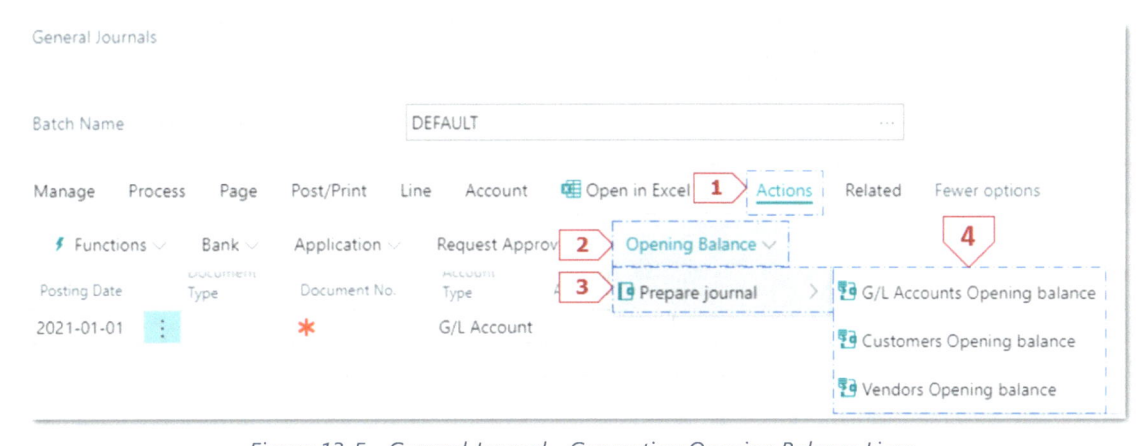

Figure 13-5 - General Journal - Generating Opening Balance Lines

In the **Actions** (**1**) section of the action bar, you will find the **Opening Balance** (**2**), the **Prepare Journal** (**3**) option has actions that will help you generate opening balances

(**4**). When you click on **Customers Opening Balance**, after a moment, it will have generated a set of journal entries for you:

Figure 13-6 - General Journal Lines Showing Customer Lines

A single entry will be made for each Customer, requiring you to fill in only what **Amount** is open for each. The best part of this routine is that it will automatically populate the **Bal. Account No.** with the correct **G/L Account** from each Customer Posting Group on the Customer to self-reverse the G/L Entry.

Any customers with no open balance can simply have their entry removed (deleted) from the journal. With **Document No.** and **Amount** populated, our entries are now ready to **Post**:

Figure 13-7 - General Journal with Customer Lines with Amounts

After this batch is posted, it is a good idea to ensure our **Chart of Accounts**, which should still have *no* accounts with a **Balance**:

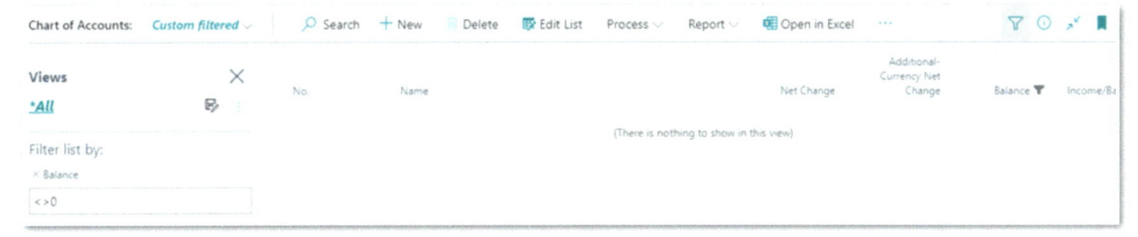

Figure 13-8 - Chart of Accounts - Showing no Accounts with Balance

And now when we look at our 🔍 **Customers** list, we can see **Balances** (**5**):

No. ↑	Name	Responsibility Center	Currency Code	Location Code	Phone No.	Contact	Balance (LCY)	Balance Due (LCY)
C0001	Zboncak LLC			ASKIM		Horatio Courtes	542.00	542.00
C0002	Muller-Wilkinson			ASKIM		Cirstoforo Bengall	1 592.15	1 592.15
C0003	VonRueden-Moen			ASKIM		Tracie Koppens	3 402.19	3 402.19
C0004	Turcotte LLC			ASKIM		Elliott Flippelli	108.90	108.90
C0005	Robel-Botsford			ASKIM		Carter Keep	795.18	795.18
C0006	Christiansen, Rosenbaum and …			ASKIM		Galen Fernan	6 513.11	6 513.11
C0007	Buckridge, Gaylord and Wunsch			ASKIM		Levey Brosini	425.69	425.69
C0008	Wisozk-Ruecker			ASKIM		Maura Hammill	73 541.99	73 541.99
C0009	Schamberger-Labadie			ASKIM		Rochell Chadney	540.45	540.45
C0010	Feeney-McGlynn			ASKIM		Sibilla Tivenan	680.29	680.29
C0011	Schaden LLC			ASKIM		Brander Moffett	22 574.44	22 574.44

Figure 13-9 - Customer List with Balances

ACTION: Create and Post Customer Balances

With help from the **Customers Opening Balance** feature in the 🔍 **General Journal**, create and post entries for all your Customers *with* balances.

Review the 🔍 **Chart of Accounts** with **Balance** filtered to "**<>0**" to ensure no accounts have balances, and then check the **Balance** on the 🔍 **Customers**.

VENDORS

To create the Vendor Opening Balances, we will handle this through the 🔍 **General Journal**:

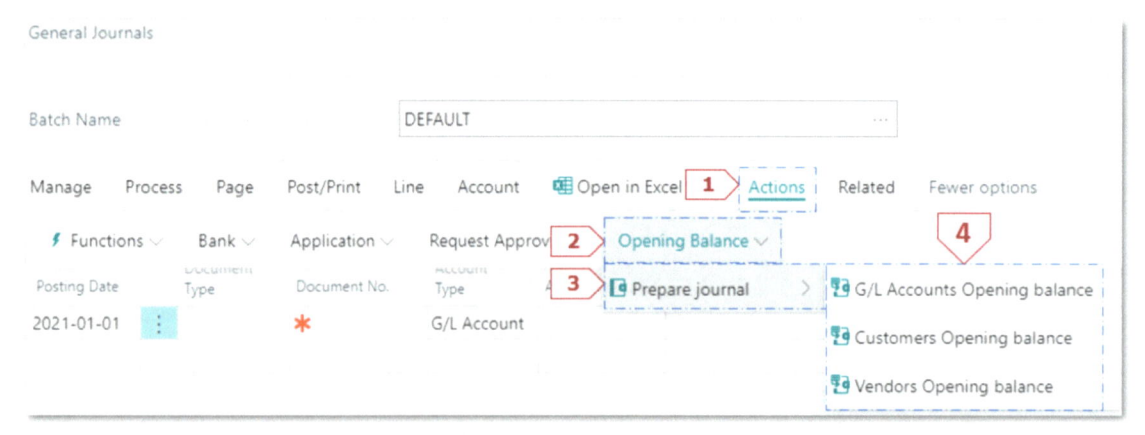

Figure 13-10 - General Journal - Generating Opening Balance Lines

In the **Actions** (**1**) section of the action bar, you will find the **Opening Balance** (**2**), the **Prepare Journal** (**3**) option has actions that will help you generate opening balances (**4**). When you click on **Vendors Opening Balance**, after a moment, it will have generated a set of journal entries for you:

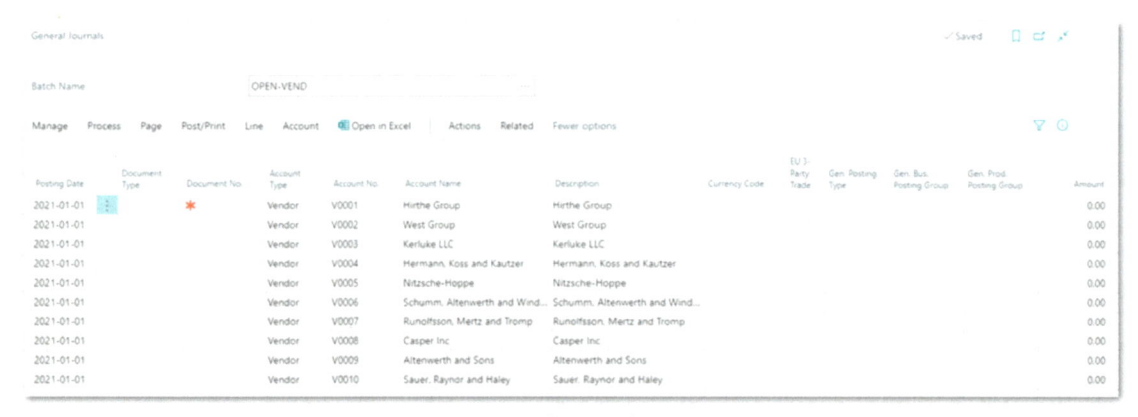

Figure 13-11 - General Journal with Vendor Lines

Similar to the Customer Opening Balance, these entries have the **Bal. Account No.** set to the correct **G/L Account** from each Vendor Posting Group on the Vendor to self-reverse the G/L Entry.

PART 3: STARTING UP
CHAPTER 13: OPENING BALANCES

Any vendors with no open balance can simply have their entry removed (deleted) from the journal. With **Document No.** and **Amount** populated (*with negative amounts!*), our entries are now ready to **Post**:

Posting Date	Document Type	Document No.	Account Type	Account No.	Account Name	Description	Currency Code	EU 3-Party Trade	Gen. Posting Type	Gen. Bus. Posting Group	Gen. Prod. Posting Group	Amount
2021-01-01		OPEN-VEND	Vendor	V0001	Hirthe Group	Hirthe Group						-4 365.20
2021-01-01		OPEN-VEND	Vendor	V0002	West Group	West Group						-406.50
2021-01-01		OPEN-VEND	Vendor	V0003	Kerluke LLC	Kerluke LLC						-125.05
2021-01-01		OPEN-VEND	Vendor	V0004	Hermann, Koss and Kautzer	Hermann, Koss and Kautzer						-600.00
2021-01-01		OPEN-VEND	Vendor	V0005	Nitzsche-Hoppe	Nitzsche-Hoppe						-450.00
2021-01-01		OPEN-VEND	Vendor	V0006	Schumm, Altenwerth and Wind...	Schumm, Altenwerth and Wind...						-1 354.21
2021-01-01		OPEN-VEND	Vendor	V0007	Runolfsson, Mertz and Tromp	Runolfsson, Mertz and Tromp						-900.00
2021-01-01		OPEN-VEND	Vendor	V0008	Casper Inc	Casper Inc						-2 281.97
2021-01-01		OPEN-VEND	Vendor	V0009	Altenwerth and Sons	Altenwerth and Sons						-1 870.32
2021-01-01		OPEN-VEND	Vendor	V0010	Sauer, Raynor and Haley	Sauer, Raynor and Haley						-1 178.10

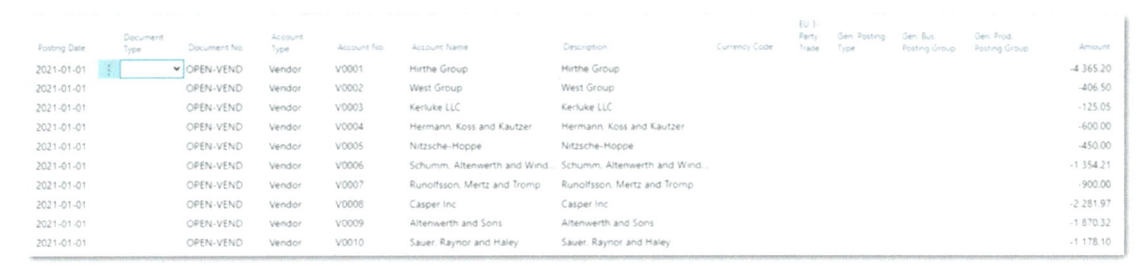

Figure 13-12 - General Journal with Vendor Lines with Amounts

With the entries **Post**ed, and the **Chart of Accounts** still *correct* at zero **Balance**, we can see **Vendors** with **Balance (LCY)** (**5**) values:

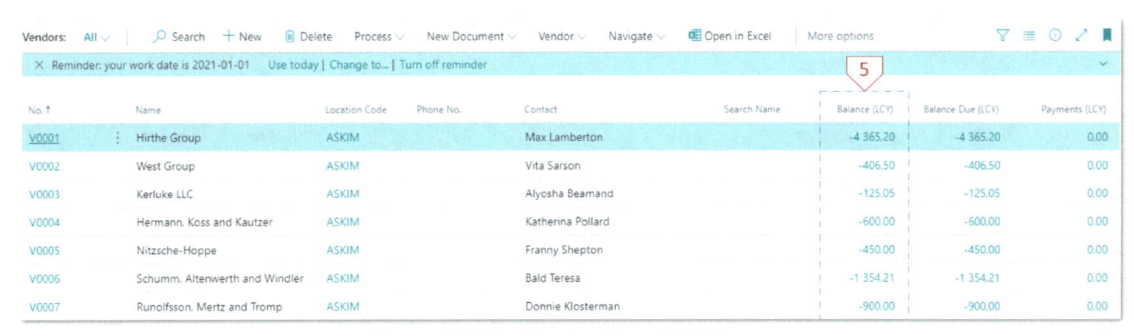

No. ↑	Name	Location Code	Phone No.	Contact	Search Name	Balance (LCY)	Balance Due (LCY)	Payments (LCY)
V0001	Hirthe Group	ASKIM		Max Lamberton		-4 365.20	-4 365.20	0.00
V0002	West Group	ASKIM		Vita Sarson		-406.50	-406.50	0.00
V0003	Kerluke LLC	ASKIM		Alyosha Beamand		-125.05	-125.05	0.00
V0004	Hermann, Koss and Kautzer	ASKIM		Katherina Pollard		-600.00	-600.00	0.00
V0005	Nitzsche-Hoppe	ASKIM		Franny Shepton		-450.00	-450.00	0.00
V0006	Schumm, Altenwerth and Windler	ASKIM		Bald Teresa		-1 354.21	-1 354.21	0.00
V0007	Runolfsson, Mertz and Tromp	ASKIM		Donnie Klosterman		-900.00	-900.00	0.00

Figure 13-13 - Vendor List with Balances

ACTION: Create and Post Vendor Balances

With help from the **Vendors Opening Balance** feature in the **General Journal**, create and post entries for all your Vendors with balances.

Review the **Chart of Accounts** with **Balance** filtered to "**<>0**" to ensure *no* accounts have balances. Check the **Balance** on the **Vendors**.

Tax & VAT Opening Balances

Because of many different regional and regulatory differences around how to handle taxes, for any VAT and other tax related opening balances, please work with your local partners to ensure that you are taking the right steps.

GENERAL LEDGERS

To create the G/L Account Opening Balances, we will handle this through the 🔍 **General Journal**:

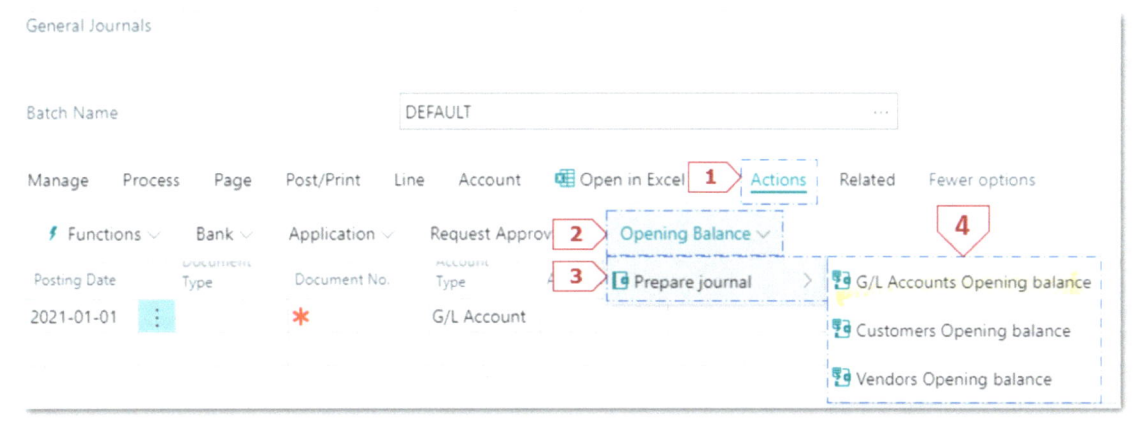

Figure 13-14 - General Journal - Generating Opening Balance Lines

In the **Actions** (**1**) section of the action bar, you will find the **Opening Balance** (**2**), the **Prepare Journal** (**3**) option has actions that will help you generate opening balances (**4**). When you click on **G/L Accounts Opening Balance**, after a moment, it will have generated a set of journal entries for you:

Figure 13-15 - General Journal with G/L Account Lines

This progress will create a General Journal Entry for each G/L Account that has an **Account Type** of **Posting** and **Income/Balance** of **Balance Sheet**. Carefully work through your journal, setting the **Amounts** as needed, and if the Amount is **0**, then the journal line can be removed.

Unfortunately, this process assumes that you have closed your Income Statement in your old system, rolling the results of Income Statement into your Balance Sheet. This makes transitioning onto Business Central at year end logical, but often other reasons factor into scheduling. This means that you will have to manually create any Income Statement journal lines if you have not done a closing process.

It can be valuable to learn from prior chapters and simply copy the existing journal lines to Excel, then populate new rows with your **Account No.**, **Account Name**, and **Amounts**:

	A	B	C	D	E	F	G	H	I	J	K	L	M	N	O
1	Posting Date	Document Type	Document No.	Account Type	Account No.	Account Name	Description	Currency Code	EU 3-Party Trade	Gen. Posting Type	Gen. Bus. Posting Group	Gen. Prod. Posting Group	Amount	Amount (LCY)	Bal. Account Type
2	2021-01-01		OPEN-GL	G/L Account	1250	Computers	Computers		No				4512.23	4512.23	G/L Account
3	2021-01-01		OPEN-GL	G/L Account	1421	Normal Inventory	Normal Inventory		No				13659.5	13659.5	G/L Account
4	2021-01-01		OPEN-GL	G/L Account	1422	Seasonal Inventory	Seasonal Inventory		No				6675	6675	G/L Account
5	2021-01-01		OPEN-GL	G/L Account	1510	Receivables, Domestic	Receivables, Domestic		No				112482.23	112482.23	G/L Account
6	2021-01-01		OPEN-GL	G/L Account	1511	Receivables, EU	Receivables, EU		No				6440.42	6440.42	G/L Account
7	2021-01-01		OPEN-GL	G/L Account	1512	Receivables, Non-EU	Receivables, Non-EU		No				3560.83	3560.83	G/L Account
8	2021-01-01		OPEN-GL	G/L Account	1940	Bank, EUR	Bank, EUR		No				50544.69	50544.69	G/L Account
9	2021-01-01		OPEN-GL	G/L Account	2441	Accounts Payable, Domestic	Accounts Payable, Domestic		No				-5711.23	-5711.23	G/L Account
10	2021-01-01		OPEN-GL	G/L Account	2442	Accounts Payable, Foreign	Accounts Payable, Foreign		No				-7820.12	-7820.12	G/L Account
11	2021-01-01		OPEN-GL	G/L Account	3041	Sales, Normal, Sweden	Sales, Normal, Sweden		No				-158079.49	-158079.49	G/L Account
12	2021-01-01		OPEN-GL	G/L Account	3045	Sales, Normal, Non-EU	Sales, Normal, Non-EU		No				-1553.94	-1553.94	G/L Account
13	2021-01-01		OPEN-GL	G/L Account	3046	Sales, Normal, EU	Sales, Normal, EU		No				-192.44	-192.44	G/L Account
14	2021-01-01		OPEN-GL	G/L Account	3051	Sales, Seasonal, Sweden	Sales, Seasonal, Sweden		No				-97340.04	-97340.04	G/L Account
15	2021-01-01		OPEN-GL	G/L Account	3055	Sales, Seasonal Non-EU	Sales, Seasonal Non-EU		No				-6457.2	-6457.2	G/L Account
16	2021-01-01		OPEN-GL	G/L Account	3056	Sales, Seasonal EU	Sales, Seasonal EU		No				-16247.98	-16247.98	G/L Account
17	2021-01-01		OPEN-GL	G/L Account	4401	Purchases, Domestic	Purchases, Domestic		No				81740.67	81740.67	G/L Account
18	2021-01-01		OPEN-GL	G/L Account	4531	Purchases, EU	Purchases, EU		No				5311.27	5311.27	G/L Account
19	2021-01-01		OPEN-GL	G/L Account	4545	Purchases, Import	Purchases, Import		No				525.33	525.33	G/L Account
20	2021-01-01		OPEN-GL	G/L Account	5910	Advertisements	Advertisements		No				754.21	754.21	G/L Account
21	2021-01-01		OPEN-GL	G/L Account	5930	Direct Marketing	Direct Marketing		No				600	600	G/L Account
22	2021-01-01		OPEN-GL	G/L Account	6040	Credit card charges	Credit card charges		No				721.01	721.01	G/L Account

Figure 13-16 - General Journal Lines Copied to Excel for Populating

These values can then be pasted back into the journal, making entry much faster:

Posting Date	Document Type	Document No.	Account Type	Account No.	Account Name	Description	Currency Code	EU 3-Party Trade	Gen. Posting Type	Gen. Bus. Posting Group	Gen. Prod. Posting Group	Amount
2021-01-01		OPEN-GL	G/L Account	1250	Computers	Computers						4 512.23
2021-01-01		OPEN-GL	G/L Account	1421	Normal Inventory	Normal Inventory						13 659.50
2021-01-01		OPEN-GL	G/L Account	1422	Seasonal Inventory	Seasonal Inventory						6 675.00
2021-01-01		OPEN-GL	G/L Account	1510	Receivables, Domestic	Receivables, Domestic						112 482.23
2021-01-01		OPEN-GL	G/L Account	1511	Receivables, EU	Receivables, EU						6 440.42
2021-01-01		OPEN-GL	G/L Account	1512	Receivables, Non-EU	Receivables, Non-EU						3 560.83
2021-01-01		OPEN-GL	G/L Account	1940	Bank, EUR	Bank, EUR						50 544.69
2021-01-01		OPEN-GL	G/L Account	2441	Accounts Payable, Domestic	Accounts Payable, Domestic						-5 711.23
2021-01-01		OPEN-GL	G/L Account	2442	Accounts Payable, Foreign	Accounts Payable, Foreign						-7 820.12
2021-01-01		OPEN-GL	G/L Account	3041	Sales, Normal, Sweden	Sales, Normal, Sweden						-158 079.49
2021-01-01		OPEN-GL	G/L Account	3045	Sales, Normal, Non-EU	Sales, Normal, Non-EU						-1 553.94
2021-01-01		OPEN-GL	G/L Account	3046	Sales, Normal, EU	Sales, Normal, EU						-192.44
2021-01-01		OPEN-GL	G/L Account	3051	Sales, Seasonal, Sweden	Sales, Seasonal, Sweden						-97 340.04
2021-01-01		OPEN-GL	G/L Account	3055	Sales, Seasonal Non-EU	Sales, Seasonal Non-EU						-6 457.20
2021-01-01		OPEN-GL	G/L Account	3056	Sales, Seasonal EU	Sales, Seasonal EU						-16 247.98
2021-01-01		OPEN-GL	G/L Account	4401	Purchases, Domestic	Purchases, Domestic						81 740.67
2021-01-01		OPEN-GL	G/L Account	4531	Purchases, EU	Purchases, EU						5 311.27
2021-01-01		OPEN-GL	G/L Account	4545	Purchases, Import	Purchases, Import						525.33
2021-01-01		OPEN-GL	G/L Account	5910	Advertisements	Advertisements						754.21
2021-01-01		OPEN-GL	G/L Account	5930	Direct Marketing	Direct Marketing						600.00
2021-01-01		OPEN-GL	G/L Account	6040	Credit card charges	Credit card charges						721.01
2021-01-01		OPEN-GL	G/L Account	6110	Office Supplies	Office Supplies						135.05

Figure 13-17 - General Journal Lines Pasted into Business Central from Excel

These entries can *now* be posted.

ACTION: Create and Post G/L Balances

With the help from the **G/L Accounts Opening Balance** feature in the 🔍 **General Journal** (and Excel), create and post journal entries for all your G/L Accounts with balances. Review the 🔍 **Chart of Accounts** to ensure that the results came in *correctly*.

SUMMARY

At this point, you now have all your key financials, inventory, and opening balances brought over.

Your system is *now* ready for daily use!

PART 4: BASIC OPERATIONS

Chapters 14 and 15 will cover basic purchasing and sales operations you will perform on a regular basis.

Chapters 16 and 17 will focus on making and receiving payments.

Chapter 18 will address some common scenarios where errors happen and how to correct them.

Chapter 19 will review some of the most commonly needed recurring tasks in the system.

Chapter 14: Purchasing

In this chapter, we are going to go over some of the common ways to create Purchase Orders to acquire items into inventory, as well as how to receive and invoice them.

We will also do a quick touch on how to create and post Invoices for purchases that are not for Items.

We will also go into how document sending in Business Central works.

CREATING PURCHASE ORDERS

The most obvious route to creating a new **Purchase Order** (PO) is via the 🔍 **Purchase Orders** list page, then clicking the **New** (**1**) button:

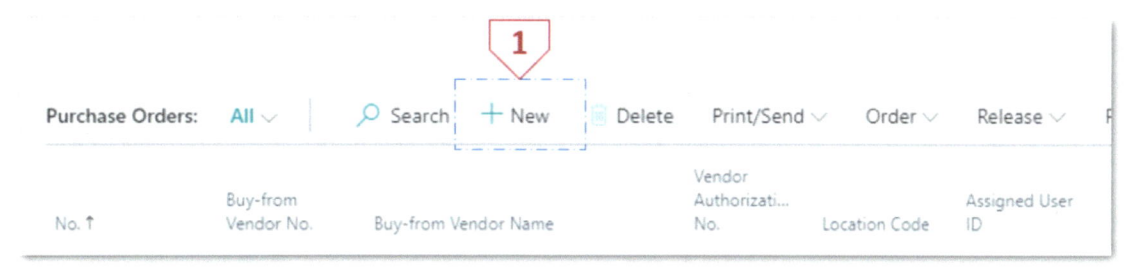

Figure 14-1 - Creating a New Purchase Order from Purchase Order List

It is also possible to create new Purchase Orders from other places in the system including directly from the 🔍 **Vendors** list itself (via **New Document** (**2**), then **Purchase Order** (**3**)):

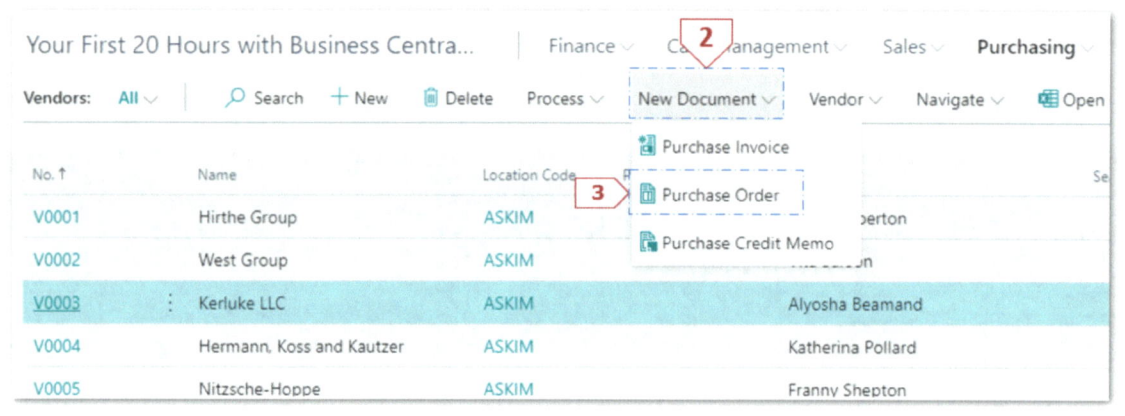

Figure 14-2 - Creating a New Purchase Order from Vendor List

When you create a new **Purchase Order**, you will get a blank Document page, with some key fields that will need to be filled in straight away.

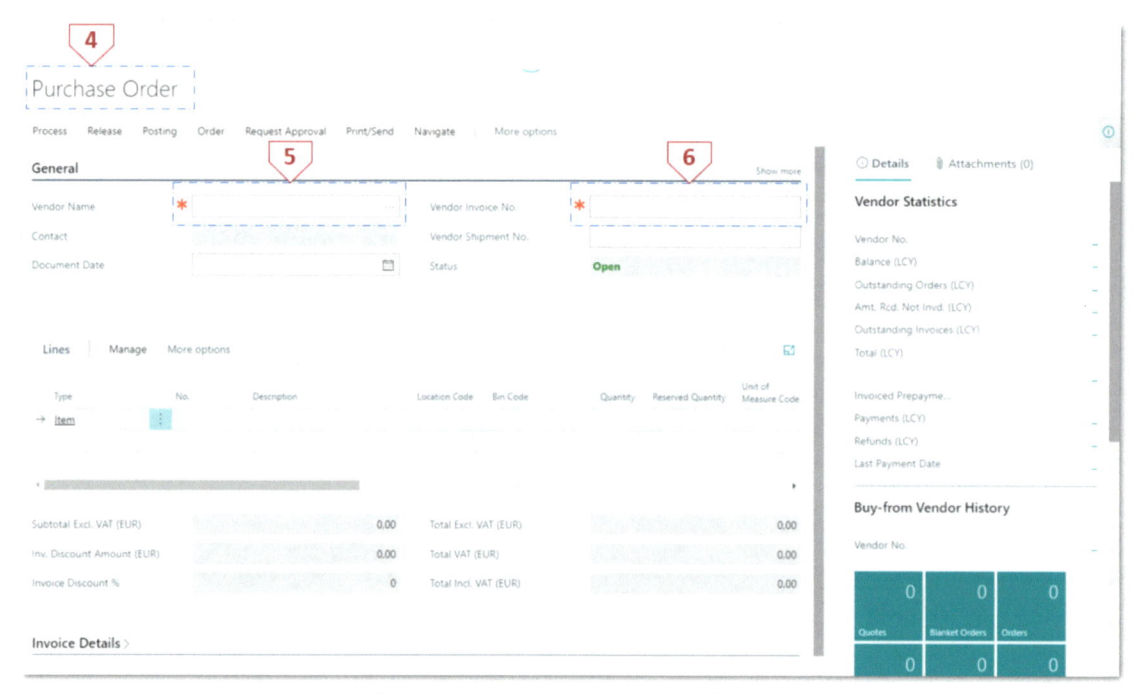

Figure 14-3 - An Empty Purchase Order

The first field that we will fill in is the **Vendor Name** (**5**) field – we can either enter the **Name** of the vendor, their vendor **No.** value or click the ⋯ (AssistEdit) button to select the vendor. As soon as we do that, the Purchase Order is started:

208 PAGE

PART 4: BASIC OPERATIONS
CHAPTER 14: PURCHASING

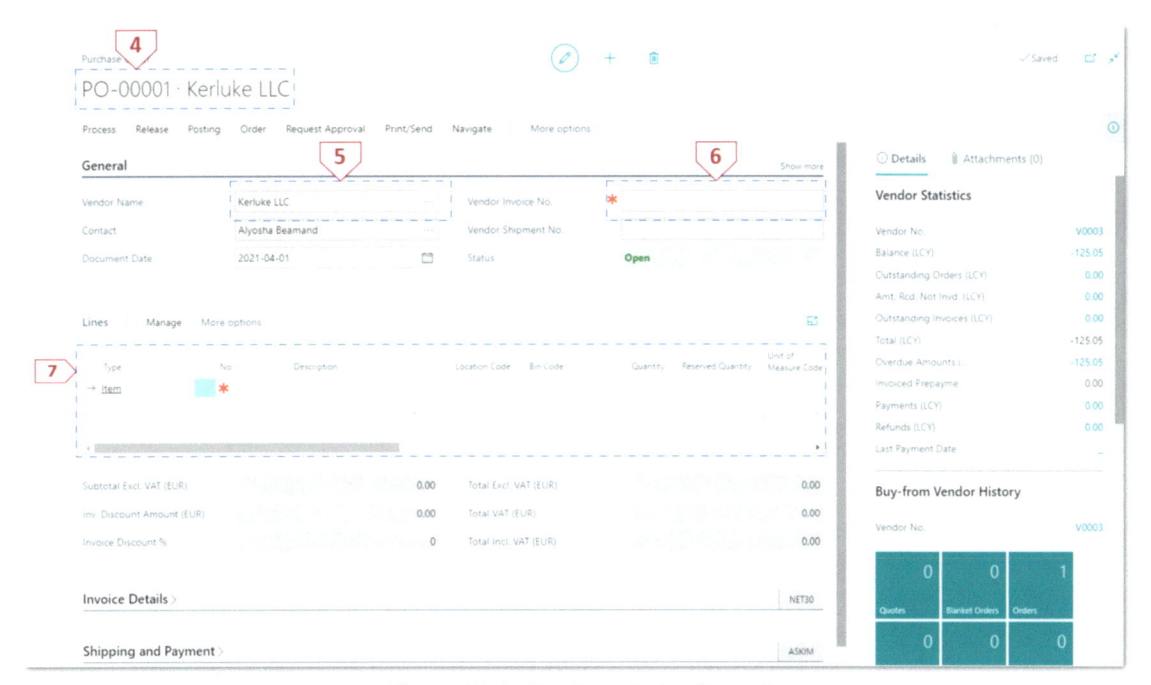

Figure 14-4 - Purchase Order Created

We can see the main caption (**4**) of the page has updated to the **Purchase Order No.**, and several other areas have updated their values from the vendor. (See more below)

We still need to enter a **Vendor Invoice No.** (**6**) had we enabled this as a requirement (see **Chapter 6** – Purchase & Payables Setup). Once we have done that, we can enter **Lines** (**7**). Since **Type** defaulted to **Item**, we can type the item's **No.**, the **Description** of an item, or select from the list:

PART 4: BASIC OPERATIONS
CHAPTER 14: PURCHASING

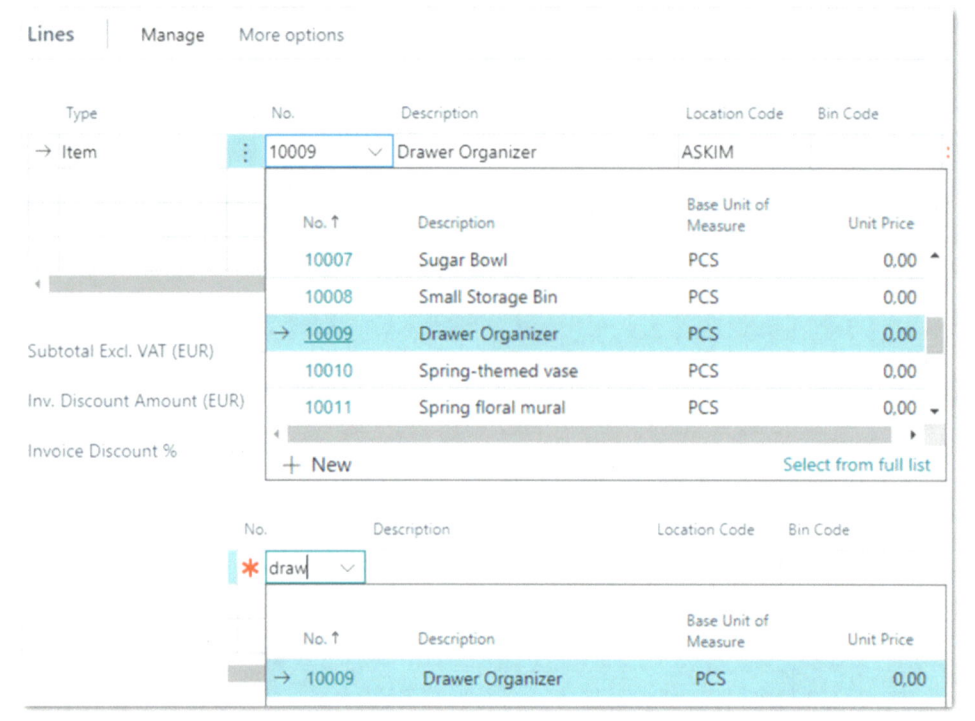

Figure 14-5 - Purchase Lines - Selecting Items by No. or Description

Then, when we enter the **Quantity** (**8**) on the line, multiple fields will update:

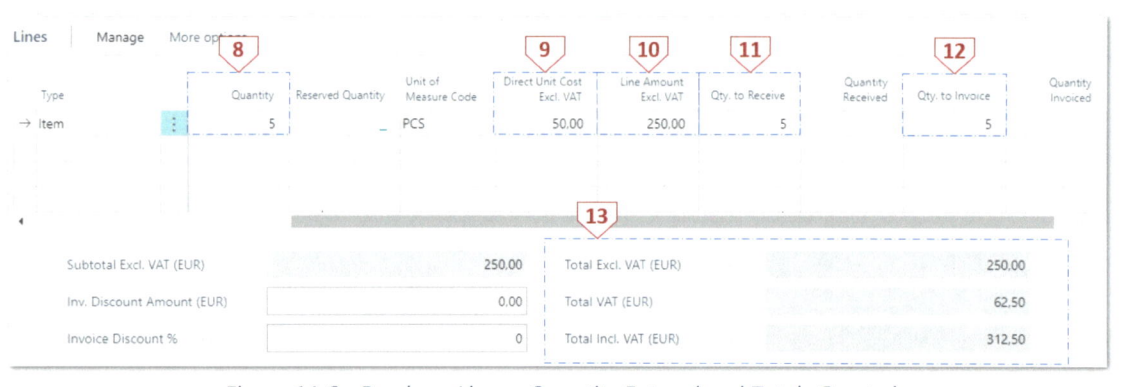

Figure 14-6 - Purchase Lines - Quantity Entered and Totals Created

- **Direct Unit Cost** (**9**) will default to the **Unit Cost** from the Item Card. Verify that *this* is the correct price that the vendor will charge you for this item.
- The **Line Amount Excl. VAT** (**10**) will be the results of the quantity (**Qty**) times (*) cost, minus (-) any discounts.
- The **Totals** (**13**) below the lines will be updated to reflect the document totals.

- **Qty. to Receive** (**11**) and **Qty. to Invoice** (**12**) will also be populated with the **Quantity**. (see Partial Receiving below)

Effectively, this is enough information to post the **Purchase Order** *now*, but before we do that process, let us look deeper at the Purchase Order.

Getting to Know the PO

Looking at the FastTabs on the Purchase Order page, there are many terrific features related to the fields, but are beyond the scope of this book.

Here are some of the highlights we can take the time to review:

General FastTab

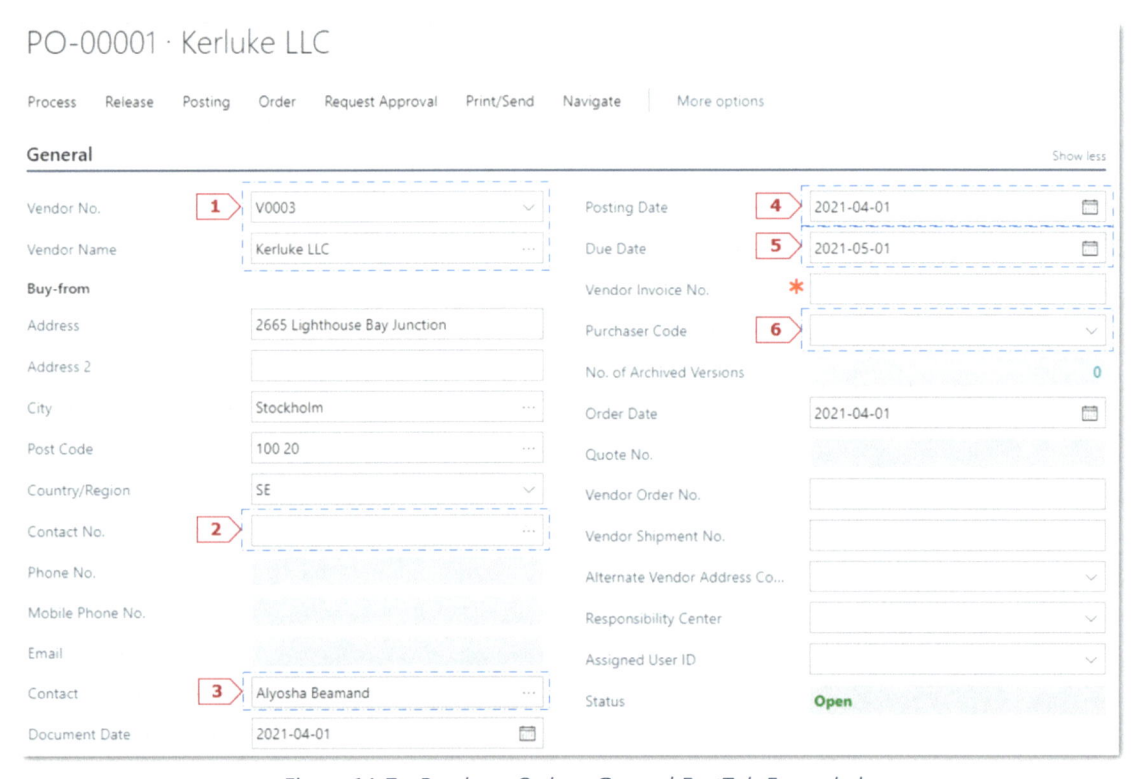

Figure 14-7 - Purchase Order - General FastTab Expanded

Element	What is it?
1	The **Vendor No.** and **Vendor Name** are stored separately, even if there appears to only be the Vendor Name.
2	If you are using the CRM module, you may have Contacts for a vendor to refer to you can choose from via the **Contact No.** field.
3	If you are not using the CRM module, it still is good to be able to enter a **Contact**.
4	**Posting Date** allows you post documents on dates that are not the *current date*.

5	**Due Date** allows you to manually set a due date, rather than use the formula from the **Payment Terms** setting, which defaulted from the **Vendor Card**.
6	It is possible to setup different purchases in the system so you can keep track of *which purchaser* oversees this document, by viewing the **Purchaser Code**.

INVOICE DETAILS FASTTAB

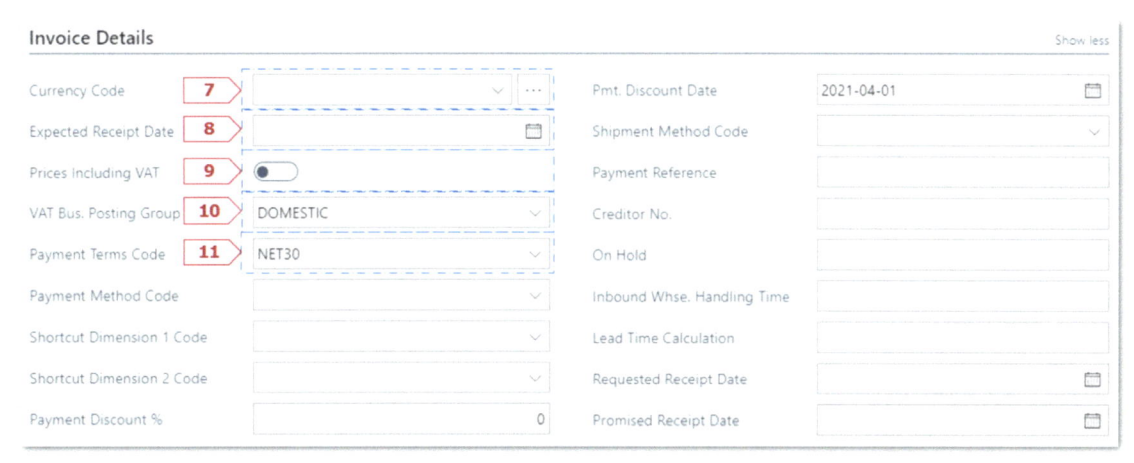

Figure 14-8 - Purchase Order - Invoice Details FastTab Expanded

Element	What is it?
7	The **Currency Code** lets you choose a specific currency to use for this single document; it is defaulted from the **Vendor Card**.
8	The **Expected Receipt Date** can be very helpful to know when something will be arriving.
9	**Prices Including VAT** will change the VAT calculation to reflect the VAT impact.
10	**VAT Bus. Posting Group** is seldom changed, but if you need to change which tax strategy to use on a *per-document* level; this is the field for it.
11	**Payment Terms Code** allows you to select alternate methods of calculating the **Due Date**.

SHIPPING AND PAYMENT

This FastTab lets you set where something should be shipped to. The default **Ship-to** (**12**) setting is **Location**, which defaults the **Location Code** (**13**) to the Location Code from the Vendor:

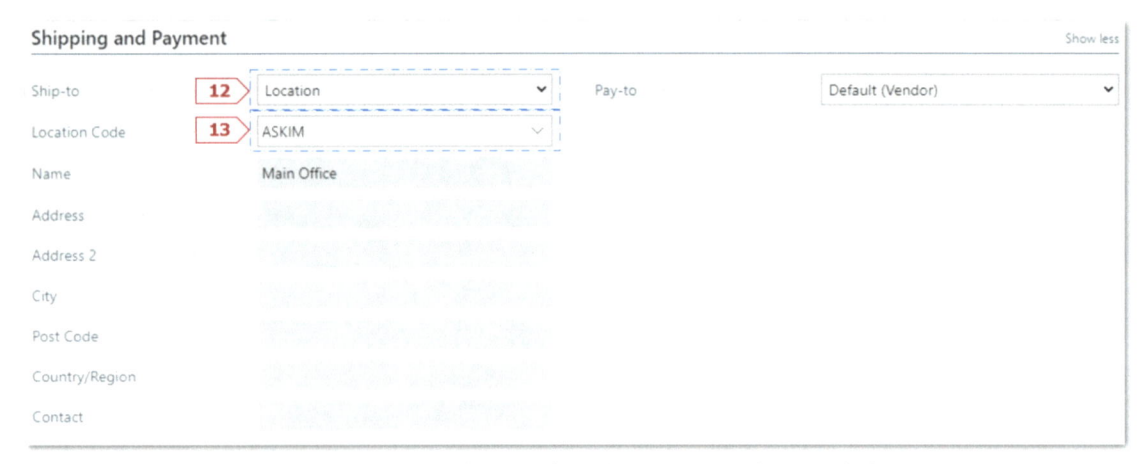

Figure 14-9 - Purchase Order - Shipping FastTab Expanded

However, there are a few alternate settings:

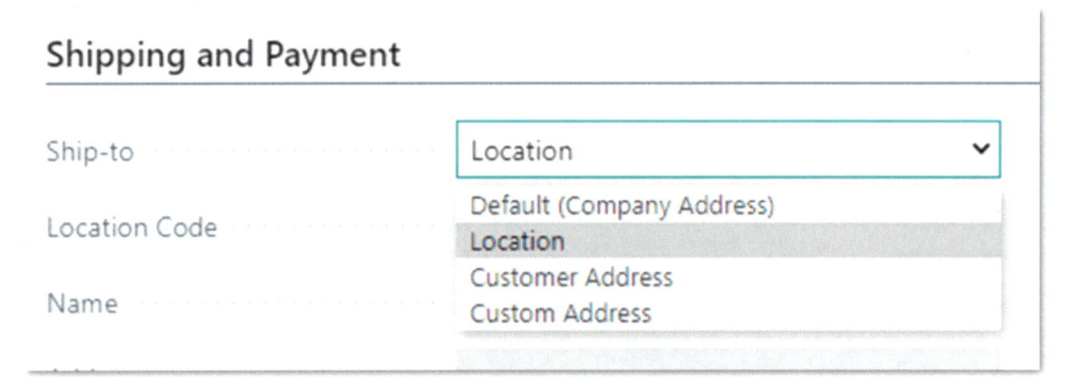

Figure 14-10 - Purchase Order - Ship-To Options

If you are not using Locations, it will default to the **Company Information** address.

Additionally, you can choose **Customer Address** and then be able to select which Customer to use for the address.

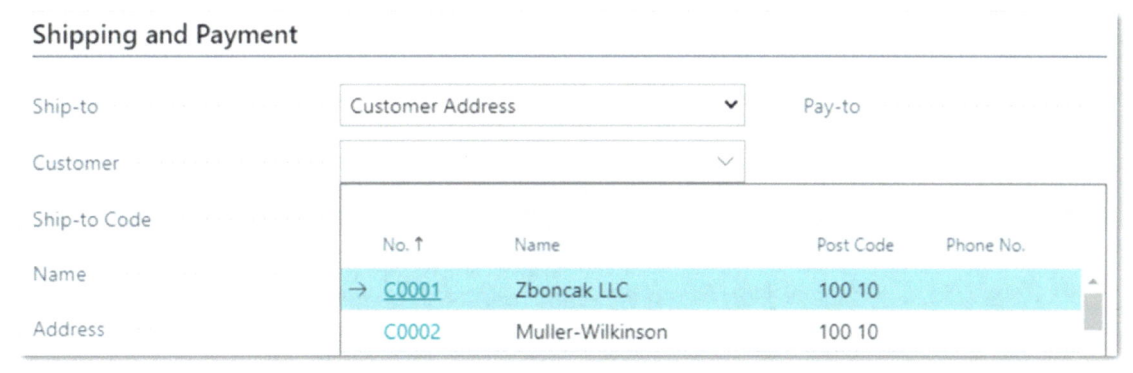

Figure 14-11 - Purchase Order - Ship-To Customer Example

Lastly, you can choose **Custom Address** and manually set the shipping information:

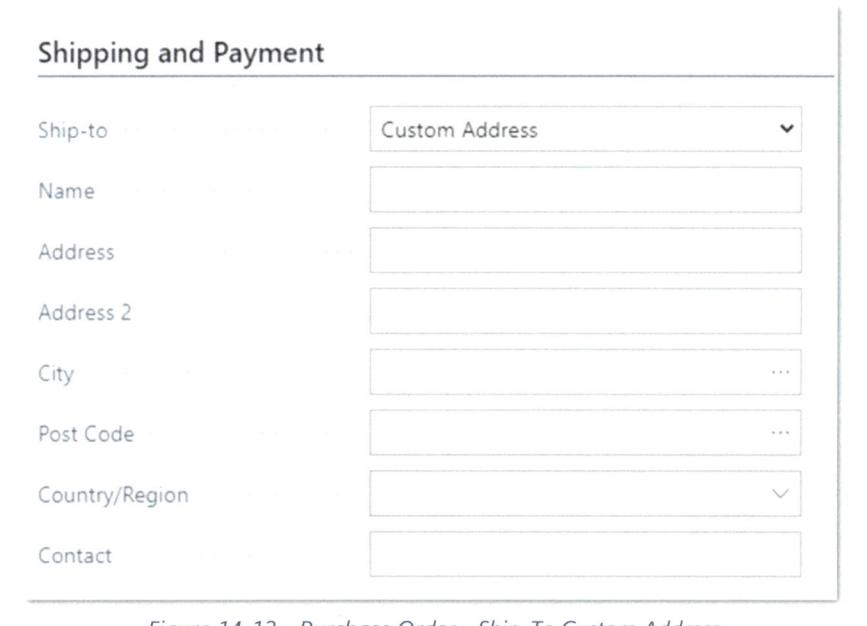

Figure 14-12 - Purchase Order - Ship-To Custom Address

ATTACHING DOCUMENTS

It is very common to want to be able to attach scanned or emailed documents to the purchase documents to be stored digitally.

Either via the **Attachments** FactBox (**1/2**) or the **Order** -> **Attachments** action bar (**3/4**):

Figure 14-13 - Purchase Order - Attaching Documents

You will get to the Attached Documents list:

Figure 14-14 - Attached Documents List

Clicking on **Select File…** (**5**) will open a dialog. You can either click **Choose…** (**6**) to browse for the file or *drag and drop* a file onto the **Choose…** button:

Figure 14-15 - Attach Document Chooser

Either way, you can attach all sorts of files. In my case, I added an *order confirmation* PDF:

PART 4: BASIC OPERATIONS
CHAPTER 14: PURCHASING

Figure 14-16 - Attached Documents List with Example File

POSTING – RECEIVE & INVOICE

Once you are done with your Purchase Order, you mainly do two different operations:

- Receive the items into Inventory.
- Register the Invoice from the Vendor for the costs of the items.

You *can* combine them into a single step. All these options are available via the Post operation. Since we are posting (meaning recording the document to ledgers), it is a good idea to preview and see what will happen:

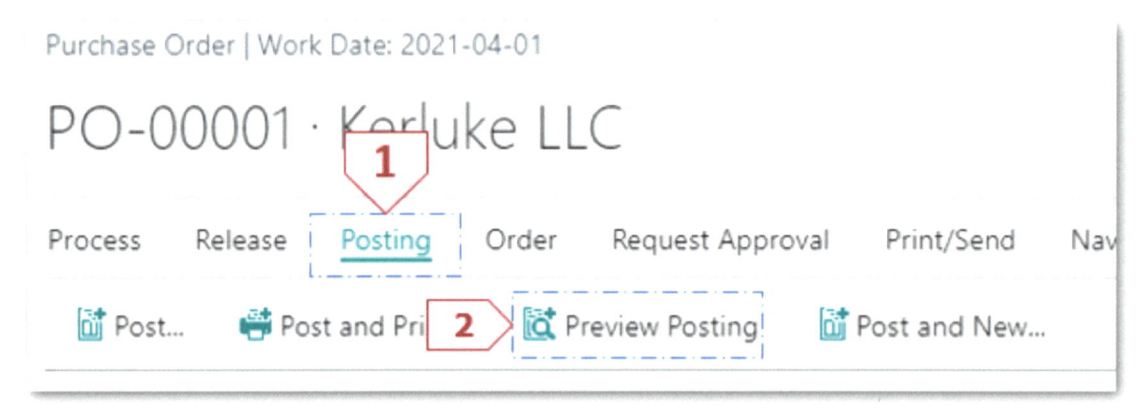

Figure 14-17 - Purchase Order - Preview Posting Action

Under **Posting** (**1**), click **Preview Posting** (**2**). This will show you the Ledger Entries, resulting in:

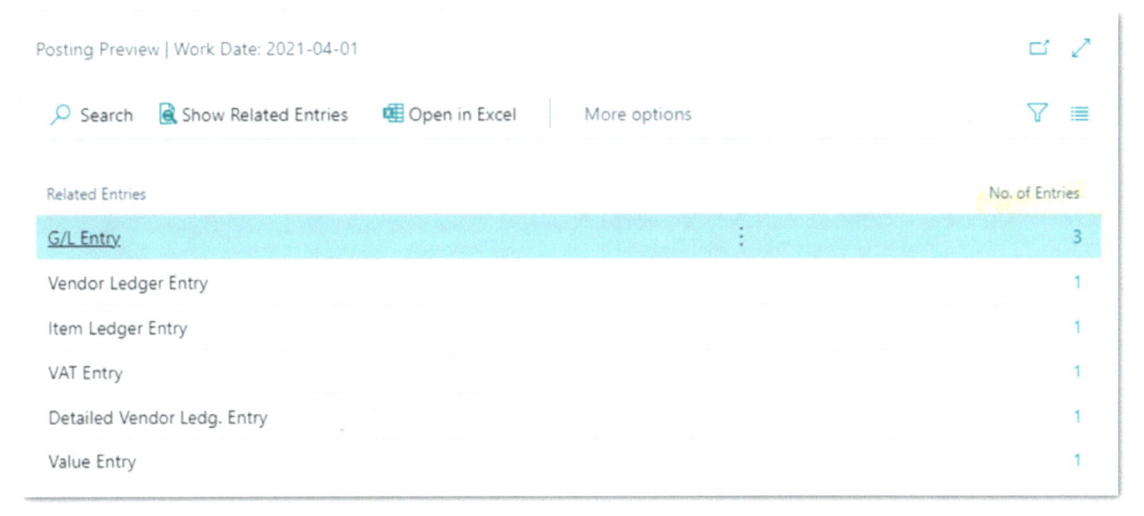

Figure 14-18 - Purchase Order - Preview Posting Summary

As you can see, we will get 3 entries to the Financials' main ledger, the G/L Entry, along with a VAT Entry. We will get some entries related to both the Inventory (Item Ledger Entry, Value Entry) and Purchasing (Vendor Ledger Entry, Detailed Vendor Ledg. Entry).

On all these **Related Entries** lines, you can click on the **No. of Entries** field to drill-down and see the details behind them. By drilling-down on the value in the No. of Entries column for **G/L Entry**, you would see:

Figure 14-19 - Purchase Order - Preview Posting - G/L Entries

(You may have to 🔧 **Personalize** to add the **G/L Account Name**)

We can see here that we would impact the following:

- The **Purchases, Domestic** account with the Amount: **250,00**.
- The **Incoming VAT, 25%** account with the Amount: **62,50**.
- The **Accounts Payable, Domestic** with the Amount: **312,50**.

After verifying this information as correct, when you **Post**, you will be asked which steps you would like to take:

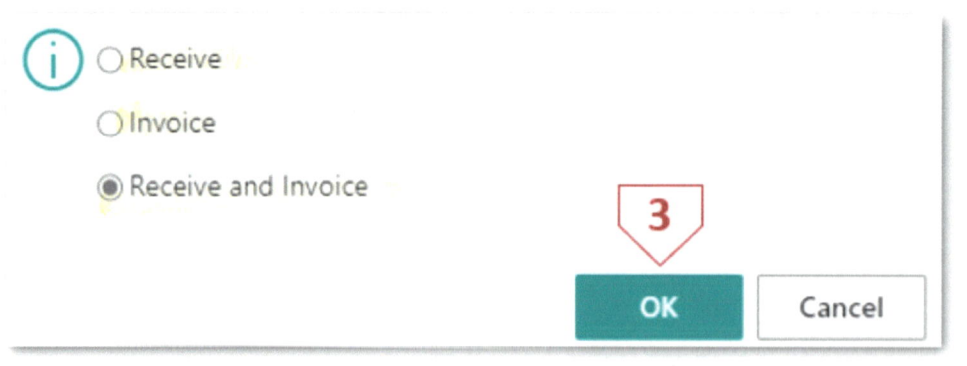

Figure 14-20 - Purchase Order - Post Options

This reflects the options listed at the top of this section. When you click **OK** (**3**) with the default **Receive and Invoice** selected, you will get a type of confirmation:

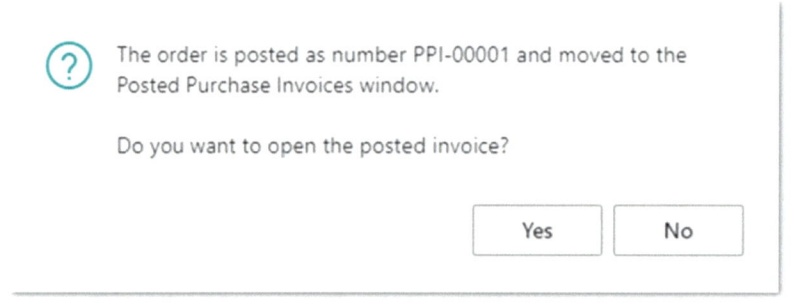

Figure 14-21 - Purchase Order - Posting Confirmation

At this point, you have created both a **Posted Purchase Receipt** *and* a **Posted Purchase Invoice**, but you are asked if you would like to open the invoice; it looks like the following:

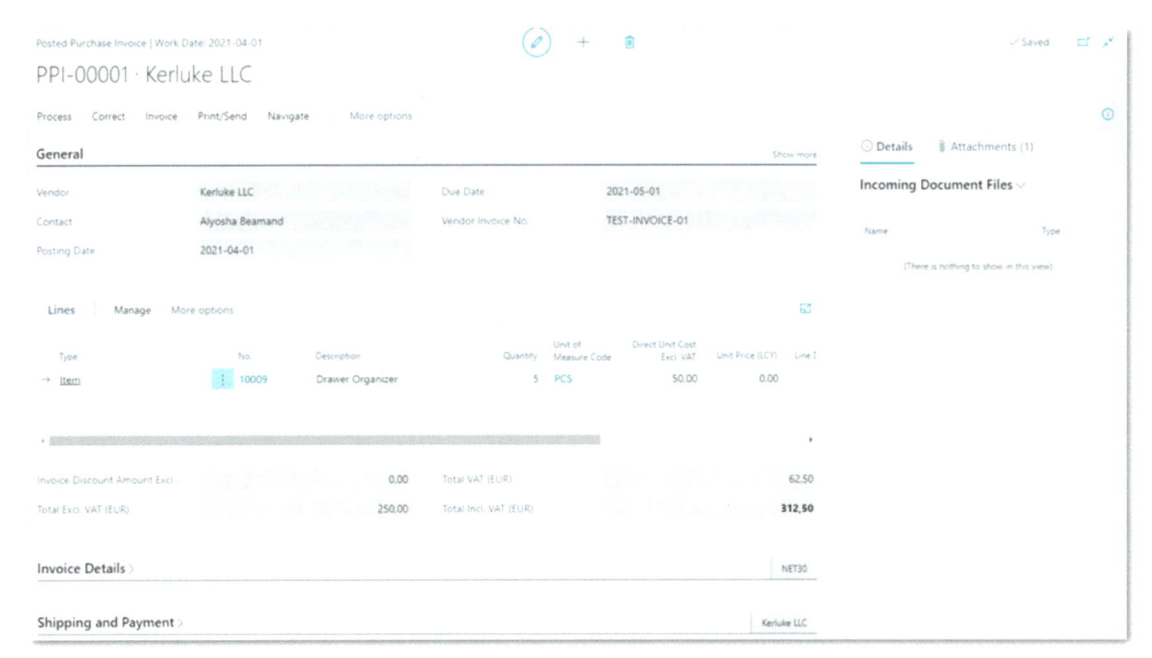

Figure 14-22 - Posted Purchase Invoice

Via the **Posted Purchase Invoices**, you can access historical documents, including reprinting them, sending them as emails, and accessing the attached files.

If we locate **V0003** in the **Vendors** list, by clicking on the **Balance** drilldown, you will see the open **Vendor Ledger Entries**:

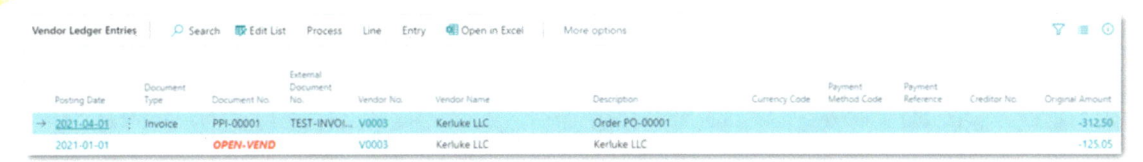

Figure 14-23 - Posted Invoice in the Vendor Ledger Entries

As you can see, Invoice **PPI-00001** is shown in the list.

Purchasing – Partial Posting

Sometimes, you receive only a portion of the items ordered. In this section, we will split a new Purchase Order.

Copying Past Orders

To make this process a little faster, we will copy the last Purchase Order. Opening a new Purchase Order, under **Actions** (**1**) -> **Functions** (**2**), and then select the **Copy Document...** (**3**) function:

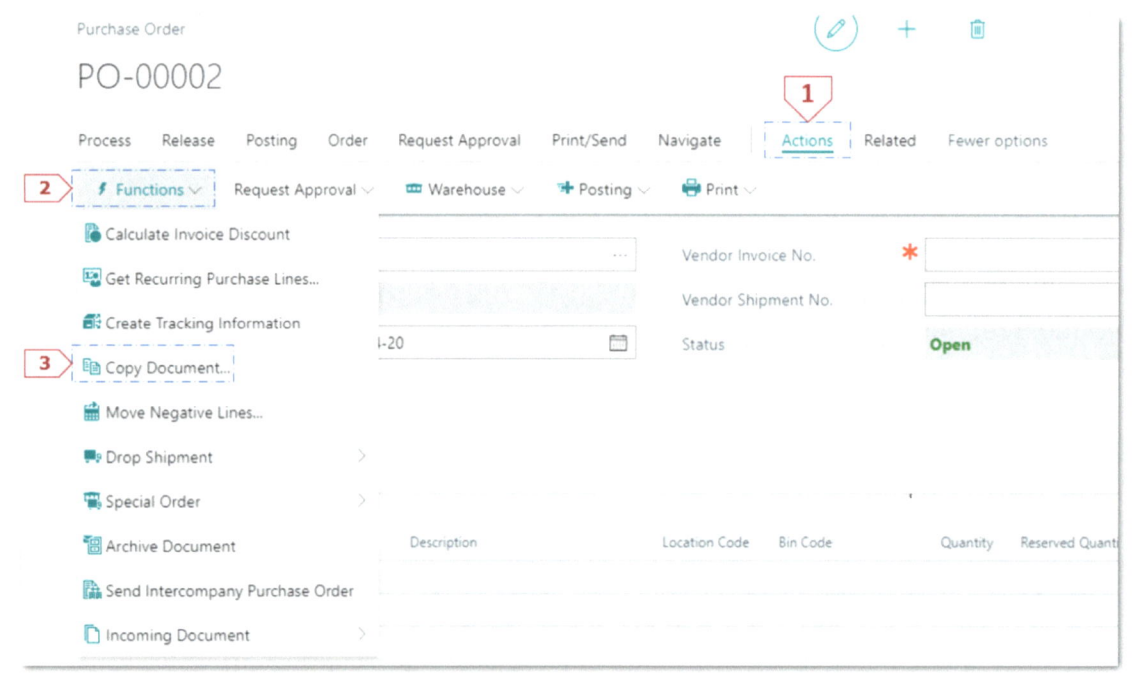

Figure 14-24 - Purchase Order - Copy Document Action

This opens the Copy Purchase Document tool:

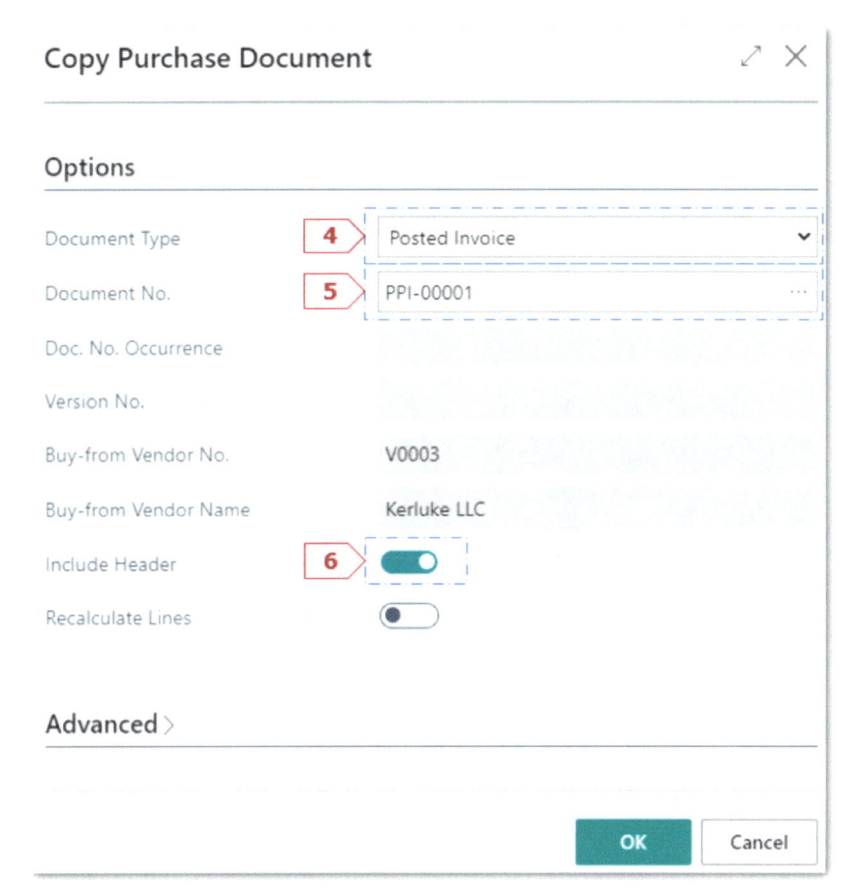

Figure 14-25 - Copy Document Settings

We will choose **Posted Invoice** as **Document Type** (**4**), and **Document No.** (**5**) will be the **PPI-00001**. In this case, we want to *exactly* duplicate the last PO, so, we will check **Include Header** (**6**). When we click OK, we will get a Purchase Order like the following:

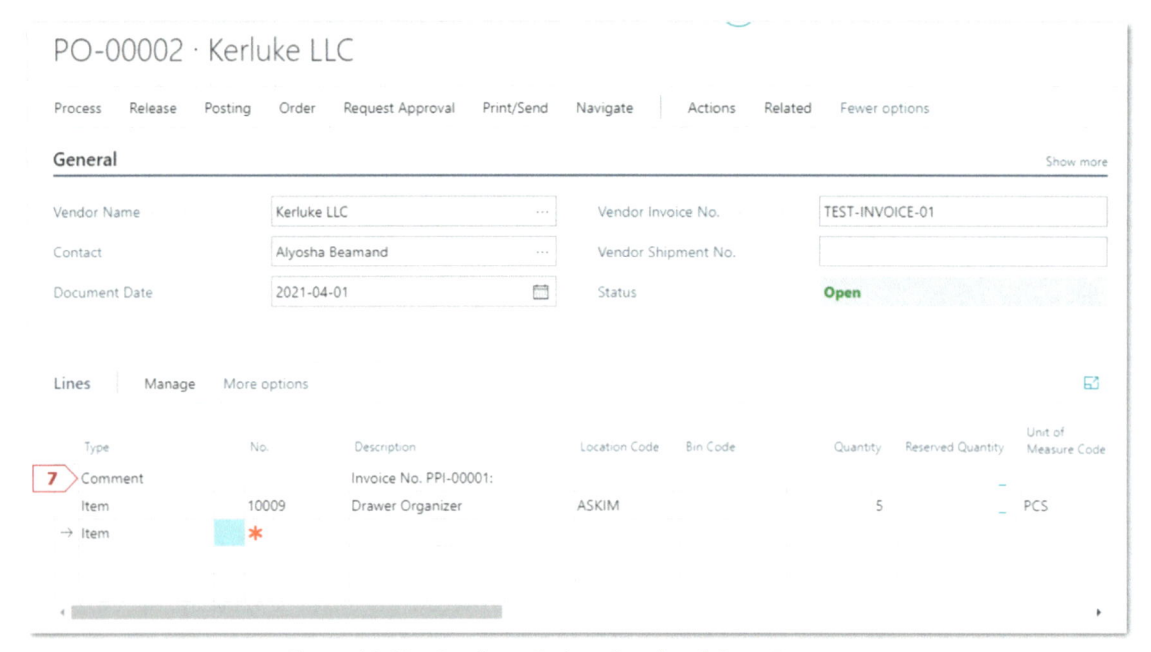

Figure 14-26 - Purchase Order - Results of Copy Document

As you can see, the only issue is that we have a **Comment Type** line (**7**), which we do not need. This can be deleted via ⋮ (**8**) -> Delete Line (**9**):

Figure 14-27 - Purchase Order - Deleting a Line

Setting the Partial Quantity

To choose how many to receive or invoice, there are fields just for that on the Lines:

Figure 14-28 - Purchase Order Line - Setting Partial Quantity to Receive

The **Qty. to Receive** (**1**) and **Qty. to Invoice** (**2**) fields control what will happen to the line when you Post, so they can be changed. In the above figure, Qty. to Receive and Qty. to Invoice are set to **2** (of the full 5).

When you **Post** the order with Receive and Invoice, those 2 will move into the *noneditable* **Quantity Received** (**3**) and **Quantity Invoiced** (**4**), while the Qty. to Receive and Qty. to Invoice resets to the remaining quantity:

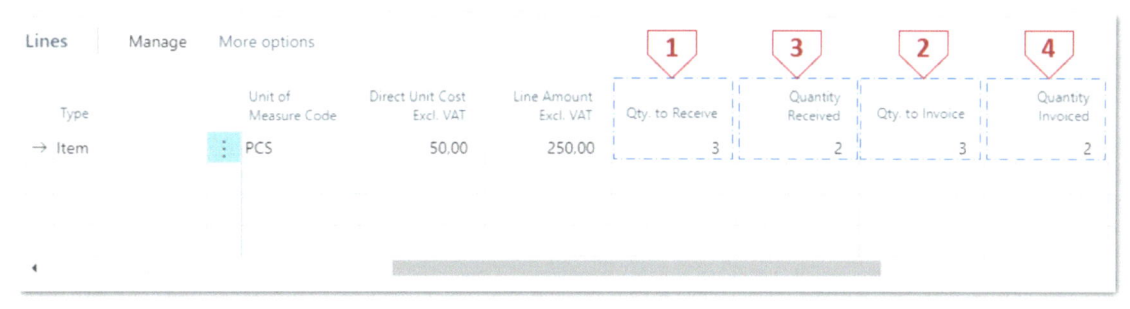

Figure 14-29 - Purchase Order Line - Partially Posted

If you **Post** (Receive and Invoice) again, the Purchase Order will be completed again, then removed.

If we locate **V0003** in the **Vendors** list, by clicking on the **Balance** drilldown, you will see the open **Vendor Ledger Entries**:

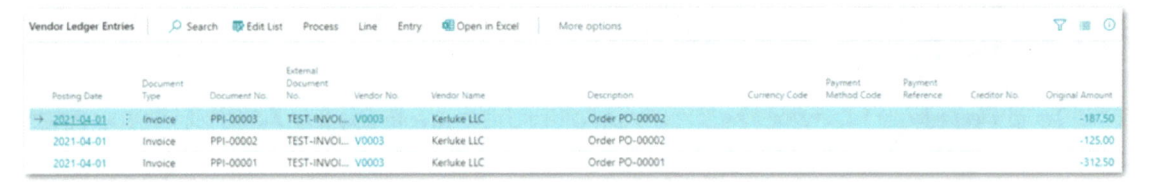

Figure 14-30 - Two Purchase Invoices in Vendor Ledger Entries

There were 2 Invoices from one Purchase Order. Because we ran the Post process two times for the same Purchase Order, two separate Invoices are created. Business Central will *not* add the second (and subsequent) postings to the same Posted Purchase Invoice.

PURCHASE INVOICES

Sometimes you purchase services, not items. For that, **Purchase Invoices** will help. Creating a new Purchase Invoice is the same process as creating a Purchase Order and looks incredibly similar:

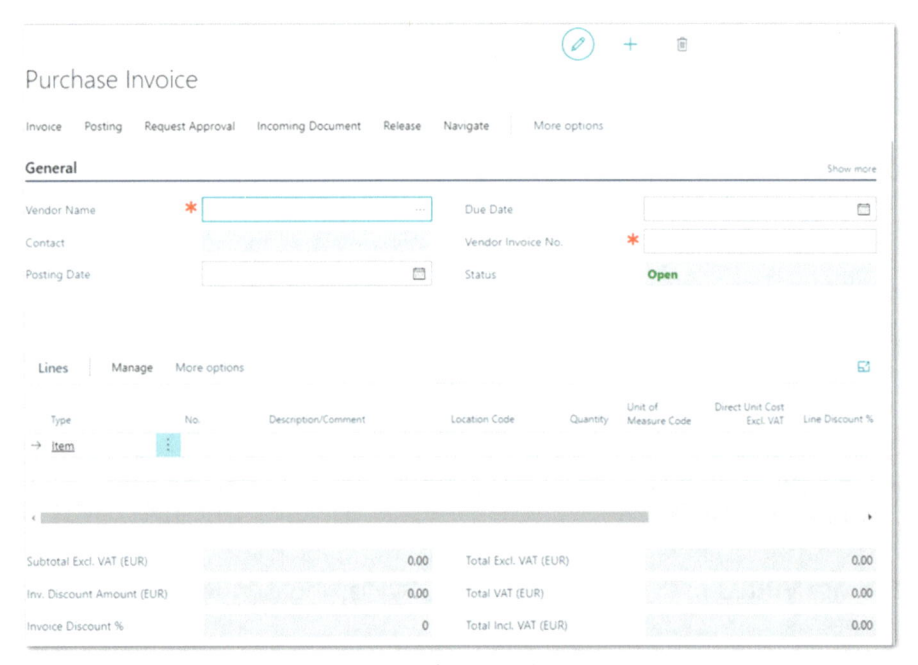

Figure 14-31 - Blank Purchase Invoice

Since we are paying for a service or a non-inventory item, we will change the **Type** (**1**) on the Line to **G/L Account** (**2**):

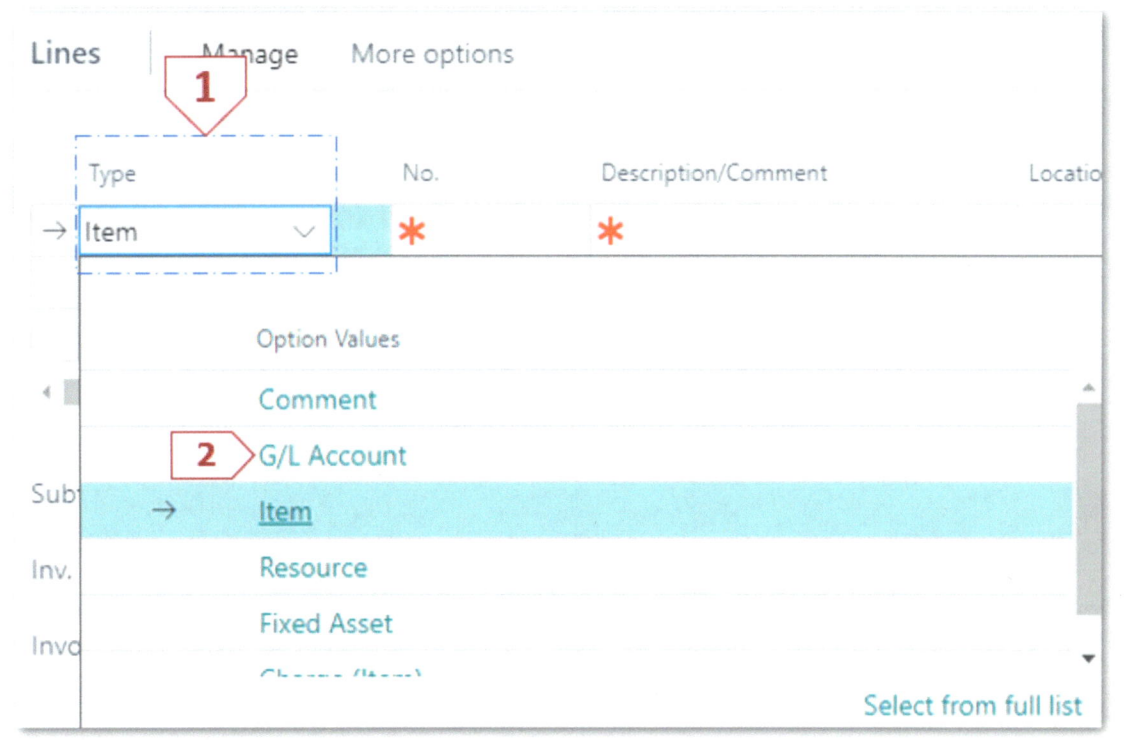

Figure 14-32 - Purchase Invoice Line - Type Selection List

Then we can set some of the other information:

Figure 14-33 - Purchase Invoice Line - Example G/L Account Line

We should set which G/L Account **No.** (**3**) to charge. For charges, it is also quite common to set the **Quantity** (**4**) to 1 and set the **Direct Unit Cost** (**5**) to the amount of the charge to be posted.

PART 4: BASIC OPERATIONS
CHAPTER 14: PURCHASING

When we **Post** the Purchase Invoice, it will appear in the **Vendor Ledger Entries** the same way that our Invoiced Purchase Orders did:

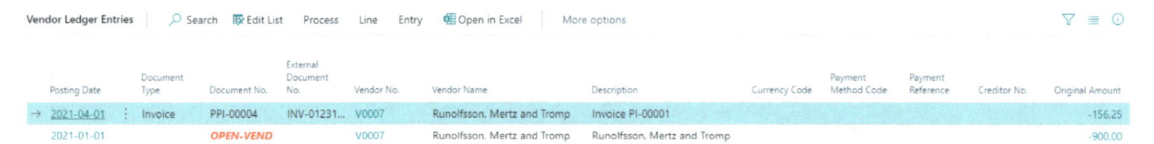

Figure 14-34 - Posted Purchase Invoice in Vendor Ledger Entries

If we look at the **6540** G/L Account (drill-down from the **Chart of Accounts** via the **Balance** field) to the General Ledger Entries, we will see the charge from the Invoice:

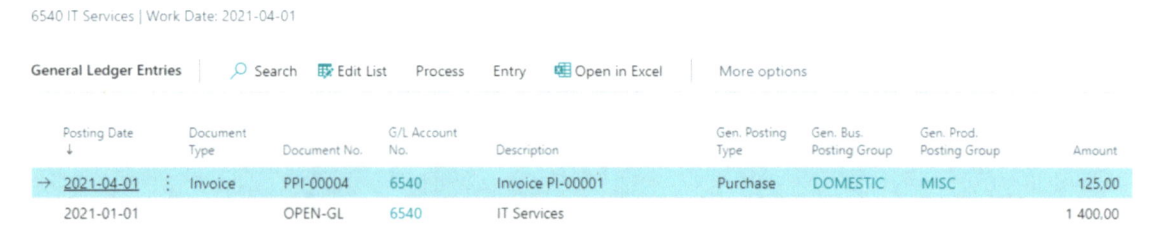

Figure 14-35 - General Ledger Entries Showing Purchase Invoice

SENDING PURCHASE DOCUMENTS

When you need to send Purchase Documents (including posted and unposted orders and invoices), there is a **Print/Send** (**1**) feature in the action bar:

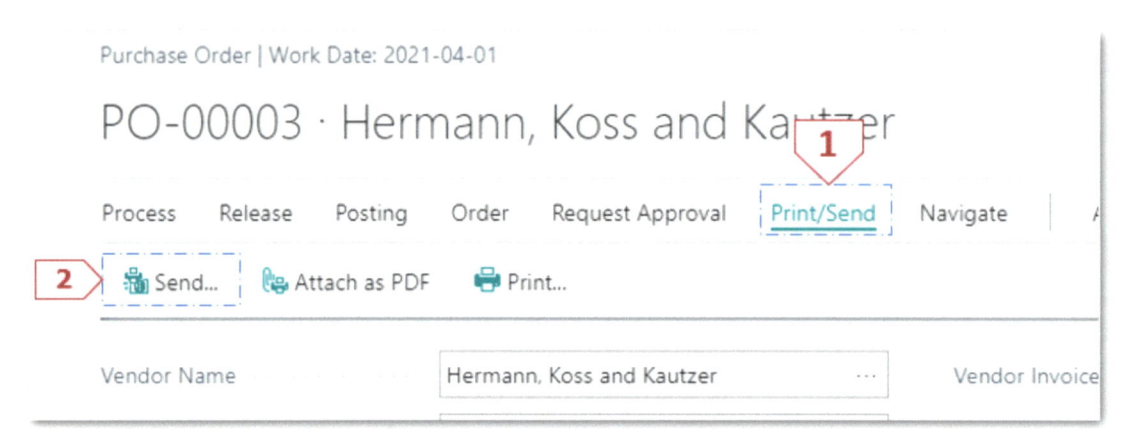

Figure 14-36 - Purchase Order - Send Action

After clicking the **Send** (**2**) option, a settings window will ask how to send it:

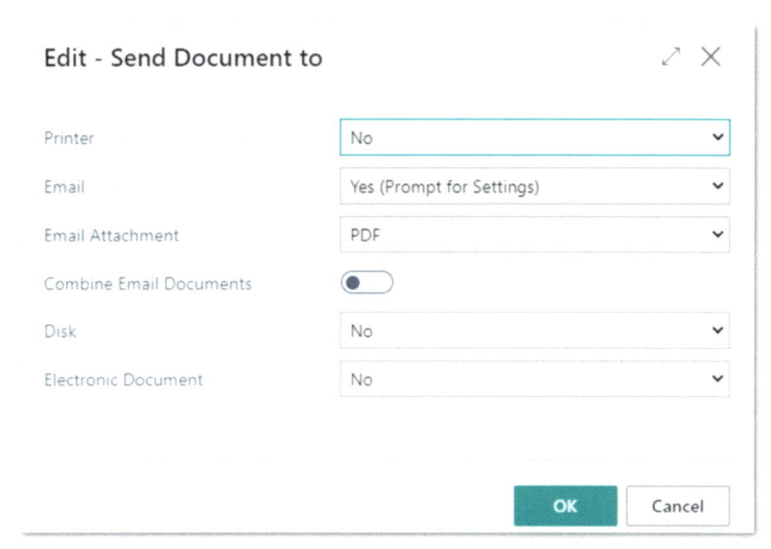

Figure 14-37 - Send Document Settings

These settings are defaulted from the **Vendor Card**'s **Document Sending Profile** field.

Leaving the field **Email** set to "**Yes**", when we click **OK**, we may get the following error:

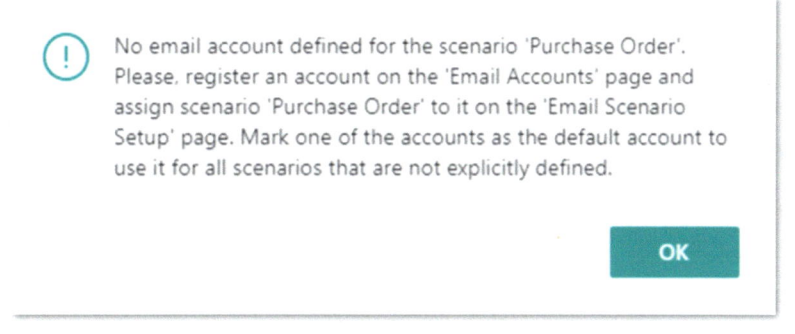

Figure 14-38 - Error Message about Missing Email Scenarios

If so, there is a little setup work. Otherwise, you can skip this next section.

EMAIL SCENARIOS

You will need to work through setting up **Email Accounts**. This varies widely by environment, so, you may need a partner or IT assistance to complete the Email Account setup. Microsoft has made it very easy to set up if you are using Business Central on their platform with Office 365, but other configurations may require assistance.

Once you have at least one Email Account configured, you also must create 🔍 **Email Scenario Assignments** that match what business process is happening to *which* Email Account you would want to use to send email *from*. As an example, you may want **Sales Order Confirmations** coming from the *user who sent it*, but invoices and credit documents to come from a *central accounting* shared mailbox.

For my test environment, I have a central **Email Account** setup, to which I will assign all **Email Scenarios**:

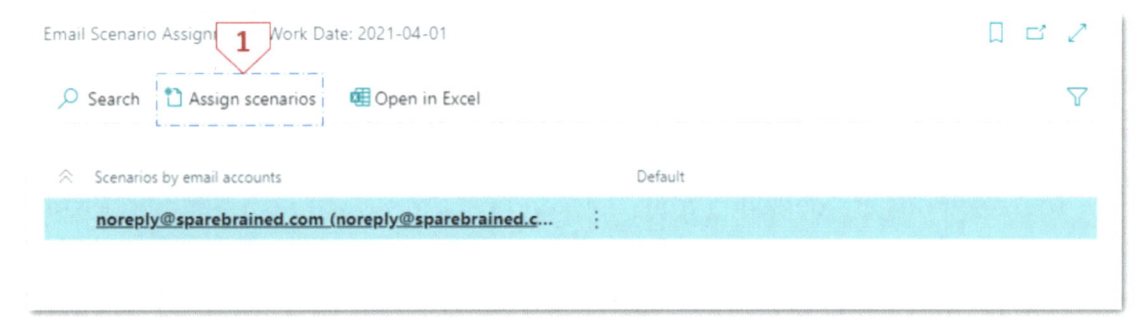

Figure 14-39 - Email Scenario Assignments - Assign Action

When you click **Assign scenarios** (**1**), you will be presented with a list to choose from. If your scenario is the same as mine, with a central email account, simply press Ctrl-A to select all rows (or select the top row, hold Shift, and click the last row):

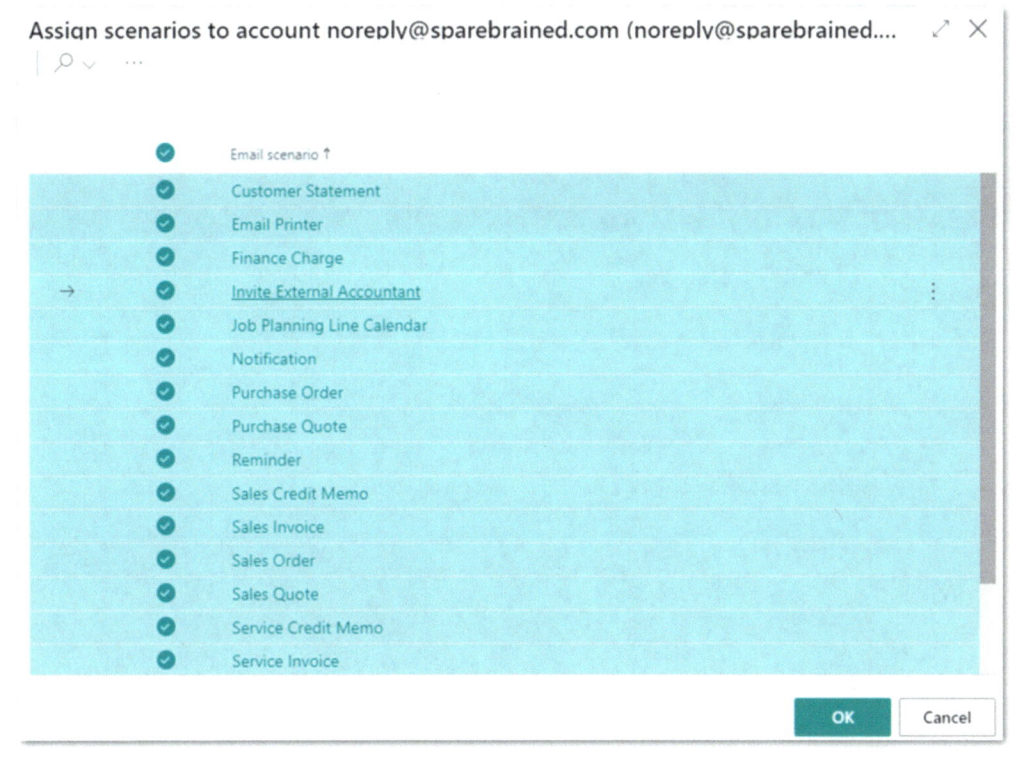

Figure 14-40 - Email Scenarios - Selecting Multiple

When you click **OK**, it will show the assignments per **Email Account**:

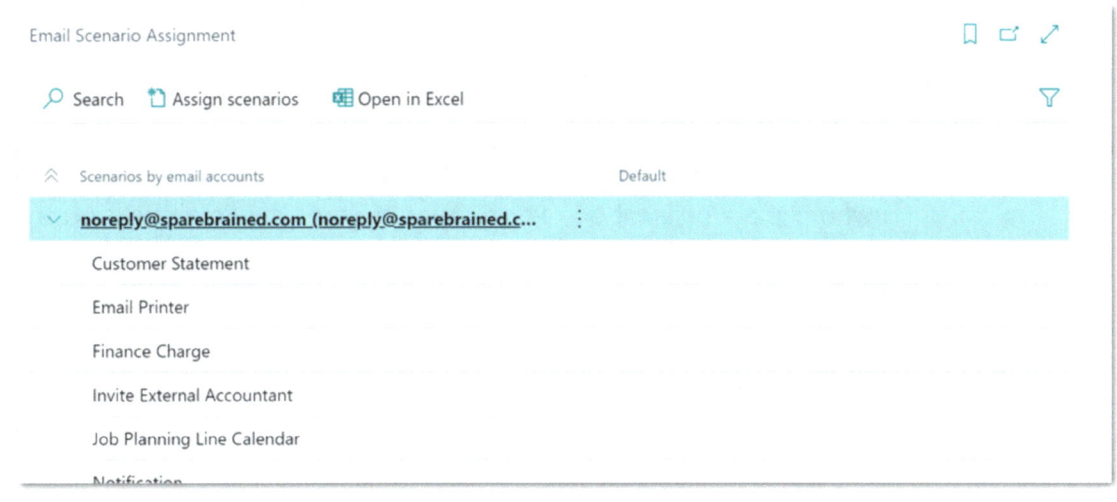

Figure 14-41 - Email Scenario Assignments - Assigned

DRAFTING EMAILS

When you **Send** (via Email) a purchase document, you are presented with an editor inside Business Central:

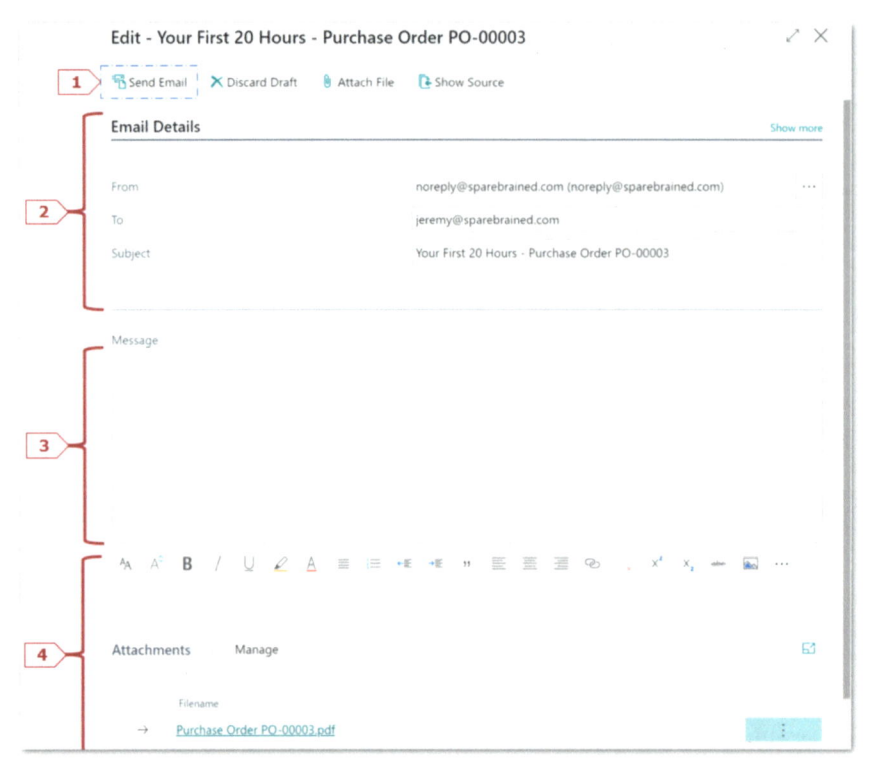

Figure 14-42 - Email Editor Window

The **Email Details** FastTab (**2**) gives the ability to:

- see (and possibly change) which **From** email to use.
- Set **To** whom the email will go, which defaults from the Email field on the purchase document.
- Behind the **Show more** functionality, you can also set **CC** and **BCC** values

Within the **Message** (**3**) editor, you can compose your email message.

The **Attachments** (**4**) area already has the PDF of the purchase document that you are sending. You can use the **Manage** button to add, and/or remove attachments as needed:

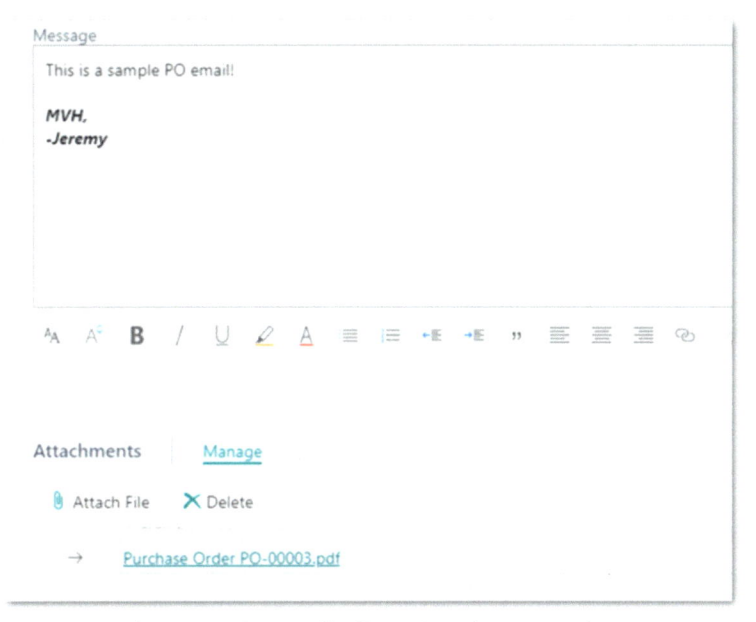

Figure 14-43 - Email Editor - Attachments Actions

Once you are done; click **Send** (**1**). Your recipient will receive the email with the content provided:

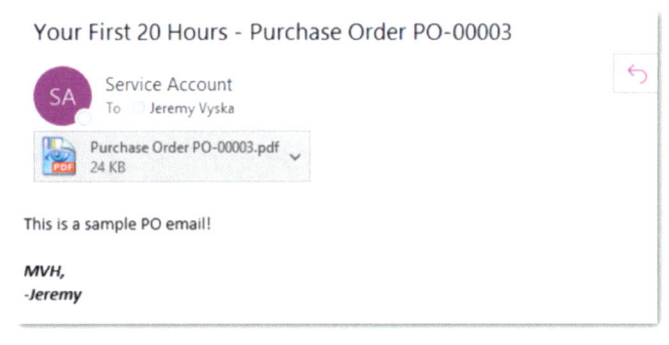

Figure 14-44 - Email Received!

SENT EMAILS

Part of the reason you send emails from Business Central through this system is that there is an archive of 🔍 **Sent Emails**, so you can be sure of who has sent documents, when documents were sent, and who received documents.

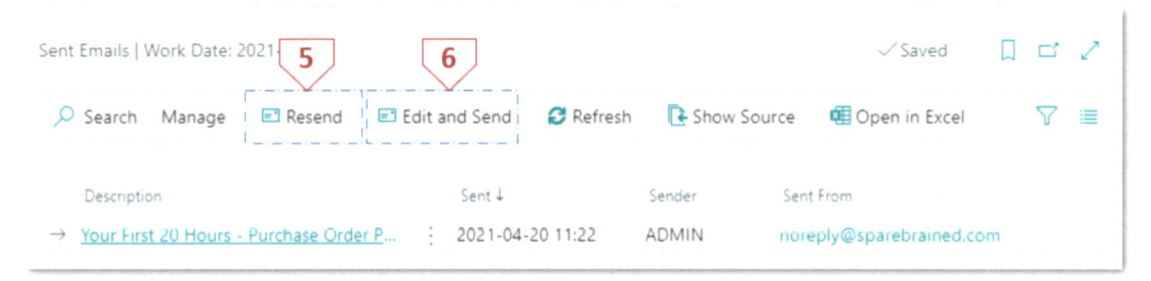

Figure 14-45 - Sent Emails List in Business Central

This shows the relevant information about the email, plus gives the ability to **Resend** (**5**); or **Edit and Send** (**6**), to send new versions of the same message.

Chapter 15: Selling

In this chapter, we are going to go over:

- Common ways to create Sales Orders, as well as how to ship and invoice them.
- How selling in another currency works.
- Creating and posting Invoices for multiple separate shipments.
- Adding package tracking information to shipment documents.
- Sending customer statements will be covered.

CREATING SALES ORDERS

The most obvious route to creating a new Sales Order (SO) is via the 🔍 **Sales Orders** list page, clicking the **New** (**1**) button:

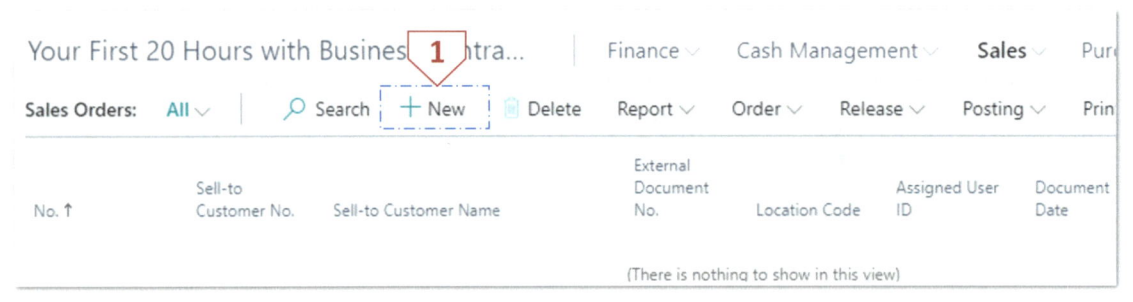

Figure 15-1 - Sales Order - Creating New from Sales Orders List

It is *also* possible to create new Sales Orders from other places in the system, including directly from the 🔍 **Customers** list itself (via **New Document** (**2**), then **Sales Order** (**3**)):

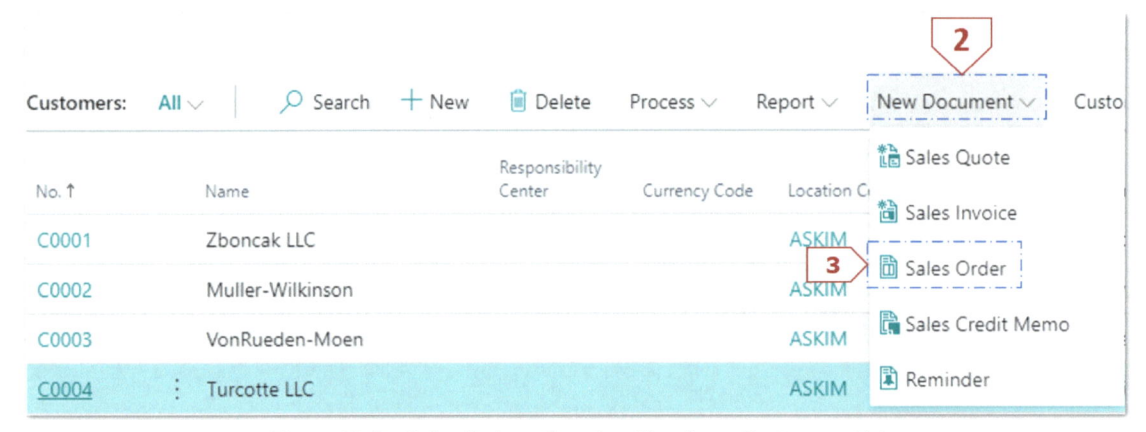

Figure 15-2 - Sales Order - Creating New from Customers List

When you create a new **Sales Order**, you will get a blank Document page:

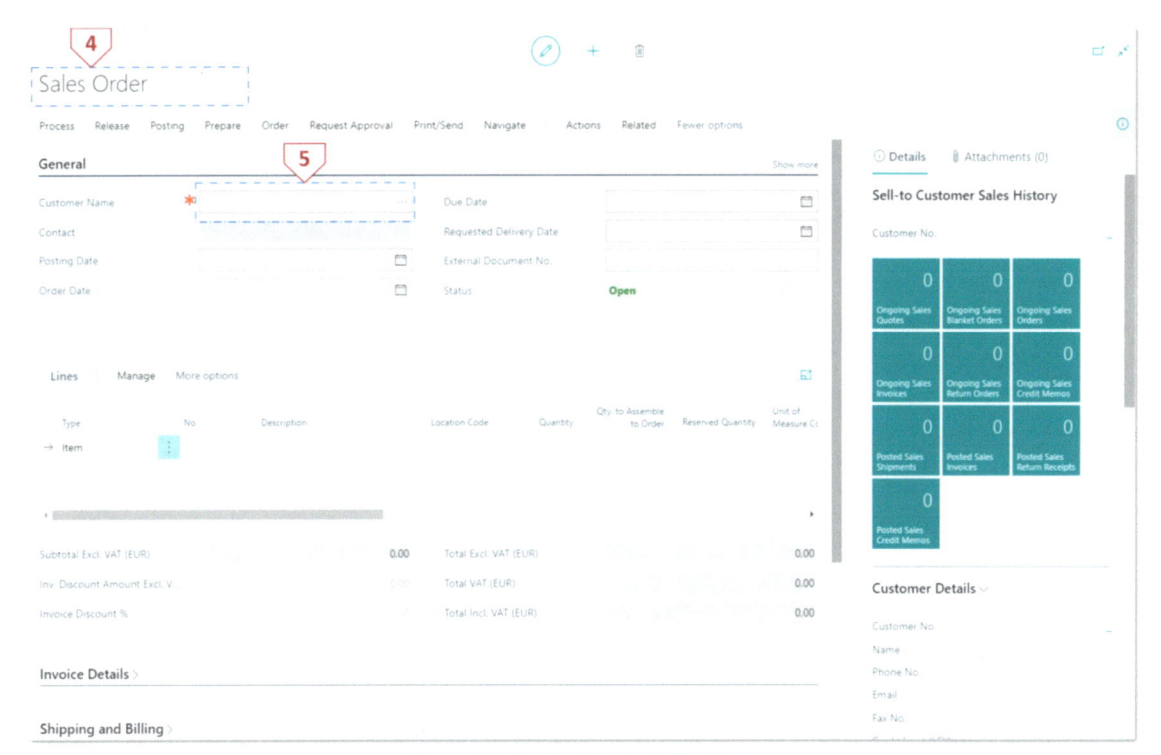

Figure 15-3 - An Empty Sales Order

The first field we will fill in is the **Customer Name** (**5**) field – we can either enter the **Name** of the customer, their customer **No.** value or click the ⋯ (AssistEdit) button to select the customer. As soon as we do that, the Sales Order is created:

PART 4: BASIC OPERATIONS
CHAPTER 15: SELLING

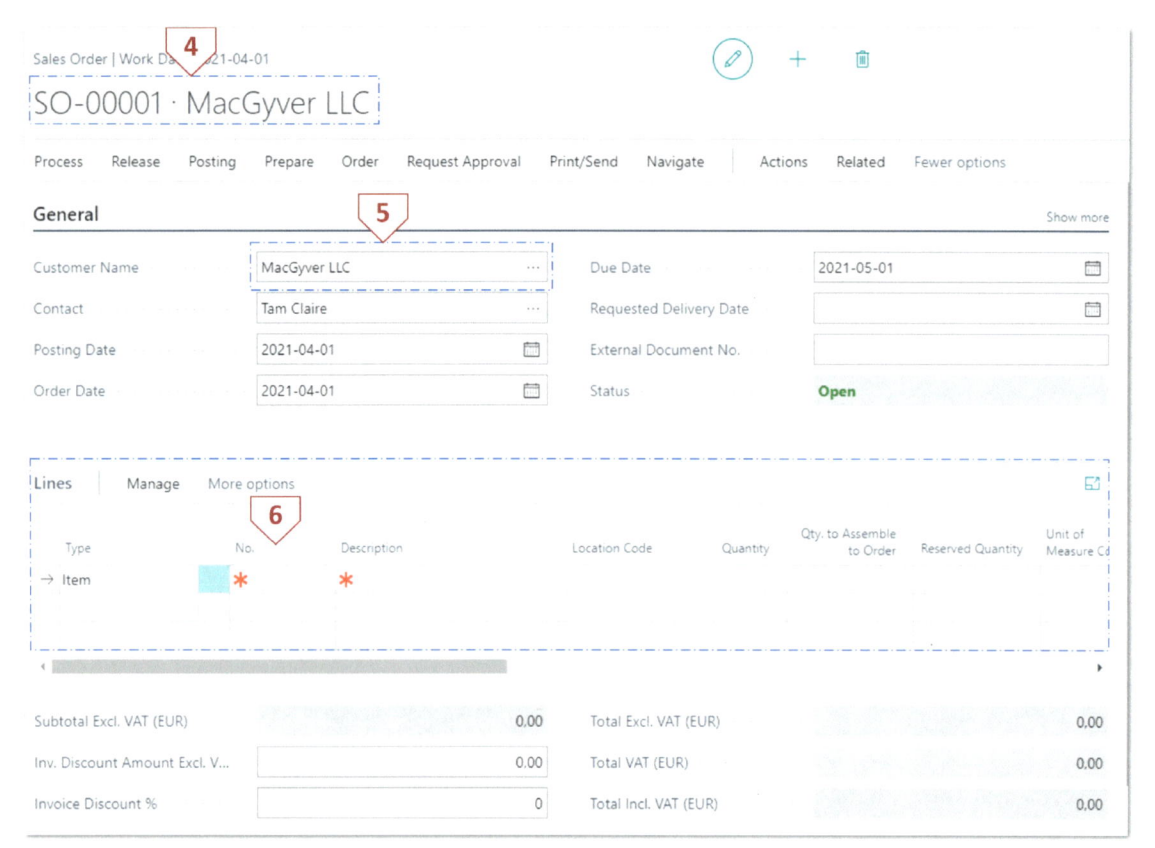

Figure 15-4 - Created Sales Order

We can see the main caption (**4**) of the page has been updated to reflect the **Sales Order No.**, and many other areas have updated their values with information from the vendor. (See more below)

In the **Lines** area, Since **Type** defaulted to **Item**, we can enter the item's **No.** (**6**), the **Description** of an item, or select from the list:

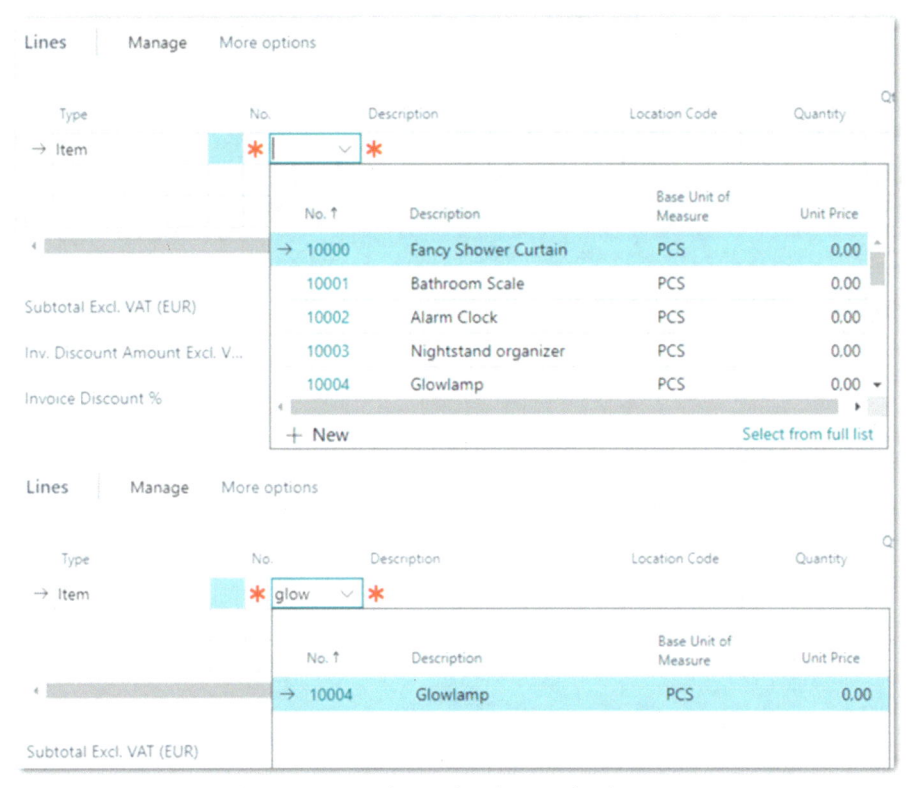

Figure 15-5 - Sales Order Line - Selecting Items

Then, when we enter the **Quantity** (**7**) on the line, other key fields will update:

Figure 15-6 - Sales Order - Entered Quantity, Missing Price

Unit Price Excl. VAT (**8**) would default from the Item Card, as would the **Line Amount Excl. VAT** (**9**) – however, there is an issue in our scenario:

ITEM PRICES

In our scenario, we had imported the Items, but the Items did not have a Unit Price assigned to them. Via the 🔍 **Items** list, opening the Item Card for the **10004 Glowlamp** and looking at the **Prices & Sales** FastTab, we can see the **Unit Price** (**10**) is missing a value:

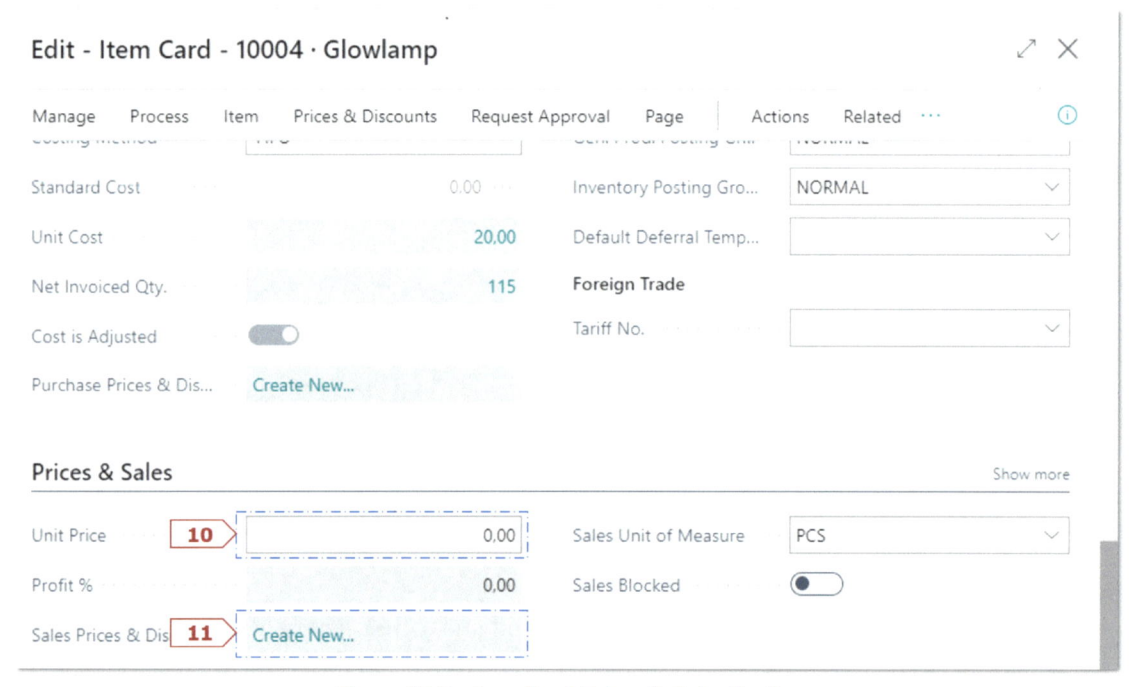

Figure 15-7 - Item Card, Prices & Sales Section

If you need to provide more complex pricing and discounts, such as special prices for customers or group of customers; the **Create New...** (**11**) link in **Sales Prices & Discounts** leads to a powerful *pricing engine*, this is, however, beyond the scope of this book.

After you set or change the **Unit Price** on the Item Card, you will need to manually assign the **Unit Price Excl. VAT** (**12**) on the Sales Order Lines:

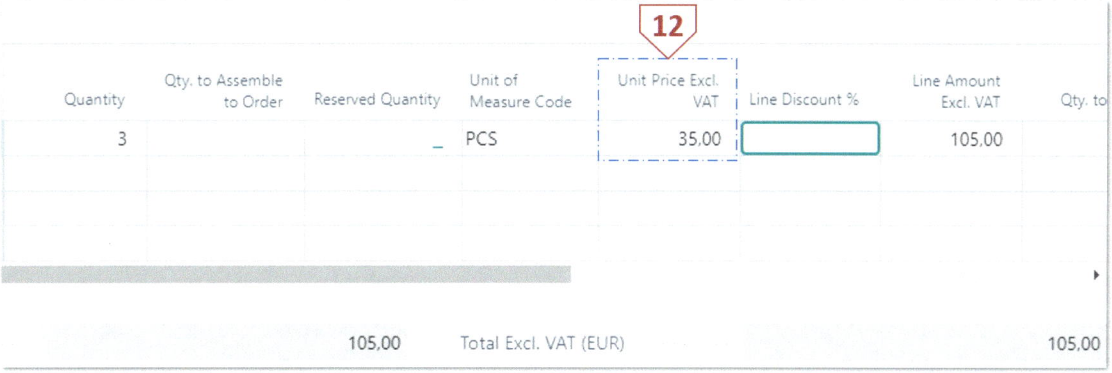

Quantity	Qty. to Assemble to Order	Reserved Quantity	Unit of Measure Code	Unit Price Excl. VAT	Line Discount %	Line Amount Excl. VAT	Qty. to
3		_	PCS	35,00		105,00	

105,00   Total Excl. VAT (EUR)   105,00

Figure 15-8 - Sales Order Line - Unit Price Set, Totals Updated

It is also possible to set manual prices as needed this way. (Note: Changing the Unit Price on an Item Card does not automatically update open Sales Orders)

Effectively, this is enough information to post the Sales Order *now*, but before we do that process, let us look deeper into the Sales Order.

PART 4: BASIC OPERATIONS
CHAPTER 15: SELLING

PAGE 241

Getting to Know the Sales Order

Looking at the FastTabs on the Sales Order page, there are many great features related to these fields, but many are beyond the scope of this book. Here are some of the highlights we can take the time to review:

General FastTab

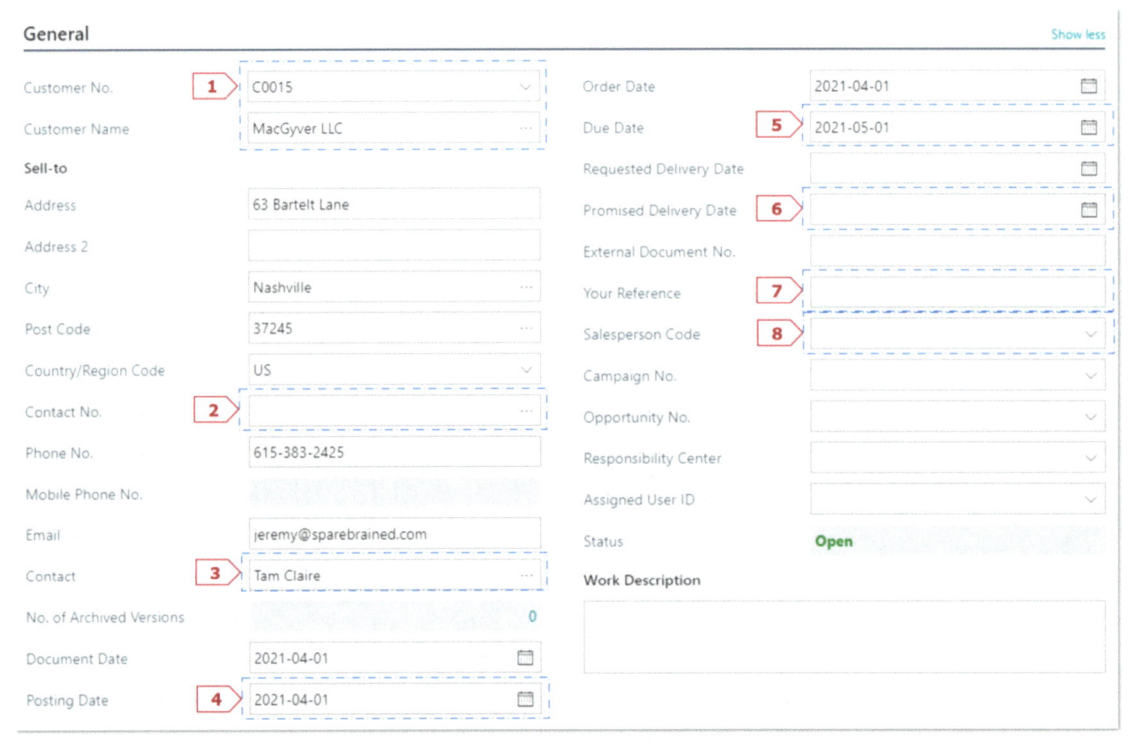

Figure 15-9 - Sales Order - General FastTab Expanded

Element	What is it?
1	The **Customer No.** and **Customer Name** are stored separately, even if in the condensed view, there appears to only be the Customer Name.
2	If you are using the CRM module, you may have a **Contact No.** for a customer to refer to.
3	If you are not using the CRM module, it is still good to be able to enter a **Contact**.
4	The **Posting Date** allows you post documents on dates that are not the current date.

242 PAGE

PART 4: BASIC OPERATIONS
CHAPTER 15: SELLING

5	The **Due Date** allows you to manually set a due date, rather than use the formula from the vendor's setup.
6	Sometimes you need to record when you have promised to deliver to a customer. While **Promised Delivery Date** is part of a great planning system for timing deliveries based on supply, you can also simply use it to record manual dates.
7	**Your Reference** is a free-form place to store extra information from the Customer about this order
8	Many organizations need to know which salesperson a Sales Order belongs to. The **Salesperson Code** field connects to a list of **Salespeople** in the system and defaults from the **Customer Card**, but you can also set it manually.

INVOICE DETAILS FASTTAB

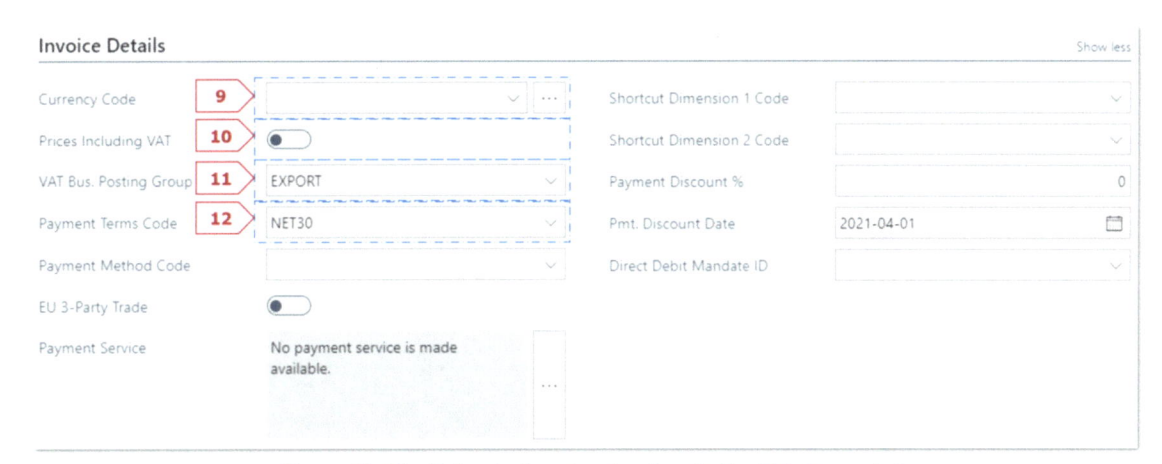

Figure 15-10 - Sales Order - Invoice Details FastTab Expanded

Element	What is it?
9	The **Currency Code** lets you choose a specific currency to use for this single document. It is defaulted from the Vendor Card.
10	The **Prices Including VAT** will change the VAT calculation to reflect the VAT impact.
11	The **VAT Bus. Posting Group** is seldom changed, but if you need to change which tax strategy to use on a *per-document* level, this is the field for it.

12 The **Payment Terms Code** allows you to select alternate methods of calculating the **Due Date**.

SHIPPING FASTTAB

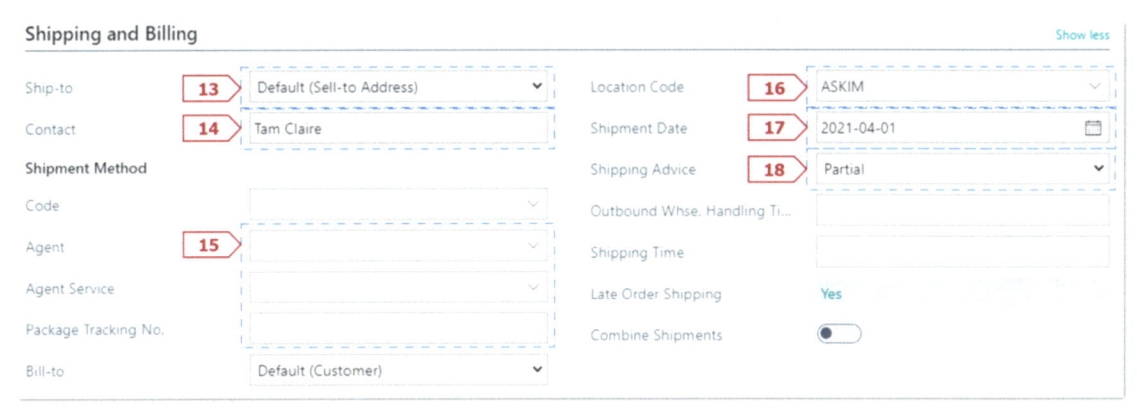

Figure 15-11 - Sales Order - Shipping and Billing FastTab Expanded

Element	What is it?
13	The **Ship-to** allows you to handle the many diverse needs of shipping to customers, including the customer's address, a separate list of customer **Ship-To Addresses**, or even custom address entry.
14	It can be helpful to be able to set a **Contact** for shipping separate from the person who ordered it.
15	While this book will not go into great detail on the **Shipping Agent** system, we will cover the very basics later on (in this chapter) because keeping the **Package Tracking No.** is very helpful.
16	While the **Location Code** defaults from the **Customer Card**, if you are using multiple Locations, you can choose to ship *from* different locations.
17	The **Shipment Date** allows you to set the date a package is shipped.
18	The **Shipping Advice** setting is a part of a complex topic, but by toggling between *Partial* or *Complete*, you can control if people are allowed to ship individual portions of the order separately.

SALES LINE DETAILS - FACTBOX

While not one of the *FastTabs* on the **Sales Order**, when you have set a Line to an **Item**, there is some great information in the **Sales Line Details** FactBox:

The **Item No.** (**1**) is a great way to quickly drill-down to the Item Card for the item on the current line.

The **Item Availability** (**2**) is a complex calculation, since it takes into account the stock, shipping demand, and more, based on the Shipment Date.

Scheduled Receipt (**3**) will show expected receipts based on open Purchase Orders.

While this book will not go into details about **Substitutions** (**4**) or the **Sales Prices** & **Sales Line Discounts** (**5**) functionality, they are very helpful and worth learning about!

Figure 15-12 - Sales Order - Sales Line Details FactBox

PAGE 246   PART 4: BASIC OPERATIONS
CHAPTER 15: SELLING

SENDING SALES ORDERS

It is very common to need to send documents to customers. This works almost identically to the process of sending purchase documents.

When you need to send Sales Orders, there is a **Print/Send** (**1**) feature in the action bar:

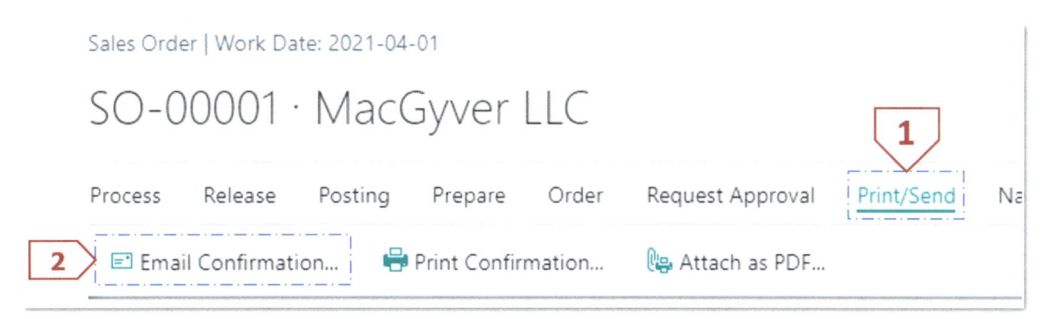

Figure 15-13 - Sales Order - Email Confirmation

The **Email Confirmation...** (**2**) option will open the Email Editor (see **Email Scenarios** in **Chapter 14** if you get an error at this step):

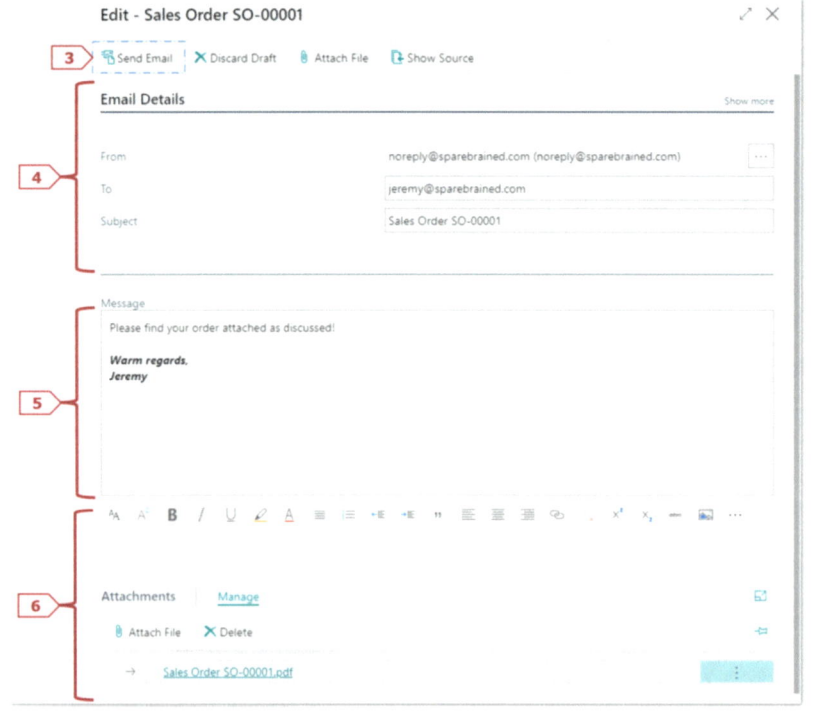

Figure 15-14 - Sales Order - Send Email Window

The **Email Details** FastTab (**4**) gives the ability to:

- see (and possibly change) which **From** email to use.
- set who the email will go **To**, which defaults from the Email field on the purchase document.
- Behind the **Show more** functionality, you can also set **CC** and **BCC** values.

Within the **Message** (**5**) editor, you can compose your email message.

The **Attachments** (**6**) area already has the PDF of the purchase document you are sending. You can use the **Manage** button to add and remove more attachments as needed.

Once you are done, click **Send** (**3**). Your recipient will receive the email with the body and attachments selected:

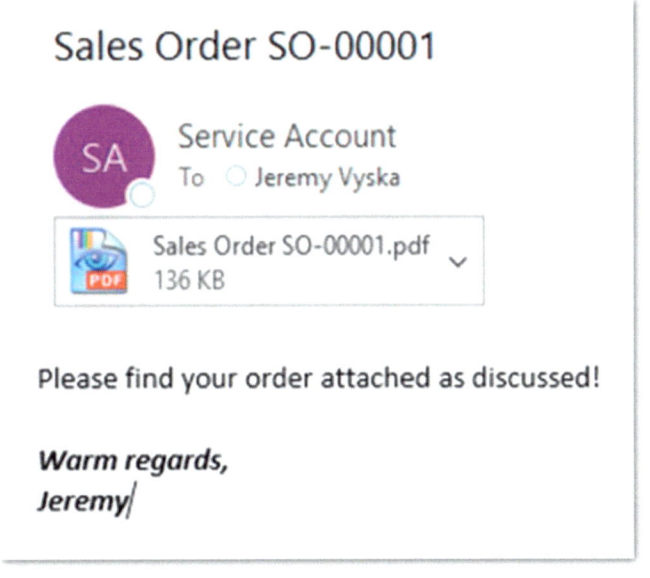

Figure 15-15 - Sales Order Email Received

SENT EMAILS

Part of the reason you send emails from Business Central through this system is that there is an archive of **Sent Emails** so you can be sure of who has been sent documents:

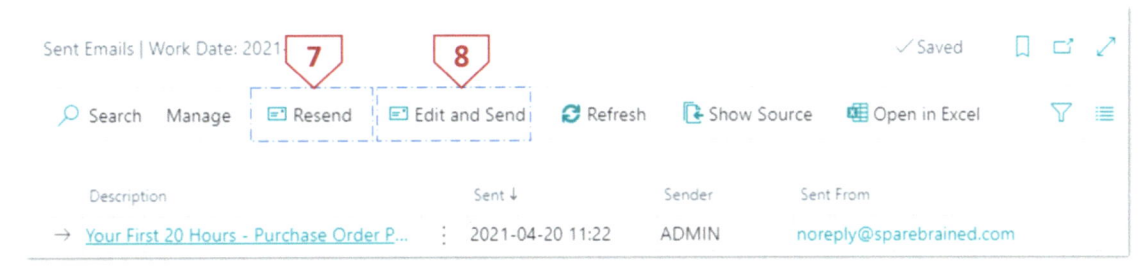

Figure 15-16 - Sent Emails Archive in Business Central

This shows the relevant information about the email, plus gives the ability to **Resend** (**7**) or **Edit and Send** (**8**) to send new versions of the same message.

PART 4: BASIC OPERATIONS
CHAPTER 15: SELLING

POSTING & REVIEW

Once you are done with your Sales Order, you primarily perform two different operations:

- Ship the items from Inventory.
- Register the Invoice to the Customer.

You *can* combine them into a single step; these options are available via the Post operation, under **Posting** (**1**) as **Post...** (**2**):

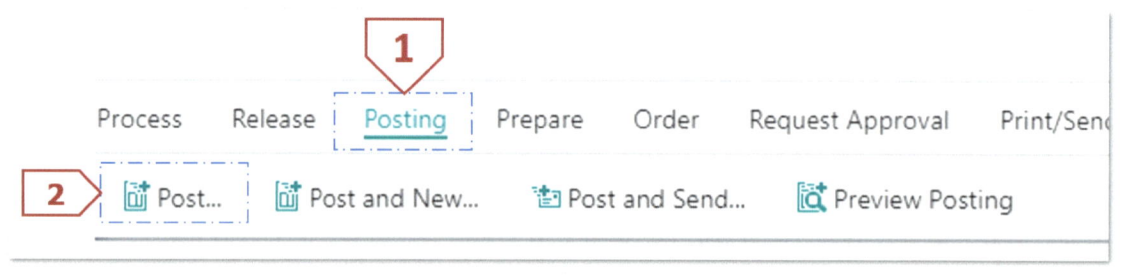

Figure 15-17 - Sales Order - Post Action

This will present you with a menu to select which combination of the operations you would like to execute:

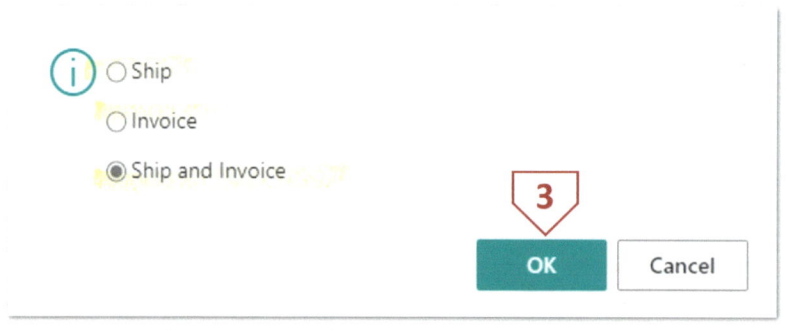

Figure 15-18 - Sales Order - Post Type Selection

When you click **OK** (**3**) with **Ship and Invoice** selected, Business Central will do the following:

- Register a Posted Sales Shipment.
- Register a Posted Sales Invoice.
- If there are no more lines with any unshipped quantity, the Sales Order is removed.

250 PAGE

PART 4: BASIC OPERATIONS
CHAPTER 15: SELLING

- Then, you are asked if you would like to open the Posted Sales Invoice:

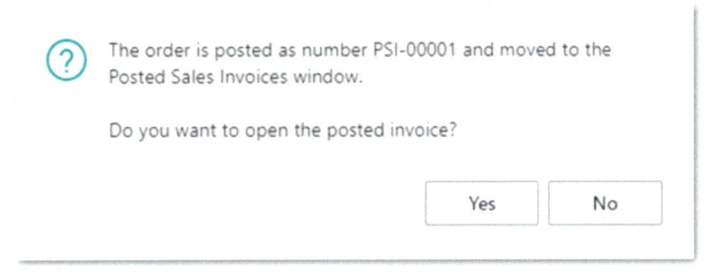

Figure 15-19 - Sales Order - Post Complete Confirmation

If you click **Yes**, you will be taken directly to the **Posted Sales Invoice**:

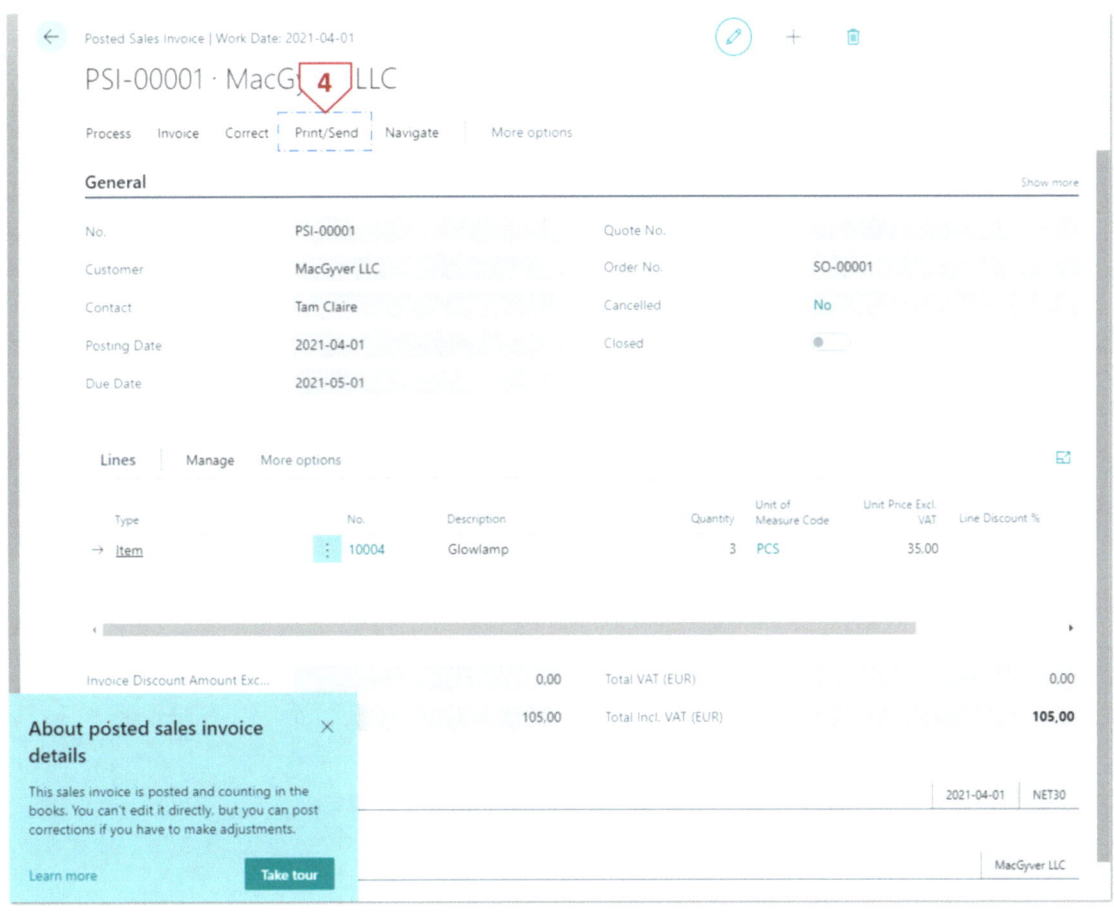

Figure 15-20 - Posted Sales Invoice

PART 4: BASIC OPERATIONS
CHAPTER 15: SELLING

As you can see, the **Posted Sales Invoice** is very similar to the **Sales Order**. Here, you can also **Print/Send** (**4**) the invoice again.

> **ⓘ** Note: In the bottom left is a new feature to Business Central as of Spring of 2021, the embedded Tour feature. This functionality is probably going to expand throughout the product in future releases.

REVIEWING THE POSTING RESULTS

This is a good time to look at the results of posting the Sales Order in the **Invoice** mode.

The best place to start reviewing this result is in the **Customer Ledger Entries**, which you can quickly get to from a **Posted Sales Invoice** by clicking: **Navigate** (**1**) -> **Customer** (**2**) – which takes you to the Customer Card – and then clicking **Customer** (**3**), you get to the **Ledger Entries** (**4**):

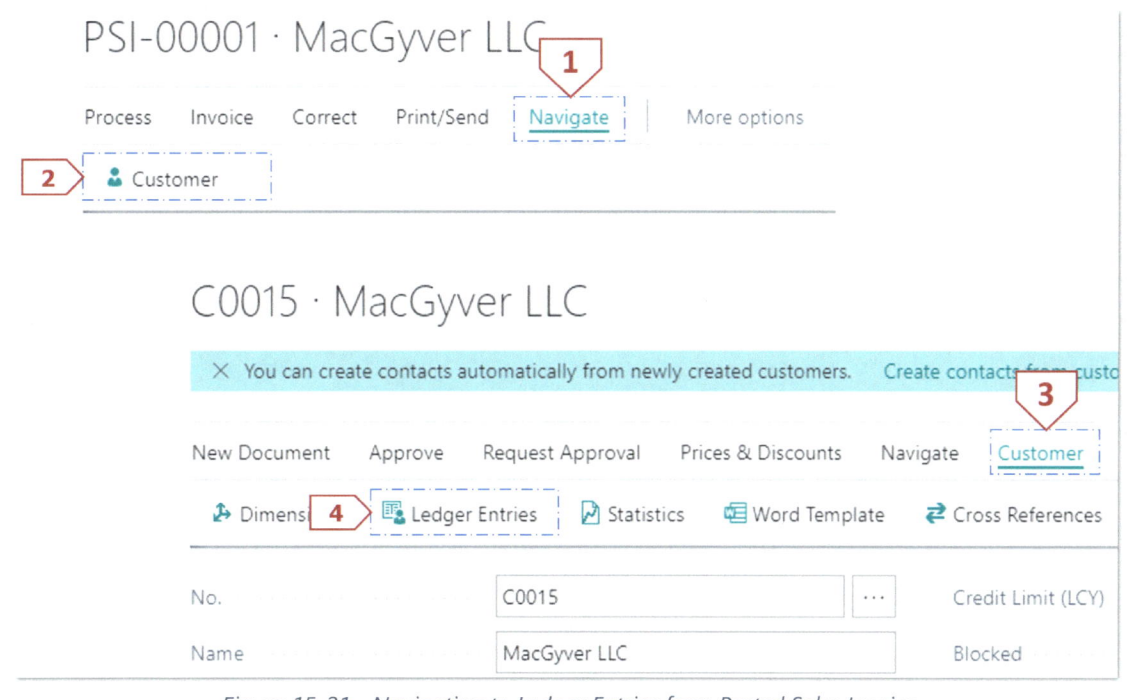

Figure 15-21 - Navigating to Ledger Entries from Posted Sales Invoice

This will show you all Ledger Entries for the specific customer, which in our scenario, includes only two – the opening balance (from **Chapter 12**) and the new Sales Invoice just posted:

PART 4: BASIC OPERATIONS
CHAPTER 15: SELLING

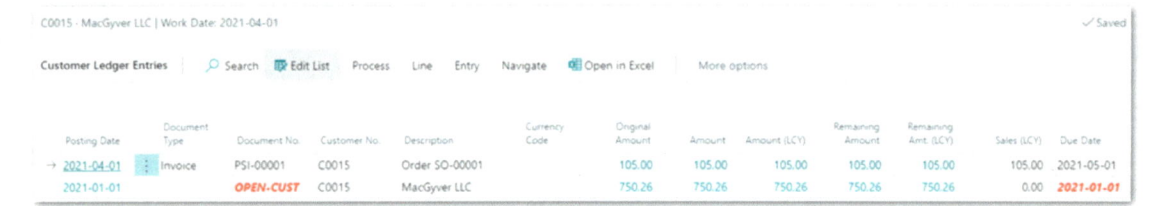

Figure 15-22 - Posted Sales Invoice in Customer Ledger Entries

With this entry selected, we can also click on **Entry** (**5**) -> **Find Entries...** (**6**) to see a list of all the related ledger entries throughout the system for this **Document No.**:

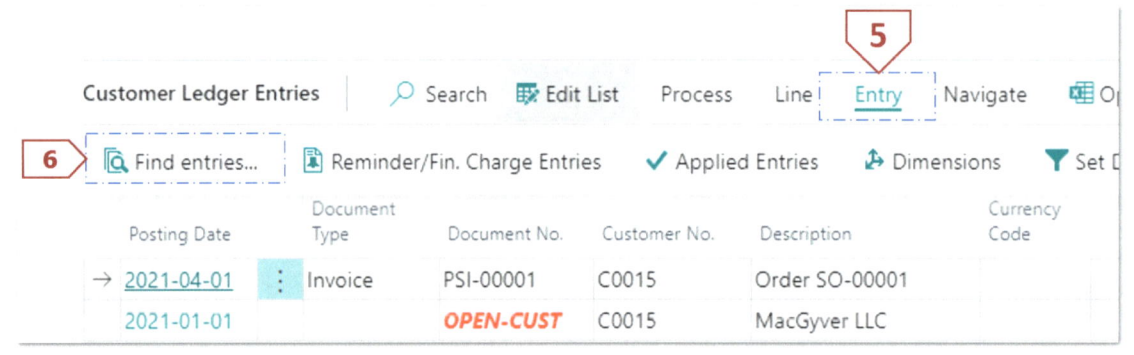

Figure 15-23 - Customer Ledger Entries - Find Related Entries

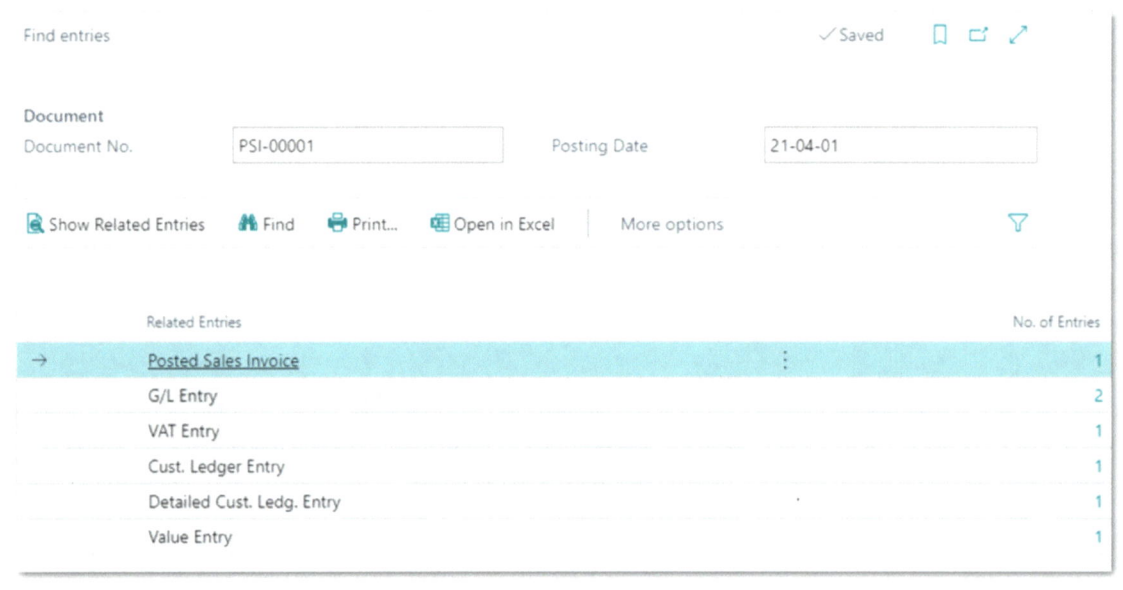

Figure 15-24 - Find Entries List for a Posted Sales Invoice

As you can see, we have the **Posted Sales Invoice**. We get 2 entries to the Financials' main ledger (the G/L Entry) along with a VAT Entry. We will get some entries related to both the Inventory (Value Entry) and Sales (Cust. Ledger Entry, Detailed Cust. Ledg. Entry).

On all these **Related Entries** lines, you can click on the **No. of Entries** field to drill-down and see the details behind them.

Drilling-down on the **2** for **G/L Entry**, you would see:

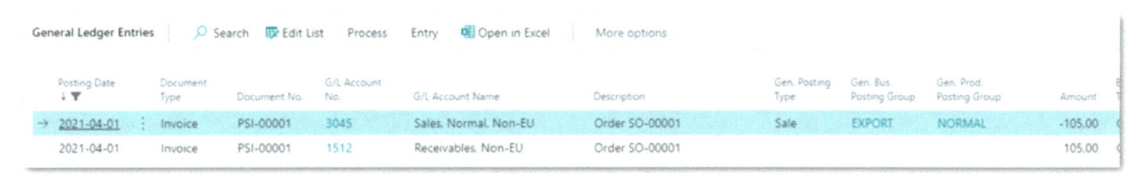

Figure 15-25 - Find Entries - G/L Entries List

Here we sold a **NORMAL** (non-seasonal) to an export customer, so the Sales is posted to the G/L Account for the **Sales, Normal, Non-EU**. We also get a new entry to our **Receivables, Non-EU**.

Selling in Another Currency

One of the great strengths of Business Central is the multicurrency functionality. To demonstrate this, we will sell an **Item** with a **Unit Price** (**1**) of **90** (in EUR, our system's local currency) to a **Customer** we have marked with the **Currency Code** (**2**) **SEK**:

No. ↑ ▼	Description	Type	Inventory	Substi... Exist	Assem... BOM	Base Unit of Measure	Cost is Adj...	Unit Cost	Unit Price
10005	Small rug	Inventory	12	No	No	PCS	☑	60.00	90.00

Customer Card | Work Date: 2021-04-01

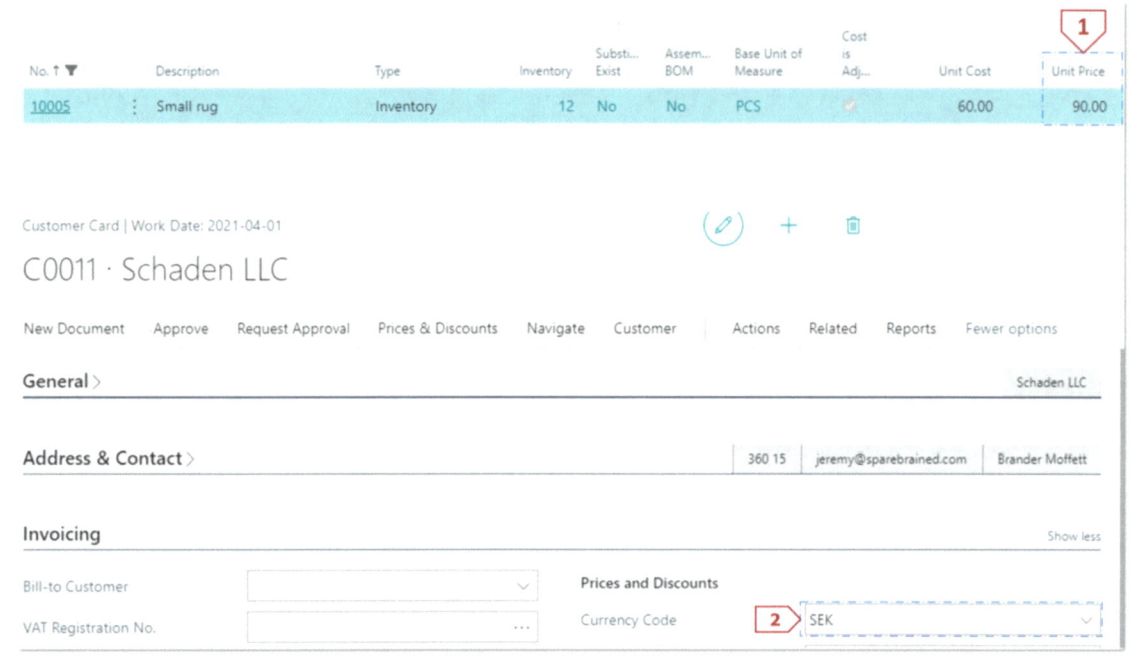

C0011 · Schaden LLC

New Document Approve Request Approval Prices & Discounts Navigate Customer | Actions Related Reports Fewer options

General >   Schaden LLC

Address & Contact >   360 15   jeremy@sparebrained.com   Brander Moffett

Invoicing   Show less

Bill-to Customer   [∨]   Prices and Discounts
VAT Registration No.   [...]   Currency Code   (**2**) [SEK   ∨]

Figure 15-26 - Item List Showing Price and Customer Card with Currency Code

When we create a new **Sales Order** for this Customer, the Sales Order will also be marked as **Currency Code** of **SEK**. Then, when we put the **10005 Item** on the **Line**:

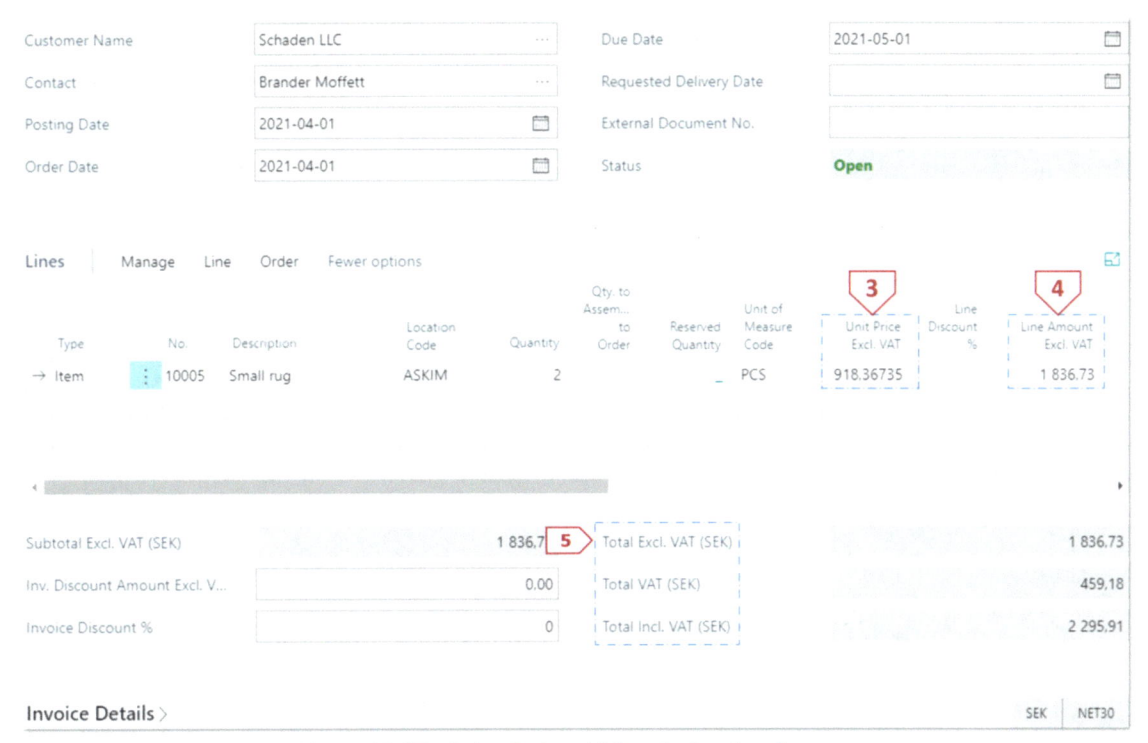

Figure 15-27 - Sales Order - Values in Another Currency

We can see that we get the **Unit Price Excl. VAT** (**3**) as **918,36735**. Multiplied by our current **Quantity** 2, we get the **Line Amount Excl. VAT** (**4**) of 1836,73, which is rounded based on the currency rounding settings. (see Chapter 10 - Currencies)

The **Totals** (**5**) are now also marked as **(SEK)** to help you know which currency this order is written in.

To see the value of this order in our currency, EUR, we need to look at the **Order Statistics**:

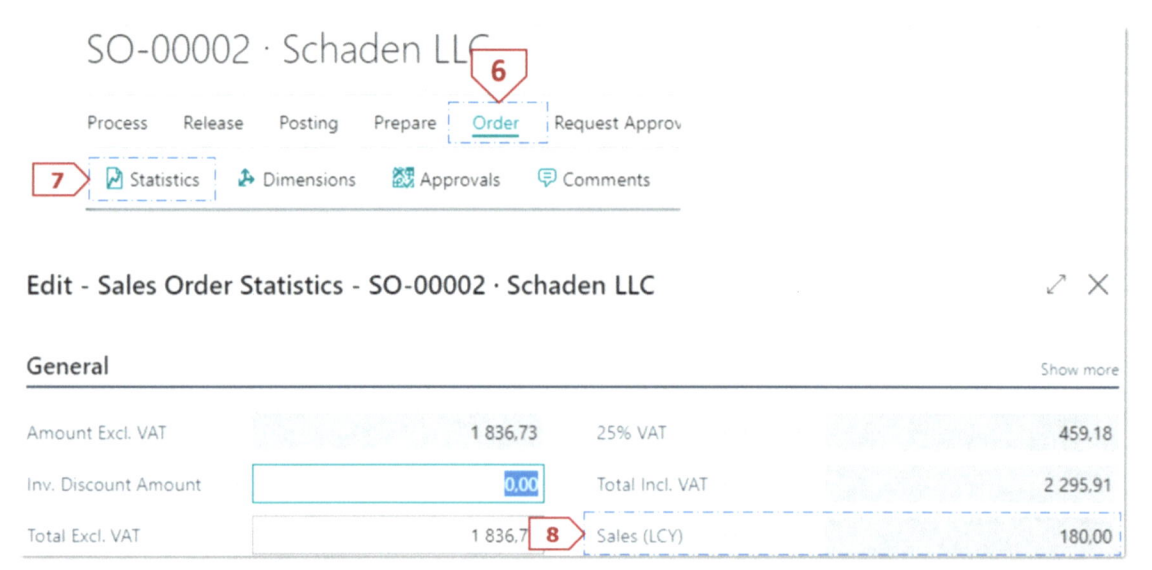

Figure 15-28 - Sales Order Statistics - Alternate Currency

Clicking on **Order** (**6**) -> **Statistics** (**7**), you will see the **Sales Order Statistics** page, which includes the **Sales (LCY)** (**8**) to show you the value in your local currency.

When this Sales Order is invoiced, if we review the **G/L Entries** (following the Review steps from above to **Preview Posting**):

Figure 15-29 - Sales Order - Posting Preview - G/L Entries

We can see that the **Amount** (**9**) is all registered in local currency values (**EUR**). However, if we review the **Customer Ledger Entries**, we will see:

Figure 15-30 - Posted Sales Invoice with Alternate Currency in Customer Ledger Entries

The line marked **SEK** and the *Amount* (**10**) is shown in the **SEK** amounts, but the *Amount (LCY)* (**11**) is shown in the system currency (**EUR**).

This is all about context – when you are looking at your financials, you need to know the information in the context of your currency. When discussing sales history or open balances with customers, they need the information in their *own* currency.

SALES – PARTIAL SHIPPING

Sometimes you need to be able to send specific portions of a **Sales Order** to a customer in multiple shipments. To demonstrate this, we will work with a Sales Order with two sets of 1 patio table, and 4 chairs, per set:

Type	No.	Description	Location Code	Quantity	Qty. to Assem. to Order	Reserved Quantity	Unit of Measure Code	Unit Price Excl. VAT	Line Discount %	Line Amount Excl. VAT
Item	10012	Patio table	ASKIM	2		_	PCS	110.00		220.00
→ Item	10013	Patio chair	ASKIM	8		_	PCS	79.00		632.00

Figure 15-31 - Sales Order Lines with Multiple Items

If we scroll the **Lines** to the right, we will see some additional fields, including the one needed, the **Qty. to Ship** (**1**) field:

Type	No.	Description	Location Code	Quantity	Qty. to Assem. to Order	Reserved Quantity	Unit of Measure Code	Unit Price Excl. VAT	Line Discount %	Line Amount Excl. VAT
Item	10012	Patio table	ASKIM	2		_	PCS	110.00		220.00
→ Item	10013	Patio chair	ASKIM	8		_	PCS	79.00		632.00

Figure 15-32 - Sales Order Lines - Set Partial Quantity to Ship

This is an editable field to set *how many of a line* will be shipped when we **Post** the Sales Order. With 1 (of 2) of the first line and 4 (of 8) of the second line, when we **Post** and **Ship** the sales order, the Lines will be updated:

Lines	Manage	Line	Order	Fewer options					2	3	
Type		Quantity	Qty. to Assem... to Order	Reserved Quantity	Unit of Measure Code	Unit Price Excl. VAT	Line Discount %	Line Amount Excl. VAT	Qty. to Ship	Quantity Shipped	Qty. to Invoice
→ Item	⋮	2		_	PCS	110,00		220,00	1	1	2
Item		8		_	PCS	79,00		632,00	4	4	8

Figure 15-33 - Sales Order Lines - Partially Shipped

Qty. to Ship (**2**) is reset to the remaining quantity so the order is ready to ship again.

Quantity Shipped (**3**) now reflects how many have already been shipped.

The **Qty. to Invoice** remains set to the total Quantity of the line (see Combined Invoicing below), as we have not yet invoiced any.

For use in the next section, the remaining set of lines should be **Post**ed with the **Ship** option.

SALES – COMBINED INVOICING

Multiple shipments and orders can be combined onto a single **Posted Sales Invoice**. To better demonstrate this, we will create another Sales Order for the customer used in "Partial Shipping" above, this time doing **Post** and **Ship** on a batch of cutting boards:

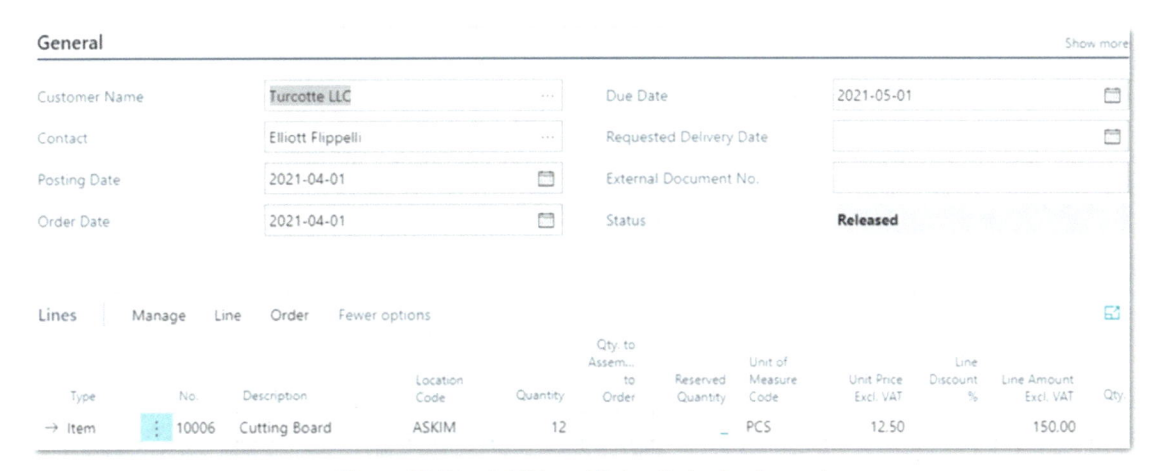

Figure 15-34 - Additional Sales Order for Example

You will notice that in the **Sell-To Customer Sales History** FactBox on the **Sales Order**, there are some interesting values:

The **Ongoing Sales Orders** (**1**) shows the two open Sales Orders for this customer.

The **Posted Sales Shipments** (**2**) shows that we now have 3 separate shipments we have posted.

The **Posted Sales Invoices** (**3**) shows that we have nothing yet.

Sell-to Customer Sales History

Customer No.

0	0	**2**
Ongoing Sales Quotes	Ongoing Sales Blanket Orders	Ongoing Sales Orders
0	0	0
On**2**es Invo	On**3**es Retu...ers	Ongoing Sales Credit Memos
3	0	0
Posted Sales Shipments	Posted Sales Invoices	Posted Sales Return Receipts

Figure 15-35 - Sales Order - Sell-to Customer Sales History

To combine multiple shipments onto a single Posted Sales Invoice, you will need to:

- Create a new **Sales Invoice** for the Customer.
- Use the **Get Shipment Lines** action to fetch the shipments onto the Invoice.
- Post the Sales Invoice.

To create the Sales Invoice, either via the **New** (**4**) button from the **Sales Invoices** list, or through the **New Document** (**5**) **Sales Invoice** (**6**) from the **Customer**:

PART 4: BASIC OPERATIONS
CHAPTER 15: SELLING

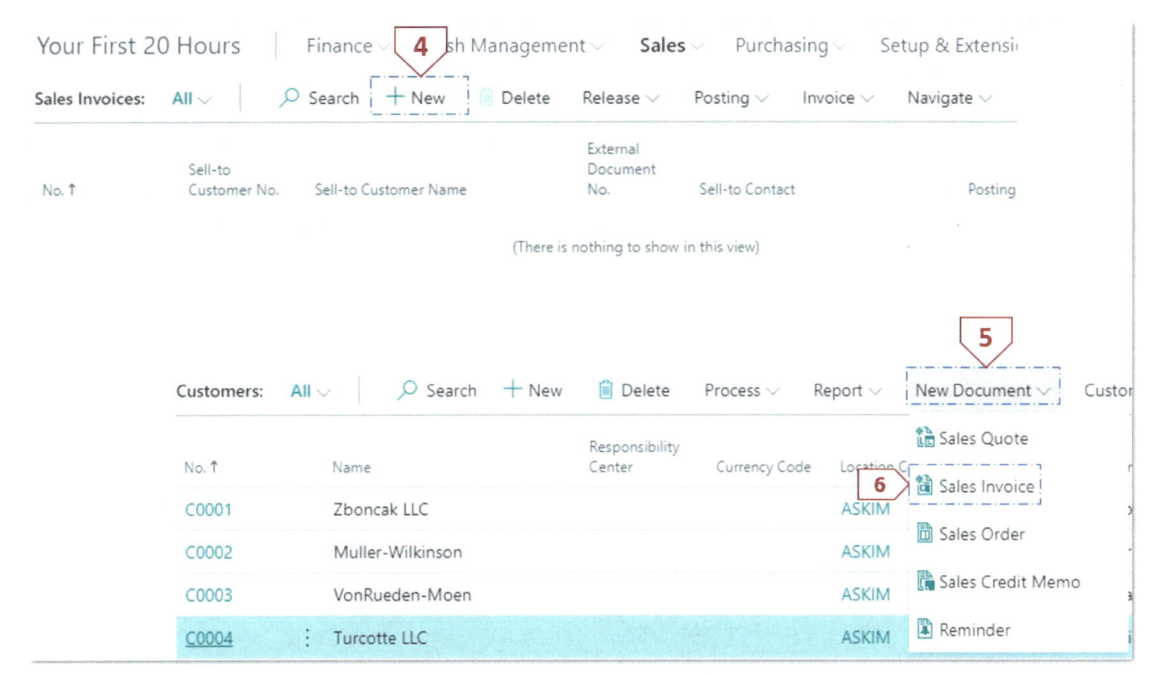

Figure 15-36 - Creating a new Sales Invoice

The **Sales Invoice** looks *almost* identical to the Sales Order:

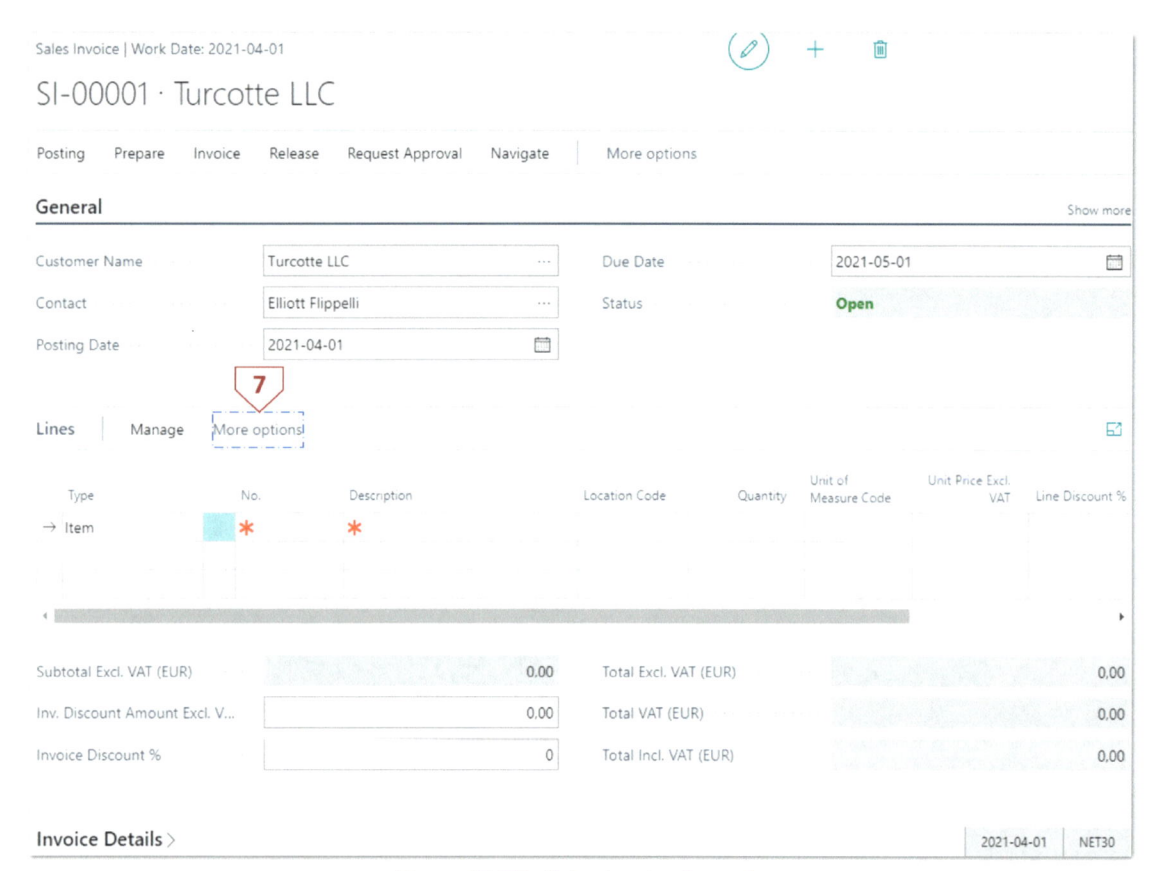

Figure 15-37 - Sales Invoice Example

To perform the **Get Shipment Lines** action to select which lines to invoice, click **Line** (**8**) (you may have to click **More options** (**7**)) -> **Functions** (**9**) -> **Get Shipment Lines…** (**10**)

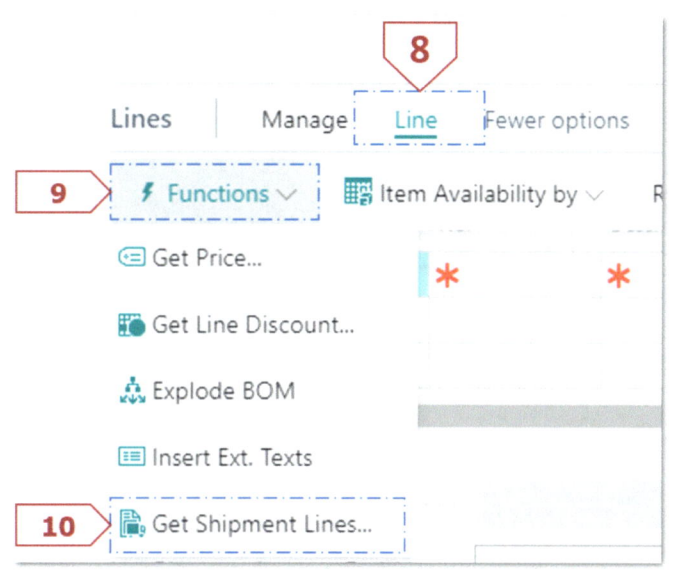

Figure 15-38 - Sales Invoice Lines - Get Shipment Lines Function

This action will open the **Get Shipment Lines** window:

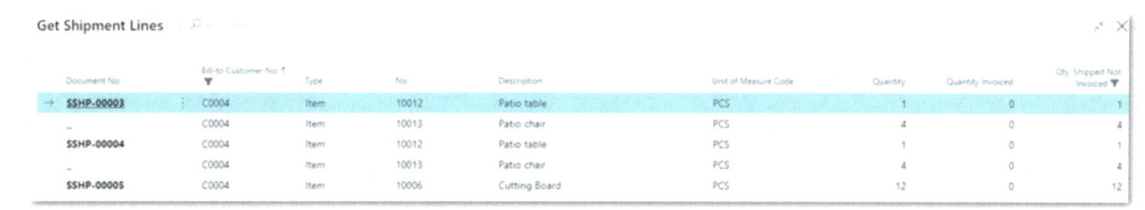

Figure 15-39 - Get Shipment Lines

This will show you a list of all shipments for that customer that have not been invoiced yet. In our scenario, we want to take all the lines, so, we will use Ctrl-A to select all, but you can also hold down control to click on each line you want. When you click **OK**, the Lines will be updated:

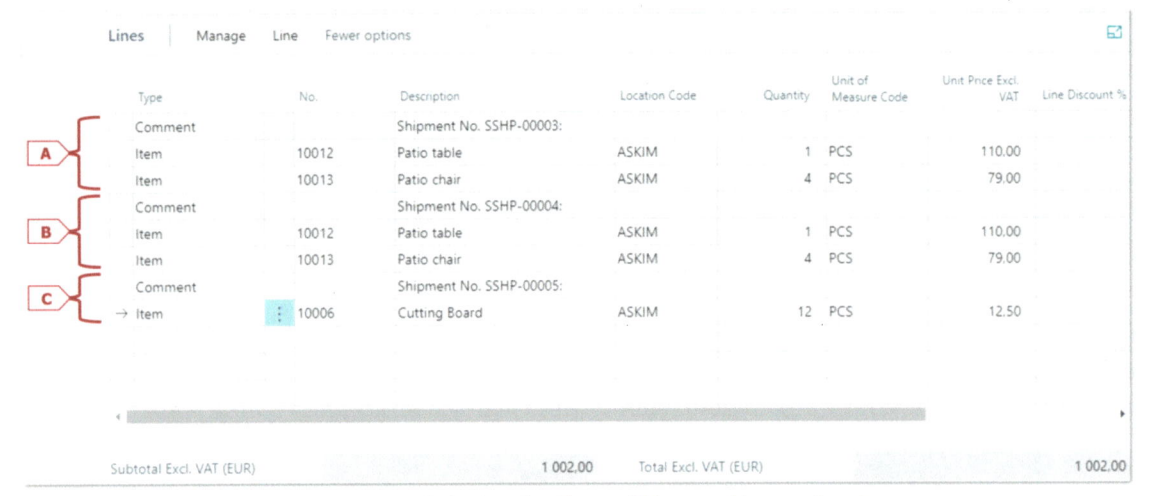

Figure 15-40 - Sales Invoice Lines - Shipment Lines to Invoice

Each of the three open shipments (**A**, **B** and **C**) are brought in, with a **Comment** line to indicate which shipment each set of lines comes from.

When you **Post** the Sales Invoice, it will register as a single entry in the **Customer Ledger Entries**:

Figure 15-41 - Posted Sales Invoice in Customer Ledger Entries

ADDING TRACKING TO A POSTED SHIPMENT

It is very common to want to keep a record of what tracking number is associated with a **Posted Sales Shipment**, but you might not have the tracking number at the time of posting.

If you want to locate a 🔍 **Posted Sales Shipment**, you can open **Process** (**1**) -> **Update Document** (**2**):

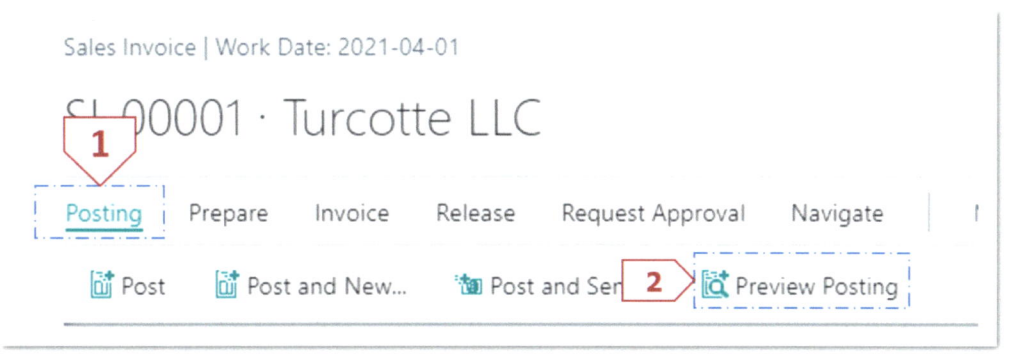

Figure 15-42 - Posted Sales Shipment - Update Document Process

This will allow you to update a limited amount of shipping information after the fact:

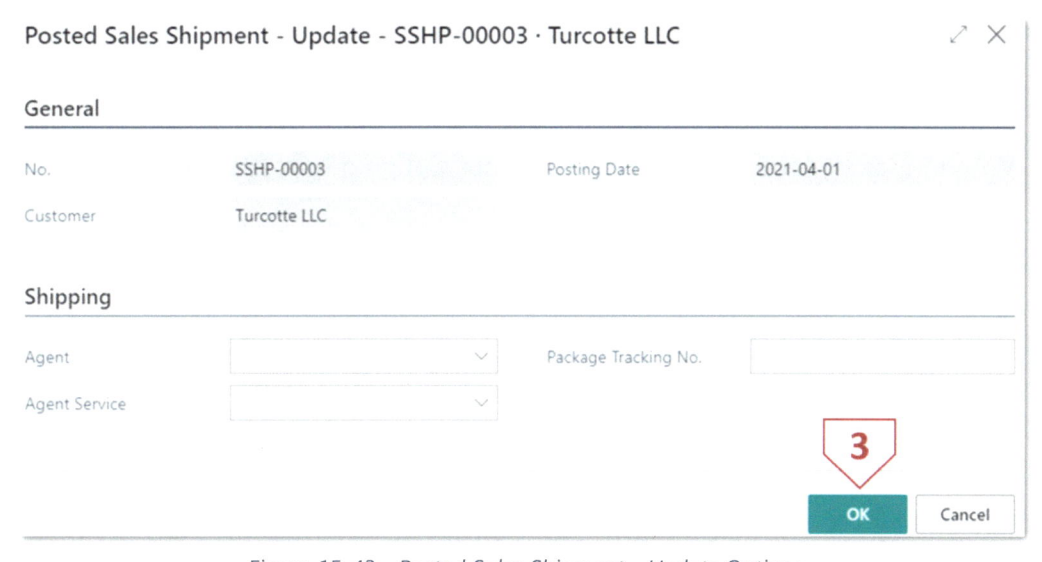

Figure 15-43 - Posted Sales Shipment - Update Options

ASIDE: SHIPPING AGENTS

While this book will not go into too much detail about **Shipping Agents**, setting up at least the basic 🔍 **Shipping Agents** information enables the use of the **Track Package** functionality.

You may need a partner's assistance, but here is an example for PostNord (a shipping company in the Nordics):

Code ↑	Name	Package Tracking URL
→ POSTNORD	PostNord	https://tracking.postnord.com/?id=%1

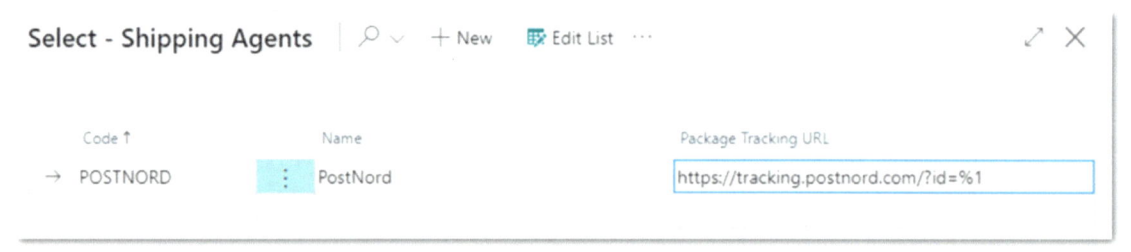

Figure 15-44 - Shipping Agents Example

In the **Package Tracking URL**, most shipping companies have some web-based tracking system that takes a package tracking number. Enter **%1** as a special kind of marker to substitute the **Package Tracking No.** In the PostNord example:

```
https://tracking.postnord.com/?id=%1
```

This will automatically turn into the right URL when we Track Package with ID of **ABC123**:

```
https://tracking.postnord.com/?id=ABC123
```

With the Agent configured, we can enter our shipping formation:

Shipping

Agent	POSTNORD	Package Tracking No.	LX▓▓▓▓▓US

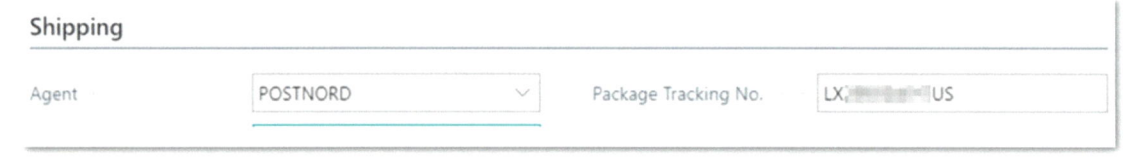

Figure 15-45 - Posted Sales Shipment - Example of Update Settings

We can click **OK** (**3**) and the Posted Sales Shipment is updated with the new information about the shipment. Now on the 🔍 **Posted Sales Shipment**, we can use the **Process** (**4**) to **Track Package** (**5**):

Posted Sales Shipment | Work Date: 2021-04-01

SSHP-00003 · Turcotte LLC

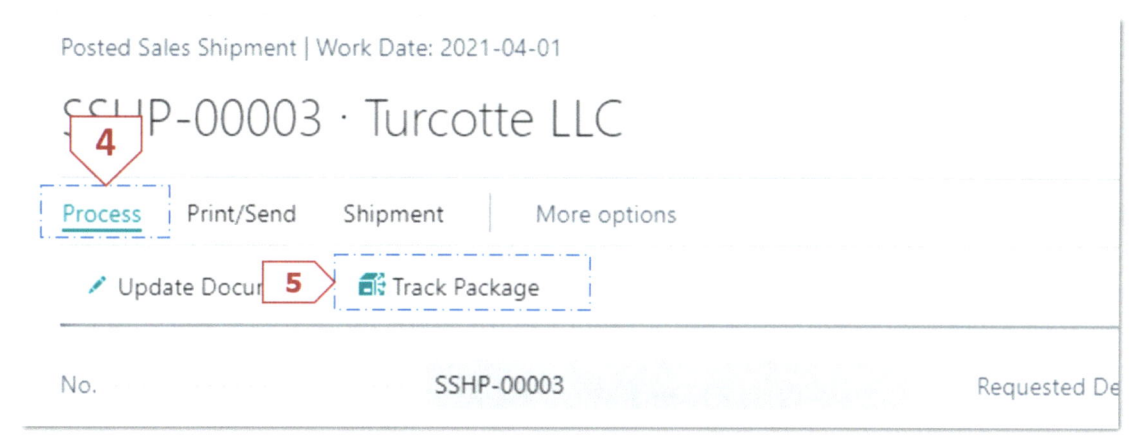

Process | Print/Send | Shipment | More options

✏️ Update Document | 📦 Track Package

No.   SSHP-00003   Requested De

Figure 15-46 - Posted Sales Shipment - Track Package Action

This will launch a browser with the URL from the shipping agent:

https://tracking.postnord.com/?id=LX........US

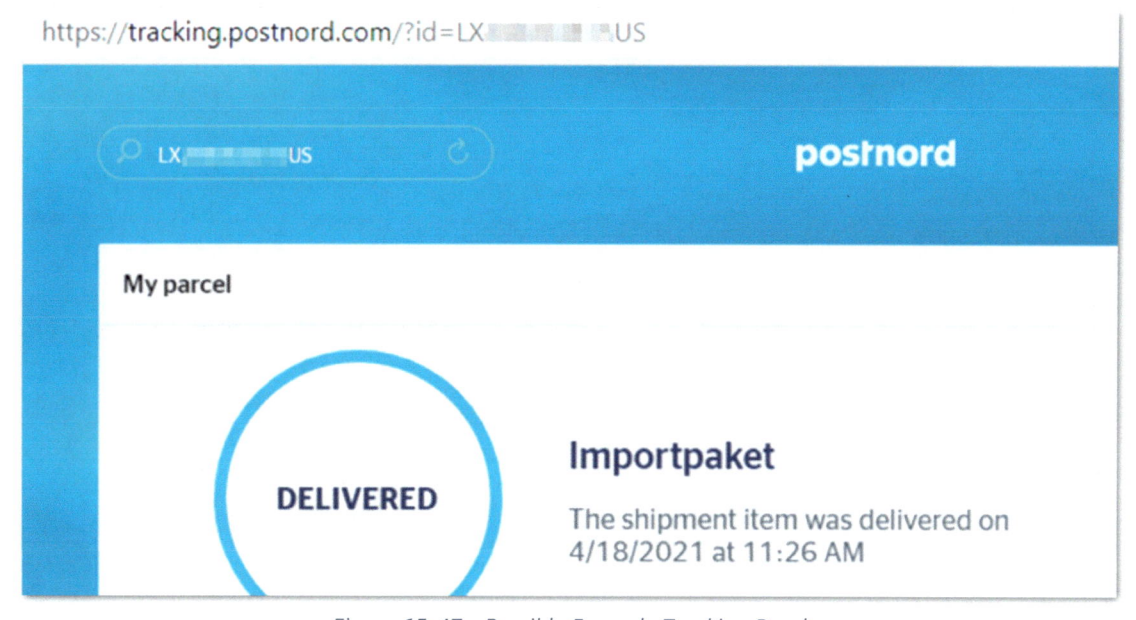

LX........US   **postnord**

My parcel

DELIVERED

Importpaket

The shipment item was delivered on 4/18/2021 at 11:26 AM

Figure 15-47 - Possible Example Tracking Result

PART 4: BASIC OPERATIONS
CHAPTER 15: SELLING

SENDING A STATEMENT

Quite often, you need to be able to send a summary statement to a customer, so they know what is *to be paid*. From the 🔍 **Customer Card**, under the **Reports** (**1**) group, select **Statement** (**2**):

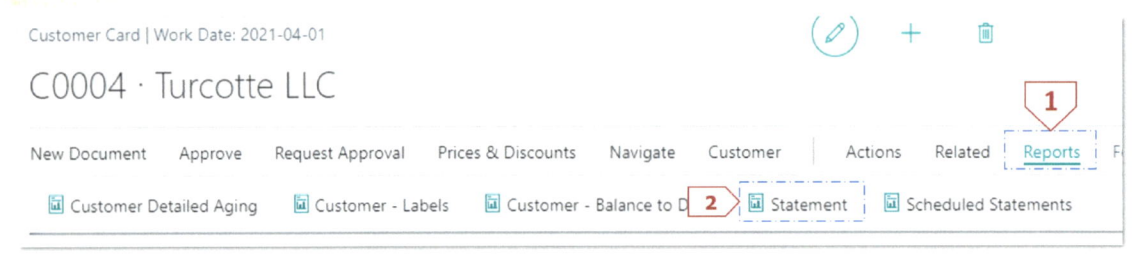

Figure 15-48 - Customer Card - Statement

This opens one of the larger report configuration windows in the system, the **Standard Statement**:

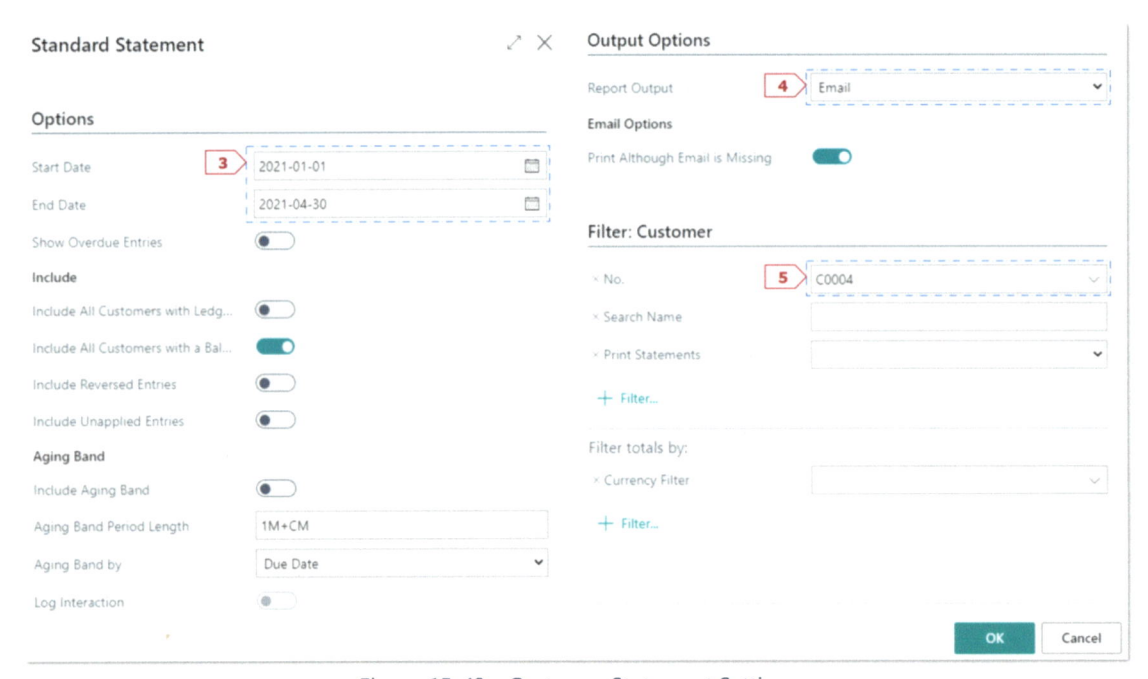

Figure 15-49 - Customer Statement Settings

There are more options here than this book will cover, but the essentials are:

3. **Start Date** & **End Date** specify what range of Posting Dates you want the statement to include.
4. When the report is run: *how would you like the **Report Output**? Email to the customer? To a PDF file? Or to a printer?*
5. If you want to run a Statement for a specific customer, you can filter on the Customer **No.**

Depending on your region, settings, extensions, and partner's help, your statement will vary widely in appearance, *but* it should result in some information about the statement, your company, the customer's company, and the open transactions:

Statement

Document Date   21-04-20
Statement   2
Starting Date   21-01-01
Ending Date   21-04-30

Turcotte LLC
Elliott Flippelli
92 Stoughton Center
100 10 Copenhagen, Denmark

Your First 20 Hours
with Business Central

Phone No.

Posting Date	Document No.	Description	Due Date	Original Amount	Remaining Amount	Running Total
Entries EUR						0,00
21-01-01	OPEN-CUST	Turcotte LLC	21-01-01	108,90	108,90	108,90
21-04-01	PSI-00003	Invoice SI-00001	21-05-01	1 002,00	1 002,00	1 110,90
					Total EUR	**1 110,90**

Figure 15-50 - Example Customer Statement

Chapter 16: Making Payments

In this chapter, we will cover how to manually register a payment to a Vendor, as well as how to use the Suggest Vendor Payments system to create payment entries.

PREPARING YOUR PAYMENT JOURNAL(S)

If you have not set up your 🔍 **Payment Journals** yet, we will need to configure some of the information. In the **Cash Management** (**1**) section, select **Payment Journals** (**2**) (or use the 🔍 Tell Me functionality, Alt-Q):

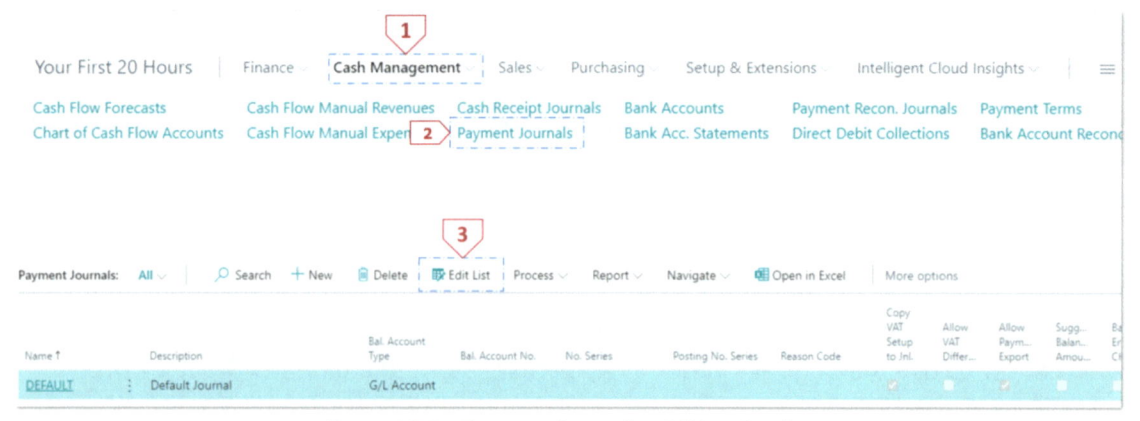

Figure 16-1 - Payment Journals - Editing Batches

To make changes, click **Edit List** (**3**):

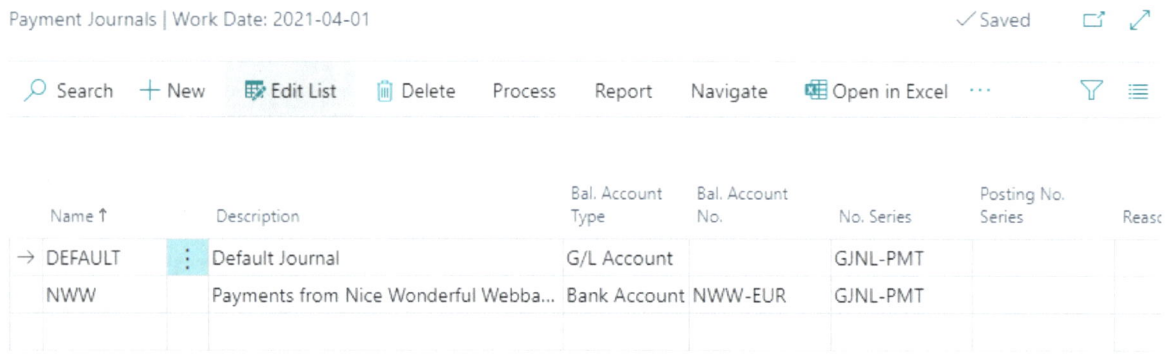

Figure 16-2 - Payment Journal Batches

For our scenario, we want to create a new batch called **NWW**, setting the **Bal. Account Type** to **Bank Account**, the **Bal. Account No.** to our **NWW-EUR** account, and using the **GJNL-PMT No. Series** to get automatic document numbers.

Close the Edit List window, and click on the name of the batch **NWW** (**4**) to open the batch:

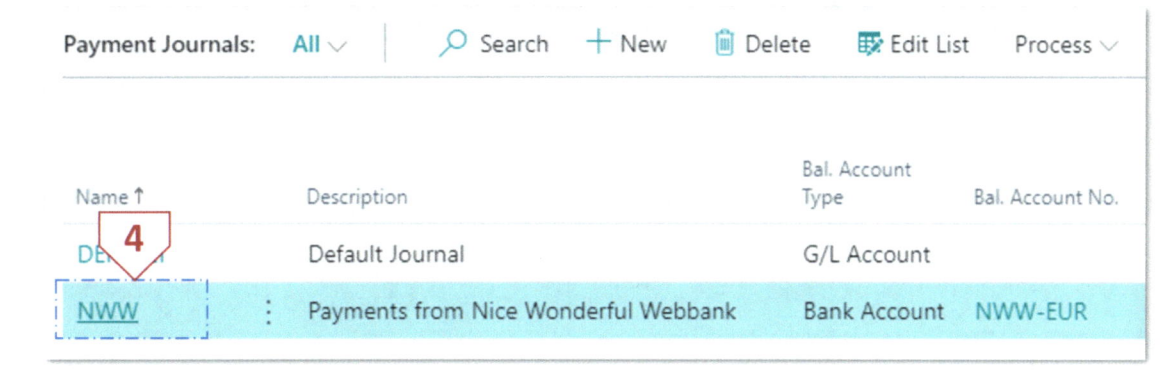

Name ↑	Description	Bal. Account Type	Bal. Account No.
DEFAULT	Default Journal	G/L Account	
NWW	Payments from Nice Wonderful Webbank	Bank Account	NWW-EUR

Figure 16-3 - Opening a Payment Journal Batch

MANUALLY CREATING A PAYMENT LINE

The Payment Journal requires some key fields:

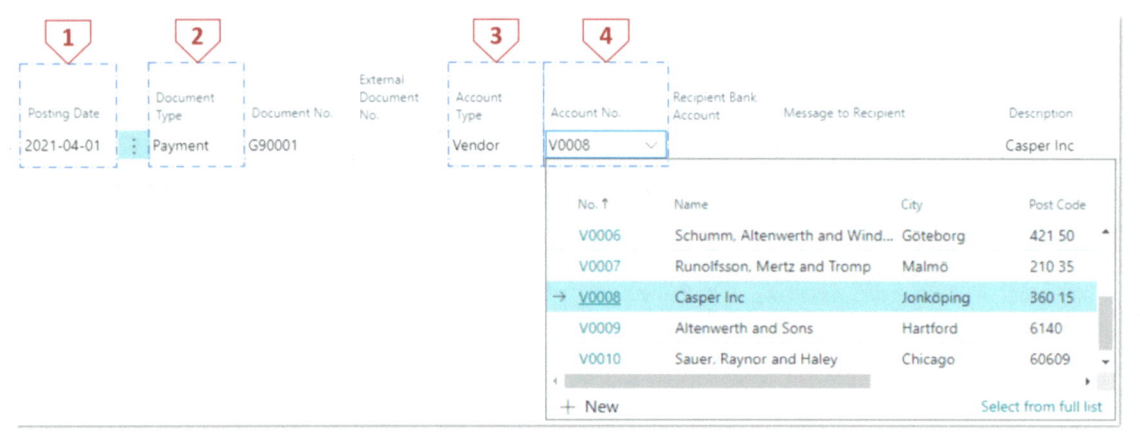

Figure 16-4 - Payment Journals - Major Fields

1. **Posting Date** controls when the payment is officially received.
2. **Document Type** should be set to **Payment**.
3. **Account Type** should be **Vendor**.
4. **Account No.** is the number of the **Vendor**, which can be selected by:
    a. Typing the number directly.
    b. Typing the name to match.
    c. Clicking the down-arrow to see the list.

Scrolling off to the right, we will see another key field: the **Applies-to Doc. No. (5)** field.

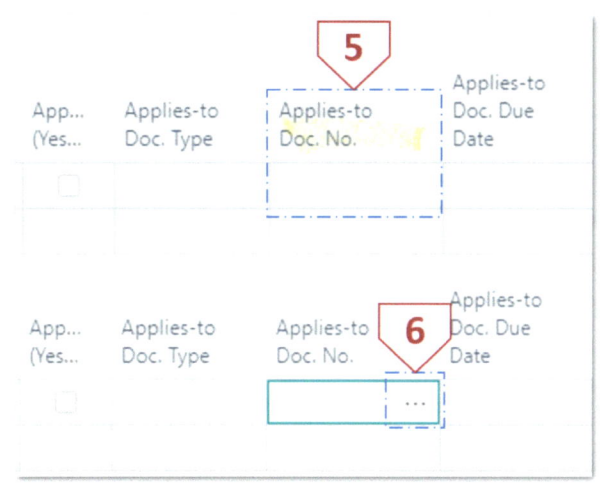

Figure 16-5 - Payment Journal - Applies-To Document Selection Access

When you click inside the field, you will see the ⋯ (**6**) (AssistEdit) button, which opens the **Apply Vendor Entries** window for you to select a single open Document that you wish to pay:

Figure 16-6 - Payment Journal - Apply Vendor Entries List

When you click on the open entry you wish to pay, and click **OK**, it will default a variety of fields on the Payment Journal Line:

PART 4: BASIC OPERATIONS
CHAPTER 16: MAKING PAYMENTS

	1		2					3		4
	Amount		Amount (LCY)	Bal. Account Type	Bal. Account No.	App... (Yes...		Applies-to Doc. Type		Applies-to Doc. No.
	2 281,97		2 281,97	Bank Account	NWW-EUR	✓				OPEN-VEND

Figure 16-7 - Payment Journal with Amounts and Application Set

1. The **Amount** will come in from the Vendor Ledger Entry you selected.
2. The **Amount (LCY)** is shown here to help you make sure you understand the local currency value of the payment. *(if you are paying in another currency)*
3. **Applies-To Doc. Type** will let you know *against which kind of document you are paying*. (In the screenshot above, we are paying against the opening balance, which has no Document Type)
4. **Applies-To Doc. No.** is *which document number you are making the payment against*. This is most often an invoice.

To understand what the result of this payment will have to the ledgers, we can preview the results via **Post/Print** (**5**) -> **Preview Posting** (**6**):

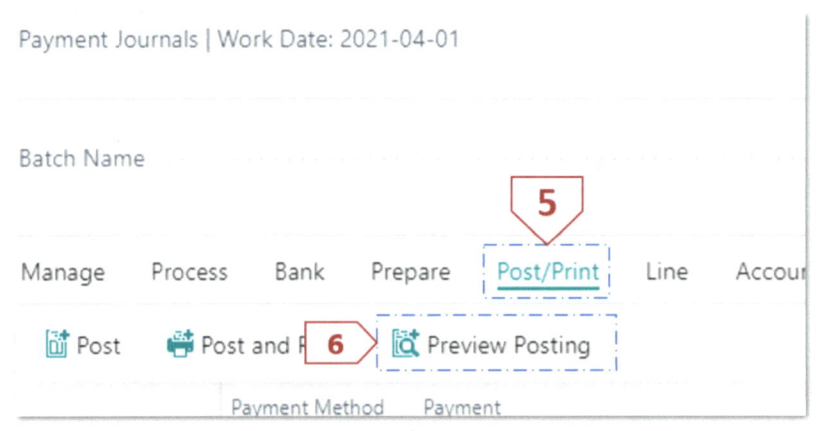

Figure 16-8 - Payment Journals - Preview Posting

This will show all the entries that will be created when we **Post** the journal:

PART 4: BASIC OPERATIONS
CHAPTER 16: MAKING PAYMENTS

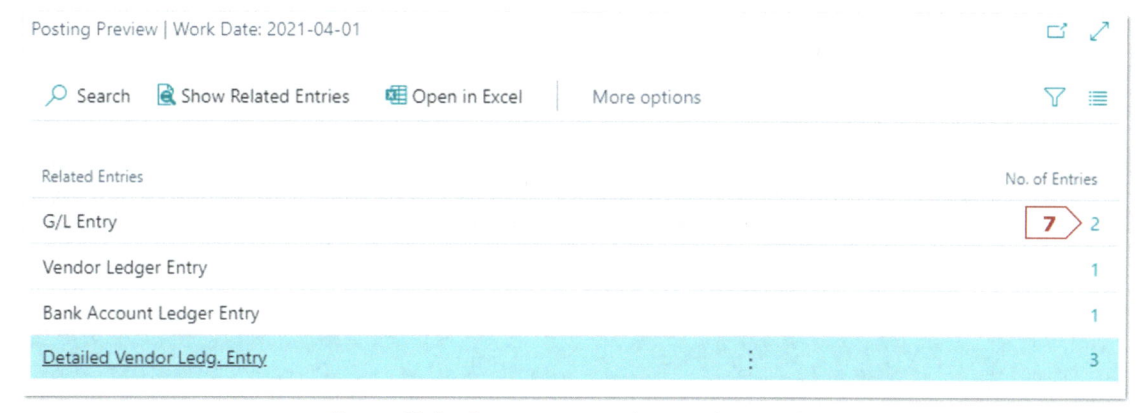

Figure 16-9 - Payment Journals - Posting Preview

For example, if we drill-down on the **2** (**7**) for the **G/L Entry**, we will see:

Figure 16-10 - Payment Journals - Posting Preview - G/L Entries

Funds will be removed from the **Bank, EUR** G/L Account and our **Accounts Payable, Domestic** will be reduced.

To Post the journals, simply click on **Post/Print** (**8**) then **Post** (**9**):

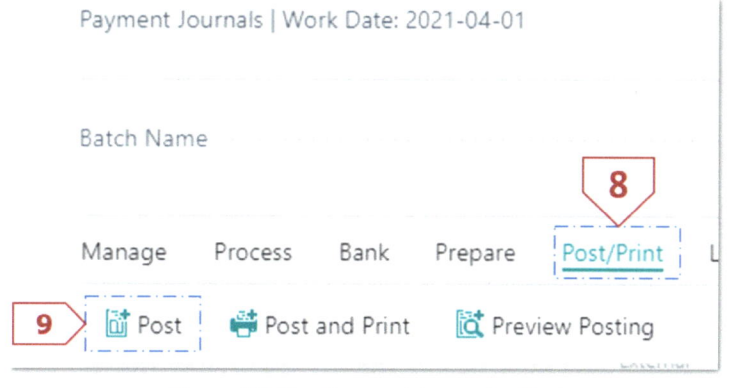

Figure 16-11 - Payment Journals - Post

To confirm this worked as we needed, let us review the **Vendor Ledger Entries**. From the 🔍 **Vendors** list, open the Vendor just paid. You should see that the **Balance (LCY)** (**10**) is reduced:

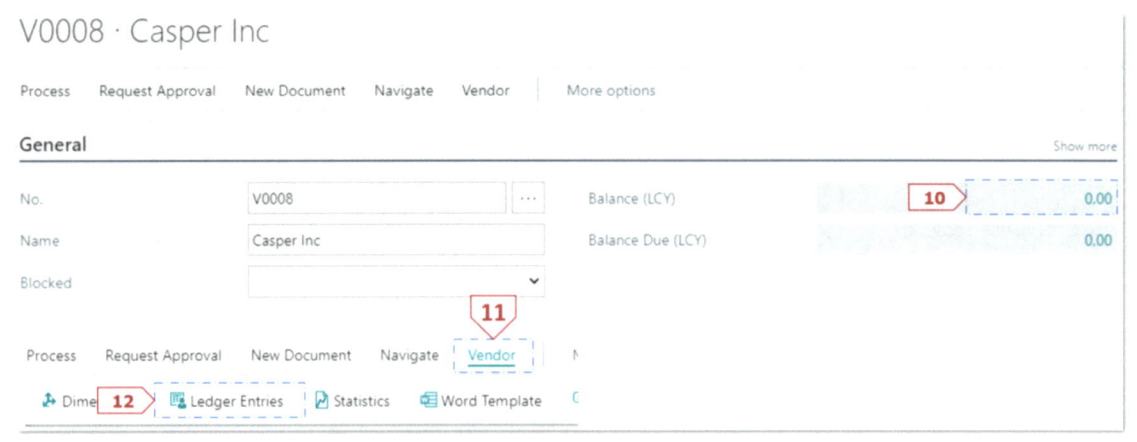

Figure 16-12 - Vendor Card with No Balance

To see all the **Vendor Ledger Entries**, locate **Vendor** (**11**) in the Action Bar, then click on **Ledger Entries** (**12**):

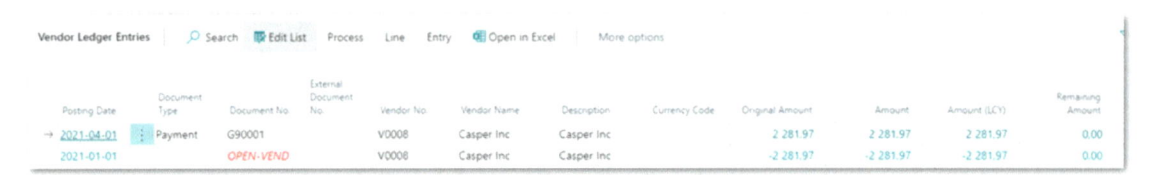

Figure 16-13 - Payment in Vendor Ledger Entries

> **Note:** On the Vendor, and Customer cards, you can drill-down on the Balance fields, but that is pre-configured to only show *open* entries. To see all entries, you need to use the action bar Ledger Entries option.

Suggest Vendor Payments

Creating payments one at a time manually works but it is hardly time efficient. The system knows how much you owe to whom and by when. To leverage that information, you use the Suggest Vendor Payments functionality.

In the Payment Journal, under **Prepare** (**1**), select **Suggest Vendor Payments...** (**2**):

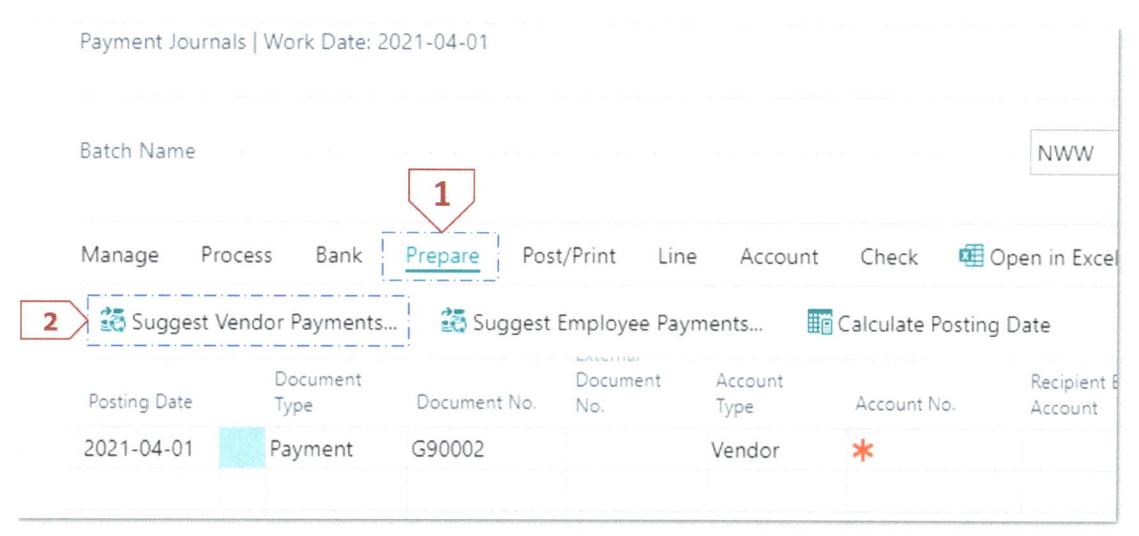

Figure 16-14 - Payment Journals - Suggest Vendor Payments

This opens a large configuration window to choose how you would like the payment journal lines to be created:

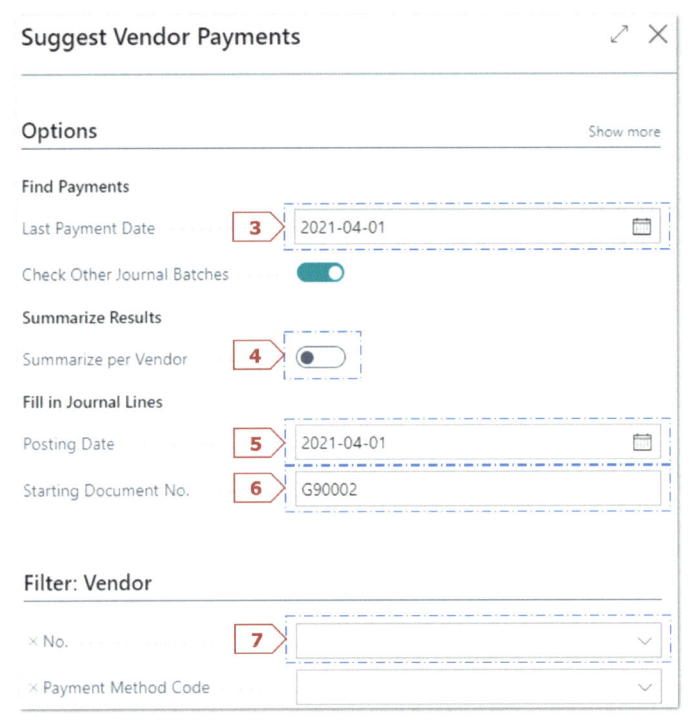

Figure 16-15 - Suggest Vendor Payments Settings Overview

Element	What is it?
1	The **Last Payment Date** setting picks the end point at which the routine should consider the Due Dates from the Vendor Ledger Entries. The example 2021-04-01 means that if an invoice is due on 03-31, it will be included; but an invoice due on 04-02 will not be. (See Future Date Suggestions below)
2	The **Summarize per Vendor** option will be covered in detail below.
3	What **Posting Date** the payment should be registered on.
4	The **Starting Document No.** is most often generated from your No. Series configuration for the Payment Journal.
5	You *can* filter the **Vendor**, which can be as specific as down to a particular vendor **No.** or include a whole range.

With the suggestion defaults, in our scenario we will mostly get opening balances. With **Summarize per Vendor** disabled, a single line in the journal matches to a single document to be paid:

Figure 16-16 - Payment Journal - Suggestion Results Example

The lines generated by the Suggest Vendor Payments routine are entirely ready to Post, making this a very efficient process.

FUTURE DATE SUGGESTIONS

In **Chapter 14**, we have posted some purchase invoices, so let us see how those get picked up by the Suggest Vendor Payments routine. We will adjust the **Last Payment Date** (**1**) filter:

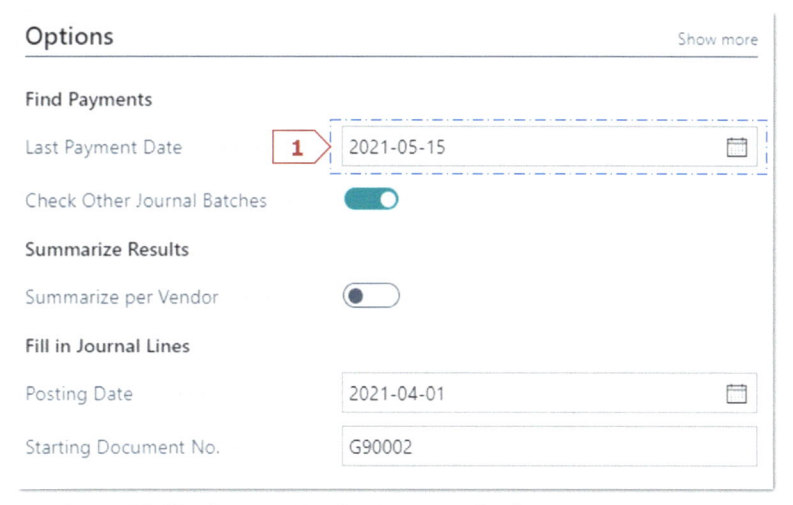

Figure 16-17 - Suggest Vendor Payments Settings - Future Payments

In this case, we are going to use a date that is 45 days out from most of our NET30 documents. This results in:

Account No.	Rec... Bank Acc...	Message to Recipient	Description	Curre... Code	Payme... Method Code	Payme... Refere...	Cre... No.	Amount	Amount (LCY)	Bal. Acc... Type	Bal. Account No.	App... (Yes...	Applies-to Doc. Type	Applies-to Doc. No.
V0001		Payment of	Hirthe Group					4 365.20	4 365.20	Bank...	NWW-EUR	☑		OPEN-VEND
V0002		Payment of	West Group					406.50	406.50	Bank...	NWW-EUR	☑		OPEN-VEND
V0003		Payment of	Kerluke LLC					125.05	125.05	Bank...	NWW-EUR	☑		OPEN-VEND
V0003		Payment of Invoi...	Kerluke LLC					312.50	312.50	Bank...	NWW-EUR	☑	Invoice	PPI-00001
V0003		Payment of Invoi...	Kerluke LLC					125.00	125.00	Bank...	NWW-EUR	☑	Invoice	PPI-00002
V0003		Payment of Invoi...	Kerluke LLC					187.50	187.50	Bank...	NWW-EUR	☑	Invoice	PPI-00003
V0004		Payment of	Hermann, Koss and...					600.00	600.00	Bank...	NWW-EUR	☑		OPEN-VEND
V0005		Payment of	Nitzsche-Hoppe					450.00	450.00	Bank...	NWW-EUR	☑		OPEN-VEND
V0006		Payment of	Schumm, Altenwerth...					1 354.21	1 354.21	Bank...	NWW-EUR	☑		OPEN-VEND
V0007		Payment of	Runolfsson, Mertz a...					900.00	900.00	Bank...	NWW-EUR	☑		OPEN-VEND

Figure 16-18 - Payment Journal Lines - Future Payments Example

As you can see, the **Kerluke LLC** vendor has their **OPEN-VEND** (opening balance) entry and we also have three lines for three invoices.

SUMMARIZING SUGGESTIONS

If we do not want to generate multiple lines for multiple payments to a single Vendor, that is where the **Summarize per Vendor** (**1**) option comes in:

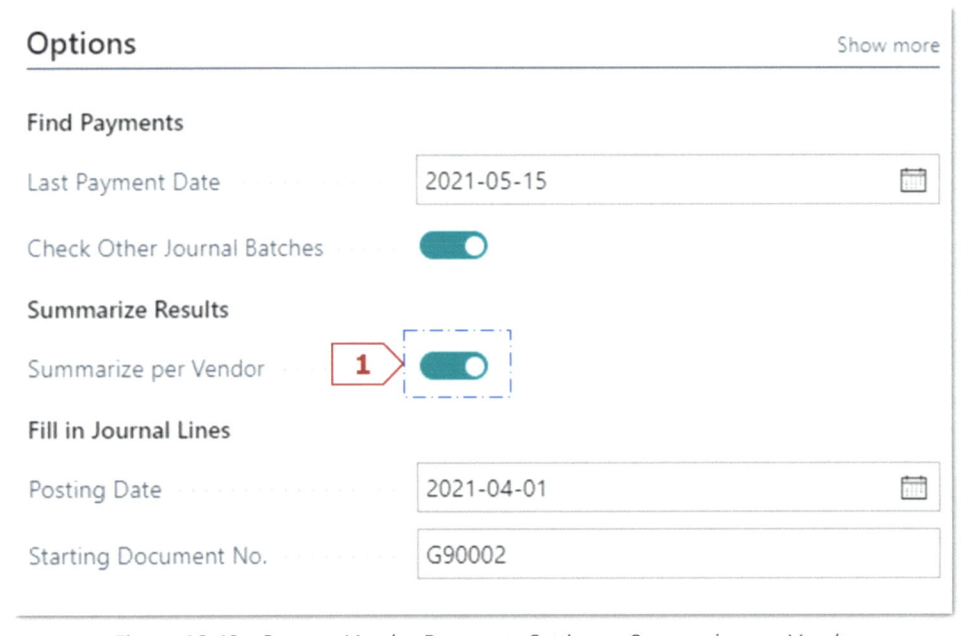

Figure 16-19 - Suggest Vendor Payments Settings - Summarize per Vendor

Now our **Kerluke LLC** vendor only gets a single line (**2**). However, you will also see that the **Applies-To Doc. No.** (**3**) field is empty:

284 PAGE

PART 4: BASIC OPERATIONS
CHAPTER 16: MAKING PAYMENTS

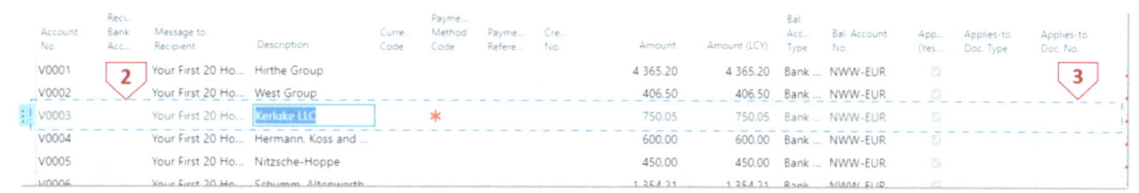

Figure 16-20 - Payment Journal Lines - Summarized Example

We no longer have a one-to-one relationship between a payment line and the document it is paying. To see the connections, we must go under the **Process** (**4**) action and select the **Apply Entries...** (**5**):

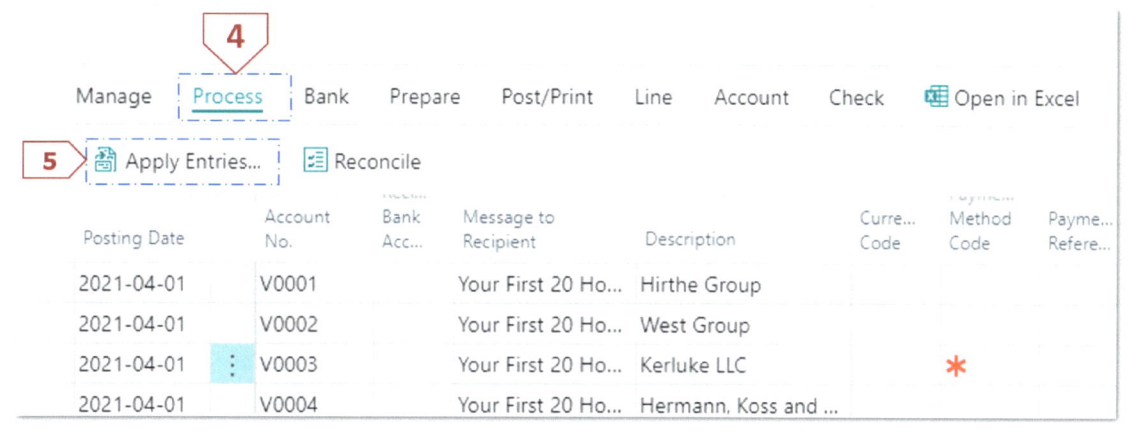

Figure 16-21 - Payment Journal - Process - Apply Entries...

This will open the **Apply Vendor Entries** window:

Figure 16-22 - Payment Journal - Application Entries

The **Amount to Apply** (**6**) column shows us which documents are involved. (**Applications** is covered in more detail in Chapter 18)

PART 4: BASIC OPERATIONS
CHAPTER 16: MAKING PAYMENTS

Chapter 17: Receiving Payments

In this chapter, we will go over how you receive payments from customers in the Cash Receipt Journal, as well as understanding how to apply partial payments.

PREPARING YOUR CASH RECEIPT JOURNALS

If you have not setup your **Cash Receipt Journals** yet, we will need to configure some information. In the **Cash Management** (**1**) section, select **Cash Receipt Journals** (**2**) (or use the Tell Me functionality, Alt-Q):

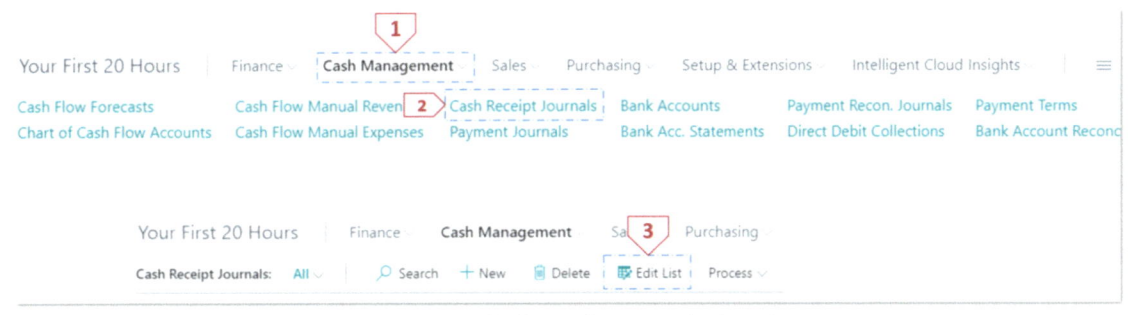

Figure 17-1 - Cash Receipt Journal - Locating

To make changes, click **Edit List** (**3**):

PART 4: BASIC OPERATIONS
CHAPTER 17: RECEIVING PAYMENTS

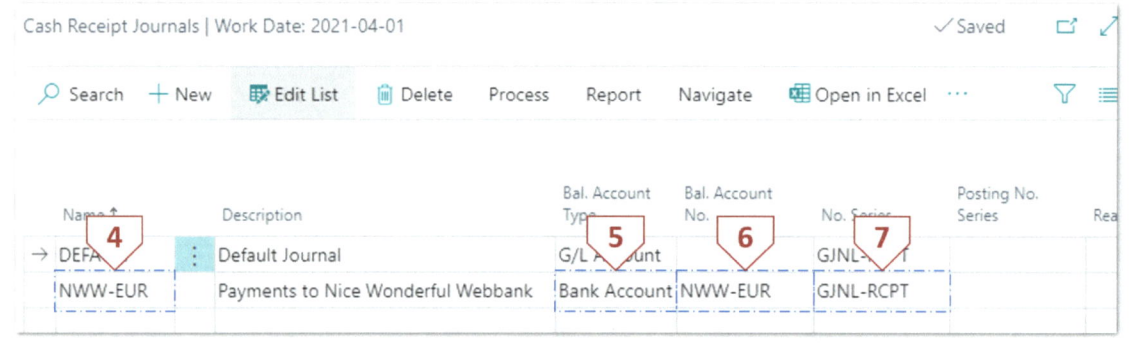

Figure 17-2 - Cash Receipt Journal - Editing Batches

For our scenario, we want to create a new batch with a **Name** (**4**) **NWW-EUR**, setting the **Bal. Account Type** (**5**) to **Bank Account**, the **Bal. Account No.** (**6**) to our **NWW-EUR** account, and using the **GJNL-PMT No. Series** (**7**) to get automatic document numbers.

Close the Edit List window and click on the name of the batch **NWW-EUR** (**8**) to open the batch:

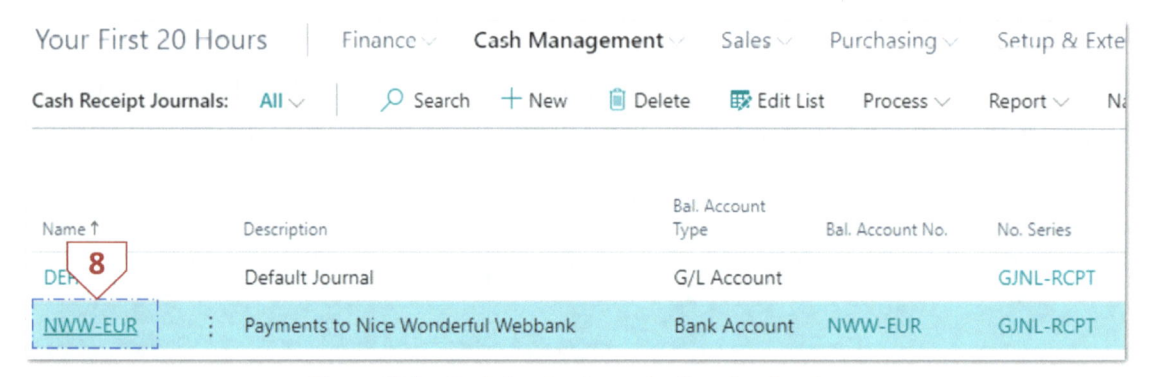

Figure 17-3 - Cash Receipt Journal - Opening Batches

> **Note:** You may come across **Customer Payments** in menus or documentation, but be aware that this is *Payments to Customers*, not receiving them.

CREATING A RECEIPT LINE

288 PAGE

PART 4: BASIC OPERATIONS
CHAPTER 17: RECEIVING PAYMENTS

The 🔍 **Cash Receipt Journal** requires a few key fields:

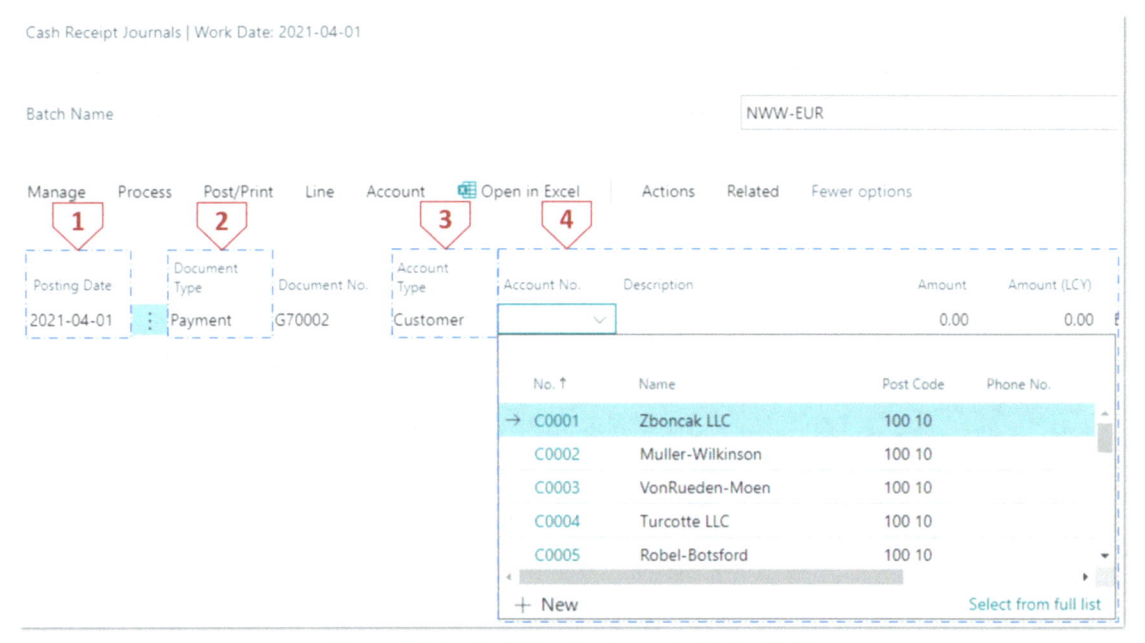

Figure 17-4 - Cash Receipt Journal - Major Fields

1. **Posting Date** controls when the Payment is officially received.
2. **Document Type** should be set to **Payment**.
3. **Account Type**. should be **Customer**.
4. **Account No.** is the number of the Customer, which can be selected by:
   a. Typing the number directly.
   b. Typing the name to match.
   c. Clicking the down-arrow to see the list.

Scrolling off to the right, we will see another key field, the **Applies-to Doc. No.** (**5**) field:

PART 4: BASIC OPERATIONS   PAGE 289
CHAPTER 17: RECEIVING PAYMENTS

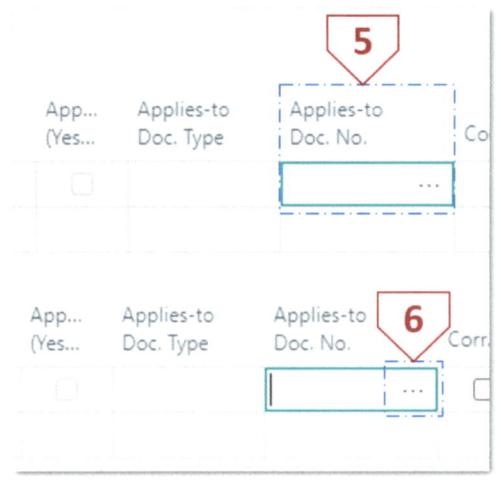

Figure 17-5 - Cash Receipt Journal - Application Fields

When you click inside the field, you will see the ⋯ (**6**) (AssistEdit) button, which opens the **Apply Customer Entries** window for you to select a single open Document that you wish to pay:

Figure 17-6 - Cash Receipt Journal - Apply Entries Window

When you click on the open entry you want to pay and click **OK**, it will default a variety of fields on the Cash Receipt Journal Line:

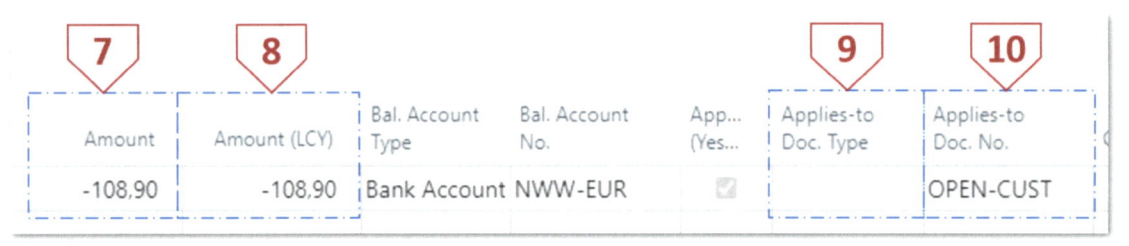

Figure 17-7 - Cash Receipt Journal - Applies-To Results

7. The **Amount** will come in from the **Customer Ledger Entry** you selected. Note that this is a *negative* value!

290 PAGE PART 4: BASIC OPERATIONS
CHAPTER 17: RECEIVING PAYMENTS

8. The **Amount (LCY)** is shown here to help you to be sure you understand the local currency value of the payment *if you are being paid in another currency*.
9. **Applies-To Doc. Type** will let you know which kind of document is being paid. (In the screenshot above, we are paid against the opening balance, which has no Document Type)
10. **Applies-To Doc. No.** is which document number you are receiving the payment against. This is most often an invoice.

To understand what the result of this receipt will have to the ledgers, we can preview the results via **Post/Print** (**11**) **Preview Posting** (**12**):

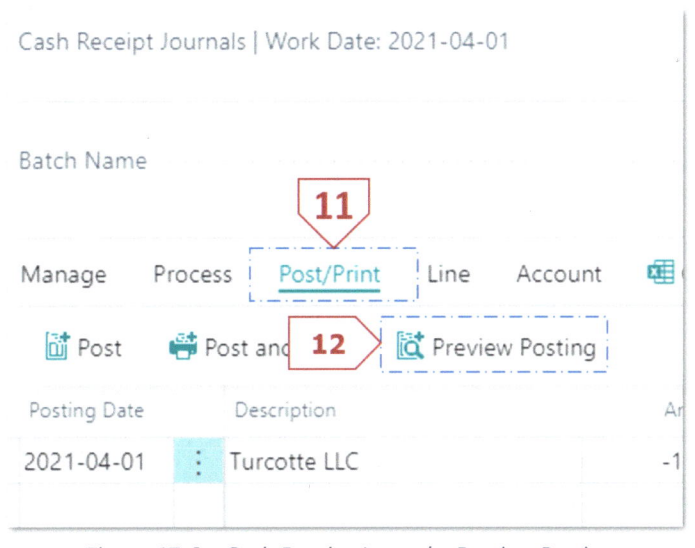

Figure 17-8 - Cash Receipt Journal - Preview Posting

This will show all the entries that will result when we Post the journal:

PART 4: BASIC OPERATIONS
CHAPTER 17: RECEIVING PAYMENTS

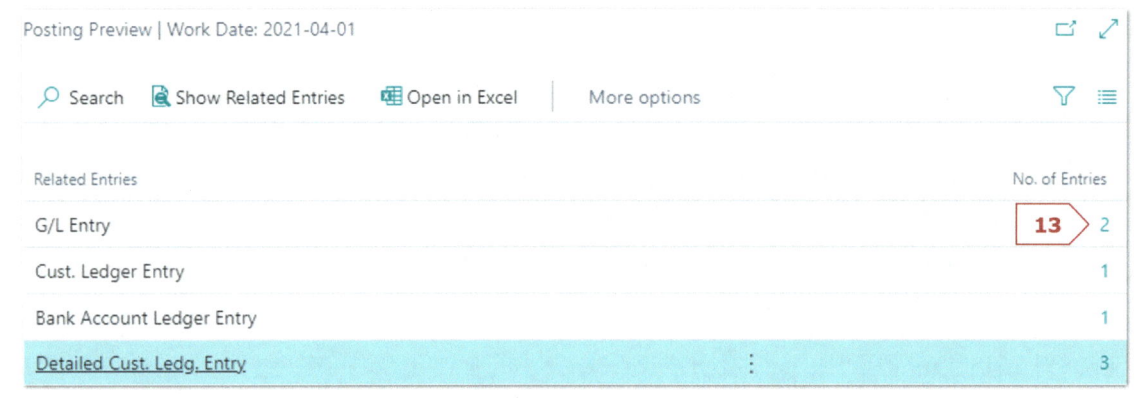

Figure 17-9 - Cash Receipt Journal – Posting Preview

For example, if we drill-down on the **2** (**13**) for the **G/L Entry**, we will see:

Figure 17-10 - Cash Receipt Journal - Posting Preview - G/L Entries

Funds will be added to the **Bank, EUR** G/L Account and our **Receivables, EU** will be reduced.

To post the journals, simply click on **Post/Print** (**14**) then **Post** (**15**):

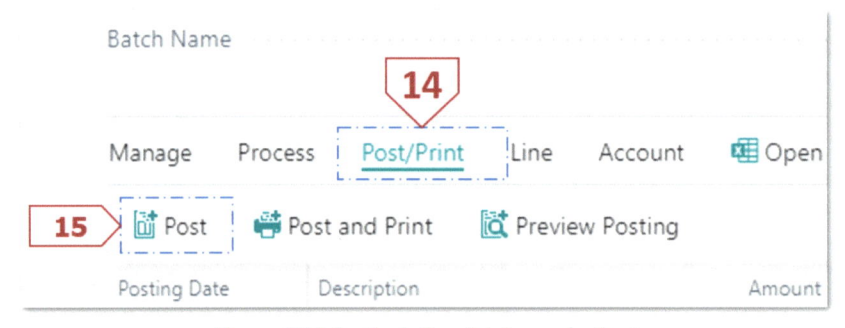

Figure 17-11 - Cash Receipt Journal - Post

To confirm this worked as we required, let us review the **Customer Ledger Entries**. From the **Customers** list, open the Customer you just paid. You should see the **Balance (LCY)** (**16**) is reduced:

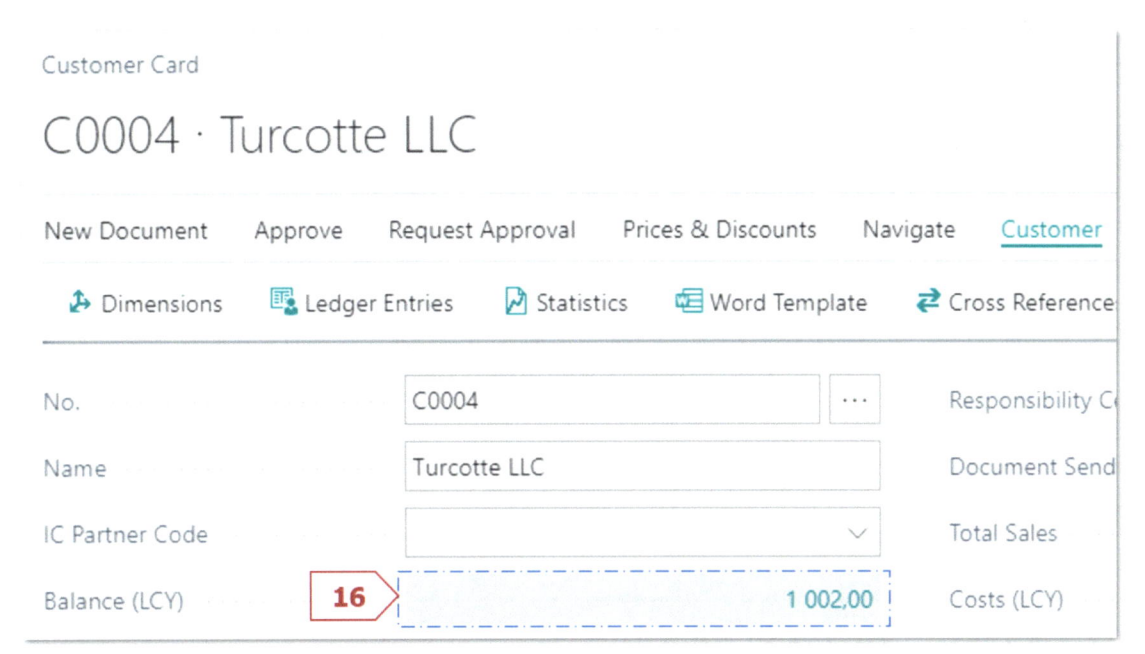

Figure 17-12 - Customer Card - Balance Changed

Under the **Customer** (**17**) action bar group, select **Ledger Entries** (**18**) to see all the **Customer Ledger Entries**:

Figure 17-13 - Customer Card - Ledger Entries

Additionally, we can drill-down on the **Remaining Amount** or **Remaining Amt. (LCY)** (**19**) fields:

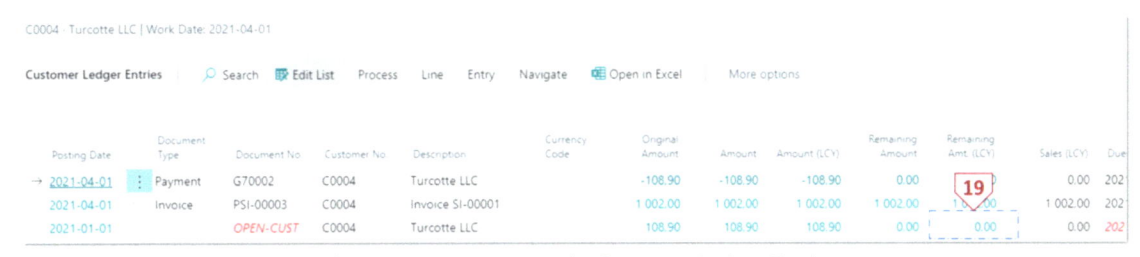

Figure 17-14 - Payment in Customer Ledger Entries

PART 4: BASIC OPERATIONS
CHAPTER 17: RECEIVING PAYMENTS

This will show you the **Detailed Customer Ledger Entries** where payments (and credits) are applied:

Posting Date	Entry Type	Document Type	Document No.	Customer No.	Currency Code	Amount	Amount (LCY)
2021-01-01	Initial Entry		OPEN-CUST	C0004		108,90	108,90
2021-04-01	Application	Payment	G70002	C0004		-108,90	-108,90

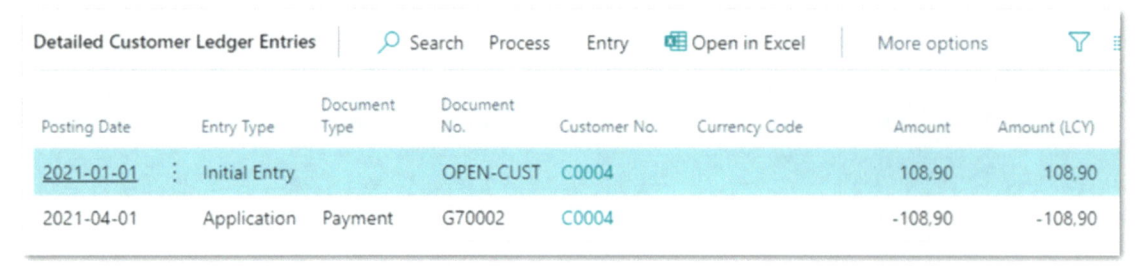

Figure 17-15 - Detailed Customer Ledger Entries Showing Application

Here (**Figure 17-15**) we can see the **OPEN-CUST** had Payment **G70002** applied to it.

CREATING PARTIAL RECEIPTS

While in a perfect world, customers might pay exactly what they owe every time, this book is not written in that perfect world.

One great example we can use for receiving partial payments in our scenario is Customer **C0008**, who had an Opening Balance of **73541,99 EUR**, which is a result of multiple documents from a prior system:

> Note: On the Vendor and Customer cards, you can drill-down on the Balance fields, but that is pre-configured to only show *open* entries. To see all entries, you need to use the action bar Ledger Entries option.

Posting Date	Entry Type	Document Type	Document No.	Customer No.	Currency Code	Amount	Amount (LCY)
2021-01-01	Initial Entry		OPEN-CUST	C0004		108,90	108,90
2021-04-01	Application	Payment	G70002	C0004		-108,90	-108,90

Figure 17-16 - Customer Ledger Entries - Open Balance

We will now receive a payment from them for **3250 EUR**. Much as we did above, we will create a 🔍 **Cash Receipt Journal** line:

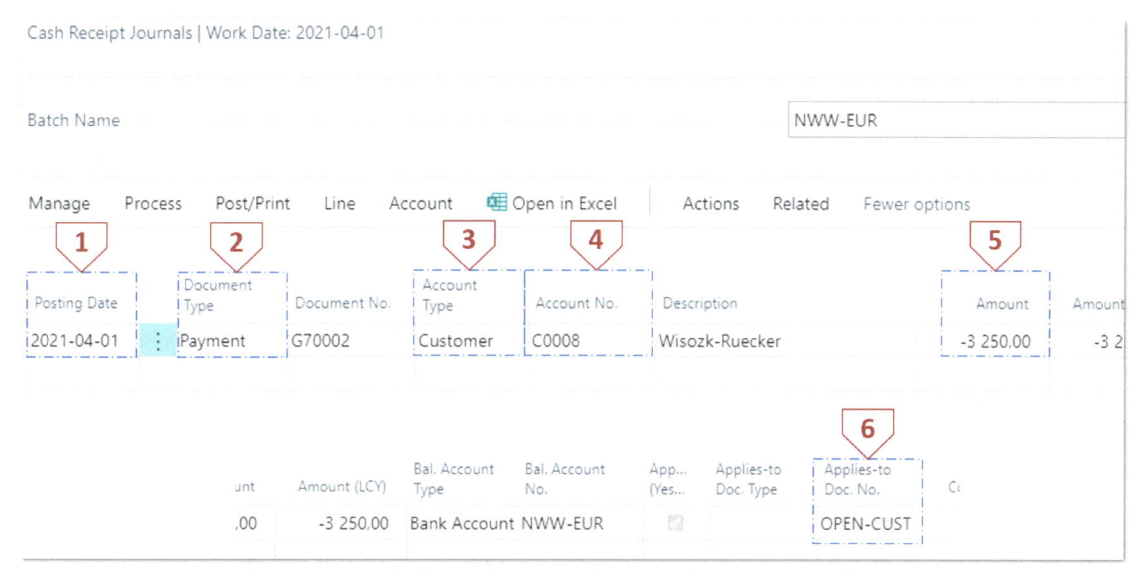

Figure 17-17 - Cash Receipt Journal - Manual Entry and Application

1. **Posting Date** controls when the payment is officially received.
2. **Document Type** should be set to **Payment**.
3. **Account Type** should be set to **Customer**.
4. **Account No.** is the number of the Customer.
5. **Amount** can be entered manually to receive a specific amount. *Make sure to enter it as a negative amount.*
6. We can still apply this cash receipt against a specific document using the **Applies-To Doc. No.** (**6**) field. By having set the line's amount first, the Amount will remain exactly what we entered.

Once we **Post** this receipt, if we go back to the **Customer Ledger Entries**, we will see the **Remaining Amount** (**7**) on the Payment is 0 (zero) as we applied it to the Invoice:

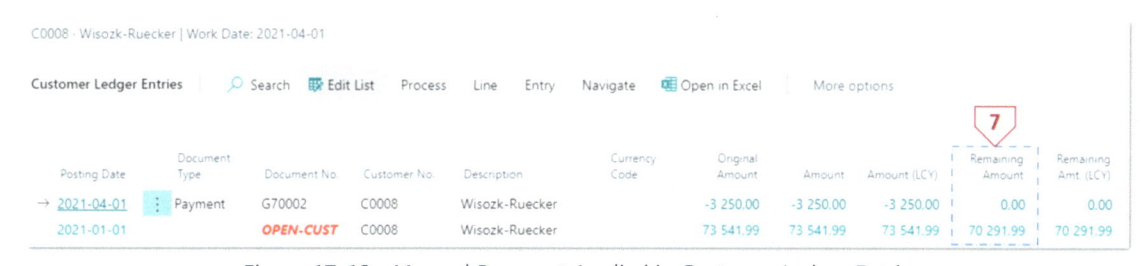

Figure 17-18 - Manual Payment Applied in Customer Ledger Entries

PART 4: BASIC OPERATIONS
CHAPTER 17: RECEIVING PAYMENTS

PAGE 295

Drilling-down on the **Remaining Amount** (**7**) of the **OPEN-CUST** document line, we can see the details of what is remaining:

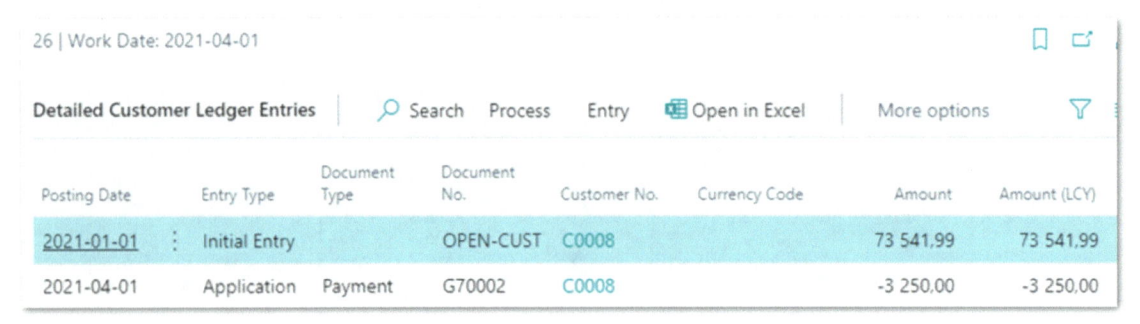

Posting Date	Entry Type	Document Type	Document No.	Customer No.	Currency Code	Amount	Amount (LCY)
2021-01-01	Initial Entry		OPEN-CUST	C0008		73 541,99	73 541,99
2021-04-01	Application	Payment	G70002	C0008		-3 250,00	-3 250,00

Figure 17-19 - Manual Application in Detailed Customer Ledger Entries

This shows that, in the **Detailed Customer Ledger Entries** (**Figure 17-19**) for this transaction, the **-3250** from Payment **G70002** was applied to the **73541,99**.

This sum makes the new **Remaining Amount** of the **OPEN-CUST** document **70291,99**, which is what we see at the **Customer Ledger Entry** level. (**Figure 17-18**)

Chapter 18: Correcting Errors

Business Central never allows you to delete posted data for accounting and business best practice. However, there are many tools for correcting errors in Business Central. This chapter will cover some of those procedures.

SALES RETURN ORDERS

To create a new **Sales Return Order**, the easiest place is from the **Sales Return Orders** list, and then click the **New** (**1**) button:

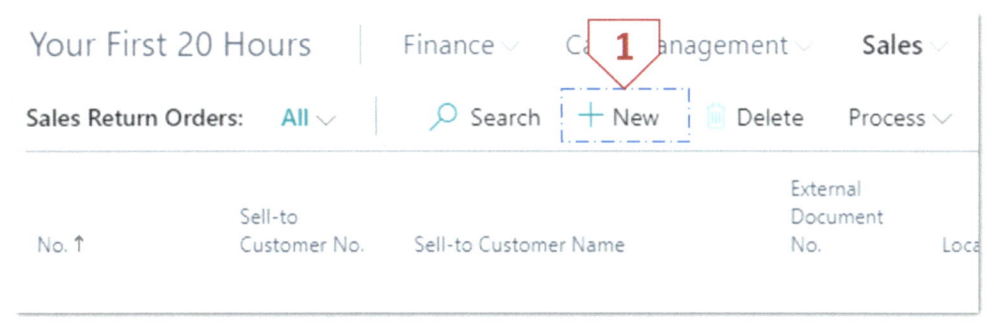

Figure 18-1 - Creating Sales Return Order

You will see that this looks just like **Sales Orders**:

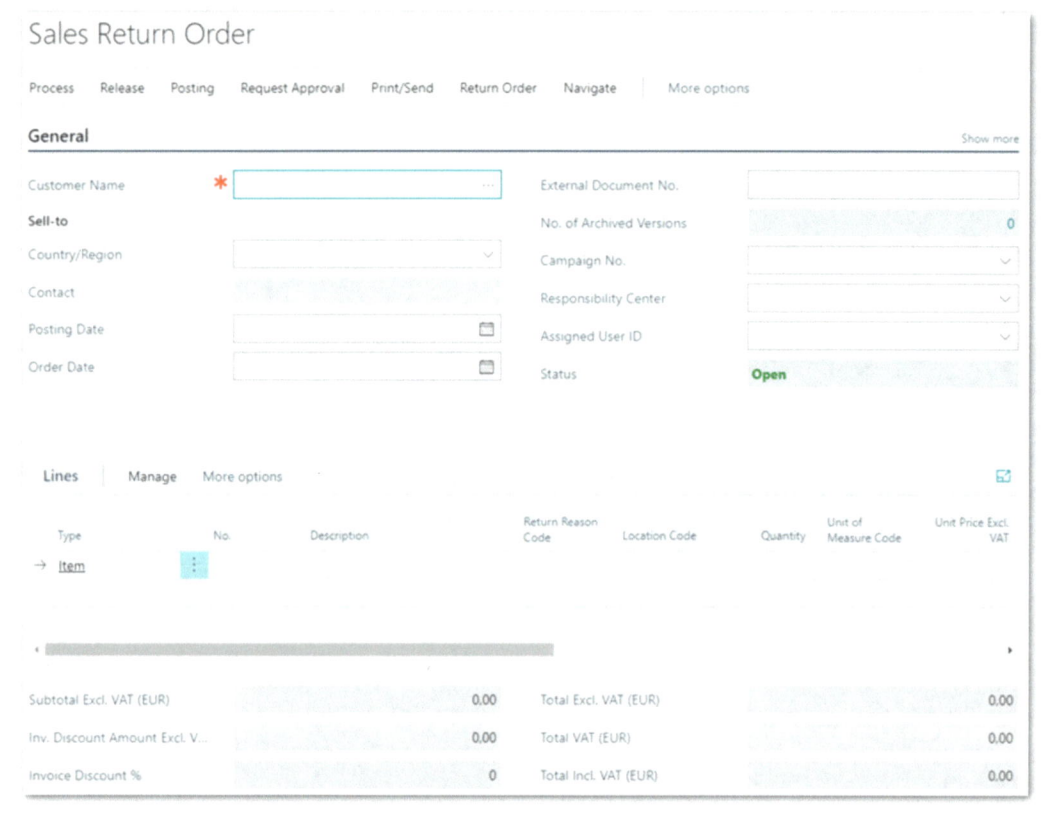

Figure 18-2 - Empty Sales Return Order

After selecting which **Customer** you will perform the return for, the next step is to select what items from which sales will be returned, via the **Process** (**2**) -> **Get Posted Document Lines to Reverse...** (**3**):

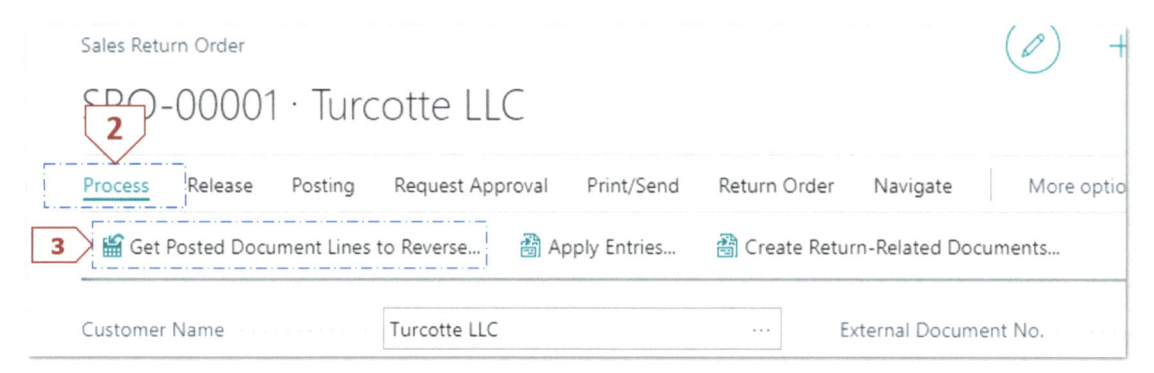

Figure 18-3 - Sales Return Order - Locating Lines to Reverse

This will open a window showing the sales history for this customer:

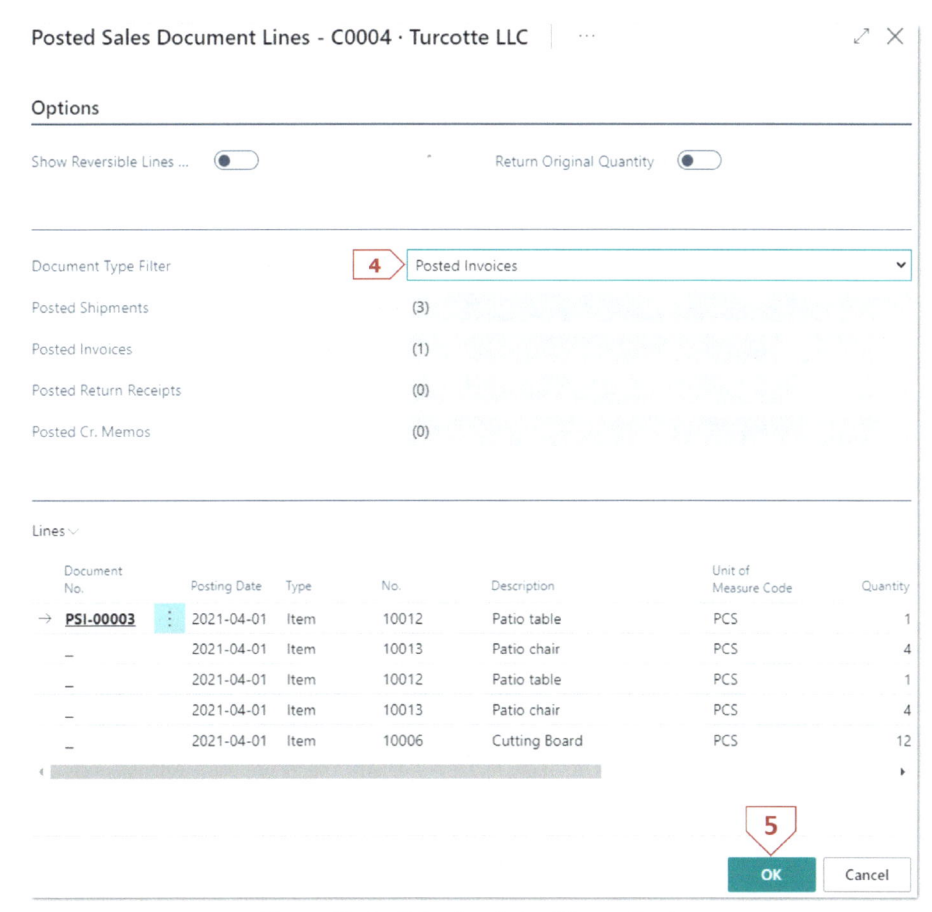

Figure 18-4 - Selecting Sales History Entries

You can toggle the **Document Type Filter** (**4**) between different posted documents, but in our case, the lines we want are already here. Holding down Shift (for a range) or Ctrl (for specific multi-select), we multi-select the lines we want to return:

Figure 18-5 - Multi-select of Sales History Entries

PART 4: BASIC OPERATIONS
CHAPTER 18: CORRECTING ERRORS

When we click **OK** (**5**) the lines we selected will be brought onto the **Sales Return Document** with all the fields needed, along with **Comment** (**6**) lines showing where the information had come from:

Type	No.	Description	Return Reason Code	Location Code	Quantity	Unit of Measure Code	Unit Price
→ Comment		Invoice No. PSI-00003:					
Comment		Inv. No. PSI-00003 - Shpt. No. SSHP-00...					
Item	10012	Patio table		ASKIM	1	PCS	11
Item	10013	Patio chair		ASKIM	4	PCS	7

Subtotal Excl. VAT (EUR)   426.00   Total Excl. VAT (EUR)   426.00

Figure 18-6 - Sales Return Order - Lines Populated

> **Note: Return Reason Codes** are a good thing to use, but sadly beyond the scope of this book. This can be a valuable way to analyze problems with products.

Return-Related Documents

Often, in a sales return situation, there could be some issues or defects. This can require you to create a short list of related documents. Business Central gives you a shortcut to handle those via **Process** (**1**) -> **Create Return-Related Documents...** (**2**):

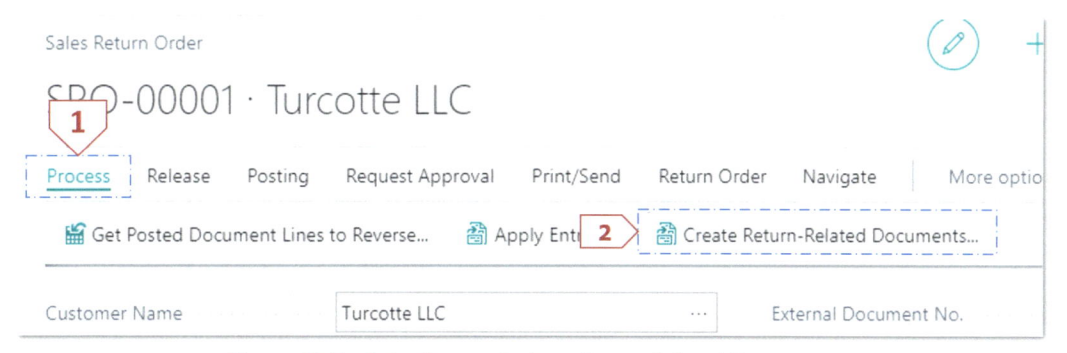

Figure 18-7 - Sales Return Order - Create Related Documents

This will open an option window that allows you to create several related documents in one step:

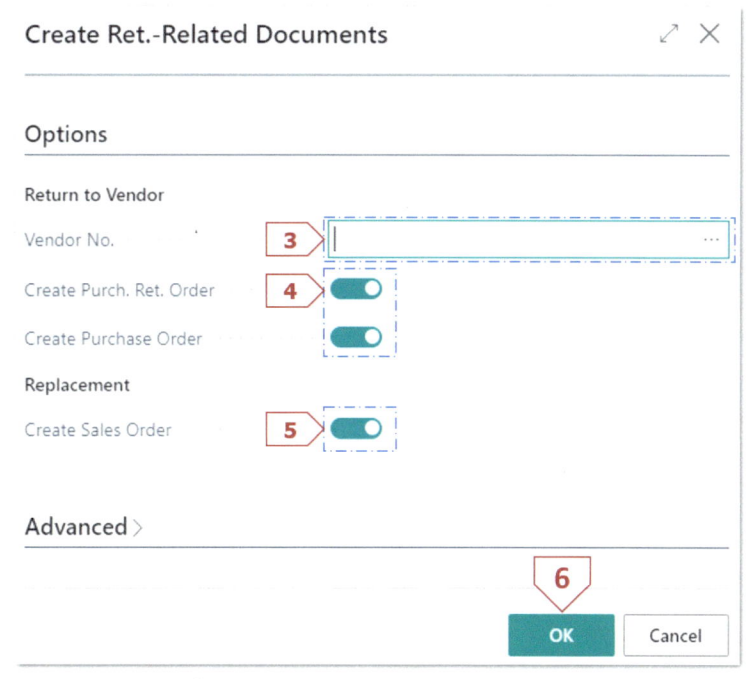

Figure 18-8 - Sales Return Order - Create Related Documents Options

Part 4: Basic Operations
Chapter 18: Correcting Errors

If you would like, you can set a **Vendor No. (3)** and create new purchase documents (**4**) for the involved items.

You can also create a new **Sales Order** (**5**) from these items for replacement. When you click **OK** (**6**), you will get a list of Document Types and Numbers:

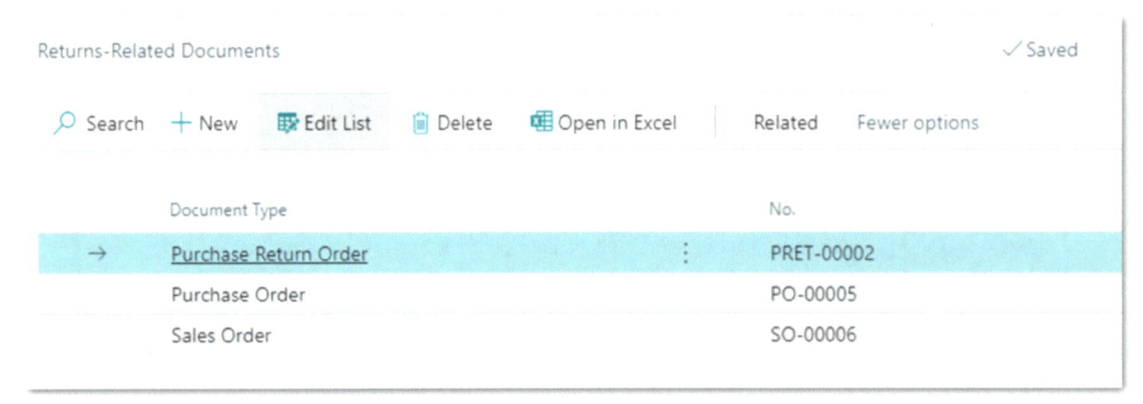

Document Type	No.
Purchase Return Order	PRET-00002
Purchase Order	PO-00005
Sales Order	SO-00006

Figure 18-9 - Sales Return Order - Related Documents List

From this list, you can navigate directly to the documents (which can be helpful to send them immediately) via the **Related** (**7**) -> **Lines** (**8**) -> **Card** (**9**) sequence:

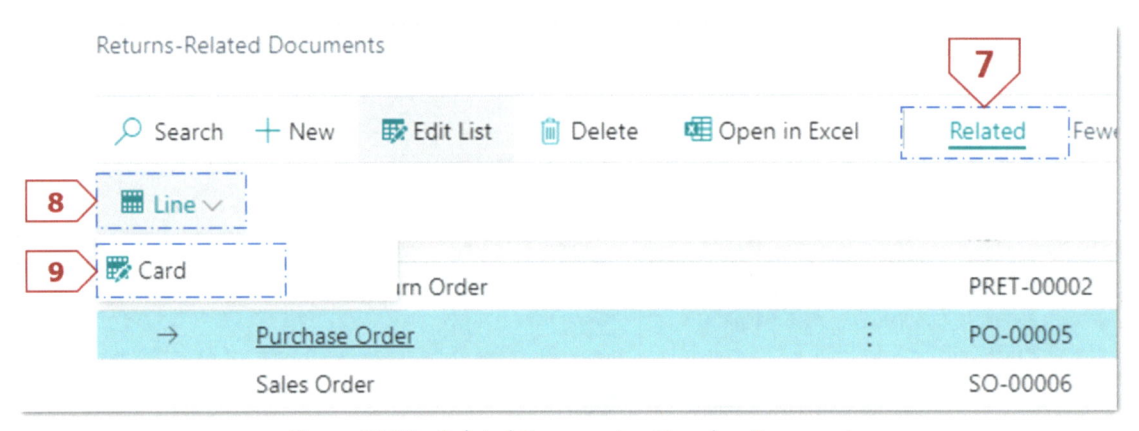

Figure 18-10 - Related Documents - Opening Document

When your return is ready, just like any Sales Document, you **Post** via **Posting** (**10**) -> **Post** (**11**):

PART 4: BASIC OPERATIONS
CHAPTER 18: CORRECTING ERRORS

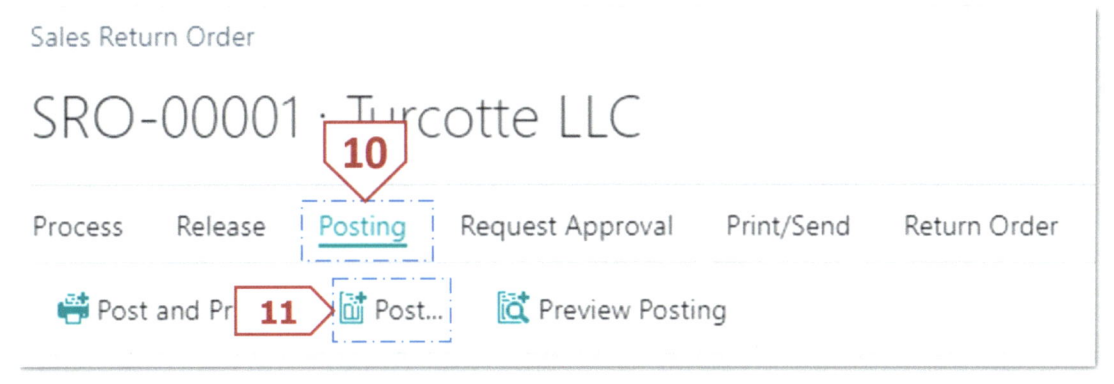

```
Sales Return Order

SRO-00001 · Turcotte LLC
                    10

Process    Release    Posting    Request Approval    Print/Send    Return Order

    Post and Pr  11  ▶  Post...    Preview Posting
```

Figure 18-11 - Sales Return Order - Post

However, since this is a return, you are receiving items, so you will see this list of options (instead of shipping):

- ○ Receive
- ○ Invoice
- ● Receive and Invoice

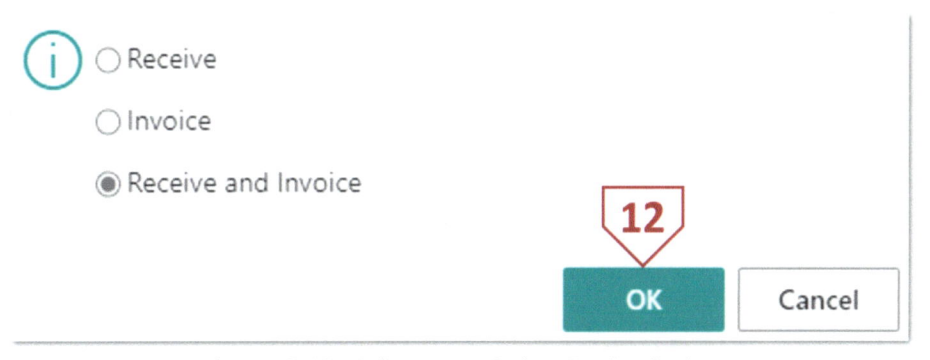

12

OK   Cancel

Figure 18-12 - Sales Return Order - Posting Options

When you select **Receive and Invoice** and click **OK** (**12**), you will be offered information about the related **Posted Sales Credit Memo**:

The return order is posted as number PSCM-00001 and moved to the Posted Sales Credit Memos window.

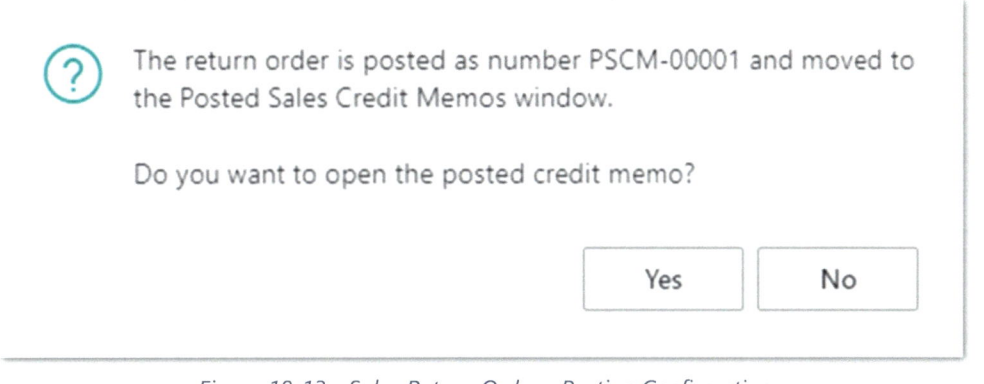

Do you want to open the posted credit memo?

Yes   No

Figure 18-13 - Sales Return Order - Posting Confirmation

PART 4: BASIC OPERATIONS
CHAPTER 18: CORRECTING ERRORS

RETURN RESULTS

If we look at the 🔍 **Customer Card**, we will see that the **Balance** (**1**) information is updated:

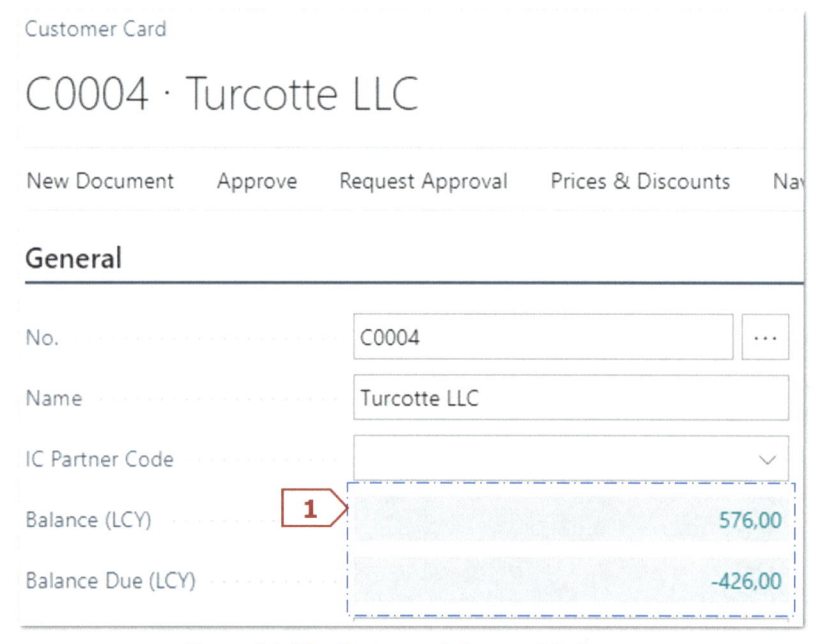

Figure 18-14 - Customer Balance with Return

The **Customer Ledger Entries** shows that the return is registered as a **Credit Memo** (**2**):

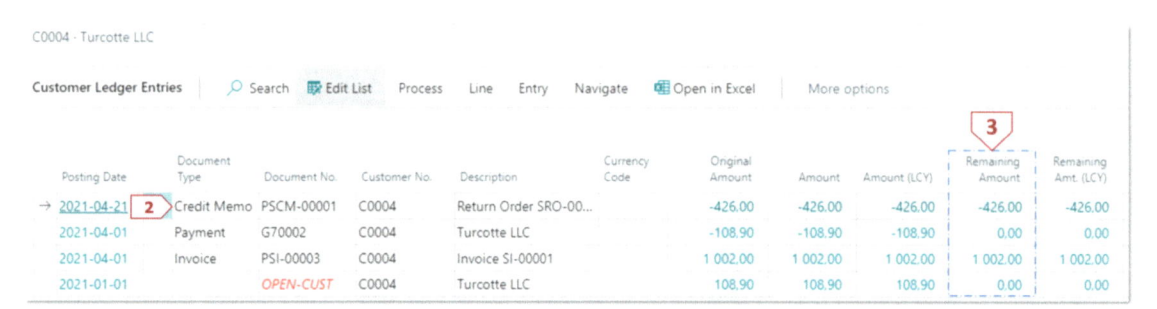

Figure 18-15 - Credit Memo (from Return) in Customer Ledger Entries

The **Remaining Amounts** (**3**) here are still open – this return was one portion of a combined invoice, so we will need to apply that manually, which is covered below in **Changing Applications**.

SALES CORRECTIVE CREDIT MEMOS

Sometimes we simply make mistakes and need to correct an incorrect sales invoice. This is handled in Business Central through Sales Credit Memos. Like any sales document, we can create a Sales Credit Memo from the **Sales Credit Memos** list with the **New** (**1**) button:

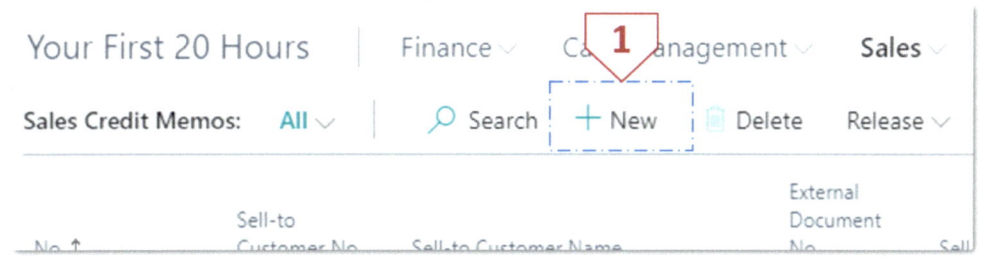

Figure 18-16 - Creating Sales Credit Memo

And then entering all the information manually:

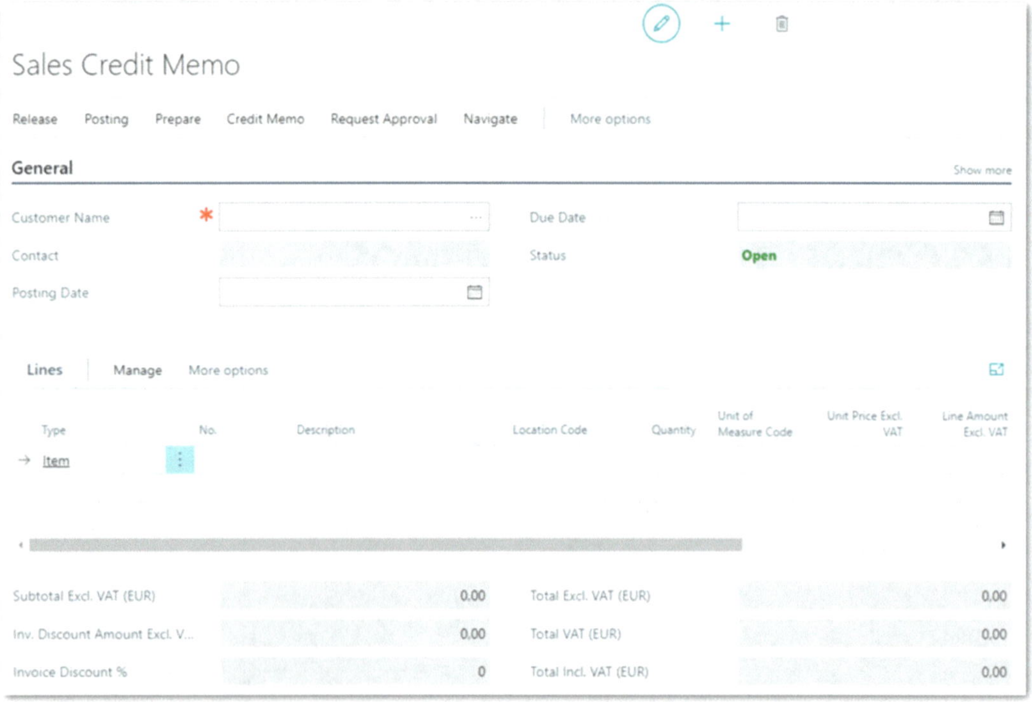

Figure 18-17 - Empty Sales Credit Memo

However, most of the time someone needs a credit memo, it is for a specific invoice. Business Central makes this easy from the **Posted Sales Invoices**. We can directly post a corrective Credit Memo from the **Correct** (**2**) action group, using the **Correct** (**3**) function:

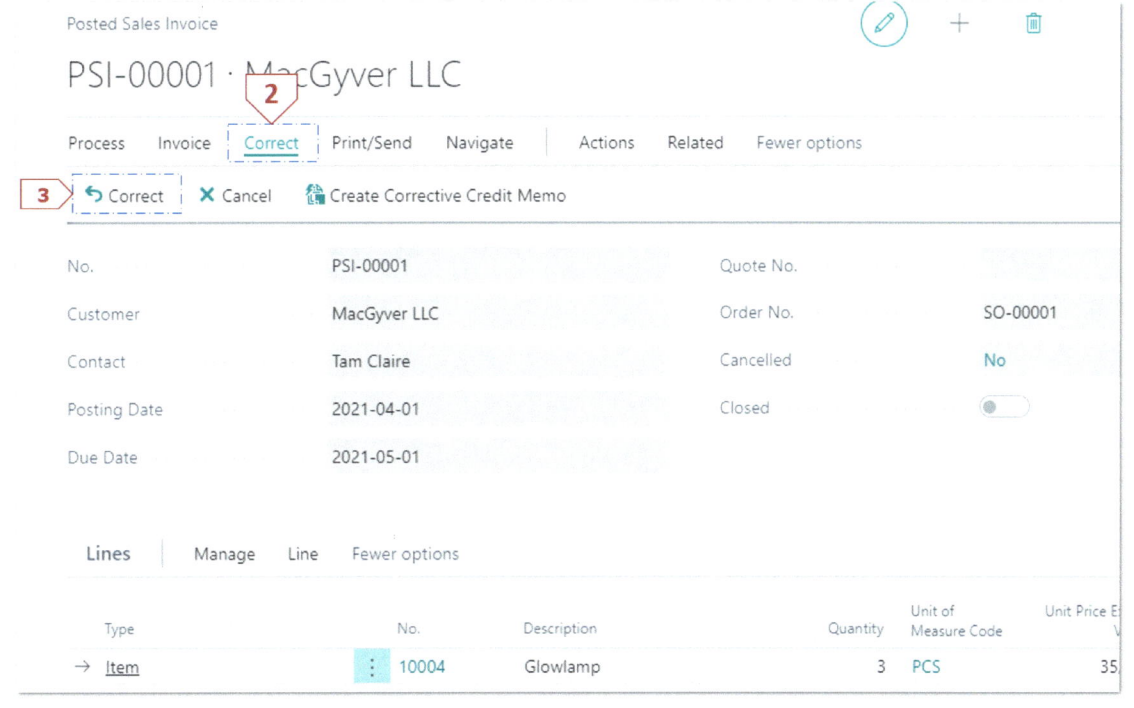

Figure 18-18 - Posted Sales Invoice - Correct Action

In this case, the invoice was created from an order, so it will tell you that it cannot create any new documents for you automatically:

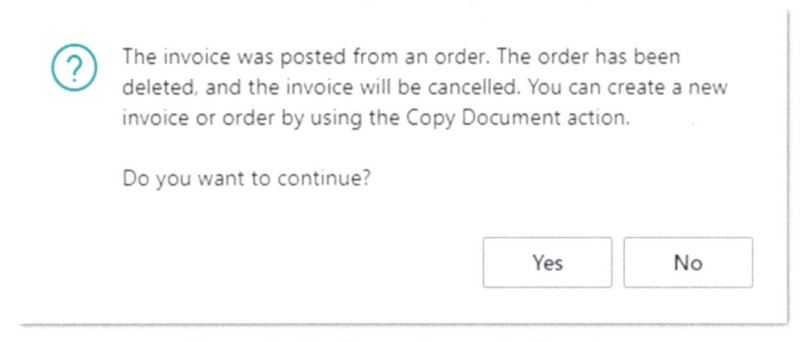

Figure 18-19 - Correct Invoice Confirmation

When you click **Yes**, it will create and post a **Sales Credit Memo** for you. When we look in the list of **Posted Sales Credit Memos**, we will see this as a corrective credit memo, which stands out with the **Remaining Amount** (**4**) already zero and **Corrective** (**4**) set to Yes:

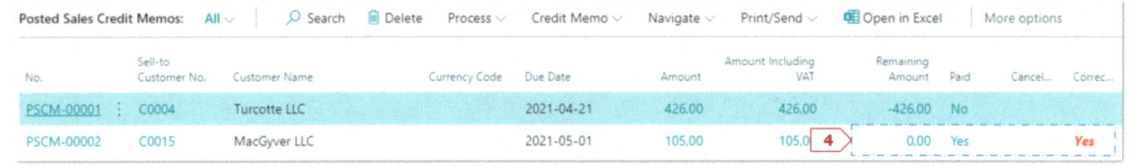

Figure 18-20 - Corrective Posted Sales Credit Memo

If we look in the Customer Ledger Entries, we see the **Credit Memo** (**5**) entry:

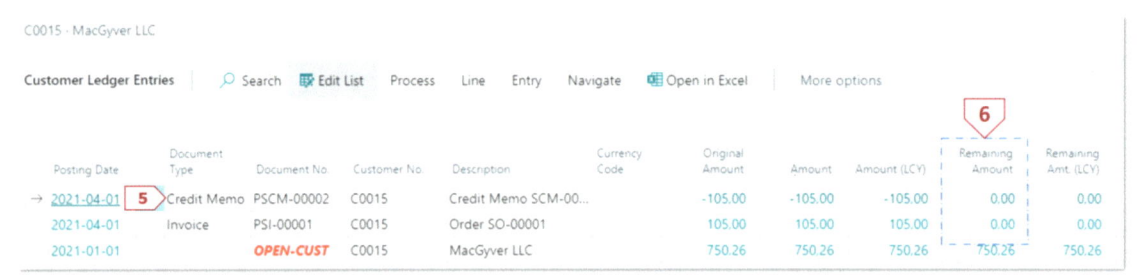

Figure 18-21 - Credit Memo in Customer Ledger Entries

We will see that the **Remaining Amount** (**6**) of both the Credit Memo and the Invoice it was correcting are now zero.

PURCHASE RETURN ORDERS

When we need to return items from our inventory to our vendors, we do this via the 🔍 **Purchase Return Order** list, by clicking the **New** (**1**) button:

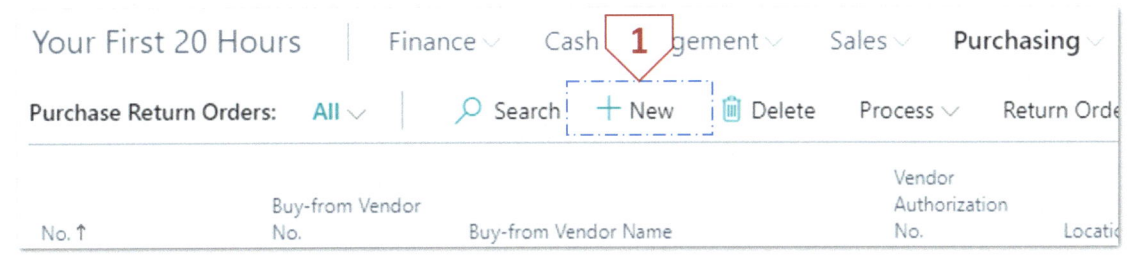

Figure 18-22 - Creating a New Purchase Return Order

The Purchase Return Order works like most purchase documents in that you select a **Vendor** (**2**) to start the document:

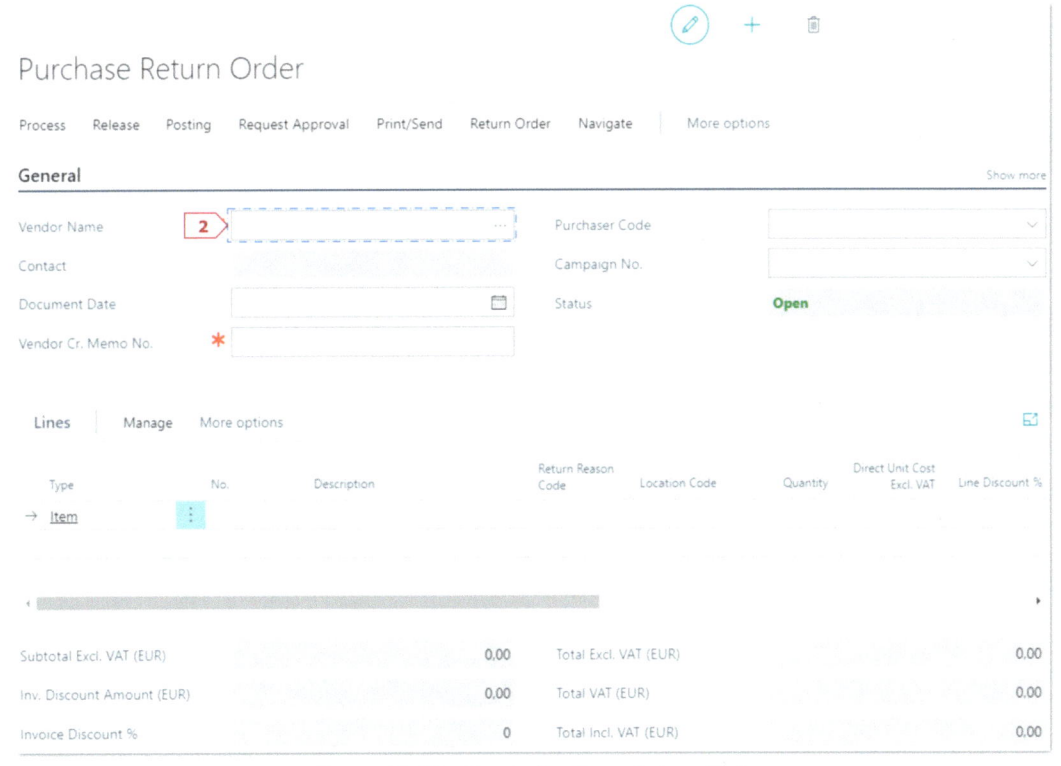

Figure 18-23 - Empty Purchase Return Order

Once the Purchase Return Order is started, you can use another efficiency function to fetch the lines of the purchase document you want to return via the **Process** (**3**) -> **Get Posted Document Lines to Reverse...** (**4**):

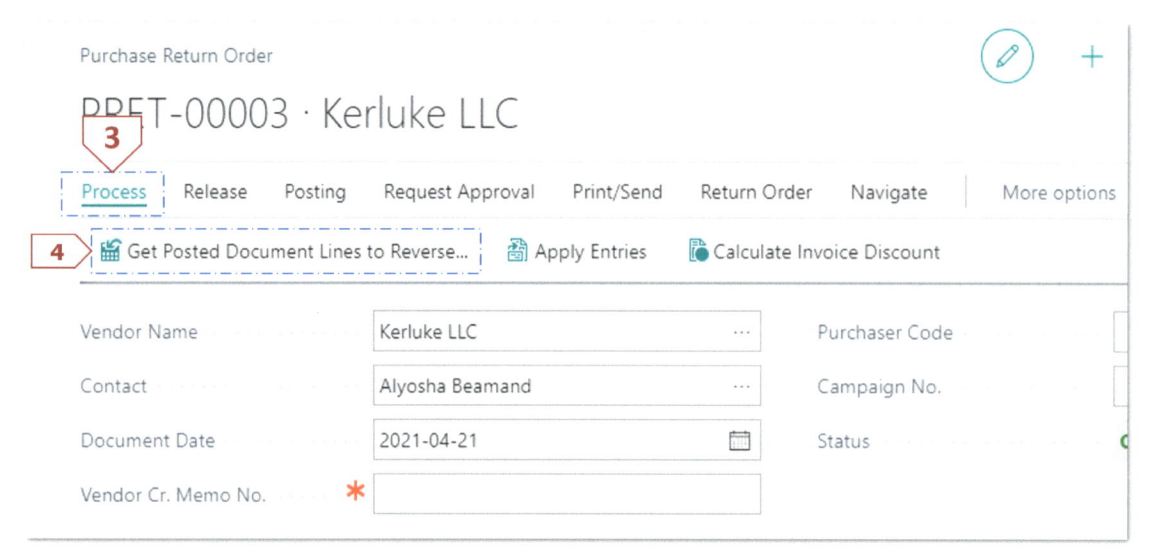

Purchase Return Order							
PRET-00003 · Kerluke LLC							
3							
Process	Release	Posting	Request Approval	Print/Send	Return Order	Navigate	More options
4 ⭲ Get Posted Document Lines to Reverse...		Apply Entries		Calculate Invoice Discount			
Vendor Name		Kerluke LLC			Purchaser Code		
Contact		Alyosha Beamand			Campaign No.		
Document Date		2021-04-21			Status		
Vendor Cr. Memo No.	*						

Figure 18-24 - Purchase Return Order - Get Lines to Reverse

This will open a history window from which you can select past purchase document lines you would like to reverse:

310 PAGE · PART 4: BASIC OPERATIONS · CHAPTER 18: CORRECTING ERRORS

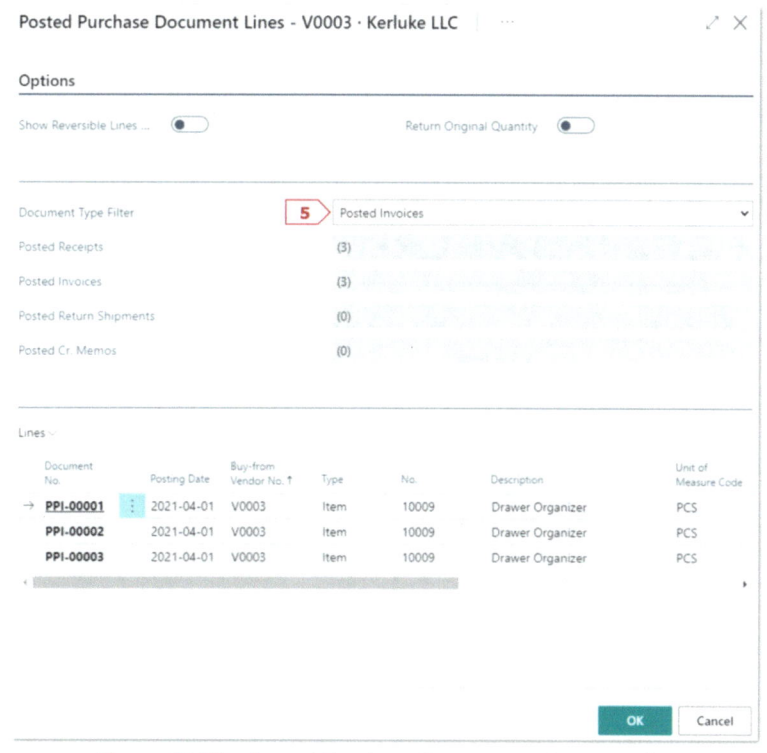

Figure 18-25 - Posted Purchase Documents Lines to Select

You can toggle the **Document Type Filter** (**4**) between different posted documents, but in our case, the lines we want are already here. Holding down Shift (for a range) or Ctrl (for specific multi-select), we multi-select the lines we want to return then click **OK**. This will bring those lines to the **Purchase Return Order Lines**:

Figure 18-26 - Purchase Return Order - Lines Populated

PART 4: BASIC OPERATIONS
CHAPTER 18: CORRECTING ERRORS

It will also bring along some **Comment Type** lines (**6**) to let you know what document these items were involved in prior to the return.

The **Purchase Return Order** can then be **Post**ed.

PURCHASE CORRECTIVE CREDIT MEMOS

While you can certainly create **Purchase Credit Memos** manually, often you need to correct a purchase invoice. Via the **Posted Purchase Invoices** list, you can create a corrective Purchase Credit Memo. Select the invoice you wish to correct in the list (**1**), then under the **Correct** (**2**) group, select the **Correct** (**3**) action:

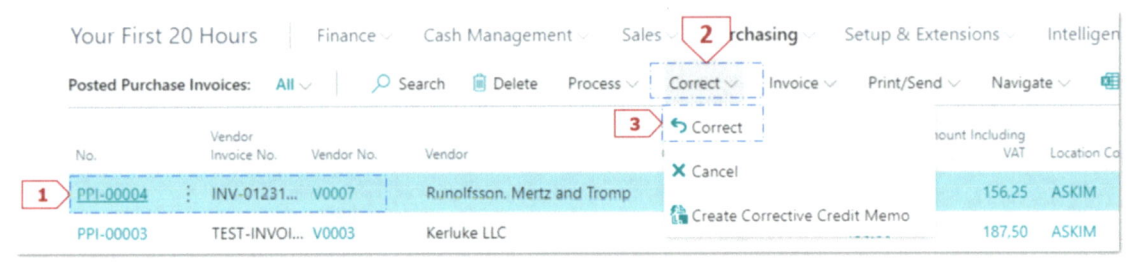

Figure 18-27 - Posted Purchase Invoice - Correct Action

In this case, we are correcting a service invoice that involved *no items*, so we are now asked:

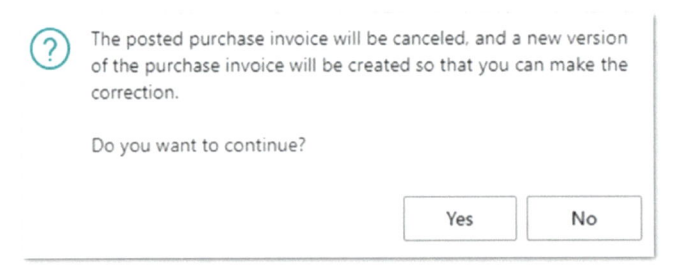

Figure 18-28 - Posted Purchase Invoice - Correct Confirmation

Because no **Purchase Order** was involved, it can recreate the **Purchase Invoice** for us so that we can make the correction(s):

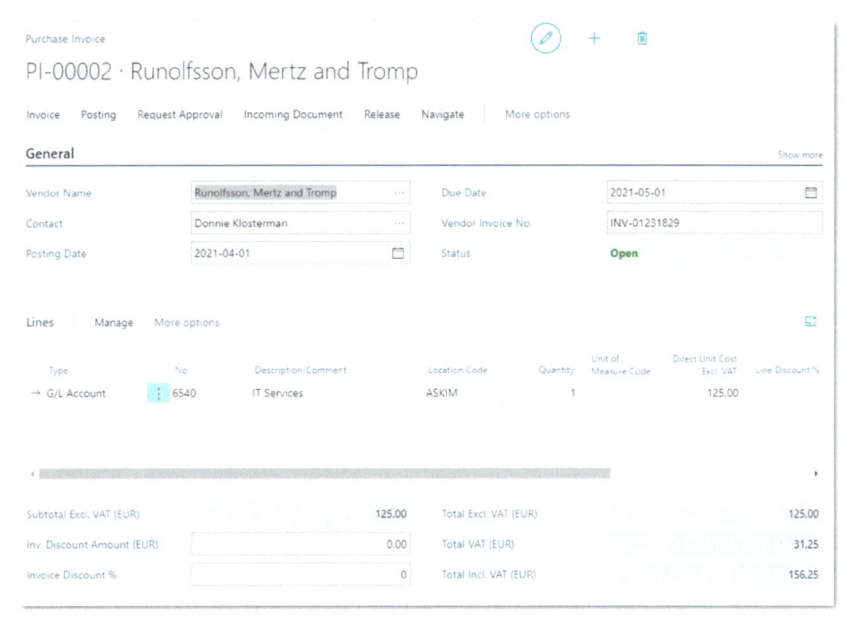

Figure 18-29 - Recreated Purchase Invoice

In the **Vendor Ledger Entries**, we will see that a **Credit Memo** (**4**) was created, and the **Remaining Amount** (**5**) for both the **Credit Memo** and the **Invoice** are now **0**:

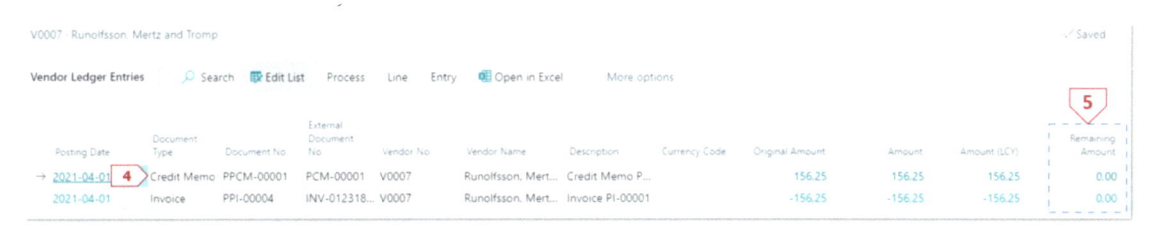

Figure 18-30 - Corrective Credit Memo in Vendor Ledger Entries

CHANGING APPLICATIONS

Sometimes a customer makes a payment to us and it is not meant for the invoice we expected. The amount of money paid to us has not changed, but we need to consider the amount for a different invoice. This is what the **Applications** system is for. We can change applications after receiving the payment.

In our scenario, we will adjust this payment that was already applied to an invoice to be applied to a different invoice, as shown here on the **Customer Ledger Entries** for **C0004** (**1**):

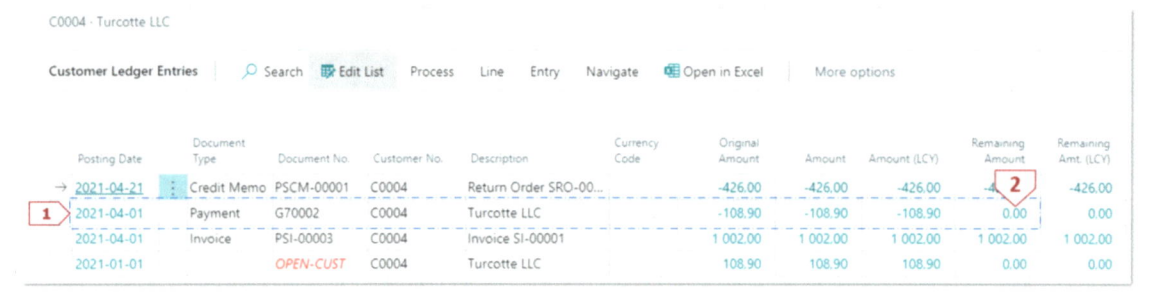

Figure 18-31 - Customer Ledger Entries - Showing Payment to Unapply

The **Remaining Amount** (**2**) of this **Payment** entry is zero, meaning it has been fully applied to an invoice.

We will now *unapply* the payment, then *reapply* the payment to a different invoice. With the **Payment Line** (**3**) selected, under **Process** (**4**) select **Unapply Entries...** (**5**):

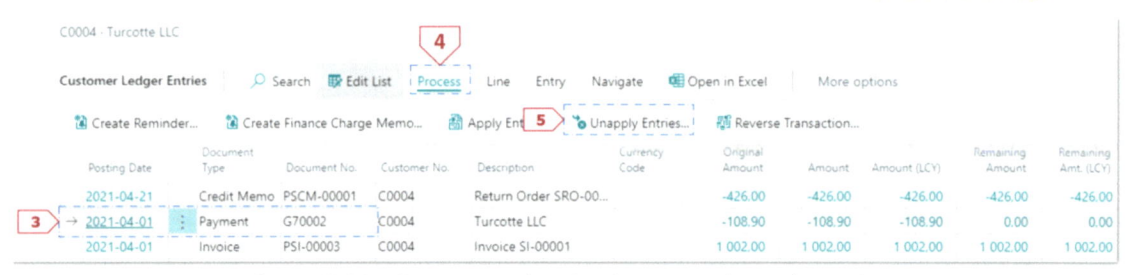

Figure 18-32 - Customer Ledger Entries - Unapply Entries Action

This opens the **Unapply Customer Entries** window:

Figure 18-33 - Customer Ledger Entries - Unapply Entries Window

Confusingly, if you click **OK** (**6**), nothing will happen. All the functionalities of this page are hidden in a *strange* menu label that looks like it is part of the title, only marked with 📋 (**7**):

Figure 18-34 - Unapply Customer Entries - Adjusting the Menu to an Action Bar

If you uncheck the **Show as menu** (**8**) option, you will find that the menu makes more sense:

Figure 18-35 - Unapply Customer Entries – Action Bar Rescued

Now, we came here to unapply an entry, so select the menu option **Unapply** (**9**):

Figure 18-36 - Unapply Customer Entries - Unapply Action

It will confirm if you want to post the correcting entries, which will change the application:

PART 4: BASIC OPERATIONS
CHAPTER 18: CORRECTING ERRORS

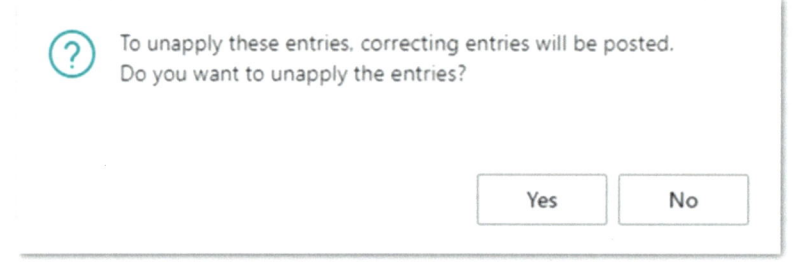

Figure 18-37 - Unapply Confirmation

When we click **Yes** in the confirmation to get back to the **Customer Ledger Entries**, we will see now that the **Remaining Amount** (**11**) fields are all reset to the full **Amount** (**10**) values:

Figure 18-38 - Customer Ledger Entries - Remaining Amounts Opened

Now we will apply the **Payment** (**14**) ledger entry using the **Process** (**12**) select **Apply Entries** (**13**):

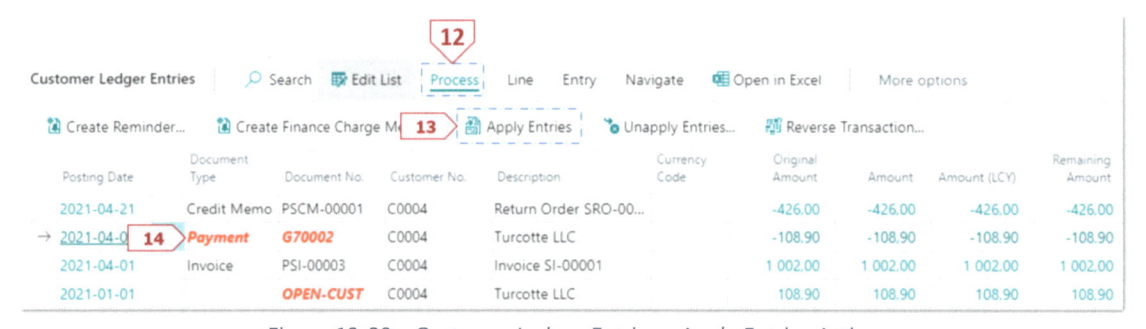

Figure 18-39 - Customer Ledger Entries - Apply Entries Action

This opens the **Apply Customer Entries** window:

Figure 18-40 - Apply Customer Entries Window

In this window, we *mark* the target documents we want to apply to using the **Applies-to ID** (**15**) field. Selecting the **Invoice** (**18**) line that we want this payment to be applied to, we then click **Process** (**16**), then select **Set Applies-to ID** (**17**):

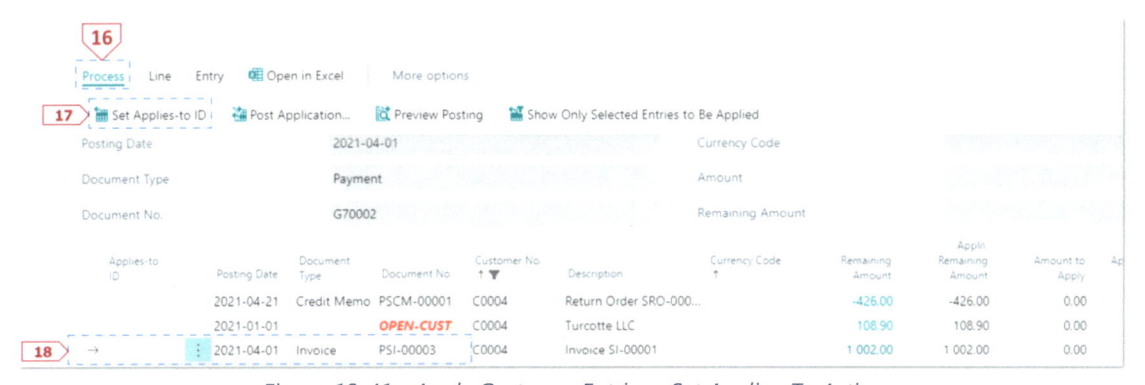

Figure 18-41 - Apply Customer Entries - Set Applies-To Action

This will mark the line with your User ID (**19**). When you are done marking lines, you click **Process** (**20**), then select **Post Application…** (**21**):

PART 4: BASIC OPERATIONS
CHAPTER 18: CORRECTING ERRORS

Edit - Apply Customer Entries - C0004 · Turcotte LLC

Process Line Entry Open in Excel More options

General

Posting Date	2021-04-01	Currency C...
Document Type	Payment	Amount
Document No.	G70002	Remaining

Applies-to ID	Posting Date	Document Type	Document No.	Customer No.	Description	Currency
	2021-04-21	Credit Memo	PSCM-00001	C0004	Return Order SRO-000...	
19	2021-01-01		**OPEN-CUST**	C0004	Turcotte LLC	
→ ADMIN	2021-04-01	Invoice	PSI-00003	C0004	Invoice SI-00001	

20

Process Line Entry Open in Excel More options

Set Applies-t **21** Post Application... Preview Posting Show O...

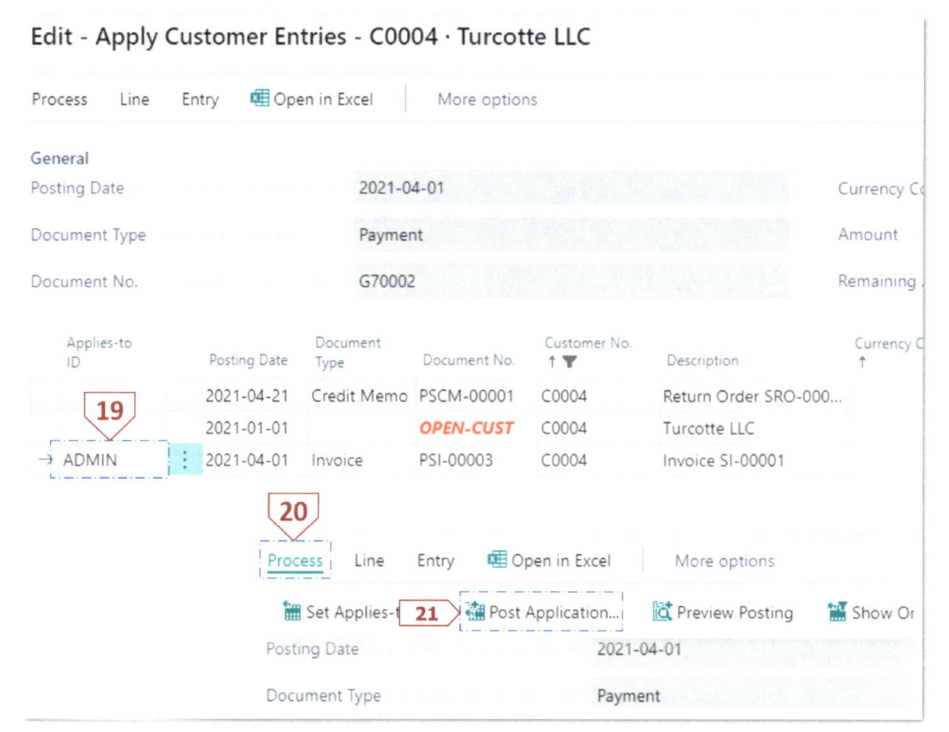

| Posting Date | 2021-04-01 |
| Document Type | Payment |

Figure 18-42 - Apply Customer Entries - Post Application Action

This will pop up a dialog confirming what date to record the application on:

Edit - Post Application

| Document No. | G70002 |
| Posting Date | 2021-04-01 |

Figure 18-43 - Post Application Confirmation

Once you click **OK** in the **Post Application** confirmation, you will be back at the **Customer Ledger Entries** and you will see that the **Remaining Amount** (**22**) of the documents is now updated:

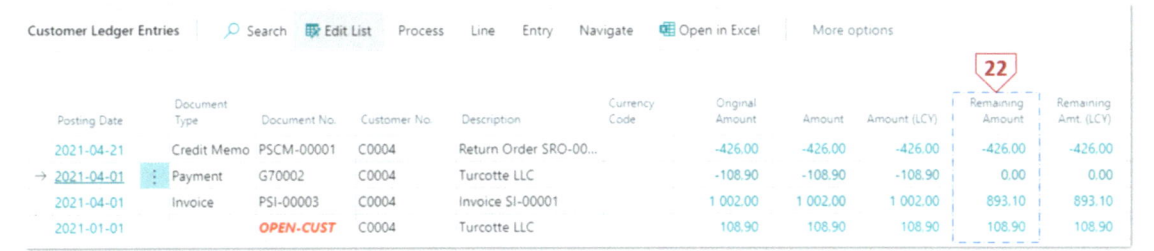

Figure 18-44 - Customer Ledger Entries - Showing Applied Results in Remaining Amount

UNDO SHIPMENTS

Sometimes when you are working quickly, you accidentally ship the wrong item, order, or quantity. If you have not invoiced the error, you can use the Undo Shipment functionality. (If you have invoiced it, you will need to create and post a return order to correct this)

On the **Posted Sales Shipment**, in the Lines action bar, in the **More Options** (**1**) section:

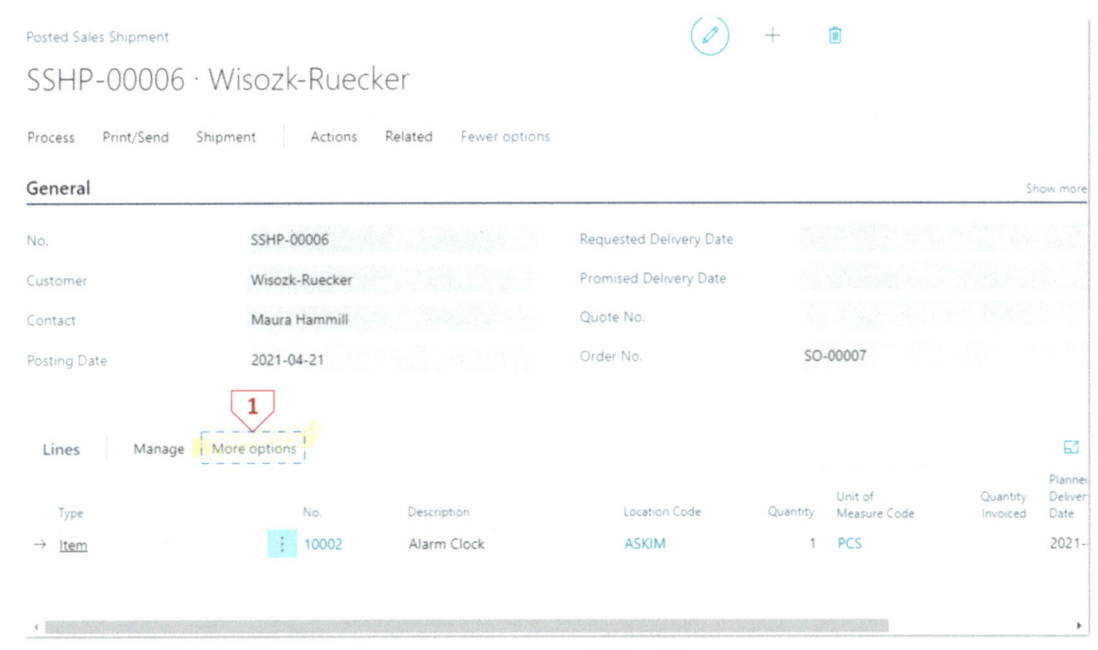

Figure 18-45 - Posted Sales Shipment

You will find the **Functions** (**1**) section with the option to **Undo Shipment** (**2**):

PART 4: BASIC OPERATIONS
CHAPTER 18: CORRECTING ERRORS

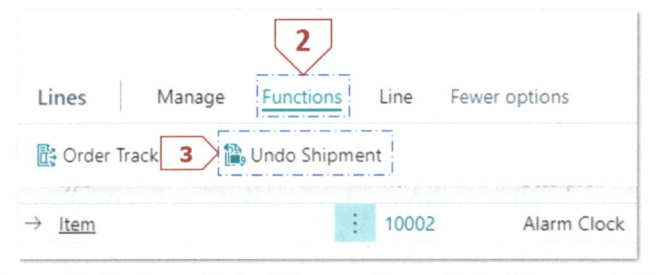

Figure 18-46 - Posted Sales Shipment Lines - Undo Shipment Action

The action applies to each line you have selected when you click the **Undo Shipment** (**3**) button, so you can undo part of, or *all* of, the shipment. It will then ask:

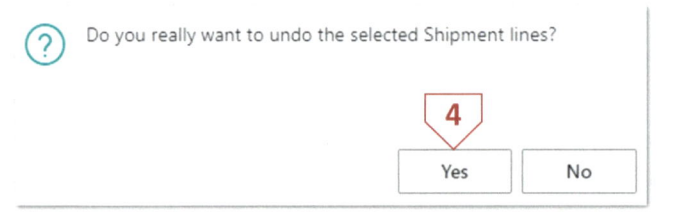

Figure 18-47 - Undo Shipment Confirmation

If you click **Yes** (**4**), you will see that it creates negative entries (**5**) on the Lines to indicate that it has been *undone*:

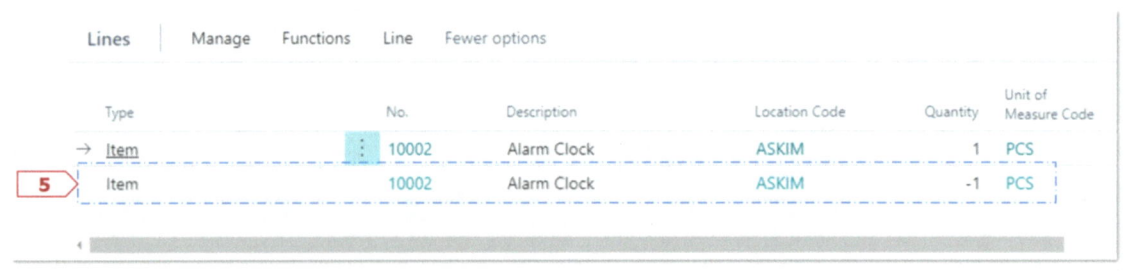

Figure 18-48 - Posted Sales Shipment Lines - Undone

It will also update the **Quantity Shipped** (**1**) of the related **Sales Order**:

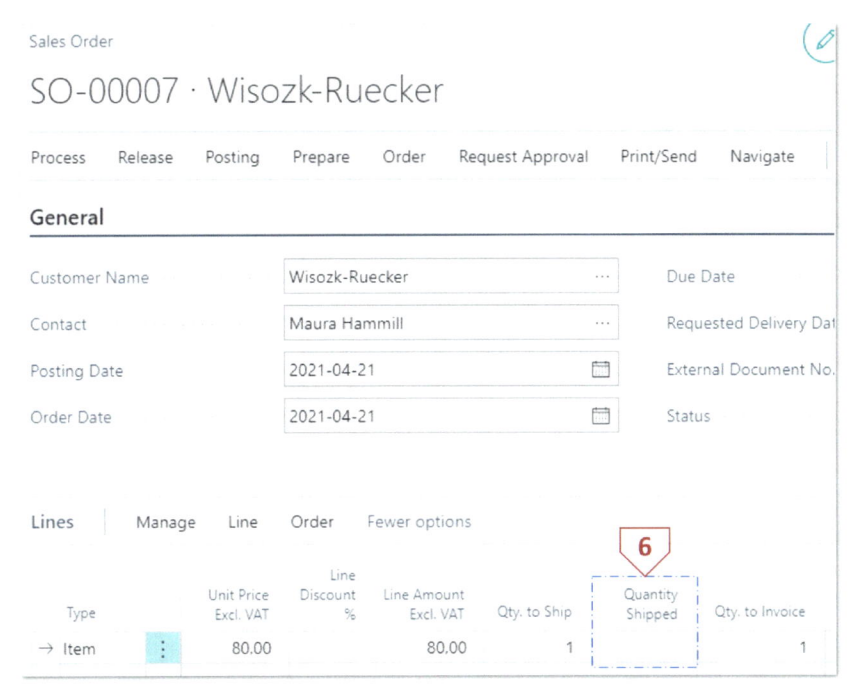

Figure 18-49 - Sales Order - Quantity Shipped Reset

Via the **Item** card, if you look at the **Item Ledger Entries** for this item, you will see that a reversing entry (**7**) has been created:

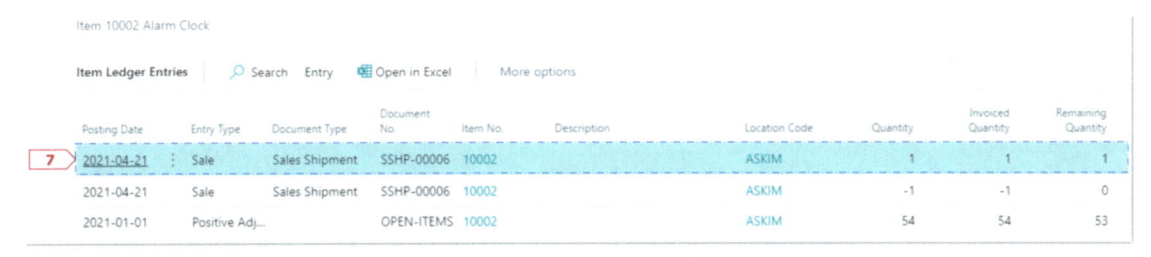

Figure 18-50 - Item Ledger Entries - Shipment Undone

UNDO RECEIPTS

The **Undo Receipts** functionality works identically to the **Undo Shipment** functionality above, except that you will find the **Undo Receipt** (**2**) under **Functions** (**1**) on the ⚙ **Posted Purchase Receipt**:

Posted Purchase Receipt

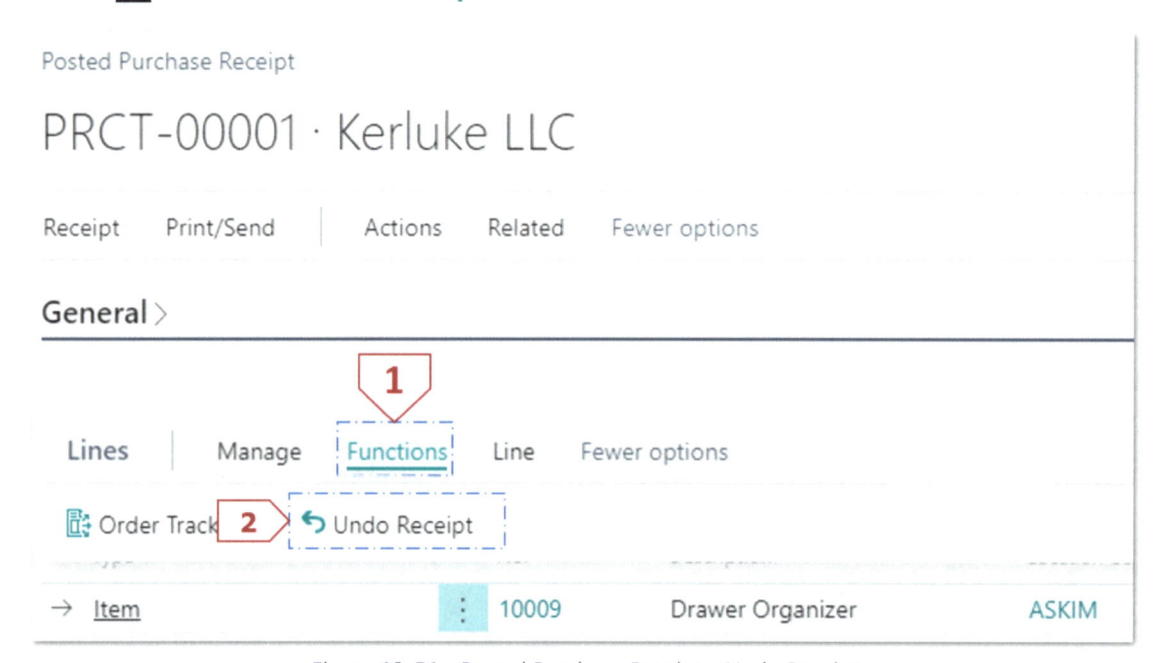

PRCT-00001 · Kerluke LLC

Receipt   Print/Send | Actions   Related   Fewer options

General >

Lines | Manage   **Functions** (1)   Line   Fewer options

📋 Order Track   (2)   ↶ Undo Receipt

→ Item   10009   Drawer Organizer   ASKIM

Figure 18-51 - Posted Purchase Receipt - Undo Receipt

Chapter 19: Recurring Tasks

There are some tasks that need to be completed in the system on a *regular basis*. This chapter will cover what those tasks are and the results of running them.

CLOSING FISCAL YEARS / INCOME STATEMENT

The two main steps to closing your year in Business Central are:

1. Close the 🔍 **Accounting Periods**.
2. Run the 🔍 **Close Income Statement** report.

Additionally, it is a good idea to update the 🔍 **General Ledger Setup** to restrict posting to the current fiscal year.

CLOSE THE ACCOUNTING PERIODS

In the 🔍 **Accounting Periods** list, we can *create* and *close* years. It is a good idea to create your new year before you close the current one. When you click the **Process** (**1**) -> **Create Year...** (**2**) action:

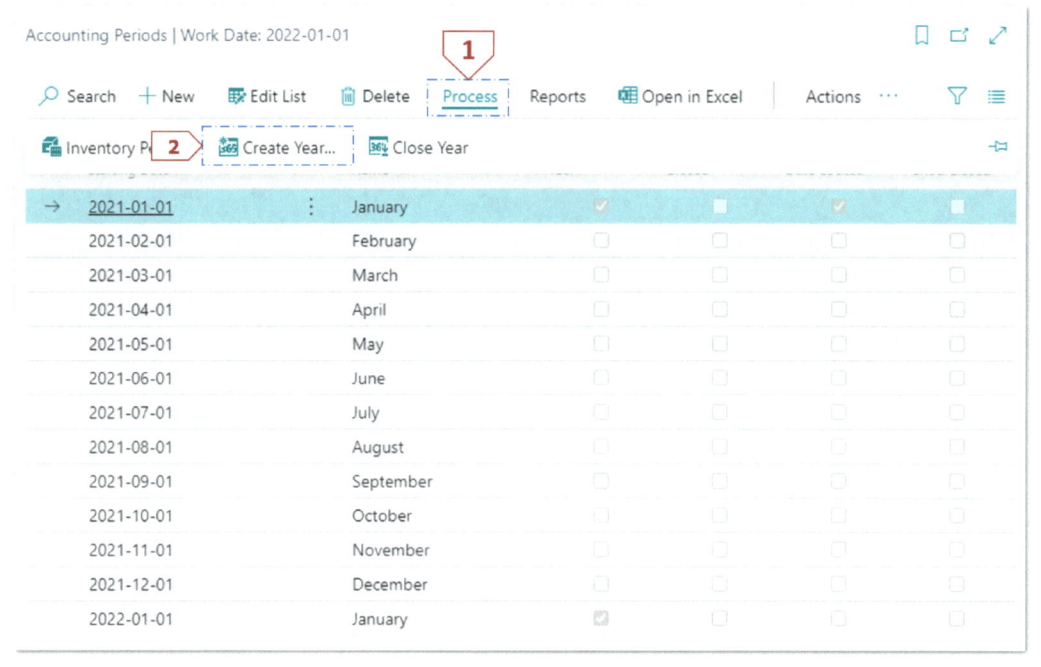

Figure 19-1 - Accounting Periods - Create Year

You will then be asked for settings, which will default most of the values:

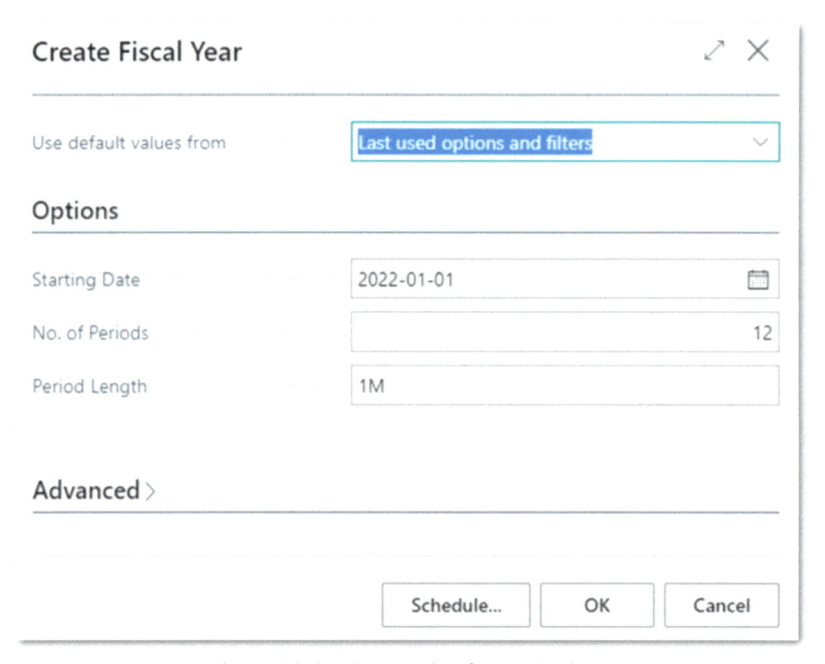

Figure 19-2 - Create Fiscal Year Options

PART 4: BASIC OPERATIONS
CHAPTER 19: RECURRING TASKS

Running this (by clicking **OK**) will create the new year. That leaves us ready to *close* the currency year.

Select the current year (**3**) in **Accounting Periods** list, then click **Process** (**4**) -> **Close Year** (**5**):

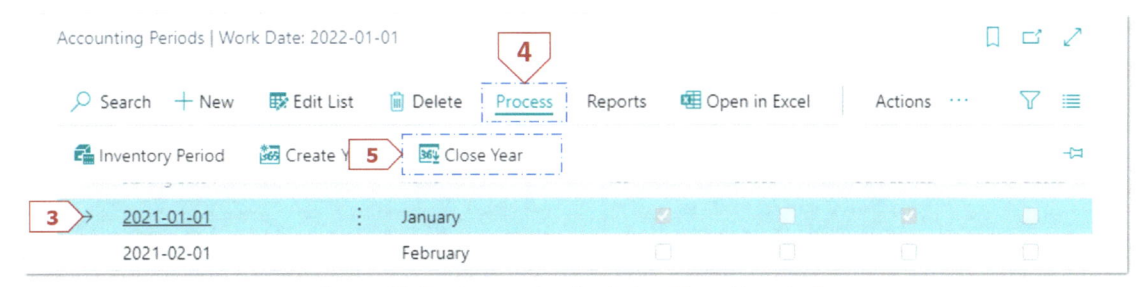

Figure 19-3 - Accounting Periods - Close Year Action

The Close Year process cannot be undone. You will be asked if you want to proceed:

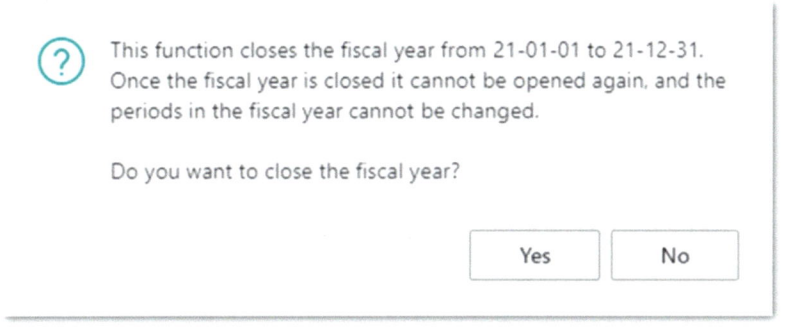

Figure 19-4 - Close Year Action Confirmation

You will now see that the periods in the *now closed* year are marked as **Closed** (**6**) and **Date Locked** (**7**):

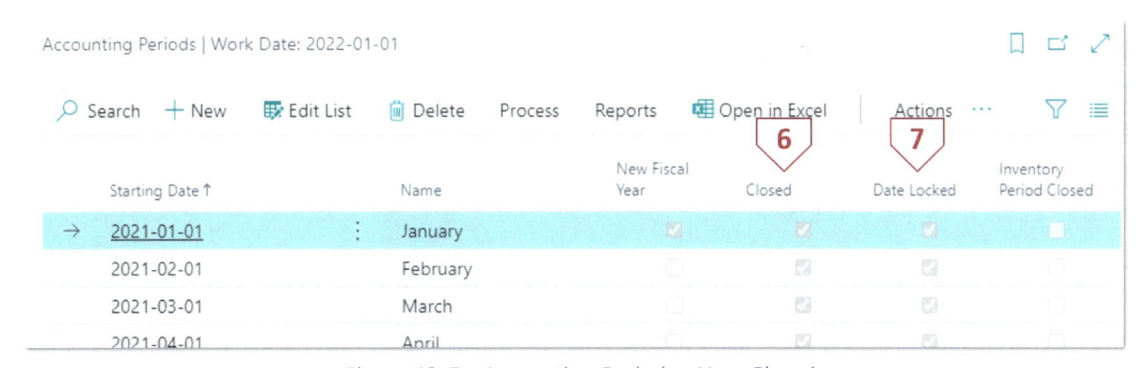

Figure 19-5 - Accounting Periods - Year Closed

PART 4: BASIC OPERATIONS
CHAPTER 19: RECURRING TASKS

Note: It is still possible to post transactions in the closed year, but they will be marked to indicate they are new entries into a prior year.

RUN THE CLOSE INCOME STATEMENT REPORT

If we look at these sample 🔍 **G/L Accounts** with **Net Change** (**1**) and **Balance** (**2**) values:

No.	Name	Net Change (1)	Additional-Currency Net Change	Balance (2)
3000	**INCOME STATEMENT**	-	-	-
3002	**Revenue**	-	-	-
3040	**Sales, Normal Stock**	-	-	-
3041	Sales, Normal, Sweden	-158 259,49	-	-158 259,49
3045	Sales, Normal, Non-EU	-1 553,94	-	-1 553,94
3046	Sales, Normal, EU	-342,44	-	-342,44
3049	**Total, Sales of Normal**	-160 155,87	-	-160 155,87
3050	**Sales, Seasonal**	-	-	-
3051	Sales, Seasonal, Sweden	-97 340,04	-	-97 340,04
3055	Sales, Seasonal Non-EU	-6 457,20	-	-6 457,20
3056	Sales, Seasonal EU	-16 673,98	-	-16 673,98
3059	**Total, Sales Seasonal**	-120 471,22	-	-120 471,22
3095	Other sales	-	-	-
3098	Sales Reductions	-	-	-
3731	Sales Discounts	-	-	-
3740	Invoice Rounding	-	-	-
3999	**Total, Revenue**	-280 627,09	-	-280 627,09

Figure 19-6 - Sample G/L Income Statement Accounts with Balances

These balances need to be moved to our retained earnings G/L Account as part of closing. This is done via 🔍 **General Journal** entries being posted. The 🔍 **Close Income Statement** process will help you to create the entries.

From the 🔍 **Chart of Accounts**, click on **Process** (**3**) -> **Close Income Statement** (**4**):

PART 4: BASIC OPERATIONS
CHAPTER 19: RECURRING TASKS
PAGE 327

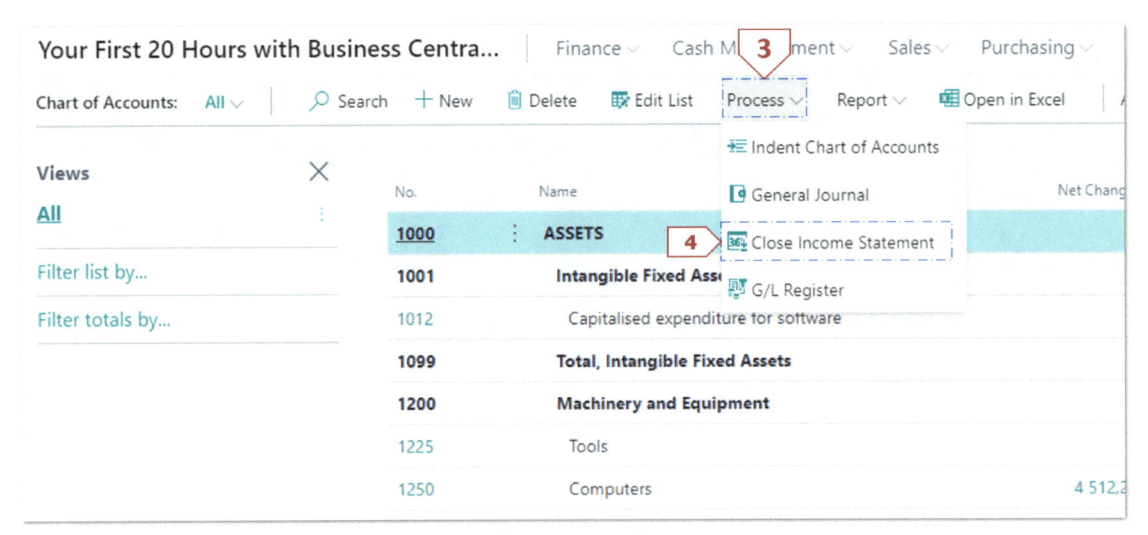

Figure 19-7 - Chart of Accounts - Close Income Statement

This will open the **Close Income Statement Options**:

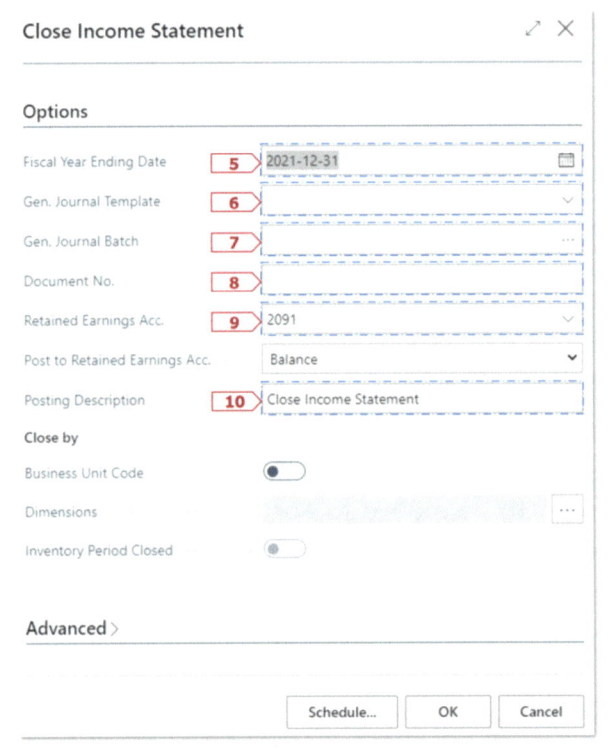

Figure 19-8 - Close Income Statement Options

Element	What is it?
1	The **Fiscal Year Ending Date** controls which year to close.

2	The **Gen. Journal Template** controls which template type the entries should be made in.
3	The **Gen. Journal Batch** controls which batch the entries should be made in.
4	The **Document No.** selected here will be used for all entries.
5	The **Retained Earnings Acc.** selects which **G/L Account** will be used to balance the entries.
6	The Posting **Description** field allows the user to enter the Description field that will appear on the journal lines. Usually, this will default to "Close Income Statement".

For the scenario we have been using in this book, we would close the year **2021** with these options:

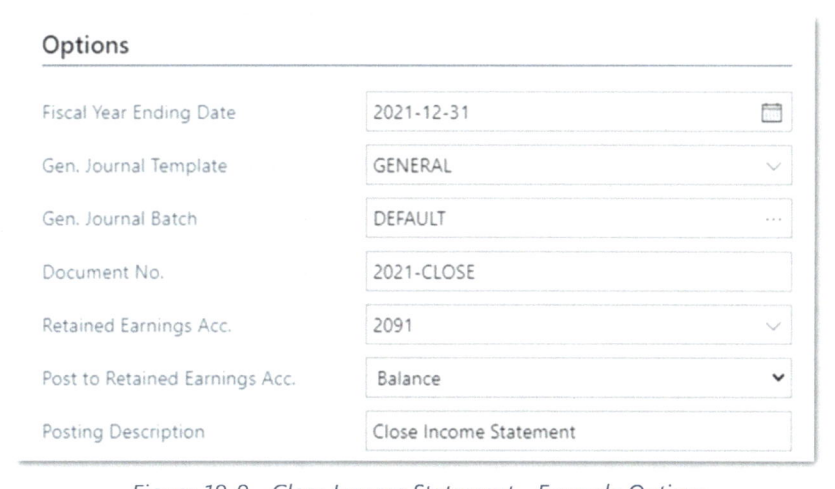

Figure 19-9 - Close Income Statement - Example Options

Once you click **OK**, it will inform you that the journal entries have been created:

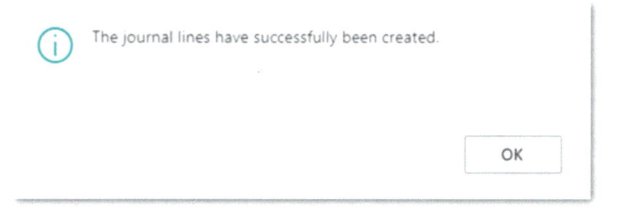

Figure 19-10 - Close Income Statement - Process Complete Message

Opening the **General Journal** batch, in our case, the **DEFAULT** batch (**11**):

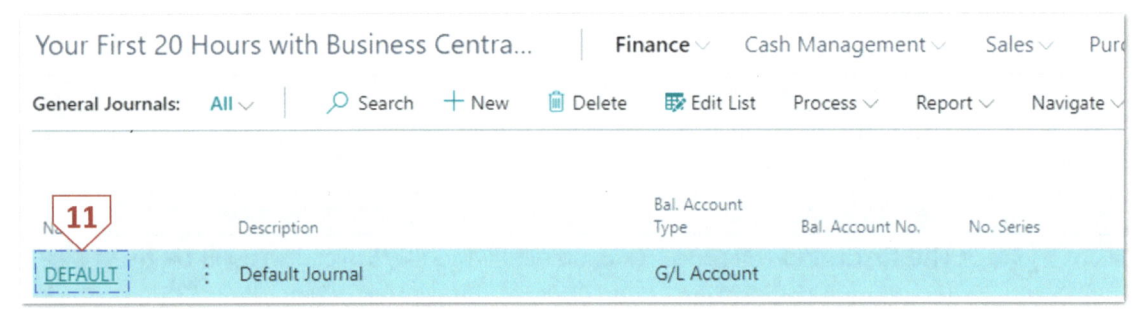

No.	Description	Bal. Account Type	Bal. Account No.	No. Series
(11) DEFAULT	Default Journal	G/L Account		

Figure 19-11 - Opening the General Journal DEFAULT Batch

We will see a prepared set of journal lines based on our income statement for the year, balanced against the **Retained Earnings** (**13**) account to ensure the journal is in balance:

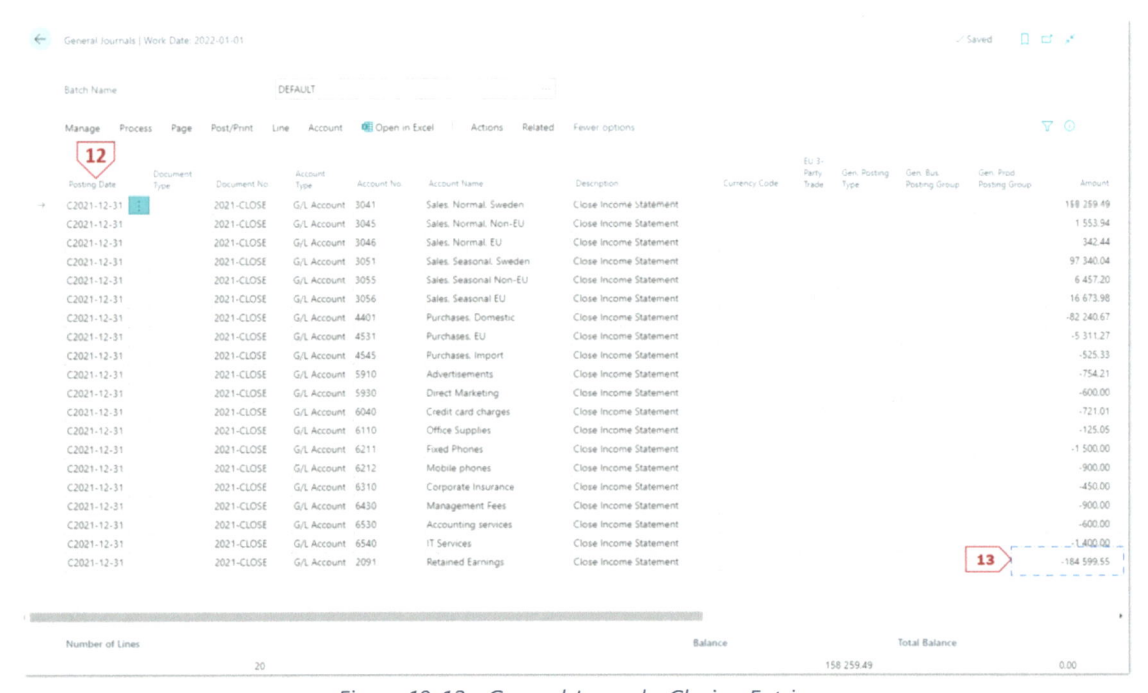

Figure 19-12 - General Jouranl - Closing Entries

You will notice the **Posting Date** (**12**) fields are all set to **C2021-12-31** in **Figure 19-12**. Dates in Business Central have a special functionality that there is a "Closing Date" between every date. So, **C2021-11-30** comes *after* **2021-11-30** but *before* **2021-12-01**. This allows filters that include the entire year to automatically exclude Closing Entries like these.

330 PAGE

PART 4: BASIC OPERATIONS
CHAPTER 19: RECURRING TASKS

After careful review and then posting, when you review your 🔍 **Chart of Accounts**, you will see the **Net Change** (**14**) and **Balance** (**15**) values are zero (blank):

No.	Name	Net Change (**14**)	Additional-Currency Net Change	Balance (**15**)
3000	**INCOME STATEMENT**	—	—	—
3002	**Revenue**	—	—	—
3040	**Sales, Normal Stock**	—	—	—
3041	Sales, Normal, Sweden	—	—	— (**16**)
3045	Sales, Normal, Non-EU	—	—	—
3046	Sales, Normal, EU	—	—	—
3049	**Total, Sales of Normal**	—	—	—
3050	**Sales, Seasonal**	—	—	—
3051	Sales, Seasonal, Sweden	—	—	—
3055	Sales, Seasonal Non-EU	—	—	—

Figure 19-13 - Income Statement - Closed Balances

Drilling-down on the **Balance** of the **3041 Sales, Normal, Sweden** account (**16**):

Posting Date	Document Type	Document No.	G/L Account No.	G/L Account Name	Description	Gen. Posting Type	Gen. Bus. Posting Group	Gen. Prod. Posting Group	Amount
→ C2021-12-31	(**17**)	2021-CLOSE	3041	Sales, Normal, Sweden	Close Income Statement				158,259.49
2021-04-01	Invoice	PSI-00002	3041	Sales, Normal, Sweden	Order SO-00002	Sale	DOMESTIC	NORMAL	-180.00
2021-01-01		OPEN-GL	3041	Sales, Normal, Sweden	Sales, Normal, Sweden				-158,079.49

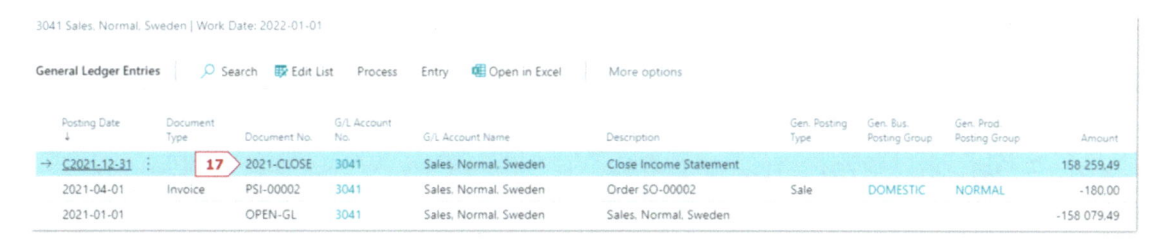

Figure 19-14 - Closing G/L Entries

We can see there is a new entry (**17**) from our **Close Income Statement** process (with the special **Closing Date** as the **Posting Date**).

If we need to be able to analyze, review, or report on the *now closed* fiscal year, we can still use the entire year in filters, such as in this view of the 🔍 **Chart of Accounts**, using **2021-01-01..2021-12-31** as the **Filter totals by** setting on the **Date Filter** (**18**):

PART 4: BASIC OPERATIONS
CHAPTER 19: RECURRING TASKS
PAGE 331

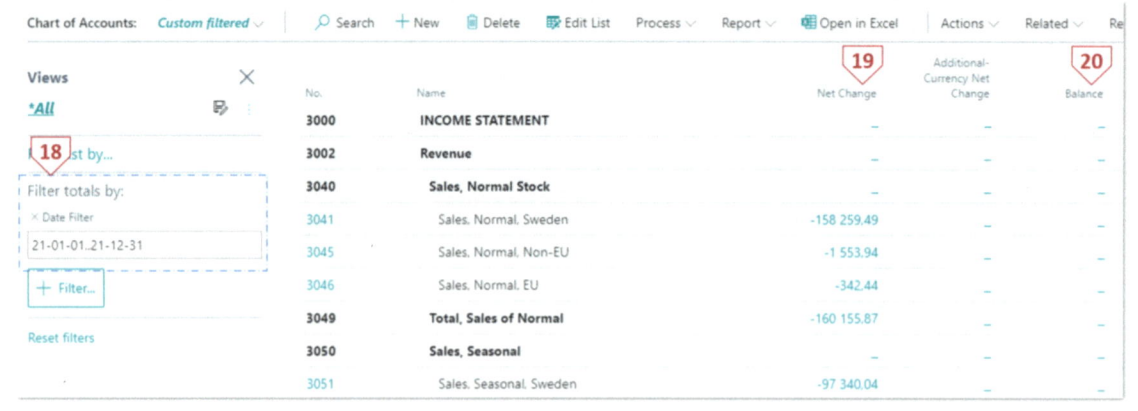

Figure 19-15 - Chart of Accounts - Net Change for Closed Year

As you can see in **Figure 19-15**, the **Net Change** (**19**) will reflect the **Date Filter** (**18**), showing you the entries for that range; but the **Balance** (**20**) shows you the *current* balance information.

ADJUST GENERAL LEDGER SETUP

It *still* needs to be possible to post in prior years, but that should be tightly controlled. As mentioned in **Chapter 6**, the **General Ledger Setup** has control fields, the **Allow Posting From** (**1**) and **Allow Posting To** (**2**) fields:

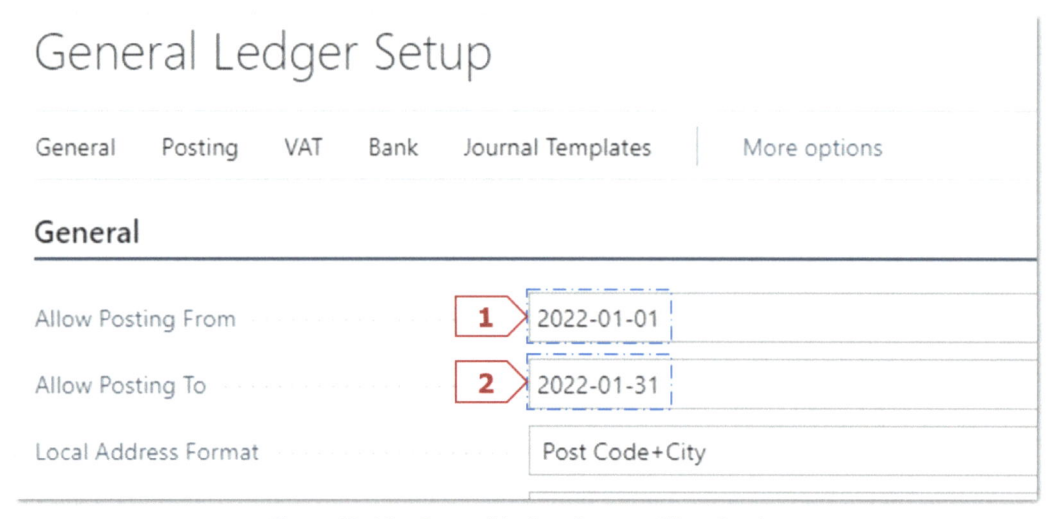

Figure 19-16 - General Ledger Setup - Allow Posting

At a minimum, these should be adjusted on a yearly basis to ensure entries are in the correct year.

It is possible to grant a user explicit permission to post to different ranges than the restriction in the **General Ledger Setup** via the **User Setup** by specifying the dates within the table's **Allow Posting From** (**1**) and **Allow Posting To** (**2**) fields:

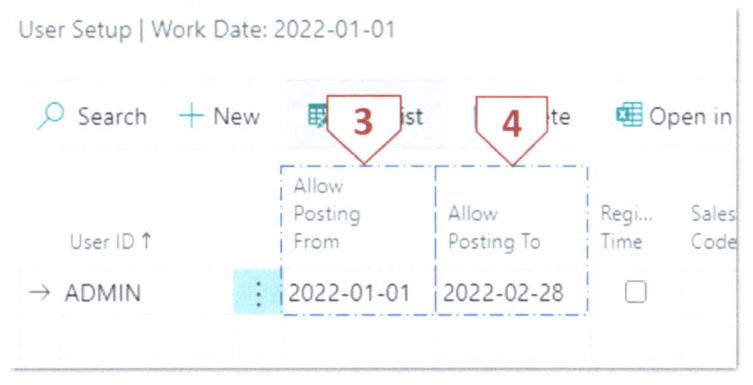

Figure 19-17 - User Setup - Allow Posting

However, user management is a lengthy topic and is, unfortunately, beyond the scope of this book.

Closing Months

There is no "month closing" process, but the question is asked often enough during ERP system configuration that this felt necessary to include.

Business Central *best practice* is to ensure users are posting in the correct period using the General Ledger Setup, per **Adjust General Ledger Setup** above.

Updating Exchange Rates

The process of updating **Currency Exchange Rates** in Business Central is very simple:

1. Set the new **Currency Exchange Rates**.
2. Run the **Adjust Exchange Rate** process to post gains/losses.

PART 4: BASIC OPERATIONS
CHAPTER 19: RECURRING TASKS
PAGE 333

To better demonstrate the gain/loss transactions, we will rely on the sales order posted in an alternate currency from **Chapter 15**, as shown in this **Posted Sales Invoice** in the **Customer Ledger Entries**:

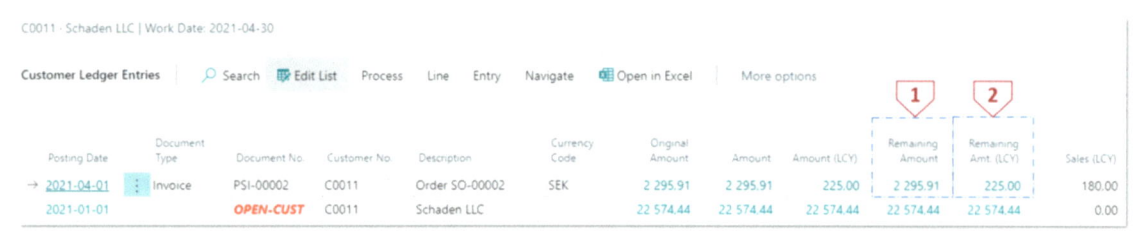

Figure 19-18 - Customer Ledger Entries - Example Alternate Currency Invoice

The **Remaining Amount** (**1**) is shown as the original **2295,91 SEK**, while the **Remaining Amt. (LCY)** (**2**) is shown in our local **225 EUR**. When we change the Exchange Rate for SEK (meaning the rate between SEK and EUR), both these remaining amounts will be affected.

SET NEW CURRENCY EXCHANGE RATES

Via the **Currencies** list, when going to the **Currency Exchange Rates**, we can see in this example that a new rate has been entered as of April 30 (**3**):

Figure 19-19 - Currency Exchange Rate - New Rate Line

All new transactions, using **SEK** as the currency, entered after **04-30** will use the newly added rate. That is all that is necessary for new transactions – just create a new line in the **Currency Exchange Rates**.

ADJUSTING OPEN TRANSACTIONS

When we invoice customers in another currency, the customer records the debt to us in that currency. When the exchange rate changes, we must track the new difference between what we recorded the receivable value (in our local currency) at the time of posting and the new value (in our local currency).

This is what the **Adjust Exchange Rate** process accounts for by creating **Unrealized Gain** or **Unrealized Loss** entries.

From the **Currencies** list, you can run this process via **Process** (**1**) -> **Adjust Exchange Rate** (**2**):

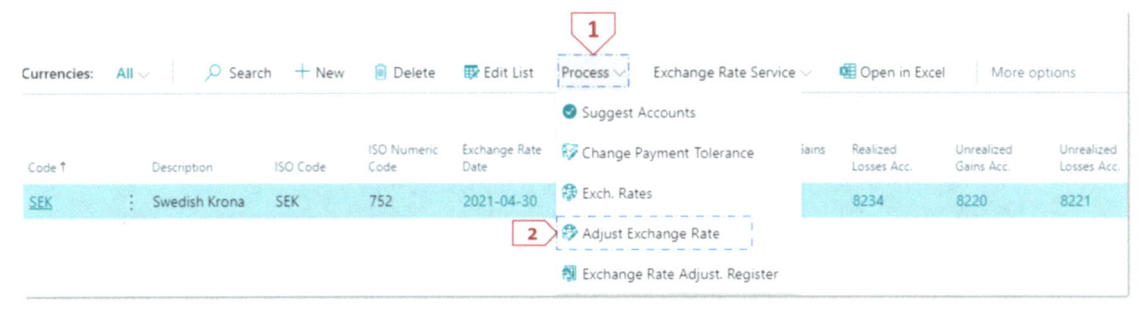

Figure 19-20 - Currencies - Running Adjust Exchange Rate

This will open the **Adjust Exchange Rates Options**:

PART 4: BASIC OPERATIONS
CHAPTER 19: RECURRING TASKS

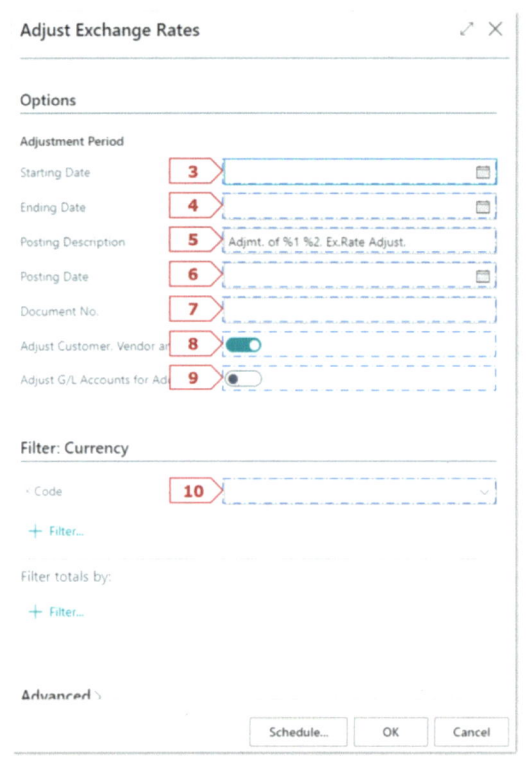

Figure 19-21 - Adjust Exchange Rates – Options

Element	What is it?
3	The **Starting Date** sets the beginning part of the range of dates you wish to be affected by this process.
4	The **Ending Date** sets the end part of the range of dates you wish to be affected by this process.
5	The **Posting Description** is the description that will be shown in the ledger entries. The default text is **Adjmt. of %1 %2, Ex.Rate Adjust.** in which %1 is replaced by the Currency Code and %2 is replaced by the amount that is adjusted. (This will vary by language) For our example Sales Invoice, the description will be: **Adjmt. of SEK 2 295,91, Ex.Rate Adjust.**
6	The **Posting Date** controls which date the gain/loss entries will be posted on.

7	The **Document No.** controls what document number the entries should have.	
8	The **Adjust Customer, Vendor and Item** controls if the adjustments should be performed on the named areas of the system.	
9	The **Adjust G/L Accounts for Add.-Currency** controls if the **Additional Reporting Currency** information on the **G/L Accounts** should be updated.	
10	Optionally, this process can be run for specific currencies by using the **Filter: Currency: Code** setting.	

To run this routine in the scenario within this book, the following settings will be used:

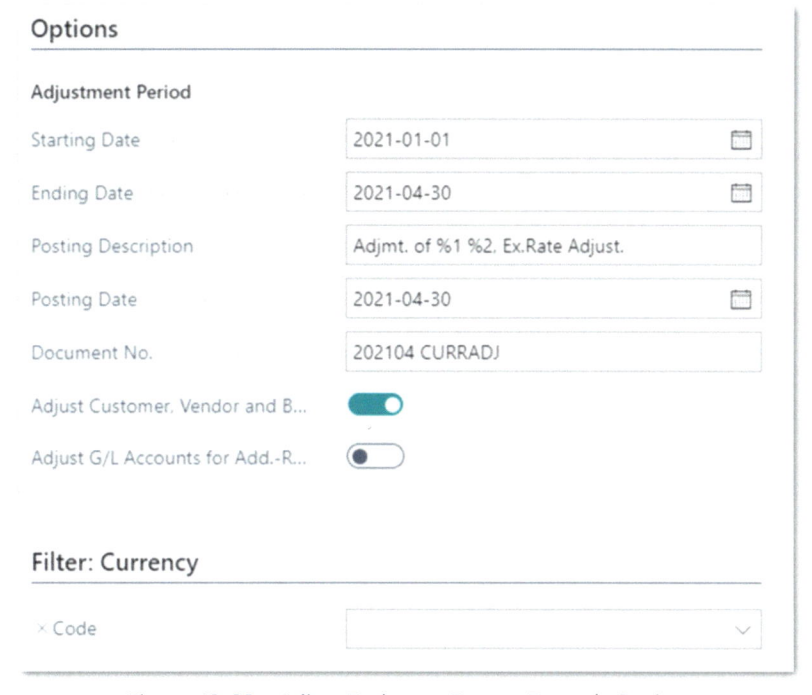

Figure 19-22 - Adjust Exchange Rates - Example Settings

When you click **OK**, the **Adjust Exchange Rates** job will proceed and once completed, it will give you a message:

Figure 19-23 - Adjust Exchange Rates - Complete Message

You can view a list of all transactions affected by the process via the 🔍 **Exchange Rate Adjustment** Registers:

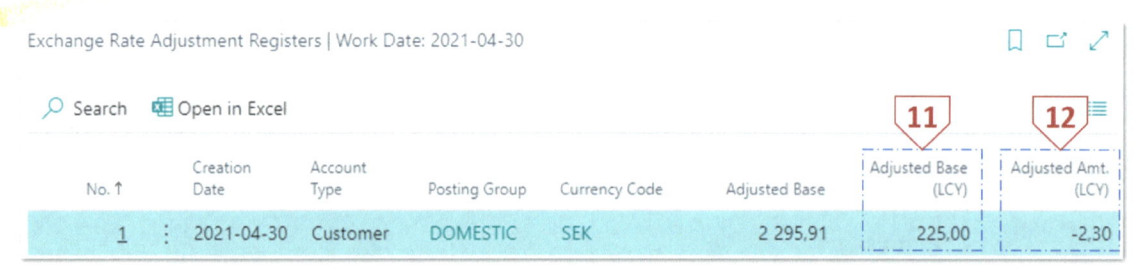

Figure 19-24 - Exchange Rate Adjustment Registers

In our scenario, only one transaction was performed in an alternate currency. We can see that the **Adjusted Base (LCY)** (**11**) was **225,00 EUR**. The process has created an **Adjusted Amt. (LCY)** (**12**) of **-2,30 EUR**, a loss of value.

When we look at the **Customer Ledger Entry** for the invoice:

Figure 19-25 - Customer Ledger Entries - Showing Adjusted Remaining Amt. (LCY)

The **Amount (LCY)** (**13**) and the **Remaining Amt. (LCY)** (**14**) have both been decreased in value by **2,30 EUR**, while the **Remaining Amount** (**15**) in **SEK** is unaffected.

Drilling-down on the **Amount (LCY)**, we can look at the **Detailed Customer Ledger Entries**:

Figure 19-26 - Detailed Customer Ledger Entries - Unrealized Loss Entry

We have the **Initial Entry** for the Invoice setting the base value. Now we also have an **Unrealized Loss** of **2,30 EUR** (seen in the **Amount (LCY)** column) and **0 SEK** (in the **Amount** column) from the **201404 CURRADJ** entry.

AUTOMATIC REALIZED GAIN / LOSS

When we receive the payment from the customer in the **Cash Receipt Journal**:

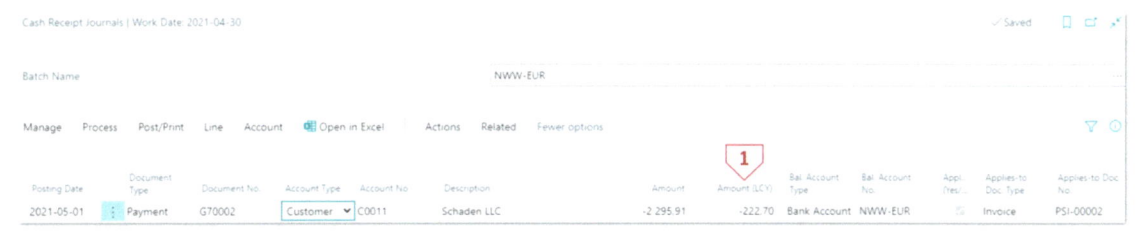

Figure 19-27 - Example Cash Receipt Journal for Realizing Loss

We can see that they are paying the **2295,91 SEK** they owe, which is currently *worth* **222,70 EUR**, shown in the **Amount (LCY)** (**1**).

Once the above payment is posted, when we look at the **Customer Ledger Entries** for the customer again:

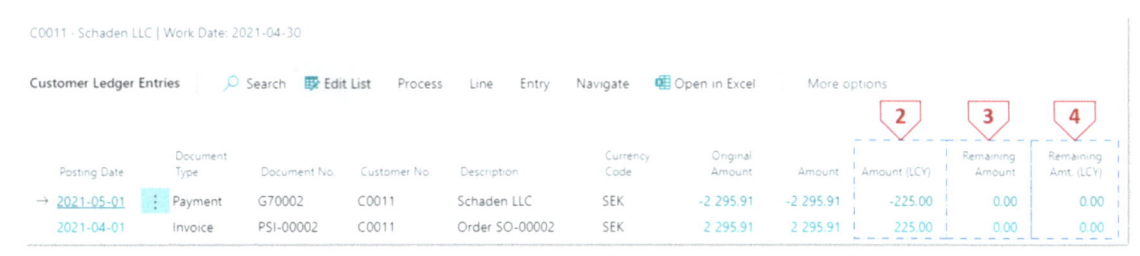

Figure 19-28 - Customer Ledger Entries - Closed and Applied after Realizing Loss

We can now see that the same **Invoice** now has no **Remaining Amount** (**3**) or **Remaining Amt. (LCY)** (**4**), however, the **Amount (LCY)** (**2**) shows as being worth **-225,00 EUR** again.

PART 4: BASIC OPERATIONS
CHAPTER 19: RECURRING TASKS

At the time the invoice was posted, the amount *was* worth **225 EUR**, so, now that we have realized the gain/loss, it shows the value when it was originally posted.

Drilling-down on the **Amount (LCY)** for the **Invoice** to the **Detailed Customer Ledger Entries**, we can see that the **Unrealized Loss** was reversed:

Posting Date ↑	Entry Type	Document Type	Document No.	Customer No.	Currency Code	Amount	Amount (LCY)
2021-04-01	Initial Entry	Invoice	PSI-00002	C0011	SEK	2 295.91	225.00
2021-04-30	Unrealized Loss		202104 CURRADJ	C0011	SEK	0.00	-2.30
2021-05-01	Unrealized Loss	Payment	G70002	C0011	SEK	0.00	2.30

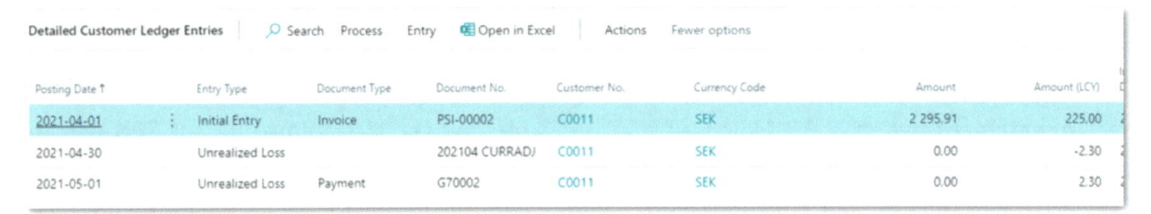

Figure 19-29 - Detailed Customer Ledger Entries - Unrealized Loss is Reversed Once Realized

Drilling-down on the **Amount (LCY)** for the **Payment** to the **Detailed Customer Ledger Entries**, we can see that the **Realized Loss** was posted:

Posting Date ↑	Entry Type	Document Type	Document No.	Customer No.	Currency Code	Amount	Amount (LCY)
2021-05-01	Initial Entry	Payment	G70002	C0011	SEK	-2 295.91	-222.70
2021-05-01	Realized Loss	Payment	G70002	C0011	SEK	0.00	-2.30

Figure 19-30 - Detailed Customer Ledger Entries - Realized Loss Entry on Payment

We will also see on the **Chart of Accounts** that the Realized Loss account (based on the settings on the **Currency** card) was affected:

8231	Currency, Realized Gain	–	–	–
8234	Currency, Realized Loss	2.30	–	2.30

Figure 19-31 - General Ledger - Realized Loss Account with Balance

POSTING INVENTORY COSTS

While inventory management and inventory costing are complex enough topics to warrant their own books, if you are not using Automatic Cost Posting (see **Chapter 6 – Inventory Setup**), you will need to adjust and post your costs to the G/L regularly.

Even though we will not cover what the processes are doing in detail, we will guide you through the steps and look briefly at the results.

The process of keeping your financials updated from the inventory is a two-step process:

1. Run the **Adjust Cost – Item Entries** (**4**) process.
2. Run the **Post Inventory Cost to G/L** (**5**) process.

Both tasks are available via **Tell Me**, and from the **Items** List under the ⋯ (**1**) -> **Actions** (**2**) -> **Periodic Activities** (**3**):

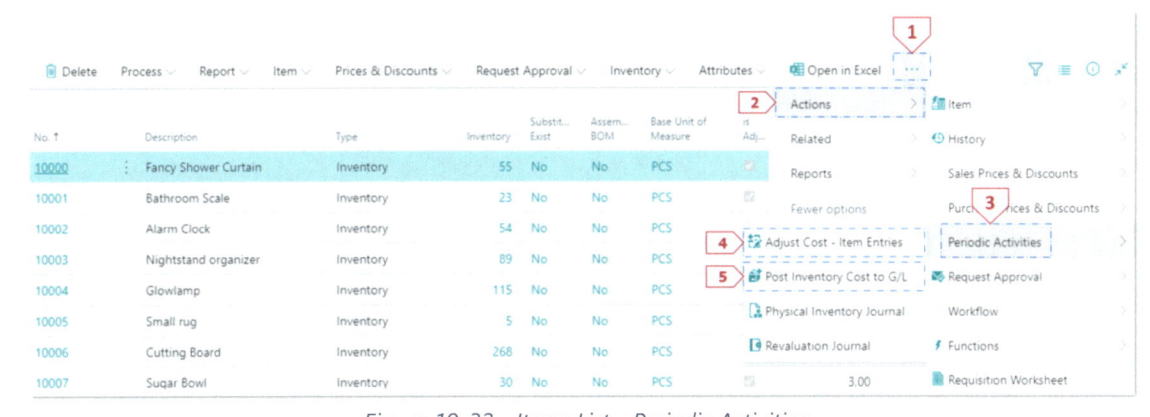

Figure 19-32 - Items List - Periodic Activities

The **Adjust Cost – Item Entries** (**4**) can be run for *all items*, a *singular item*, or *by category*:

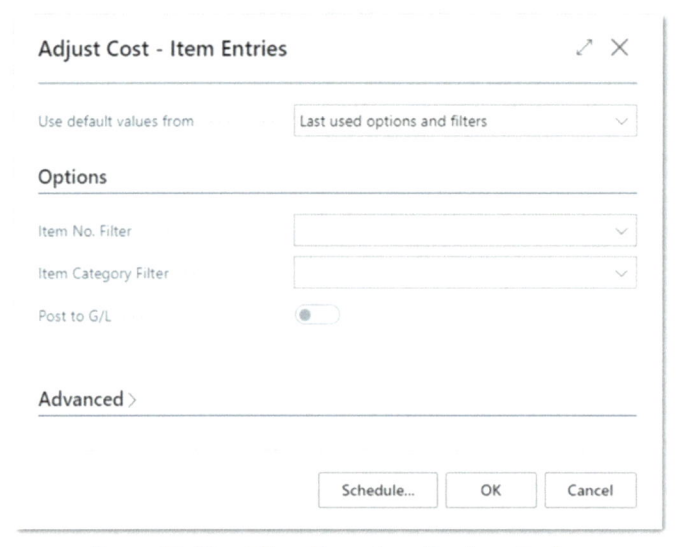

Figure 19-33 - Adjust Cost - Item Entries - Options

When you click **OK**, this job will allocate costs to items in preparation for posting to the G/L.

Running the **Post Inventory Cost to G/L** (**5**) process will require information about the ledger entries it will create for you. There are three required settings and optional filters:

Post Inventory Cost to G/L

Printer	(Handled by the browser)

Options

Posting Method	**6**	Per Posting Group
Document No.	**7**	202104 INVTADJ
Post	**8**	⬤

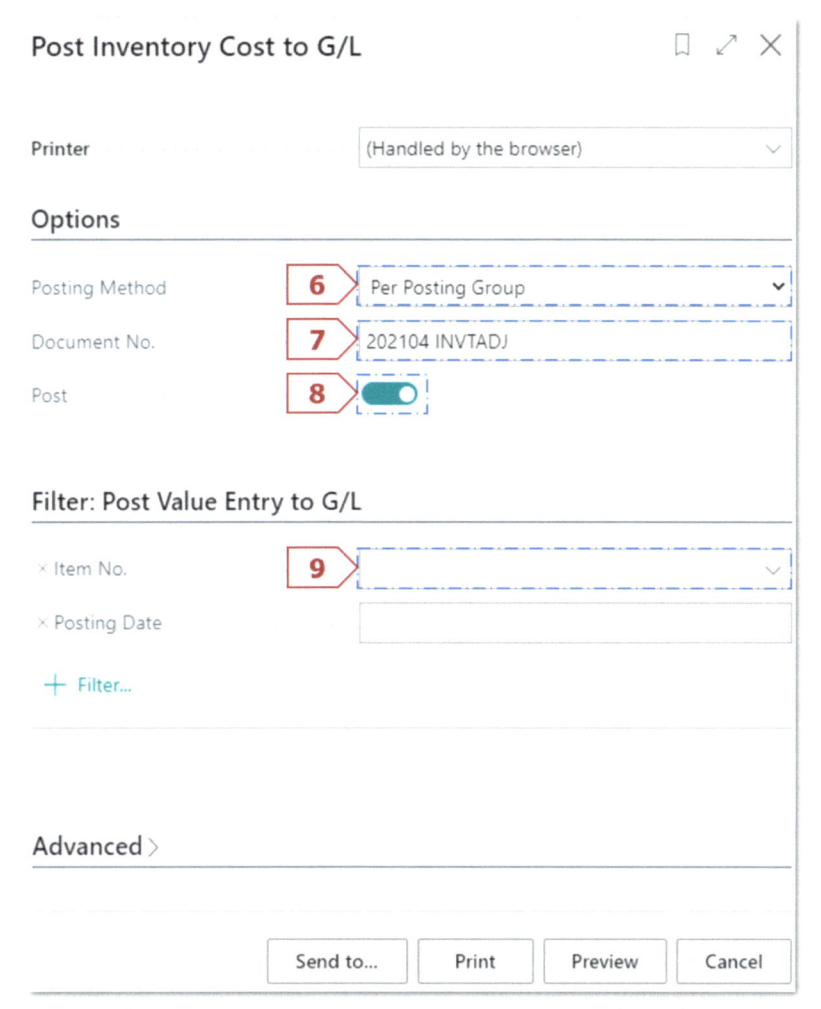

Filter: Post Value Entry to G/L

× Item No. **9**

× Posting Date

＋ Filter…

Advanced ›

[Send to…] [Print] [Preview] [Cancel]

Figure 19-34 - Post Inventory Cost to G/L - Example Options

Element	What is it?
6	The **Posting Method** controls if you want the process to post entries to the G/L by **Per (Inventory) Posting Groups**, making the number of entries smaller, or by **Item**, making it easier to see where costs came from.
7	The **Document No.** written here will be used for all entries.
8	The **Post** option controls if you want the entries to be posted when you run this report. You can disable this to preview the results.
9	Optionally, you can filter which **Item No.** you wish to post costs for.

When you run this report, entries will be posted to the G/L to affect COGS, inventory, direct costs, *and more*.

USING G/L REGISTERS TO REVIEW POSTED COSTS

A helpful tool in Business Central to review posted transactions is the 🔍 **G/L Registers** list:

Figure 19-35 - G/L Registers Showing Inventory Cost Posting Entries

When any transaction in the system posts to the **G/L Accounts**, Business Central will create an entry here for the entire posting batch, whether 2 entries or 200. This will show which user, posting date, time (one of the only places that shows posting time) and the range of the entries involved.

Here we can see an entry marked **INVTPCOST**, which in my region is the default setting for posting inventory costs. (**Source Codes** are beyond the scope of this book)

To see all the entries for that transactional batch, click on **Process** (**1**) -> **General Ledger** (**2**):

Figure 19-36 - G/L Registers - Viewing Related Entries Actions

This will show you the list of *all* General Ledger Entries from the whole batch:

Posting Date	Document Type	Document No.	G/L Account No.	G/L Account Name	Description	Gen. Posting Type	Gen. Bus. Posting Group	Gen. Prod. Posting Group	Amount
2021-04-21		202104 INVT...	4586	Cost of Goods Sold	COGS - Inventory. ASKIM.SEAS...				-320.00
2021-04-21		202104 INVT...	4586	Cost of Goods Sold	COGS - Inventory. ASKIM.NOR...				-55.00
2021-04-21		202104 INVT...	4586	Cost of Goods Sold	COGS - Inventory. ASKIM.NOR...				55.00
2021-04-01		202104 INVT...	4586	Cost of Goods Sold	COGS - Inventory. ASKIM.SEAS...				640.00
2021-04-01		202104 INVT...	4586	Cost of Goods Sold	COGS - Inventory. ASKIM.NOR...				-60.00
2021-04-01		202104 INVT...	4586	Cost of Goods Sold	COGS - Inventory. ASKIM.NOR...				60.00
2021-04-01		202104 INVT...	4586	Cost of Goods Sold	COGS - Inventory. ASKIM.NOR...				60.00
2021-04-01		202104 INVT...	4586	Cost of Goods Sold	COGS - Inventory. ASKIM.NOR...				120.00
2021-04-01		202104 INVT...	4580	Invt. Adjustment - Normal	Direct Cost Applied - Inventory...				-500.00
2021-04-21		202104 INVT...	1422	Seasonal Inventory	Inventory - COGS. ASKIM.SEAS...				320.00
2021-04-01		202104 INVT...	1422	Seasonal Inventory	Inventory - COGS. ASKIM.SEAS...				-640.00
2021-04-21		202104 INVT...	1421	Normal Inventory	Inventory - COGS. ASKIM.NOR...				-55.00
2021-04-21		202104 INVT...	1421	Normal Inventory	Inventory - COGS. ASKIM.NOR...				55.00
2021-04-01		202104 INVT...	1421	Normal Inventory	Inventory - COGS. ASKIM.NOR...				-60.00
2021-04-01		202104 INVT...	1421	Normal Inventory	Inventory - COGS. ASKIM.NOR...				60.00
2021-04-01		202104 INVT...	1421	Normal Inventory	Inventory - COGS. ASKIM.NOR...				-60.00
2021-04-01		202104 INVT...	1421	Normal Inventory	Inventory - COGS. ASKIM.NOR...				-120.00
2021-04-01		202104 INVT...	1421	Normal Inventory	Inventory - Direct Cost Applied...				500.00

Figure 19-37 - General Ledger Entries from Post Inventory Cost to G/L

PART 5: WRAPPING UP

Chapter 20 is the final step, guiding you towards several resources and assets to learn more about Business Central.

Chapter 20: Continued Learning & Resources

There is *always* so much more functionality in Business Central to cover than can fit into a single book.

This last chapter focuses on some additional places that you can turn to for more information.

All resources in this chapter are linked at:

https://sparebrained.com/yourfirst20-files

BOOKS

FIELD GUIDE

Most of the books in the industry are more oriented towards the professionals within the industry. An exception to that pattern (besides this one you are reading right now) is "Microsoft Dynamics 365 Business Central Field Guide" by **Erik Hougaard**:

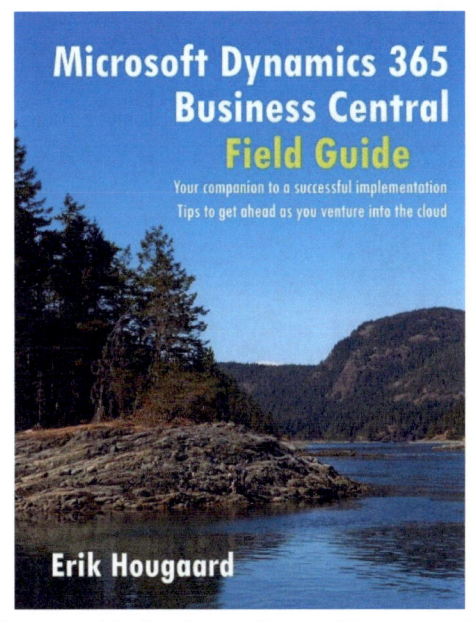

While "Your First 20 Hours with Business Central" is a step-by-step guide from having an empty system to being able to operate some core modules, the ***Field Guide*** is less sequential, but significantly more in-depth and well worth adding to your collection.

Implementing Business Central

If you have bought this book before implementing Business Central in your environment as a way to learn more about the product, there is also the "Implementing Microsoft Dynamics 365 Business Central On-Premise - Fourth Edition" by **Roberto Stefanetti** and **Alex Chow**.

While this book focuses on the On-premises version, this neatly outlines the whole project process, helping you understand the whole *team* (partner and customer) perspective of how the implementation can be done.

MICROSOFT LEARN

The Microsoft Learn platform is an ever-increasing list of courses and content about their products, Business Central included. These courses are 2-8 hour online self-paced educational resources on a variety of topics:

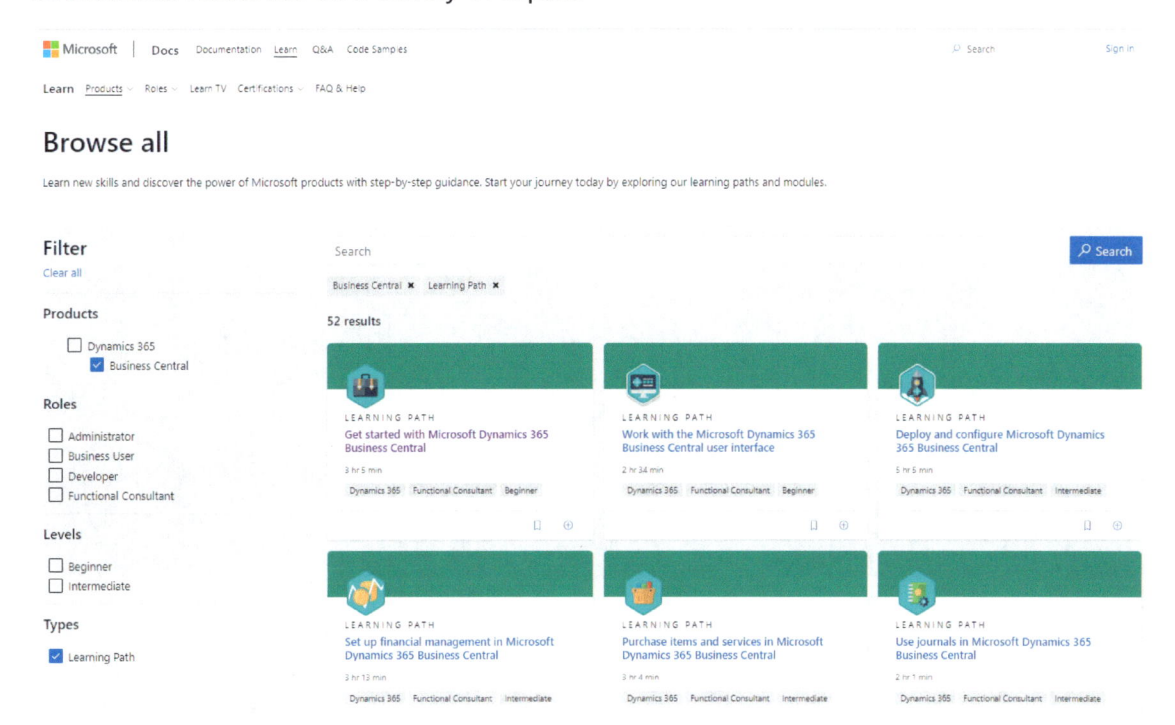

ONLINE COURSES

Self-paced online courses can also be another valuable tool. The Dynamics Community has a resource platform particularly aimed towards this industry:

Welcome to Dynamics User Group Skill-Up Training Marketplace
Your global online marketplace for high quality Microsoft business application on demand training

Microsoft Business Application Courses
Purchase these online, elearning Power Platform & Microsoft Dynamics 365 courses today.

As of the time of this book's release, the site has only recently launched, so the course list is short for now, but there are many discussions about the value this can bring for the users of the Dynamics products.

COMMUNITY RESOURCE OVERVIEW

The author of *this book*, **Jeremy Vyska**, recorded a session for **DynamicsCon 2021** on the useful resources and tools within the community.

The entire video presentation is available on **YouTube** here:

https://sparebrained.com/dynamicscon-2021-session-now-available

Links to all the toured resources are available here on the Spare Brained Ideas site:

https://sparebrained.com/map

PART 6: APPENDICES

APPENDIX A: EXAMPLE IMPORTS

The sample data for the scenario used throughout this book is available to download at:

https://sparebrained.com/yourfirst20-files

The data needed for **Chapter 9 - Data Import** is included below as simple tables for completeness, but downloading the data instead is strongly encouraged, as not all columns can fit on the pages.

Opening Balances data for **Chapters 12 – Adjusting Inventory into Stock** and **Chapter 13 – Opening Balances** is not practical to include and must be downloaded.

GL Account Sheet

No.	Name	Account Type	Account Category	Income/Balance	Debit/Credit	Blocked	Gen. Posting Type	Gen. Bus. Posting Group	Gen. Prod. Posting Group	Account Subcategory Entry No.
1000	ASSETS	3		1	0	No	0			
1001	Intangible Fixed Assets	3		1	0	No	0			
1012	Capitalised expenditure for software	0	1	1	0	No	0			
1099	Total, Intangible Fixed Assets	4		1	0	No	0			
1200	Machinery and Equipment	3		1	0	No	0			
1225	Tools	0	1	1	0	No	0			
1250	Computers	0	1	1	0	No	0			
1259	Depreciation of computers	0	1	1	0	No	0			
1299	Total, Machinery and Equipment	4		1	0	No	0			
1400	Inventory	3		1	0	No	0			
1421	Normal Inventory	0	1	1	0	No	0			
1422	Seasonal Inventory	0	1	1	0	No	0			
1499	Total, Inventory	4		1	0	No	0			
1500	Accounts Receivable	3		1	0	No	0			
1510	Receivables, Domestic	0	1	1	0	No	0			
1511	Receivables, EU	0	1	1	0	No	0			
1512	Receivables, Non-EU	0	1	1	0	No	0			
1525	Doubtful Receivables	0	1	1	0	No	0			
1599	Total, Accounts Receivables	4		1	0	No	0			
1900	Liquid Assets	3	1	1	0	No	0			
1910	Cash	0	1	1	0	No	0			
1940	Bank, EUR	0	1	1	0	No	0			
1998	Total, Liquid Assets	4	1	1	0	No	0			
1999	Total, ASSETS	4		1	0	No	0			
2000	EQUITY AND LIABILITIES	3		1	0	No	0			
2001	Equity, Owners	1	3	1	0	No	0			
2010	Equity, Owner 1	0	3	1	0	No	0			
2020	Equity, Owner 2	0	3	1	0	No	0			

2091	Retained Earnings	0	3	1	0	No	0		
2098	Year Result	2	3	1	0	No	0		
2300	Long-Term Liabilities	3		1	0	No	0		
2399	Total, Long-Term Liabilities	4		1	0	No	0		
2400	Current Liabilities	3		1	0	No	0		
2440	Accounts Payable	3	2	1	0	No	0		
2441	Accounts Payable, Domestic	0	2	1	0	No	0		
2442	Accounts Payable, Foreign	0	2	1	0	No	0		
2449	Total, Accounts Payable	4	2	1	0	No	0		
2499	Total, Current Liabilities	4		1	0	No	0		
2510	Other Tax Liabilities	0	2	1	0	No	0		
2600	VAT	3	2	1	0	No	0		
2610	Outgoing VAT, 25%	0	2	1	0	No	0		
2620	Outgoing VAT, 12%	0	2	1	0	No	0		
2630	Outgoing VAT, 6%	0	2	1	0	No	0		
2640	Incoming VAT, 25%	0	2	1	0	No	0		
2641	VAT Only	0	2	1	0	No	0	MISC	
2642	Incoming VAT, 12%	0	2	1	0	No	0		
2645	Incoming VAT, 6%	0	2	1	0	No	0		
2650	Total, VAT	4	2	1	0	No	0		
2998	Total, EQUITY/LIABILITIES	4		1	0	No	0		
2999	Net Income for Year	2		1	0	No	0		
3000	INCOME STATEMENT	1		0	0	No	0		
3002	Revenue	3		0	0	No	0		
3040	Sales, Normal Stock	3	4	0	0	No	0		
3041	Sales, Normal, Sweden	0	4	0	0	No	2	DOMESTIC	NORMAL
3045	Sales, Normal, Non-EU	0	4	0	0	No	2	EXPORT	NORMAL
3046	Sales, Normal, EU	0	4	0	0	No	2	EU	NORMAL
3049	Total, Sales of Normal	4	4	0	0	No	0		
3050	Sales, Seasonal	3	4	0	0	No	0		
3051	Sales, Seasonal, Sweden	0	4	0	0	No	2	DOMESTIC	SEASONAL
3055	Sales, Seasonal Non-EU	0	4	0	0	No	2	EXPORT	SEASONAL
3056	Sales, Seasonal EU	0	4	0	0	No	2	EU	SEASONAL
3059	Total, Sales Seasonal	4	4	0	0	No	0		
3095	Other sales	0	4	0	0	No	0		
3098	Sales Reductions	0	4	0	0	No	0		

3731	Sales Discounts	0	4	0	0	No	0	
3740	Invoice Rounding	0	4	0	0	No	2	NO VAT
3999	Total, Revenue	4	4	0	0	No	0	
4000	Operating Expenses	3		0	0	No	0	
4002	Purchase of Goods	3		0	0	No	0	
4099	Total, Purchase of Goods	4		0	0	No	0	
4200	Resource Costs	3		0	0	No	0	
4299	Total, Resource Costs	4		0	0	No	0	
4400	Purchases	3		0	0	No	0	
4401	Purchases, Domestic	0	5	0	0	No	1	DOMESTIC
4531	Purchases, EU	0	5	0	0	No	1	EXPORT
4545	Purchases, Import	0	5	0	0	No	1	EU
4580	Invt. Adjustment - Normal	0	5	0	0	No	0	
4581	Invt. Adjustment - Seasonal	0	5	0	0	No	0	
4586	Cost of Goods Sold	0	5	0	0	No	0	
4598	Total, Purchases	4		0	0	No	0	
4599	Total, Operating Expenses	4		0	0	No	0	
5000	External Operating Costs	3		0	0	No	0	
5001	Rental Expenses	3		0	0	No	0	
5099	Total, Rental Expenses	4		0	0	No	0	
5600	Transportation	3		0	0	No	0	
5611	Passenger Car, Fuel	0	6	0	0	No	0	
5612	Passenger Car, Insur/Tax	0	6	0	0	No	0	
5613	Passenger Car, Maintenance	0	6	0	0	No	0	
5699	Total, Transportation	4		0	0	No	0	
5700	Freight	3		0	0	No	0	
5710	Freight, Goods	0	6	0	0	No	0	
5720	Freight, Customs	0	6	0	0	No	0	
5799	Total, Freight	4		0	0	No	0	
5800	Travel Expenses	3		0	0	No	0	
5810	Tickets	0	6	0	0	No	0	
5820	Rental Car	0	6	0	0	No	0	
5830	Board & Lodging	0	6	0	0	No	0	

5899	Total, Travel Expenses	4		0	0	No	0	
5900	Advertising/PR	3		0	0	No	0	
5910	Advertisements	0	6	0	0	No	1	MISC
5930	Direct Marketing	0	6	0	0	No	0	
5940	Exhibitions / Fairs	0	6	0	0	No	0	
5980	PR Sponsorship	0	6	0	0	No	0	
5999	Total, Advertising/PR	4		0	0	No	0	
6000	Selling Expenses	3		0	0	No	0	
6040	Credit card charges	0	6	0	0	No	0	
6071	Business entertaining, tax-deductible	0	6	0	0	No	0	
6072	Business Entertaining, Non-deductible	0	6	0	0	No	0	
6099	Total, Selling Expenses	4		0	0	No	0	
6100	Office Supplies / Printing	3		0	0	No	0	
6110	Office Supplies	0	6	0	0	No	0	
6199	Total, Office Supplies / Printing	4		0	0	No	0	
6200	Phones and Postage	3		0	0	No	0	
6211	Fixed Phones	0	6	0	0	No	0	
6212	Mobile phones	0	6	0	0	No	0	
6230	Data Fees	0	6	0	0	No	0	
6250	Postal Fees	0	6	0	0	No	0	
6299	Total, Phone / Postage	4		0	0	No	0	
6300	Insurance and Risks	3		0	0	No	0	
6310	Corporate Insurance	0	6	0	0	No	0	
6350	Bad Debt Losses	0	6	0	0	No	0	
6399	Total, Insurance and Risks	4		0	0	No	0	
6400	Costs of Administration	3		0	0	No	0	
6420	Audit	0	6	0	0	No	0	
6430	Management Fees	0	6	0	0	No	0	MISC
6491	Payables Invoice Rounding	0	6	0	0	No	0	NO VAT
6499	Total, Costs of Administration	4		0	0	No	0	
6500	External Services	3		0	0	No	0	
6530	Accounting services	0	6	0	0	No	0	
6540	IT Services	0	6	0	0	No	1	MISC
6570	Banking Costs	0	6	0	0	No	1	NO VAT
6599	Total, External Services	4		0	0	No	0	
6900	Other External Expenses	3		0	0	No	0	
6993	Donations and Gifts	0	6	0	0	No	0	

6998	Total, External Expenses	4		0	0	No	0	
6999	Total, Other External Expenses	4		0	0	No	0	
7000	Personnel, Depreciation	3		0	0	No	0	
7200	Salaries	3		0	0	No	0	
7211	Salaries, Employees	0	6	0	0	No	0	
7221	Salaries, Managers	0	6	0	0	No	0	
7299	Total, Salaries	4		0	0	No	0	
7400	Pensions	3		0	0	No	0	
7410	Pension Insurance Premiums	0	6	0	0	No	0	
7460	Pension Payments	0	6	0	0	No	0	
7499	Total, Pensions	4		0	0	No	0	
7500	Social Security	3		0	0	No	0	
7510	Statuatory social contributions	0	6	0	0	No	0	
7580	Group Insurance Premiums	0	6	0	0	No	0	
7590	Other social contributions	0	6	0	0	No	0	
7599	Total, Social Security	4		0	0	No	0	
7600	Other Personnel Costs	3		0	0	No	0	
7610	Training	0	6	0	0	No	0	
7620	Health Care	0	6	0	0	No	0	
7630	Entertainment of Personnel	0	6	0	0	No	0	
7693	Leisure Activities	0	6	0	0	No	0	
7698	Other personnel costs	0	6	0	0	No	0	
7699	Total, Other Personnel Costs	4		0	0	No	0	
7800	Depreciation	3		0	0	No	0	
7835	Depreciation of computers	0	6	0	0	No	0	
7899	Total, Depreciation	4		0	0	No	0	
7990	Other Operating Expenses	0	6	0	0	No	0	
7999	Total, Personnel, Depreciation	4		0	0	No	0	
8220	Currency, Unrealized Gain	0	4	0	0	No	0	
8221	Currency, Unrealized Loss	0	6	0	0	No	0	
8231	Currency, Realized Gain	0	4	0	0	No	0	
8234	Currency, Realized Loss	0	6	0	0	No	0	
8311	Interest income, banks	0		0	0	No	2	NO VAT

PART 6: APPENDICES
CHAPTER 20: CONTINUED LEARNING & RESOURCES

Customer Sheet

No.	Name	Search Name	Address	City	Post Code	Country/Region Code	Contact	Customer Posting Group	Payment Terms Code	Gen. Bus. Posting Group
	Christiansen, Rosenbaum and Murray						Galen Fernan			DOM
	Buckridge, Gaylord and Wunsch						Levey Brosini			DOM
	Wisozk-Ruecker						Maura Hammill			DOM
	Schamberger-Labadie						Rochell Chadney			DOM
	Feeney-McGlynn						Sibilla Tivenan			DOM
	Schaden LLC						Brander Moffett			DOM
	Kilback-Shanahan						Hurleigh Eskell			DOM
	Goodwin LLC						Gabi Pomery			DOM
	Zboncak LLC						Horatio Courtes			EU
	Muller-Wilkinson						Cirstoforo Bengall			EU
	VonRueden-Moen						Tracie Koppens			EU
	Turcotte LLC						Elliott Flippelli			EU
	Robel-Botsford						Carter Keep			EU
	Vandervort-Bechtelar						Val Castellone			EXPORT
	MacGyver LLC						Tam Claire			EXPORT
	Nitzsche-Hahn						Hollie Littlejohn			EXPORT
	Wehner-Mitchell						Constantino Fabbri			EXPORT
	Frami-Swaniawski						Caz Warlowe			EXPORT
	Schmidt Inc						Victor Gottelier			EXPORT
	Pfeffer-Kertzmann						Bonni MacDearmaid			EXPORT

Vendor Sheet

No.	Name	Search Name	Address	City	Post Code	Contact	Vendor Posting Group	Payment Terms Code	Gen. Bus. Posting Group
	Kerluke LLC					Alyosha Beamand			DOM
	Hermann, Koss and Kautzer					Katherina Pollard			DOM
	Nitzsche-Hoppe					Franny Shepton			DOM
	Schumm, Altenwerth and Windler					Bald Teresa			DOM
	Runolfsson, Mertz and Tromp					Donnie Klosterman			DOM
	Casper Inc					Quinton Savaage			DOM
	Hirthe Group					Max Lamberton			EU
	West Group					Vita Sarson			EU
	Altenwerth and Sons					Debby Hunnicot			EXPORT
	Sauer, Raynor and Haley					Sigismundo Anstiss			EXPORT

ITEM SHEET

No.	Description	Search Description	Base Unit of Measure	Unit Price	Unit Cost	Standard Cost	Inventory	Maximum Inventory	Prevent Negative Inventory	Reorder Point	Reorder Quantity	Unit List Price	Gross Weight	Net Weight	Minimum Order Quantity	Maximum Order Quantity	Safety Stock Quantity
	Fancy Shower Curtain																
	Bathroom Scale																
	Alarm Clock																
	Nightstand organizer																
	Glowlamp																
	Small rug																
	Cutting Board																
	Sugar Bowl																
	Small Storage Bin																
	Drawer Organizer																
	Spring-themed vase																
	Spring floral mural																
	Patio table																
	Patio chair																
	Winter-themed vase																
	Winter snowscape mural																
	Boot tray																
	Boot and glove dryer																

APPENDIX B: COMPANIES

In Microsoft Dynamics 365 Business Central, business data is kept entirely separate via the **Companies** system. There are a few system components, like Users and User Permissions, which apply to the whole system, but Companies are kept separate – which is why there are the Consolidation and Intercompany modules. Extensions apply to all Companies as well.

This means, for example, you can create a *Test Company* that is either blank or a copy of a *Production Company* to test if transactions work the way you need them to.

> Note: If you have automatic jobs, integrations, or send information out of a *Test Company*, this can be *majorly* disruptive and cause data problems.
>
> Please consult with a partner about any steps you would need to take to generate testing companies in your specific situation.

Generating new companies, copying companies, and removing companies tends to be an intense process for your system to execute. It is often recommended to do this during an *off-hour* or a *light-use* period.

Companies are managed via the **Companies** list. Depending on your version, this list will vary a little, but the core concept is that each record in the **Companies** list has the **Name** of each of your companies.

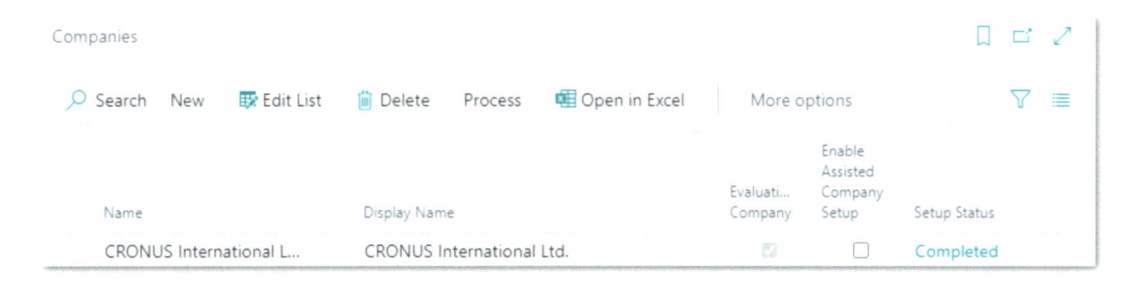

Name	Display Name	Evaluati... Company	Enable Assisted Company Setup	Setup Status
CRONUS International L...	CRONUS International Ltd.	☑	☐	Completed

PART 6: APPENDICES
CHAPTER 20: CONTINUED LEARNING & RESOURCES

Just like any list, you can create **New** companies or **Delete** them (on-premises users can also rename them, not just adjust the **Display Name**). As you can probably imagine, this is a dangerous part of the system, so *frequent* backups and *heavily enforced* permissions are highly advised.

In older versions of this system, you only had the option to click **New** to create a new Company, and upon entering the **Name**, it would generate an empty Company.

In the current version (as of publishing this book), there is the **Create New Company** wizard, which will give you some additional options:

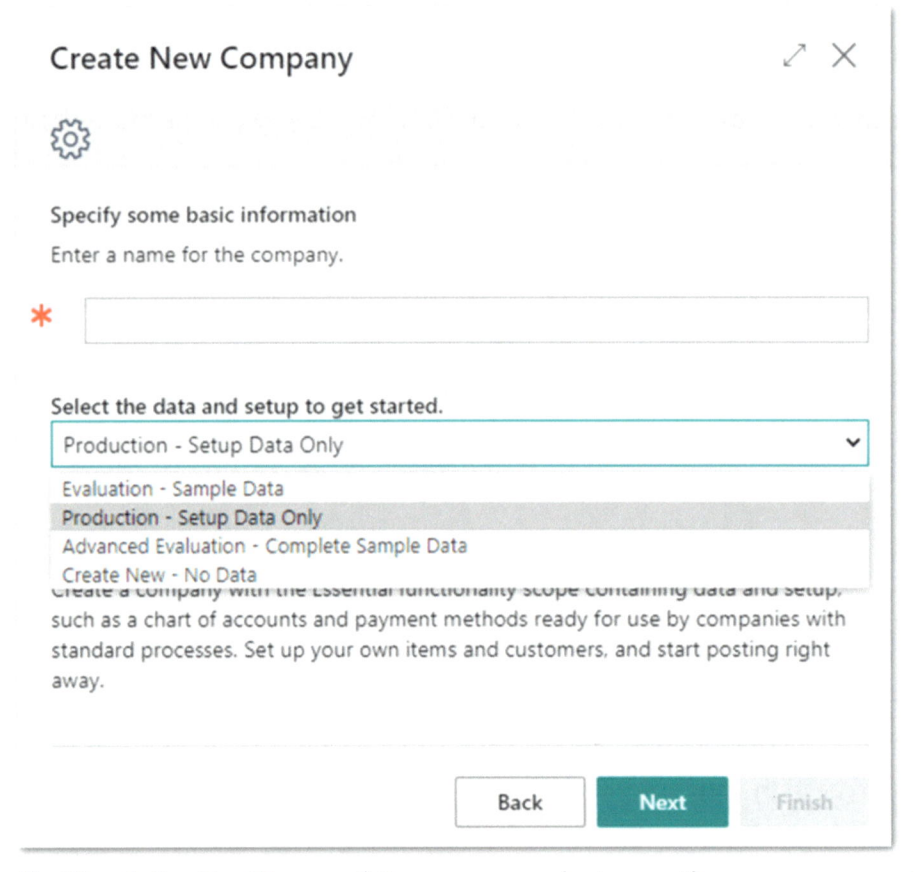

Create New Company

Specify some basic information
Enter a name for the company.

Select the data and setup to get started.

Production - Setup Data Only

- Evaluation - Sample Data
- Production - Setup Data Only
- Advanced Evaluation - Complete Sample Data
- Create New - No Data

Create a company with the Essential functionality scope containing data and setup, such as a chart of accounts and payment methods ready for use by companies with standard processes. Set up your own items and customers, and start posting right away.

[Back] [Next] [Finish]

It will still ask for the **Name** of the company, but now there are some additional options:

- **Evaluation – Sample Data** – This creates a CRONUS company with most of the system setup for testing and use.

- **Production – Setup Data Only** – This creates a *mostly* empty company, but using the CRONUS setup data, such as Posting Groups, Chart of Accounts, and many other setup elements.
- **Advanced Evaluation – Complete Sample Data** – This creates a CRONUS company with all the additional demo data, including the Manufacturing and Service modules.
- **Create New – No Data** – An *entirely blank* company.

This book is written to help you from the start, with the selected option **Create New – No Data**.

You could *also* use it as a reference guide for the other available options to understand them better.

Once you have set up your **Companies**, the user(s) with the required permissions (to the relevant companies) will be able to change them via the ⚙ **Settings** window:

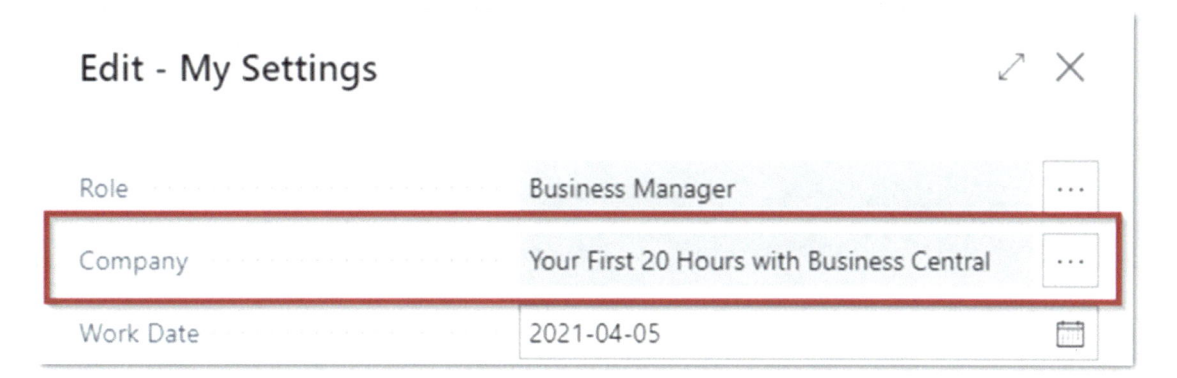

Edit - My Settings

Role	Business Manager
Company	Your First 20 Hours with Business Central
Work Date	2021-04-05

PART 7: INDEX

A

Account Category 123, 149
Account Name 204
Account No 204, 276, 289, 295
Account Schedules 144
Account Subcategory 141
Account Type 122, 124, 149, 203, 276, 289, 295
Accounting Periods 82, 84, 323, 325
Action Bar 24, 25, 28, 30, 31, 32
Actions 187, 197, 200, 203, 222, 341
Additional Reporting Currency 164, 337
Additional-Currency Balance 167
Additional-Currency Net Change 166, 167
Addition-Currency Balance 166
Adjust Cost – Item Entries 187, 188, 189, 192, 341
Adjust Customer, Vendor and Item 337
Adjust Exchange Rate 335
Adjust Exchange Rates 337
Adjust G/L Accounts for Add.-Currency 337
Adjusted Amt. (LCY) 338
Adjusted Base (LCY) 338

Advanced Evaluation – Complete Sample Data 369
Allow Posting From 91, 332, 333
Allow Posting To 91, 332, 333
Amount ... 169, 180, 182, 198, 201, 204, 258, 259, 278, 290, 295
Amount (LCY) 169, 259, 278, 291, 338, 339, 340
Amount to Apply 285
Applies-to Doc. No. 276, 289
Applies-To Doc. No. 278, 284, 291, 295
Applies-To Doc. Type 278, 291
Apply Customer Entries 290, 316
Apply Entries 285, 316
Apply Vendor Entries 277, 285
Archive Orders 98
Archived Sales Orders 98
Archiving 98
Assign scenarios 230
Attachments 215, 232, 248
   Choose 216
   Select File 216
Automatic Cost Posting 99, 187

B

Bal. Account No. 196, 198, 200, 274, 288
Bal. Account Type.................................... 196, 274, 288
Balance.....50, 122, 123, 142, 191, 192, 193, 196, 197, 198, 199, 201, 221, 225, 228, 304, 327, 331, 332
Balance (LCY).................................... 49, 160, 280, 292
Bank Acc. Posting Group 173
Bank Account 172, 173, 174, 197
Bank Account No.. 92
Bank Account Nos. 92
Bank Account Posting Groups 153
Bank Accounts.................................... 176, 196, 197
Base Unit of Measure..............114, 115, 118, 119, 127
Batch Name.. 179
BCC 232, 248
Begin-Total 122
Bill-To Customer 35
Bookmark 25

C

Card.. 28, 30, 302
Cash Management 274, 287
Cash Receipt Journal 295, 339
Cash Receipt Journals....................................... 287, 289
CC 232, 248
Change when I receive notifications 47
Chart of Accounts.....50, 122, 125, 136, 140, 145, 146, 166, 167, 176, 191, 192, 193, 196, 197, 198, 199, 201, 205, 228, 327, 331
Close Income Statement 323, 327
Close Year... 325
Closed... 325
Closing – Trial Balance... 166
Code 78, 115, 337
Companies... 367
Company Information 58, 81, 214
Configuration 130
Configuration Templates 105, 107, 110, 111, 113, 114, 118, 119, 134
Contact.. 212, 242, 245
Contact No. 212, 242
Content Area 24, 25
Copy Config. Template 110
Copy Customer Name to Entries 96
Copy Document… 222
Copy Vendor Name to Entries 94

Correct 306
Cost is Adjusted 186, 187
Cost is Posted to G/L.. 187
Create Item from Description 96
Create Item from Item No. 93, 96
Create New – No Data 369
Create New Company 368
Create New… 240
Create Return-Related Documents… 301
Create Year...82, 84, 323
Credit Warnings 95
Currencies 58, 160, 162, 163, 164, 167, 334, 335
Currency Card 161, 164
Currency Code ..42, 168, 169, 170, 174, 213, 243, 256
Currency Exchange Rates.......................162, 333, 334
Customer . 60, 107, 126, 168, 253, 256, 262, 270, 293, 298
Customer Card 49, 67, 243, 245, 304
Customer Ledger Entries..49, 253, 258, 266, 292, 293, 295, 304, 313, 316, 318, 334, 339
Customer Ledger Entry 60, 62, 338
Customer List 136
Customer Name 237, 242
Customer No. 242
Customer No. Series 126
Customer Posting Group..75, 107
Customer Posting Groups 76, 126, 152
Customer Posting Setup 151
Customer Statistics 160
Customer Templates... 108
Customers.17, 38, 42, 45, 58, 107, 169, 170, 176, 199, 236, 292
Customers Opening Balance 198, 199

D

Data Migration.................................120, 121, 130, 132
Data Templates... 102
Date Filter 331, 332
Date Locked 325
Debit/Credit 123
Def. VAT Bus. Posting Group..................................... 73
DEFAULT 329
Default Costing Method... 100
Default Item Quantity 96
Delete 368
Description..................... 115, 159, 179, 209, 238, 329
Detailed Customer Ledger Entries 294, 338, 340

Detailed Customer Ledger Entry 60, 62
Direct Unit Cost 210, 227
Document 30
Document No. 179, 182, 189, 198, 201, 223, 254, 329, 337, 343
Document Sending Profile 229
Document Type 35, 223, 276, 289, 295
Download Template 121
Due Date 213, 243, 244

E

Edit and Send 234, 249
Edit List 84, 274, 287
Email 229
Email Accounts 229, 231
Email Confirmation 247
Email Details 232, 248
Email Scenario Assignments 230
Email Scenarios 230
End Date 85, 271
Ending Date 336
Ending No. 87
End-Total 123
Entry 254
Entry Type 179, 182
Evaluation – Sample Data 368
Exchange Rate 161, 162
Exchange Rate Adjustment 338
Expand Lines 31
Expected Receipt Date 213
Explore All 51
Ext. Doc. No. Mandatory 94
Extensions 46

F

FactBox Area 24
FastTab 28, 29, 30
Filter 25, 35
Filter List By 38
Filter Pane 24
Filter totals by 50, 331

Find Entries... 254
Finish 132
Fiscal Year Ending Date 328
From 232, 248
Functions 222, 264, 322

G

G/L Account 133
G/L Account Categories 140, 141, 142, 143
G/L Account Name 219
G/L Account No. 153
G/L Accounts in Category 142, 143
G/L Accounts Opening Balance 203, 205
G/L Entries 258
G/L Registers 344
Gain/Loss Accounts 161
Gen. Bus. Posting Group 107, 124, 148
Gen. Business Posting Groups 73, 126
Gen. Journal Batch 329
Gen. Journal Template 329
Gen. Posting Type 124
Gen. Prod. Posting Group 124, 133, 134
Gen. Prod. Posting Groups 134, 148, 191
General 106
General Business Posting Groups 74
General Journal 32, 178, 192, 193, 195, 197, 199, 200, 201, 203, 205
General Ledger 63, 344
General Ledger Account 122, 141
General Ledger Setup 90, 92, 160, 164, 167, 323, 332, 333
General Posting Setup 147, 150
General Product Posting Groups 73, 74
Generate Account Schedules 143
Get Posted Document Lines to Reverse 298, 310
Get Shipment Lines 262, 264, 265

H

Heading 122
Help 17, 45

I

Include Header 223
Income/Balance 123, 203
Indent Chart of Accounts 145, 146
Info 25
Inspect 36
Inspect pages and data 45
Inventory 128, 179, 186
Inventory Account 154
Inventory Account (Interim) 155
Inventory Posting Group 133
Inventory Posting Group Code 154
Inventory Posting Groups 76, 77, 154
Inventory Posting Setup 154, 189
Inventory Setup 99, 100, 127
Invoice 262
Invoice Rounding 93, 96
Invoices 262
Invoicing 107
Item 114, 158, 179, 256, 321
Item Attributes 116, 117
Item Availability 246
Item Card 23, 68, 179
Item Categories 116, 117
Item Category Code 114
Item Journals 178, 179, 180, 181, 184, 186
Item Ledger Entries 179, 321
Item List 137
Item No. 127, 179, 180, 181, 246
Item No. Series 127
Item Nos. 100, 343
Item Translations 158
Item Units of Measure 58
Items 58, 114, 118, 158, 186, 188, 192, 240, 341

J

Journal Batches 180

L

Language Code 158, 159
Languages 58, 156, 157
Last Date Used 89
Last No. Used 89
Last Payment Date 282

LCY 164
LCY Code 92
Ledger Entries 253, 280, 293
Line 256, 264
Line Amount 257
Line Amount Excl. VAT 210, 239
Lines 87, 209, 302
List 24
List Display Mode 25
Local Address Format 91
Local Currency Symbol 92
Location Code 43, 108, 154, 179, 214, 245
Location Mandatory 100
Locations 77, 78, 79, 154

M

Magnifying Glass 46
Manage 232, 248
Manual Setup 71
Message 232, 248
Migrate 131
Mobile UI 36
My Notifications 47
My Settings 17, 21

N

Name 122, 145, 146, 173, 208, 237, 367, 368
Navigate 87, 253
Net Change 50, 122, 123, 327, 331, 332
New 207, 236, 262, 305, 309, 368
New Document 207, 236, 262
New Window 28, 30
No126
No. 35, 122, 123, 126, 127, 134, 173, 208, 209, 227, 237, 238, 271, 282
No. of Entries 219, 255
No. of Periods 83
No. Series 85, 87, 89, 92, 94, 274, 288
No. Series Line 87, 89
Number Series 94, 96

O

OK ... 165, 188, 229, 231, 250, 265, 268, 277, 290, 302, 311, 314, 318, 325, 337, 342
Ongoing Sales Orders 262
Opening Balance 197, 200, 203
Options 35
Order 215, 258
Order Nos. 94
Order Statistics 257
Orders 168
Original Amount 169

P

Package Tracking No. 245, 268
Package Tracking URL 268
Page 45
Page Filters 46
Page Inspection 45
Page Inspector 45
Page Toggle 25
Payables Account 152, 153
Payment Journals 274
Payment Line 314
Payment Methods 101
Payment Terms 100, 101, 126, 213
Payment Terms Code 38, 107, 213, 244
Payments 107
Period Length 83
Periodic Activities 187, 341
Personalization 45
Personalize 42, 219
Post 62, 63, 185, 186, 189, 190, 193, 197, 198, 201, 220, 225, 228, 250, 259, 260, 261, 266, 279, 292, 295, 343
Post Application… 317
Post Inventory Cost to G/L 187, 189, 192, 193, 341, 342
Post/Print 278, 279, 291, 292
Posted Purchase Invoice 220
Posted Purchase Invoices 221, 312
Posted Purchase Receipt 220, 322
Posted Sales Credit Memo 59
Posted Sales Credit Memos 307
Posted Sales Invoice 62, 251, 255, 261
Posted Sales Invoices 262, 306
Posted Sales Shipment 267, 268, 319
Posted Sales Shipments 262
Posting 123, 218, 250
Posting Date... 179, 182, 193, 212, 242, 276, 282, 289, 295, 331, 336
Posting Description 336
Posting Groups 119
Posting Method 343
Prepare 281
Prepare Journal 197, 200, 203
Prevent Negative Inventory 100
Preview 35, 189, 190
Preview Posting 218, 278, 291
Prices & Sales 240
Prices Including VAT 213, 243
Print 35, 190
Print/Send 228, 247
Printer 35
Process 82, 145, 267, 268, 285, 298, 301, 310, 314, 316, 317, 323, 325, 327, 335, 344
Production – Setup Data Only 369
Promised Delivery Date 243
Promoted 25
Promoted Actions 24
Promoted Fields 29
Purch. Account 149
Purchase Credit Memos 312
Purchase Invoices 226
Purchase Order 207, 208
Purchase Order No. 209
Purchase Orders 207
Purchase Return Order 309
Purchaser Code 213
Purchases & Payables Setup 93, 95, 96

Q

Qty. to Invoice 225, 260
Qty. to Receive 225
Qty. to Ship 259, 260
Quantity 179, 181, 210, 227, 239, 257

Quantity Invoiced 225
Quantity Received 225
Quantity Shipped 260, 320

R

Receivables Account 152
Related 158, 302
Related Entries 219, 255
Remaining Amount. 293, 296, 305, 308, 313, 314, 316, 318, 334, 338, 339
Remaining Amt. (LCY) 293, 334, 338, 339
Report
    Settings & Filtering 34
Report Inbox 35
Report Output 271
Reporting 164
Reports 34, 270
Resend 234, 249
Retained Earnings 330
Retained Earnings Acc. 329
Role Center 16
Rounding
    Amount 91
    Decimal Places 91
    Invoice 91
    Unit-Amount 91

S

Sales 262
Sales – Confirmation 34
Sales & Receivables Setup 95, 98, 126
Sales (LCY) 169, 258
Sales Account 149
Sales Credit Memo 307
Sales Credit Memos 305
Sales Invoice 262, 263
Sales Line Discounts 246
Sales Order .. 30, 62, 159, 168, 236, 256, 259, 261, 320
Sales Order Confirmations 230
Sales Order No. 238
Sales Order Statistics 169, 258
Sales Orders 236
Sales Prices 246
Sales Prices & Discounts 240
Sales Quote 59

Sales Return Order 297
Sales Return Orders 297
Salespeople 243
Salesperson Code 243
Saving Indicator 28, 30
Schedule 35
Scheduled Receipt 246
Search 24
Sell-To Customer Sales History 261
Send 228, 232, 233, 248
Send To 35
Sent Emails 234, 249
Set Applies-to ID 317
Settings 17, 21, 42, 47, 48, 81, 130, 369
Shipment Date 245
Shipping 107, 108
Shipping Advice 245
Shipping Agent 245
Shipping Agents 268
Ship-to 214, 245
Ship-To Addresses 245
Show as menu 315
Show Errors 132
Show more 28, 187, 232, 248
Slim/Wide Toggle 28, 30
Source Codes 344
Standard Cost 128
Standard Statement 270
Start Date 85, 88, 271
Starting Date 83, 163, 336
Starting Document No. 282
Starting No. 87
Statement 270
Statistics 168, 258
Stockout Warning 96
Substitutions 246
Suggest Vendor Payments... 281
Sum Index Flow Technology 50
    FlowField 50
    FlowFilter 50
Summarize per Vendor 282, 284
System Actions 28, 30

T

Table 46
Table Fields 46
Tell Me 17, 20, 75, 156

Templates 130
To 232, 248
Total Balance... 193
Totaling 123
Totals.. 210, 257
Track Package.. 268
Translations.. 158
Type 209, 224, 226, 238
Types of Pages.. 23

U

Unapply 315
   Unapply Entries 314
Unapply Customer Entries 314
Undo Receipt.. 322
Unit Amount 180, 182
Unit Cost 128, 180, 210
Unit of Measure 115
Unit of Measure Code 180
Unit of Measures.. 114, 115
Unit Price...............................127, 186, 240, 256, 257
Unit Price Excl. VAT 239, 240
Units of Measures 58, 114
Update Document.. 267
User Setup.. 333

V

VAT Bus. Posting Group 150, 213, 243

VAT Business Posting Groups 71, 72
VAT Posting Setup...150, 151
VAT Prod. Posting Group 150
VAT Prod. Posting Groups......................................150
VAT Product Posting Groups............................71, 72
Vendor 168, 280, 282, 309
Vendor Card..213, 229
Vendor Invoice No. 209
Vendor Invoice Number..94
Vendor Ledger Entries 221, 225, 228, 280, 313
Vendor List...137
Vendor Name...208, 212
Vendor No...212
Vendor Posting Groups 76, 153
Vendor Posting Setup 152
Vendors 170, 176, 201, 207, 221, 225, 280
Vendors Opening Balance..............................200, 201
View Controls..24, 25
View Table 46

W

Warn about unreleased orders................................47
Work Date..41, 48
Worksheet 32

Y

Your Reference 243

Manufactured by Amazon.ca
Bolton, ON